The Habsburgs

The Dynasties
Series Editor: Nigel Saul, Professor of Medieval History
                        Royal Holloway, University of London, UK

Also in the series:

The Habsburgs

The History of a Dynasty

BENJAMIN CURTIS

B L O O M S B U R Y
LONDON • NEW DELHI • NEW YORK • SYDNEY

Bloomsbury Academic

An imprint of Bloomsbury Publishing Plc

50 Bedford Square	175 Fifth Avenue
London	New York
WC1B 3DP	NY 10010
UK	USA

www.bloomsbury.com

First published 2013

British Library Cataloguing-in-Publication Data
A catalogue record for this book is available from the British Library.

ISBN: HB: 978-1-4411-8023-0
PB: 978-1-4411-5002-8
ePDF: 978-1-4411-4549-9
ePub: 978-1-4411-0053-5

Typeset by Newgen Imaging Systems Pvt, Ltd, Chennai, India

CONTENTS

LIST OF ILLUSTRATIONS

Cover: Maximilian I and family, by Bernhard Strigel (after 1515). In the collection of the Kunsthistorisches Museum, Vienna. Image courtesy of the Bridgeman Art Library.

Figures

Maps by C. James Carter

Table

Habsburg Family Tree

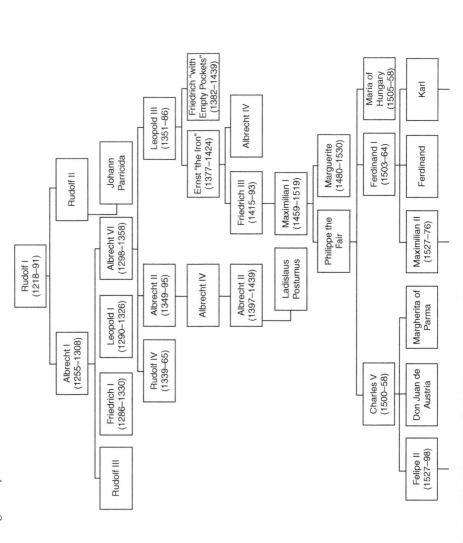

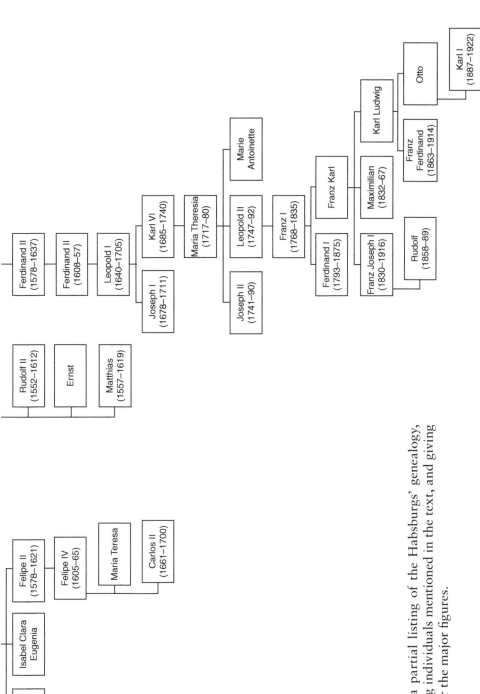

This is a partial listing of the Habsburgs' genealogy, depicting individuals mentioned in the text, and giving dates for the major figures.

PREFACE

There is no shortage of books about the Habsburgs. That is only fitting for the family that can stake a credible claim to being the most important in European history. However, English has long lacked a concise overview of the dynasty, covering its first king to its last, and embracing both the Spanish and the Austrian branches of the family. This book seeks to fill that gap by answering some of the basic questions—Who were these people? What did they do?—while always keeping the dynasty itself at the center of the analysis. It was a family business, after all, whose individual members should be seen in the context of both their predecessors and successors. The task is to understand how the dynasty worked as a unit, and did so in a way that elevated it to the first rank of European royal houses. In surveying such broad territory chronologically and geographically, I hope that I have not sacrificed scholarly rigor in my attempt to make the narrative at least somewhat accessible to and engaging for nonspecialists. Contemporary academia tends to reward the narrow rather than the broad. But sometimes the educational mission demands a breadth comparable to the Habsburgs' own expansive ambit.

Like any book, this one required the hard work of many people besides my own. The staff at Seattle University's Lemieux Library were outstanding in fetching material from far and near for the long research process. I am grateful to my colleagues in Matteo Ricci College for providing a worthy intellectual home. In particular, I cannot thank Dan Doyle, Emily Lieb, and Daniel Washburn enough for their comments on the manuscript. Thanks also to the other anonymous readers, and to Nigel Saul, the series editor, who provided feedback. All inadequacies are solely mine, as the standard disclaimer goes. My old friend Christopher Carter did excellent work on the maps. Rick Steves, Steve Smith, Michelle Michael Kono, and many other estimable compatriots in Edmonds have made it possible for me to go teach and learn in central and eastern Europe every year. Claire Lipscomb and Rhodri Mogford at Continuum-Bloomsbury were invaluable editors throughout this process. To these people and many others, for their support over the years of writing this book, Danke, gracias, köszönöm, děkuji, merci, obrigado, dzękuję, hvala, grazie, mulţumesc—in only some of the many languages of the Habsburg domains.

Introduction

AEIOU. The vowels themselves symbolized the Habsburg destiny: *Austriae est imperare orbi universo* ("Austria is to rule the whole world"). Another version of the motto was *Alles Erdreich ist Österreich untertan* ("All the world is subject to Austria"). This rather audacious usurpation of the alphabet was quite characteristic of the ambition—and the confidence—of the House of Habsburg. The family's members were sure that they were born to rule. And though they shared this ideology of divine right with other European dynasties, several things make the Habsburgs distinct from the rest. Their preeminence was longer lasting, and their ambitions more grandiose, than any other modern royal family. For almost 650 years, from 1273 to 1918, Habsburg sons (and even a few daughters) ruled lands at the heart of Europe. There are only a few current countries on the continent whose lands were not at one point ruled by a Habsburg. From England to Serbia, Portugal to Poland, in the early modern period the dynasty's dominions extended still further, encompassing nearly all of the Americas, touching territories in Africa and Asia as well. Not content with their near-monopoly of the highest crown in the West, that of the Holy Roman Empire, Habsburg rulers up to the eighteenth century truly believed that it was their destiny to rule the "universal orb," to govern as much of the globe as possible.

The AEIOU motto is but one example of how the Habsburgs wove a mythology of glory about themselves. They concocted genealogies to make their ancestors Roman nobles and Trojan heroes. They built lasting architectural monuments to their own majesty, such as the great palaces of Schönbrunn outside Vienna or El Escorial outside Madrid. They assembled a legendary treasury, now in the Viennese Hofburg, to show off the family's fabulous wealth. It holds objects such as the Holy Lance that supposedly pierced Christ's side, and the garishly bejeweled crown of the Holy Roman Emperor, once believed to have sat on the head of Charlemagne himself.

They commissioned the greatest artists of their day such as Dürer, Titian, and Velázquez to create regal portraits of Habsburg family members. These paintings, and much other art besides, gave rise to the incomparable collections of the Museo del Prado in Madrid and the Kunsthistorisches Museum in Vienna, which also serve as enduring reminders of Habsburg refinement.

Such practices were not uncommon among European dynasties. But where the Habsburgs are again distinct is that no other dynasty has so thoroughly penetrated the popular imagination. The Habsburgs' reputation among the general public includes elements rather more dubious than those many old emperors would prefer. Another of the House's celebrated mottos— "Let others wage war; you, happy Austria, marry"—is often inextricably associated with tales of the family's inbreeding. Those marital connections were indeed for a long time tightly linked within the family, which did produce a rather watery genetic stew, incarnated above all in the disabled Carlos II, the dead end of the Spanish Habsburgs. The marriage policies also perpetuated the family's most characteristic physical inheritance: the protuberant jaw known as the "Habsburg lip," easily visible in many of those same regal portraits by the great artists.

Out of this long, intertwined line, an unprecedented number of the Habsburgs' cast of characters still strut the stage of popular culture. Felipe II is usually seen as a villain, stained with the "Black Legend" of Spanish fanaticism, guilty of murdering his own son and brutalizing the freedom-loving people of the Netherlands. Rudolf II is imagined as the Habsburg Prospero, hidden away in the labyrinthine chambers of Prague castle, pursuing the dark arts of alchemy while his kingdom falls apart. Maria Theresia is the indomitable, fecund matron of Rococo Europe, mother to 16 children even as she ruled an empire on the upswing. One of her children, Marie Antoinette, symbolizes the cake-eating, doomed *ancien régime.* Her brother, Joseph II, has been portrayed as the brittle ultra-rationalist of the Enlightenment, infamous for his supposed comment to Mozart that the latter's opera had "too many notes." The lives of the last ruling Habsburgs in particular have been reconceived as a soap opera. Empress Elisabeth (known as "Sisi"), romanticized as the beautiful, misunderstood Princess Diana of her day, was murdered on the shores of Lake Geneva. Her son Rudolf is sketched as the brilliant, unstable heir who took his own life, while Franz Joseph himself, the emperor, husband, and father who saw his family die and his realm crumble around him, has attained a strange, tragic, plodding grandeur.

The truth about the dynasty lies, predictably, somewhere in between its ostentatiously constructed self-image and the rather pock-marked public perception. The Habsburgs can be justifiably called the foremost family of Europe, and the paradigmatic European dynasty. The family owes these superlatives to its longevity, the prestige of its ruling titles, and its geographic reach. It attained all three via the astute manipulation of a number of key strategies for dynastic aggrandizement. These practices enabled the Habsburgs to rise from their original, modest power base in what is now Switzerland and southwestern Germany, to expand all the way across Europe and the planet, and to remain so important in European power politics for so many centuries. The Habsburgs' astonishing record of success (along with some equally astonishing failures) offer a fascinating window through which to observe these strategies; they are nothing less than the work of dynasties, and the Habsburgs are the most consistently accomplished practitioners of European dynasticism.

The strategies were intentional, even if they were not always practiced exclusively by a member of the family. The definition of a dynasty is a kinship-based political organization promoting the interests of a family across generations, which claims a right to power grounded in medieval notions of lineage and inheritance. This book studies the Habsburgs precisely as an organization, focusing on the strategies that reinforced the dynasty's rule and maintained familial cohesion. Though the book is organized around the individual sovereigns, dynastic monarchy encompasses not just discrete rulers but a whole ruling cooperative, including the advisors, ministers, and underlings who assisted in governance. Why this is important is that a number of rather colorless Habsburg monarchs such as Karl VI or the nineteenth-century Ferdinand matter less for their personalities or decisions than for the position they occupied. Quite a few Habsburg rulers were thus place-holders, pale figureheads whose story is really their functional role in the perpetuation of the dynasty and its associated power structure.

Dynastic strategies

If a dynasty is in a sense a family business, then the Habsburgs' family business was ruling. Dynasties were the most prominent actors behind the creation of the modern state. They provided the most influential and durable "continuity of interest" (in Wolfgang Reinhard's phrase) that transcended individual rulers and the slowly developing conceptions of the impersonal, public state.[1] The evidence that dynasties were the most successful creators of states is that many currently existing European countries trace their origins and consolidation to the work of individual families, even if those families are now long gone. Indeed, especially in the later medieval and early modern periods, key processes of state-building such as the growth of an administrative apparatus and the increased extraction of fiscal resources were very often measures taken to consolidate and centralize a *dynasty's* rule.[2] In most cases, the state and the dynasty were conceived as essentially identical; whatever was good for the dynasty was good for the state, and *raison de dynastie* became *raison d'état*. This fused identity of individual sovereign, family, and polity was vital because as the state consolidated out of many competing jurisdictions, creating some unity and harmony out of fragmented medieval polities, it was far easier for the sovereign to stand over all those tentatively fusing polities and represent (incarnate!) the developing state community. Before there was any shared state identity per se, there was thus the shared identity of being a sovereign's subject. This means that the Habsburg dynasty had a mixed private-public character that is a particular characteristic of early modern state development.

Over several centuries, a small number of dynasties out-competed other polities (such as city-states or ecclesiastical principalities) and even other aristocratic families to build up many of the state structures that persist in Europe today. The most successful dynasties such as the Habsburgs were those that competed most effectively using common strategies of dynastic furtherance, which also typically formed vital parts of building the dynastic state. This book studies four key dynastic strategies and how the Habsburgs used them:

1   How the dynasty produced and reproduced itself, which includes succession and marriage politics and territorial acquisition.

2   How the dynasty created legitimacy and loyalty for itself and its political system.

3   How the image and function of the ruler changed, which involves the evolution from the sacralized medieval warrior king to the demystified constitutional monarchy.

4   How the dynasty institutionalized and improved its government structures.

There is certainly some overlap between these processes; legitimation can be related to the function of the ruler and the institutionalization of administrative structures, for instance.[3] In any case, the four strategies require a brief, further explanation.

The first, production and reproduction of the dynasty, involves not only producing heirs and securing marital alliances, but also the continuance of family traditions and the preservation of the patrimonial territorial complex. These activities are really the dynastic *sine qua non*. The essence of a dynasty is a family with a heightened sense of (a) its own identity and (b) exclusivity of membership. A dynasty is not just a familial group; it is also a culture. This culture of identity and exclusivity allows for common possession of certain goods via bequest across subsequent generations, all in the interest of preserving and increasing the family's possessions. The idea of the dynasty as bigger and more important than any one member is fundamental to the dynastic ideology. The obsessiveness with which dynasties propagate this ideology is one of the things that separates them from ordinary families or even other, minor familial empires. Each member of the dynasty is really only a trustee whose duty is to pass on the dynasty's domains. The head of the family, typically the oldest ruling male, oversees this project. However, it depends not just on the royal leader, since other members of the family also contribute, as do the extra-family advisors, clients, or groups who are interested in benefits (whether riches or power) they can accrue by supporting the dynasty.[4]

For the dynasty to work as a corporate, trans-generational unit, an essential aspect of its reproduction is socialization: dynasties must inculcate their members with certain norms, including a sense of identity with and responsibility to the dynasty itself. This is indispensable for the perpetuation of the family's possessions (territorial and material) as well as its symbolic image of authority. A dynasty's claim of a right to rule a territory depends on inheritance, whose terms were not surprisingly of intense concern to most dynasties. There was a tension here between medieval traditions of partible inheritance and the succession imperative of producing as many legitimate children as possible to continue the line and serve the dynasty's interests. Partible inheritance—the division of territory among sons—tended to weaken and scatter dynastic patrimonies, while primogeniture passed on the inheritance to the oldest son. The Habsburgs throughout the Middle Ages and into the early modern period grappled with partible inheritance versus primogeniture, the latter only gradually becoming dominant through various legal codes and other familial agreements. The persistence of partible inheritance helps account for intra-dynastic conflicts, such as those that bedeviled the family in the fourteenth century between the "Albertine" and "Leopoldine" branches. Though primogeniture was not definitively established in the dynasty until the Pragmatic Sanction of 1713, a part of Habsburg success in this strategy was that they commonly managed to resolve conflicts within the family and maintain solidarity.

Despite primogeniture's benefits in stabilizing dynastic rule by serving as a legal foundation for succession, it also brought drawbacks. When the oldest male child is automatically the family's leader, this works against a meritocratic system by which younger but more talented members of the family could take over the leadership. Such was the problem on a few occasions in the Habsburg monarchy, perhaps most famously with Franz I's younger brothers Karl and Johan, both of whom were more intelligent than he. Even with such drawbacks, primogeniture was recognized as an acceptable tradeoff, since it prevented an insecure succession, which historically was one of most destabilizing factors to the evolution of dynastic states. Moreover, the Habsburgs learned to use younger sons and daughters in productive ways, appointing them to rule parts of the family's lands such as the Low Countries or northern Italy, or to key ecclesiastical positions. Indeed, another factor in the dynasty's success was its occasional surplus of cadet lines that could still represent dynastic interests in far-flung outposts.[5] The cadet lines also helped out in the case of succession crises in the ruling line, such as in the later years of Franz Joseph's reign.

Multiple sons and daughters were also essential for the other vital aspect of dynastic production and reproduction, namely marital alliances. The Habsburgs' fame of ascending through marriage rather than war rests above all on a series of alliances involving Maximilian I by which Burgundy, Castile-Aragon, and Bohemia-Hungary all came into the house over the course of 50 years from 1477. Marrying off sons and daughters to other dynasties brought such territorial gains and solidified diplomacy with other powers (such as Marie Antoinette marrying into the French royal house in 1770). But the practice also brought risks. Marrying outside the family could lead to other dynasties claiming parts of the Habsburg patrimony through marriage. Such was the case when Felipe IV's daughter María Teresa married Louis XIV of France, which became the basis for later Bourbon succession claims to Spain in 1700. This danger led to another risk, that of inter-breeding. To keep the patrimony all in the family, and encourage strong collaboration between the Spanish and Austrian branches of the dynasty, cousins married cousins and uncles married nieces. It was this debacle of consanguinity that finally felled the Spanish Habsburgs.

The second dynastic strategy is legitimation and loyalty creation. Legitimation justifies the dynasty's right to rule, and loyalty creation means inculcating a sense of allegiance to the dynasty and its rule among its subject populations. Blood itself was an aspect of legitimacy, and is obviously crucial to dynasties. Though Carlos II because of his many infirmities was incapable of governing, he was nonetheless legitimate because he was Felipe IV's son. A ruler owed his prestige and position only partially to his individual attributes and abilities, but often more to his family line. Related to blood is an assiduous cultivation of a historical identity, to emphasize the dynasty's longevity and hence its obligations for its currently living members. The Habsburgs were appropriately dedicated to the cultivation of a genealogical mythology which would legitimize their rule. Maximilian I in particular sponsored fabulistic investigations to legitimize Habsburg supremacy by tracing the family lineage back to the Carolingians, Merovingians, and Trojans. Legitimacy was also firmly grounded in persistent ideas of a Habsburg divine mission. This mission was simply one to rule. It said that the Habsburgs were anointed by God to defend Christendom. In part because the era of the Habsburgs' hegemonic position in Europe coincided with the Reformation and Counter-Reformation, religious claims were more fundamental to their sense of legitimacy than they were for any other European house.[6] Though the belief in divine right and the necessity of religious homogeneity declined as society secularized, it never fully disappeared from the family's traditions.

The Habsburgs' legitimation strategies until the end of their rule in 1918 were intertwined with particular imperial and dynastic principles. The Habsburgs believed very strongly in the imperial ideology, which postulated a continuity of Western empire from Rome, to Charlemagne, and onward into the later medieval and early modern periods. Seizing on this ideology, family members envisioned themselves as the supreme, overarching rulers of much of Europe. Because of this imperial mindset, the family was less inclined to regard the territories over which it ruled as one state that needed to be consolidated and centralized. Certainly there was consolidation and centralization of administrative structures and authority, which some monarchs such as Joseph II pushed more than others. But a number of scholars have advanced the argument that the family's privileging of the imperial idea, rooted in its long hold on the crown of the Holy Roman Empire, helps explain why the Habsburgs did not work as persistently to fuse their territories into a more tightly bound state, as did say the French Bourbons or the Hohenzollerns.[7] Bound up with this imperial legitimacy, though, was also a particular strand of dynastic legitimacy. Habsburg rulers always regarded themselves as the key point of unity among their diverse domains. The dynasty was what connected its subjects in the Netherlands and Naples—and to the Habsburgs' traditionalist thinking, that dynastic connection was sufficient as justification for rule over such distant and disparate lands.

The Habsburgs' strategies of legitimation and loyalty creation for the most part remained fundamentally rooted in medieval ideas of patrimony and sixteenth-century ones of confessional loyalty. Just as the medieval notions of divine right carried through to the end of the monarchy, so to a lesser extent did the Augsburg ideology of *cuius regio, eius religio* and the sovereign's attendant responsibility for his subjects' salvation.[8] The Habsburgs never fully made the transition to territorial legitimacy—the idea of a common polity arising from common territorial bounds—and they certainly never made it to national legitimacy. The structural impediments to these other forms of legitimacy are obvious. Habsburg territories did not even become contiguous until after 1815, when Belgium was hived off. Even subsequently it would have been difficult to create a sense of territorial legitimacy subsuming regions as diverse as Lombardy and Transylvania. Moreover, that endeavor was already compromised by the middle nineteenth century with the rise of national identities. The Habsburgs tried only in the most modest way to create some sort of legitimating and loyalty-building identity to supplant a sense of national identity. Though the dynastic state did have significant legitimacy and loyalty even until World War One, in that cataclysm it lost both, and so the family's rule was ended. This is not to say that legitimation strategies went without change. The justification of the rational, multinational state came to supersede that of divine anointment; the supranational gradually displaced the supernatural. The idea of the dynasty serving its subjects grew especially under Maria Theresia and her sons. This was associated with the state's improved provision of things such as education and social welfare. Throughout the long nineteenth century the Habsburg state did enjoy legitimacy from the relatively efficient services it delivered.

The expanded role of state services in legitimation is related to the third dynastic strategy, the function and image of the ruler. The understanding of the role of the last Habsburg monarch, Karl I in 1916–18, evolved dramatically but not unrecognizably from that of the first, Rudolf I from 1273–91. Over these 645 years, the Habsburg rulers demonstrated many of the broader trends of European monarchy, including personal, patrimonial rule; the codification of law, the sovereign's legal authority, and the legal rights of subjects; the Renaissance emergence of bureaucratic kingship; Baroque notions of "absolute" monarchy; the Enlightenment de-mystification of royal power and the growing primacy of kings as servants of the state; and the collision of aristocratic privilege with mass politics in the later nineteenth century.[9] The image of the monarch accordingly also changed in many ways: compared to the armored knight of Titian's portrait of Charles V in 1548, monarchs by Franz Joseph's time still wore a military outfit, but it was now a simpler officer's uniform, configuring the monarch as merely the highest of many state officials. No Habsburg ruler was ever "absolutist" in the ideal type sense, but there was nonetheless a definite growth in monarchical power from, say, Friedrich III's almost continual inability to impose his will, to Felipe II's thorough control of the available levers of power. Habsburg rulers in the nineteenth century continued to yearn for absolutism, but after 1867 found their role reduced to that of constitutional monarch.

The rules, display, and cultural patronage of the court were vital in shaping the monarch's role and image. An oft-discussed feature of the Habsburgs is their supposed "Spanish ceremonial" which made the courts in Vienna or Madrid particularly austere and formal. The growth of royal ceremonial after Maximilian I's time gradually made the ruler more distant from the people, limiting access to him as a way of asserting his power and status. Charles V introduced a strictly regulated court etiquette in 1548, which a century later was further adjusted by Felipe IV. These regulations were an amalgam of Burgundian and Spanish traditions, and though elements of them lasted into the nineteenth century, they were also continually modified and even jettisoned. The size of the court grew enormously into the seventeenth century; where the Viennese court included some 500 people in the early 1500s, by the time of Karl VI it was over 2000. Joseph II, who disliked much of the pseudo-divine exaltation of the monarch, introduced his own changes, radically cutting back on court ceremonial, even refusing coronations. As in so many other areas, the Habsburgs evolved but remained traditional too. The court by the end of the 1800s was quite insular, less public than it had been, but still stamped with ideas of the ruler's authority that were archaic in the context of obstreperous parliamentary politics.

The fourth strategy, institutionalizing the dynasty's rule, refers to the administrative structures through which the Habsburgs exercised control of their realms. This is the evolution of the dynastic state in its purest sense, and it involves many different aspects, from the monopolization of the powers of coercion (i.e. the rise of standing armies), to the development of a professional bureaucracy (typically motivated by the need to extract resources to pay for the army), to the expansion of representative and consultative systems fundamental to governance.[10] The reigns of the Habsburg rulers chart a distinct if fitful evolution from the very limited governance of the Middle Ages, with its relatively basic judicial, peacekeeping, and extractive functions, through the consolidation, intensification, and professionalization of government in the early modern period. Well into the eighteenth century, the Habsburgs had comparatively weak central power; they lacked the administrative apparatus to carry out their decisions without the help of other elites. Habsburg rule was therefore founded on cooperation with the landed aristocracy and the Church, especially in the Danubian domains. The aristocracy dominated the provincial representative bodies known as the estates, and consistently resisted encroachments on their own power. It took many centuries to wrest from these estates the power to raise taxes and to centralize in Vienna authority over legislation, defense, and even such things as maintaining roads. The Church was less essential to administration, but it supported the dynasty in a variety of ways, including sacralization (and thereby legitimation) of the sovereign's authority, and ensuring the obedience of his subjects through doctrine and education. In return for the Habsburgs' promotion of the Catholic faith, the Church promised to remain loyal to the dynasty's rule, and to cultivate that loyalty among the population.

Apart from the relatively innovative and effective administrative institutions developed in Castile during the sixteenth century, the dynasty cannot lay claim to particularly efficient institutionalization until the middle of the eighteenth century under Maria Theresia. Indeed, the period from Ferdinand I to Maria Theresia saw few momentous developments. This is indicative of the family's contentment with existing if ramshackle administrative institutions, but also the difficulty of creating better ones in such a scattered, heterogeneous set of territories. From 1740 onward, though, the dynasty's government did penetrate society much more deeply. This was thanks in large part to the growth of the bureaucracy and the army, the two institutions most consistently essential to Habsburg central control. They facilitated the gradual move from indirect rule via local elites to direct rule by Vienna. This was part of the general evolution of European monarchical states by which the aristocracy and the Church were gradually subordinated to the dynasty's vertical hierarchy of power, their autonomy reduced, and their own governance functions integrated into the state.[11] In the Habsburg realms this development was slower and more partial than in some other monarchies such as the French. Nonetheless, by the middle of the nineteenth century the institutions of government had expanded, centralized, and largely separated from the dynastic court. These institutions became to a certain extent distinct from the dynasty, and operated without it. Of the structures that had grown up to carry out the monarch's will, by Franz Joseph's time only the military was still firmly under dynastic control. It was an odd transformation from the medieval sovereign, one of whose limited governance duties was warmaking, to the modern constitutional monarch, who had surrendered much of the institutional authority his ancestors acquired in seventeenth and eighteenth centuries.

Taken as a whole, the dynastic dynamics outlined above constitute a very tough set of tasks for any family and its leaders to manage. A dynasty's overall objective is to continue its rule over its patrimony. This required among other things that the dynasty always persuade its various realms that the dynasty's rule was legitimate and in some ways profitable. At the very least, as Wolfgang Weber has remarked, the dynasty had to convince its subjects and perhaps especially the elite that maintaining the relationship to the dynasty was more sensible than dissolving that relationship.[12] The difficulty of these dynamics is apparent in that relatively few families actually succeeded at them. Most noble families with their own patrimonies witnessed their authority erode and eventually dissolve by the twentieth century. Very few families managed to make the system work for themselves, to survive and even thrive. Fewer still were able to work the system so that they came out on top. For instance, of the 136 leading families in England in 1300, only 16 survived to 1500, and of the 120 leading families in western German principalities in the early Middle Ages, only 9 lasted into the middle 1500s.[13] This makes the Habsburgs' achievements all the more remarkable.

The Habsburg realms

The Habsburgs' achievements also have to be considered in the context of the challenges of the multifarious realms over which they ruled. These challenges included consolidating and centralizing enough to assert control, without antagonizing the provincial elites who were necessary for governance. Other rulers in the late medieval and early modern period faced similar challenges of heterogeneous cultures and polities within their realms, but the Habsburgs' difficulties were much greater. The family's core domains in the southern portion of German-speaking Europe were partially contiguous and had linguistic commonalities, but the situation was dramatically altered after the acquisition of the Bohemian and Hungarian crowns in the sixteenth century. The Spanish branch had to deal with disconnected territories in Italy and the Netherlands as well as the contiguous, more culturally similar lands in the Iberian peninsula. From its "big bang" of expansion thanks to Maximilian I, up to 1918, the Habsburgs always ruled a composite monarchy.

A composite monarchy is a dynastic agglomeration under one ruler of different territories that typically have distinct political and cultural histories.[14] Most large European states today are the outcomes of composite monarchies. These heterogeneous monarchies were themselves the product of the personally based political organization of the Middle Ages, in which people commonly owed their allegiance not to a state or a territory, but rather to a person, to a family. In their agglomerative nature, the Habsburgs' realms were therefore not unique. The Spanish Habsburgs ruled over the compounded realms of Castile and Aragon, with their possessions in Italy and overseas, plus the formerly Burgundian lands of the Netherlands. The Austrian Habsburgs ruled over several multiply composite monarchies. The Hungarian kingdom was a compound of Hungary, Croatia-Slavonia, and Transylvania, while the Bohemian kingdom compounded Bohemia, Moravia, Silesia, and Lusatia. In the case of the central European domains, the compound parts were closer to equal in their relative populations than in Iberia (where Castile was clearly dominant) or even Britain (where the English far outnumbered the Welsh or the Scots). This fact always impeded centralization impulses from the dynasty's main Austrian lands.

Another challenge of the dynasty's geography was that its central European domains had no necessary connection to each other. Its western lands could easily have belonged to Switzerland, the Tyrol could naturally have been associated with Bavaria, and Carinthia and Carniola were part of the Adriatic hinterland. And yet the dynasty forged these realms into a sturdy polity that, over time, became not only one of the most powerful European states but also a monarchy under one of the longest continuous dynastic reigns in all of Europe. Alongside the challenges, it is important to recognize that these diverse realms shared some sources of cohesion too. To the traveler, the Habsburg heritage is still visible in much of eastern central Europe, evidence of a cultural unity that reinforced an admittedly often halting political unity: Baroque churches in cities and towns; main squares with a plague column at their center; pastel-painted administrative buildings, often colored "Maria Theresia yellow"; showy theaters and opera houses from the late nineteenth century. All testify that despite the heterogeneity of the Habsburgs' realms, one thing overarched and united them all, namely the dynasty itself. As A. J. P. Taylor pithily observed, "In other countries dynasties are episodes in the history of the people; in the Habsburg Empire peoples are complications in the history of the dynasty."[15]

The central difficulty of the dynasty's rule was paradoxically also its greatest success. It proved so adept at the first strategy of production and reproduction that the fourth strategy, institutionalizing rule, took a decentralized form. The unheard-of windfall in the late medieval and early modern periods—suddenly acquiring a worldwide territorial reach as no family in human history ever had before—collided with the technological and other limitations of government in this time. Thus the family had to strike deals with the elites in its lands to ensure the continuity of Habsburg rule. Those deals, coupled with the diversity of the dynasty's domains, in the long run often worked against the development of a state that could extract sufficient resources to remain a major military power. The Habsburgs' remarkable accomplishments in assembling a patrimony also in the long run created a realm where the dynasty could represent a state, but not the multiple nations that emerged there. In this way the dynasty remained stamped and even hampered by its sixteenth-century gains; it was never exactly stuck in the early modern period, but its achievements in that period constricted its options in the future.

Finally, a few practical considerations on terminology and the book's approach. Though the Habsburgs are often known as the "House of Austria," their domains extended far beyond Austria, and even the definition of Austria itself was contestable into the nineteenth century. Austria proper was often divided into "Upper Austria" (roughly, the northwestern part bordering mostly on Germany) and "Lower Austria" (the northeastern part bordering the Czech lands and Hungary), with the River Enns as the dividing line. There was also "Inner Austria," which referred to the southern areas of Carinthia, Styria, and Carniola (the latter of which is now mostly Slovenia). When the term "Austria" is used in this book, it will usually refer to the whole complex of the dynasty's domains centering on the Danube, excluding Hungary. Another term, "the Danubian domains," more accurately embraces Hungary as well. The term "Hereditary Lands" (*Erblande* in German) refers to the strictly Austrian domains, but after 1627 also includes the Bohemian kingdom. Within the Hereditary Lands, the family's oldest territories in what is today mostly Switzerland and southwest Germany have a more precise definition, the *Vorlande*; the English-language term "Further Austria" is too clumsy to use. "The Habsburg monarchy" refers to all the lands under Habsburg rule, from the Netherlands, to the Vorlande, to Transylvania. This is the name of the state, even when the state was rather weak, and I prefer it to another sometimes-used term, "the Habsburg empire," which legitimately covers the Iberian overseas possessions but is much too grandiose to describe the Danubian domains, even after Franz I proclaimed the Hereditary Lands an "empire" in 1804. The Habsburg monarchy in Iberia presents fewer terminological difficulties, though the term "Spain" will sometimes be used when in fact there was no unified Spanish state throughout the time the Habsburgs ruled there.

My naming of places and people is admittedly idiosyncratic. For towns, I most often employ the name currently in use in whatever country the place is located. For instance, I will typically refer to Bratislava even though during Habsburg rule it was almost always known by its German name, Pressburg, or Hungarian, Pozsony. A few exceptions are made for place names that are too well established in English, thus Vienna instead of Wien. Regions that have a commonly used name in English will use that name; hence Styria rather than the German Steiermark. For people, I will use the name they themselves used in whatever was their main language. Rather than Philip II of Spain, then, it is Felipe II since his primary language was Spanish. Other, highly multilingual Habsburgs are trickier, and expose my choices to quibbling. Since Felipe's father grew up favoring French, he is Charles V rather than the Spanish "Carlos" or the German "Karl." I acknowledge that this nomenclature will occasionally present readers whose first language is English with unfamiliar orthography. Therefore, in the chapters that follow, as well as in the index, when a person's name is first mentioned, the English version (if it is not obvious) will be given in brackets. In any case, I hope that such difficulties are requited by the more respectful approach of using the names that these people would actually have used for themselves.[16]

In compressing so many centuries of one family's and multiple lands' histories into what will hopefully be a relatively manageable text, I have made many sacrifices. This book focuses unapologetically on "high politics," that is, battles, diplomacy, royal marriages, and other matters central to the dynasty's rule. Given short shrift are cultural and social history. Broader developments in society, and the conditions of those who did not live in palaces, had to give way in order to do some justice to the crowned heads. Similarly, because the dynasty is the star of this show, and it was most deeply connected to Austria, the other realms such as Hungary or the Netherlands do not receive as much attention as do the Hereditary Lands. Also in an effort to do justice to the Habsburgs themselves, I have tried to sketch them as individuals, to put some flesh on their old bones. Hence each chapter begins with a mostly "narrative" section detailing the major events of the reign. Each ends with a more "analytical" section evaluating the relevant rulers according to the four dynastic strategies outlined above. I also regret that the book is mostly a parade of dead white men. Where possible I have devoted attention to some of the dynasty's remarkable women, but the first duty has to be to the family's heads, who were almost always males. In the end, many other books were cut out of this one, ending up on the "editing room floor," so to speak. Yet since the Habsburgs are an inexhaustible topic, those less-explored areas may yet find books of their own.

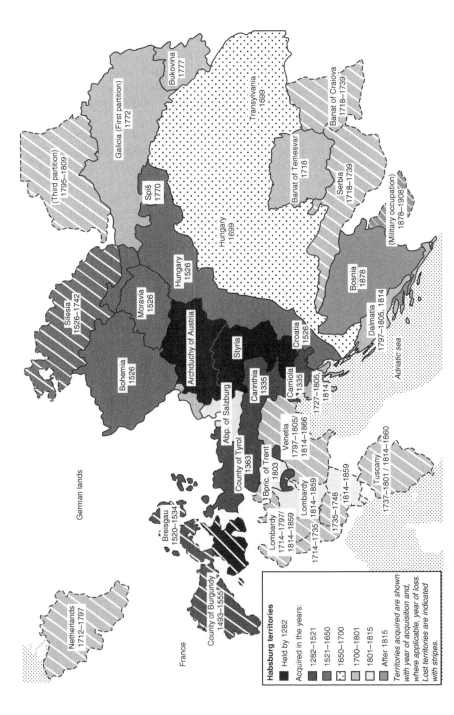

MAP 1. *Growth of Habsburg territories.*

(Third partition)
1795–1809

Galicia (First partition)
1772

Bukovina
1777

Transylvania
1699

Banat of Craiova
1718–1739

Spiš
1770

Banat of Temesvar
1718

Serbia
1718–1739

(Military occupation)
1878–1908

Silesia
1526–1742

Moravia
1526

Hungary
1526

Hungary
1699

Bosnia
1878

Bohemia
1526

Archduchy of Austria

Styria

Croatia
1526

Dalmatia
1797–1805, 1814

Adriatic sea

Carinthia
1335

Carniola
1335

1727–1805

1814

Abp. of Salzburg

County of Tyrol
1363

Bpric. of Trent
1803

Venetia
1797–1805/
1814–1866

Tuscany
1737–1801 / 1814–1860

German lands

Breisgau
1520–1534

Lombardy
1714–1797/
1814–1859

Lombardy
1714–1735/ 1814–1859

Lombardy
1735–1748

1814–1859

County of Burgundy
1493–1555

Netherlands
1712–1797

France

Habsburg territories

Held by 1282

Acquired in the years:

1282–1521
1521–1650
1650–1700
1700–1801
1801–1815

After 1815

*Territories acquired are shown
with year of acquisition and,
where applicable, year of loss.
Lost territories are indicated
with stripes.*

CHAPTER ONE

From not so humble beginnings
(c. 1000–1439)

On a hill above the Aare River in the Swiss canton of Aargau stands a thousand-year-old castle, a modest structure consisting now of a square, crenellated tower attached to an austere residential building of rough-hewn stone. This is the original Habichtsburg, sometimes known as "Hawk Castle," the ancestral seat and source of appellation for the Habsburg dynasty. The family was thus named after a place, a fortress dating back to the early eleventh century, which occupies a strategic position near the upper Rhine and important passes over the Alps. These were the Habsburgs' earliest lands, though they were eventually lost: after 1415 the Habsburgs no longer owned the Habsburg castle itself, since it fell under the control of the Swiss Confederation. That surprising setback illustrates how the family's history in its first few centuries does not presage its later dominance. At times it rose to become one of the elite German dynasties, but at others experienced major defeats such as being expelled from its original homelands. In response, the Habsburgs moved their center of gravity eastward to the Austrian duchies, where they gradually built up administrative structures to buttress their rule and their status. Their territorial patrimony thereby expanded, though it also came to be divided among multiple family lines. During this period, several lasting patterns of Habsburg dynastic practice were established, including a conscientiously pious image and a grandiose belief in the family's eminence. The Habsburgs' oldest castle may have been modest, and only a few family members truly significant, but even in its beginnings the dynasty was never humble.

Much of the dynasty's earliest history is uncertain, a mélange of mythology and conjecture. Standing as the hazy first figure in a long lineage is a duke named Guntram the Rich, who lived in the middle 900s. The details of Guntram's life are little known, but he had a son, Lanzelin, the count of

Altenburg, who in the later 900s owned land where the Habichtsburg was later built. Lanzelin himself may have had three sons. One was Rudolf—a name which created a precedent in Habsburg history—and another was Radbot, who married a woman named Ita and died sometime around 1045. A certain Werner, who became the bishop of Strasbourg circa 1002, may have been Lanzelin's third son, or perhaps Ita's brother; in any case, it was he and Radbot who began the construction of the Habsburg Castle. These men were all minor nobles in what was then the Duchy of Swabia. Lanzelin's sons Rudolf and Radbot, and their sons in turn, grew rich from transalpine trade and tolls and amassed land in the areas of Alsace, southwestern Germany, and Switzerland. They received commensurately appropriate authority and titles: Radbot's grandson Otto was named the first "count of Habsburg" in 1090.

During the 1100s the Habsburgs forged a political alliance with the Hohenstaufens, one of the most prominent European dynasties by virtue of ruling the Holy Roman Empire for much of the twelfth century. The imperial crown was elective, chosen by several of the highest German princes. Another Rudolf (known as "the Benevolent") supported the Hohenstaufens in the election of 1198. This loyalty was rewarded in land and prestige: Emperor Friedrich II subsequently took Rudolf the Benevolent's grandson (whose name was also Rudolf) as his godson, which helped elevate the family into the highest imperial circles. Thanks to such astute alliances, by the early 1200s the Habsburgs had established themselves as one of the wealthiest, most prominent families of southwestern Germany. The dynasty was now positioned for a sudden jump in its power and status. That opportunity came after the end of Hohenstaufen rule in the Empire (1254), which led to the Interregnum, an almost 20-year period when the German kingship was split between multiple claimants. The lack of an acknowledged royal authority led to a gradual breakdown of public order, with rogue knights marauding the countryside and no strong king to bring them to justice. Finally in 1273 the electoral princes moved to remedy the situation and elect a compromise candidate. In that year Rudolf von Habsburg attained the German kingship.

Rudolf I (1218–91)

Rudolf I (actually the fourth Habsburg Rudolf) is the dynasty's first figure of major importance and represented a zenith that no successor would equal for several generations. He was chosen because the electoral princes calculated that he was rich and powerful enough to restore order in the Empire, but not *too* rich and powerful to overstep the monarch's bounds by encroaching on the princes' sovereignty. Rudolf was 55 years old when elected, but had been head of his family for more than 30 years. From both his parents' sides he had claim to valuable territories that made him one of the richest lords in Swabia. Though it can be difficult to cut through mythical obfuscation and simple inadequacy of historical sources to ascertain the personalities of the early Habsburgs, contemporary accounts and family tradition coincide in their descriptions of Rudolf. He was known as a wise, modest, decent person, famed not only for his astute political skills but for his sense of humor as well. Tall and thin, with a prominent aquiline nose, stories relate that he would mend his own clothes, pick grapes with his men, and dress in a style quite subdued for a great lord. Contrary to the allegations made by those who opposed Rudolf's candidacy, he was no parvenu "poor count" unworthy of the German kingship, the office still regarded as the highest secular power in Europe.

Rudolf's reign in fact proved quite successful in spite of the lingering unrest from the Interregnum and the institutional limitations of the king's authority. From the outset, he focused on the situation in Germany, relegating the imperial territories in Italy to secondary importance—and indeed he was never officially crowned by the pope in Rome, so he was king but never emperor. He diligently worked with the electoral princes to share authority. In order to strengthen these relationships and his dynasty's position, he married four of his daughters to these princes. He also formed an advantageous relationship with the imperial cities, respecting their rights while at the same time drawing tax revenue and military support from them. Such military support was essential in one of Rudolf's prime tasks in the Empire, namely to restore law and order after the breakdown of the Interregnum years. He combated private feuds, abolished illegal tolls imposed by local lords, and traveled about Germany destroying robber knights and their castles. As one example, in December 1289 he had 29 malefactors executed for flouting imperial law, then displayed their heads before Erfurt's town gates. He also improved administrative structures in the Empire by appointing loyal men to temporary positions in which they would carry out his laws, but not accumulate too much influence. He attempted, with less success, to reform the fiscal basis of royal power through his tax programs, record keeping, and efforts to recover former royal domains in Alsace and elsewhere. Overall, Rudolf managed to steer an effective course between restoring some central authority in the realm without upsetting the various other stakeholders in the Empire's tangled web of authority.

Rudolf's most lasting achievement, and certainly his most important for the future of the dynasty, was to bring the Austrian duchies into his house. Austria as a whole was a territory of the Holy Roman Empire, but had considerable independence thanks to privileges given in 1156 by Emperor Friedrich I Hohenstaufen to the ruling Babenberg family. In 1246 the last male Babenberg died leaving no heir. Because of the chaos of the Interregnum, no emperor could designate an acknowledged successor in the Austrian duchies, which experienced their own attendant collapse of law and order. To correct this situation, in 1251 nobles in Austria and Styria turned to Otakar Přemysl, the margrave of Moravia who subsequently became king of Bohemia. Otakar aggressively solidified his hold on the Austrian domains—gaining Carinthia by an inheritance, conquering Carniola, and even marrying a Babenberg. Otakar, disappointed that he had not been chosen as German king, refused to acknowledge Rudolf's authority or to cede some lands in Austria that had formerly belonged to the German crown. Rudolf then created a strong alliance with other German princes and went to war. The conflict culminated in the battle of Marchfeld on 26 August 1278, in which Otakar was killed. Rudolf claimed the Austrian lands for himself, and they belonged to the dynasty until 1918, giving rise to the Habsburg moniker as "the House of Austria."

Having claimed the Austrian lands, it was then necessary to assert control over them. As did any high lord in the medieval period, Rudolf had to negotiate with the nobles below him to have his authority recognized. In return he had to recognize the nobles' rights, including that the major Austrian nobles would form a council that would advise the Habsburgs' rule. The nobles also had to accept Rudolf's plans to make his sons Albrecht and Rudolf counts of Austria and Styria in 1282. Rudolf granted rule over Carinthia to his vassal Meinhard of Gorizia-Tyrol. This division of authority was necessary partly because the imperial electors were always wary of the king accruing too much power. They therefore insisted on limiting Rudolf's domains now that his family held the second biggest collection of territories in the Empire, after the Bohemian kingdom. Rudolf lived to the advanced age of 73. Fittingly for a man who was so methodical in life, his death was also carefully planned. In his waning days, he rode to the city of Speyer specifically to die there, since he considered it the traditional burial place of his ancestors. He also contracted an artist to design his tomb monument. This monument, which has been credited as the first realistic portrait of a king of the Holy Roman Empire, was placed in the cathedral of Speyer after Rudolf's death on 15 July 1291.

Rudolf's contributions to his dynasty were momentous. His territorial acquisitions alone would have won him an honored place. In addition to the Austrian domains, Rudolf added a number of smaller lands to the patrimony, including several in southern Germany and a few cities in present-day Switzerland. He also achieved success in another essential duty of any dynast, namely marriage politics. Besides marrying his six daughters to high lords in Bavaria, Brandenburg, Saxony, and Hungary, he made a double marital arrangement in which one of Rudolf's daughters married one of Otakar's sons, and one of Rudolf's sons married one of Otakar's daughters. All of these links were intended to cement the Habsburgs' newly lofty status, to forge the kind of alliances that followed from such personal liaisons, and even to establish inheritance claims for the future. The chief area where Rudolf failed in his aims to advance the family was with his inability to get his son Albrecht accepted as his successor to the German kingship. That failure came in part because Rudolf was never able to make the journey to Rome, where he would have been crowned emperor by the pope. Lacking the emperor's prerogative of suasion in naming an heir, Rudolf's desire to designate Albrecht also ran into the electors' resistance to the family's increased power after the acquisition of Austria.

Albrecht I (1255–1308)

Albrecht's rather intimidating character made many people wary. He had only one eye as a result of a botched medieval cure for poisoning, which directed that he be suspended upside down so that the poison could "drain out" of him. What this prescription actually achieved was a blood clot in his eye that caused him to lose it. His appearance only added to his reputation as a harsh, occasionally brutal person. One medieval chronicler described Albrecht as "hard as a diamond," his heart as "a red-hot iron."[1] He certainly lacked his father's affability. But he was also highly intelligent, energetic, and competent. As the oldest son, his task was to further the dynasty's prospects. His duties in that regard were, first of all, to manage the rule in the new Austrian territories as well as its older domains in the Vorlande. It was only some years later, after a short-lived rival's rule, that Albrecht followed in his father's path as German king.

Albrecht became duke in the Austrian lands in 1282. There was significant initial resistance to his taking over there. He was regarded as an outsider from Swabia who brought too many foreigners into his court. He made concessions to the Austrian nobility to win their support—but he also sometimes used an iron fist. He put down an uprising in Vienna in 1287, a rebellion in Styria in 1291–2, and a nobles' revolt in 1295–6. He was fairly moderate in his punishment of the rebels, however, and attempted to win over his new subjects by giving his sons the names Friedrich and Leopold, which had been common names among the Babenbergs and then became traditional among Habsburgs. As he was trying to cement the dynasty's control in the Austrian duchies, he also faced resistance in its Swiss lands. In August 1291, after Rudolf's death, the cantons of Uri, Schwyz, and Unterwalden joined in an "Eternal League," and shortly thereafter the towns of Zürich and St. Gall were brought in to solidify this defensive alliance. Though not directly antagonistic to the Habsburgs, the purpose of this league was to preserve the signatories' independence against all powers, including their Habsburg overlords. The formation of the Eternal League is often cited as the birth of the eventual state of Switzerland, and it foreshadowed the escalating problems the dynasty would have there over the next two centuries.

Albrecht was chosen as German king only in 1298 after his predecessor Adolf of Nassau was deposed by the princes for overreaching his royal prerogatives. Given Albrecht's harsh reputation it is not surprising that his ten years on the throne were rocky. He pursued a line of action not dissimilar from the deposed Adolf's, hoping to strengthen his monarchical authority via efforts to take control of Thuringia and a number of other key territories. Albrecht arranged a marital alliance with Philippe IV of France, which alarmed a number of the electors who suspected that Albrecht was maneuvering to gain French support to make the Habsburgs hereditary monarchs in Germany in return for giving away certain lands of the Empire. Three electors—the archbishops of Cologne, Mainz, and Trier—actually signed a pact to depose Albrecht. The latter responded forcefully, convincing the lesser nobility and the cities to remain on his side, and then sent armies to subdue the three archbishops. Their rebellion had collapsed by 1302, but not before involving the trouble-making pope Boniface VIII, eternal object of Dante's scorn. Albrecht placated Boniface by swearing an oath of allegiance and renouncing certain aspects of his imperial authority over Lombardy and Tuscany.

As an audacious part of his plan to reinforce his own dynasty within the Empire, Albrecht took advantage of the death of the last male member of the Přemyslid dynasty to put his own son Rudolf on the throne of Bohemia. In 1306 he sent an army to Prague that chased away Heinrich, Duke of Carinthia, who claimed to be the legitimate heir. Albrecht's soldiers also managed to "persuade" the Bohemian nobles to choose the Habsburg as their new king. Rudolf thus became the first Habsburg to wear the Bohemian crown, albeit only for a short stint, as he died prematurely in 1307. Albrecht's other major venture to gain Thuringia also unraveled at this time. The Wettin family, who had been feuding over the right to rule the territory for a number of years, finally found in Albrecht a sufficient threat to settle their differences and unite against him. They made common cause with the new king of Bohemia, Heinrich of Carinthia, and together they defeated an army of Albrecht's in May of 1307.

Like his father before him, Albrecht failed to secure for his son succession to the German kingship. He was prevented from doing so by one of the most nefarious turns of Habsburg family history, when he was murdered by his nephew Johann. Johann had for years aggressively protested that his share of the family's patrimonial lands should be larger. He raised claims to Austria, Styria, and even argued that he should succeed as German king rather than Albrecht's own son. Albrecht, not surprisingly, intended to keep primacy for his own branch of the family. This led Johann to form a conspiracy with four other nobles, and on 1 May 1308 they attacked and killed Albrecht as he rode toward the city of Brugg, now in Switzerland. Johann was never brought to justice for his crime, though he did have to flee the ferocious campaign of vengeance pursued by Albrecht's heirs. Johann was much later given the appellation "Parricida," and he died in Pisa in 1313. Albrecht's murder was a disaster for the dynasty's prestige. Though it is by no means certain that the Habsburgs could have retained their hold on the imperial crown, once Albrecht was gone the family was shut out of the kingship for the next 130 years. Certainly Albrecht's own pugnacious politics helped bring about his downfall, and he must bear some of the blame for this disaster.

Albrecht's sons: Friedrich I (1289–1330), Leopold I (1290–1326), and Albrecht II (1298–1358)

The failures of Albrecht's two oldest sons—who shared their father's and grandfather's ambition, but not their ability—also help explain the family's long drought. The brotherly team of Friedrich and Leopold can at least be faintly praised for their dynastic solidarity and close cooperation. Albrecht before he died had tasked Friedrich with leading the charge for the Bohemian crown following his older brother Rudolf's death, but he was repelled on the battlefield. Friedrich was then outmaneuvered in the election to choose Albrecht's successor as king in 1309, and the winner was Heinrich of the Luxemburg dynasty. The latter died suddenly in 1313, however, setting up perhaps the most controversial election of the late medieval period. The two main contenders were Friedrich and Duke Ludwig of Upper Bavaria, a Wittelsbach. The electors split: in September 1314, meeting on opposite sides of the Main River, four of the electors opted for Ludwig while three chose Friedrich. Ludwig was then crowned in the traditional coronation city, Aachen, but without the traditional imperial crown. That was in Friedrich's hands, so his coronation took place in Bonn—the wrong city, but the right crown. The disputed vote led to an eight-year war between Friedrich and Ludwig. In this war, unrest in the Swiss lands was weakening the Habsburgs' western possessions, which Ludwig used to his advantage. The Eternal League that the communities of Uri, Schwyz, and Unterwalden had formed in 1291 saw several new communities join, forming what is known in Swiss history as the Waldstätten or "Forest Cantons."

This League took an increasingly hostile stance toward the Habsburgs' attempts to assert their authority in the area. It was Leopold's job to suppress the unrest, but at the battle of Morgarten in November 1315 Habsburg forces suffered a terrible defeat. Leopold barely escaped with his life after his knights were ambushed and butchered by heavily armed Swiss farmers. It took another major battle to settle the conflict between Friedrich and Ludwig over their claims to the German crown. In the battle of Mühldorf in 1322, Friedrich had the larger force, and exemplified chivalric ideals by fighting alongside his men, but was defeated and taken prisoner. Mühldorf was one of the last large knightly battles fought on German soil, and was the very last fought without any firearms. Surprisingly, after the battle Friedrich and Ludwig's relationship improved immensely. In 1325 Ludwig released

Friedrich from prison on condition that he convince Leopold to give up the fight and return to Ludwig some territories that he had captured. When Leopold refused, Friedrich again honorably upheld the chivalric ideal by returning to imprisonment voluntarily. This gesture so impressed Ludwig that he made Friedrich his regent in Bavaria and eventually his coruler in the empire, allowing him to use the title *rex*, the only time in German history this occurred. Ultimately this arrangement meant very little: Leopold died in 1326, and Friedrich thereby lost his best strategist. He accomplished nothing important in the last years of his own life, dying in 1330.

After the Habsburgs' impressive rise in the previous two generations, with Friedrich and Leopold gravity reasserted itself and the family entered a long period where it played little role in imperial politics. Despite Friedrich's and Leopold's ambitions, they achieved very little of what they had aspired to. They did further the family's reorientation of its power base eastwards, which change can be traced through the increasing numbers of churches and monasteries they endowed in the Austrian lands. Friedrich and Leopold themselves had no children, so it was left to two of Albrecht I's other children to further the dynastic ambitions. The first of these was his daughter Agnes, an intelligent, energetic woman who, as the widowed Queen of Hungary, became an important advisor to the male heads of the family. After Friedrich and Leopold were gone, the head of the family became the surviving fourth son, also known as Albrecht. In contrast to his two rash, underachieving brothers, Albrecht II concentrated on prudently building up the family's rule in the Austrian lands, making him the first truly "Austrian" Habsburg.

Albrecht was known as "the Wise," but also as "the Lame." An illness had left him nearly paralyzed, such that he often had to be borne about on a palanquin carried by two horses. Like many younger sons in the Middle Ages, he had been prepared for a career in the Church; the solid education he received contributed to both his intellect and character once he became the family's leader. A humble, conciliatory man, Albrecht took a number of smart steps. He fully reconciled with King Ludwig in 1335, and in return for renouncing any further disputes over the imperial crown was enfeoffed with Carinthia and Carniola, which added to the family's lands in what is now Austria and Slovenia. Albrecht married one of his daughters to the last count of Tyrol, helping prepare the eventual Habsburg acquisition of that territory. In another worthy dynastic marriage, in 1353 Albrecht betrothed his oldest son Rudolf to the daughter of Ludwig's successor as German king, Charles IV of Luxemburg. Also during Albrecht's reign, the Habsburgs lost further fights with the Swiss Waldstätten and their allied cities of Zürich and Bern in the 1350s. At this time, too, the Black Death struck the Austrian lands, killing some 30 percent of the population.

His efforts to institutionalize rule in the Austrian lands were Albrecht's most lasting legacy for the dynasty. In 1341 Albrecht stated that his goal in Austria was to create "one people, one ruler, one house."[2] This phrase implies much more unity than Albrecht ever intended or could have achieved. But it does accurately represent his achievements in standardizing and integrating administrative structures and legal rights across the two Austrian duchies as well as Styria, Carinthia, and Carniola. He also improved the financial basis of rule in these lands, gaining greater control over tax policy, for instance. This helped him raise revenues to pay off debts. His economic policies promoted the growth of towns and cities, which in turn also contributed to his government's coffers. His government itself became somewhat more professional as he staffed it with more trained jurists. For all these reasons, Albrecht can be considered the true founder of the Austrian state. Essential to dynastic control of this growing state were the rules he decreed in 1355 to preserve the unity of the patrimony for inheritance purposes. Though these rules were not fully implemented, they were important for asserting dynastic solidarity, the indivisibility of the territories, and the identification of the noble magnates with the dynasty, since they all had to assemble in Vienna to approve them. Albrecht, in his peaceful way, secured the family's control especially of its eastern lands more than his brothers' belligerence ever did.

Rudolf IV "the Founder" (1339–65)

Rudolf IV was a comet that burned brightly if briefly, blazing a trail that all subsequent Habsburgs would follow—hence his sobriquet as "the Founder." He came to head the family when he was only 19, upon Albrecht's death, and did so until his own death just 7 years later at 26. The urgency of his ambition and the boldness of his deeds are very much those of a young man. The shrewdness of his politics would have been remarkable in someone twice his age, however. That he was raised from the time he was 9 as the son-in-law of the Emperor Charles IV, almost a crown prince while Charles had no sons, may help explain his self-assurance. So, too, may the fact that his brothers were all underage, allowing Rudolf to act alone, unhemmed by fraternal jealousies. He was also supported by the counsel of his aunt Agnes. There were four main areas of Rudolf's achievements: completing the acquisition of Tyrol for his house, building up Vienna as the nascent dynastic capital, reforming governance and especially taxes in his lands, and concocting the extraordinary, myth-making document known as the *Privilegium maius*.

Tyrol and Vienna are the two territorial symbols of Rudolf's reign. Though Albrecht had arranged the marriage of his daughter to give the Habsburgs a claim to inherit Tyrol, it fell to Rudolf to make good that claim. Rudolf had to fight off the Bavarian Wittelsbachs' attempt to grab the territory when its last count, Rudolf's brother-in-law, died in 1363. He marched over the Alps in winter with a small contingent of soldiers to the city of Bressanone, where he convinced Countess Margarete, the surviving daughter of the family that had ruled Tyrol, to agree to Habsburg suzerainty. Acquiring Tyrol was tremendously valuable for the dynasty because of its rich mines and its geographical connection between the Habsburg lands in Austria and those in the Vorlande. Rudolf's efforts to build up Vienna as the dynasty's main city include his laying of the foundation stones for the great Gothic expansion of St. Stephan's cathedral in 1359. He also founded Vienna's university in 1365, which made it the third in central Europe, after those in Prague and Kraków. Though the Vienna University nearly folded after Rudolf's death, it was a vital endeavor for the prestige it lent the city and as an institution that supported the state through training officials and elaborating the legal basis of princely power. In both these projects Rudolf was inspired by (and competing with) his father-in-law Charles IV, who had made Prague a glittering capital through his many building projects, including Charles University and St. Vitus Cathedral.

Prestige was also a key motivation behind the *Privilegium maius*, promulgated by Rudolf in 1359. The "privileges" enunciated therein were many. According to the document, the Habsburgs were entitled to call themselves "archdukes"—which is to say, they were no mere dukes, but something considerably higher than that, as an archbishop is to a bishop. All sorts of other titles, both ceremonial (like the Holy Roman Empire's "Master of the Imperial Hunt") and regnal (like duke of Swabia) were also claimed for the Habsburgs. The family was exempted from any imperial military operations they did not want to participate in, and likewise exempted from any of the imperial diets they did not feel like attending. Legitimizing this special position over and above nearly all other noble families were letters from Julius Caesar and Nero emphasizing Austria's unique rights. The trouble with these claims was that the *Privilegium* was a forgery; Rudolf purported to have conveniently "rediscovered" these ancient guarantees. In actual fact, the *Privilegium maius* was directly inspired by the *Privilegium minus*, an authentic set of privileges granted by Emperor Friedrich Barbarossa to the Babenbergs in 1156. Rudolf had Barbarossa's seal removed from the older document and attached to the *Privilegium maius* to make it seem legitimate. When he received the *Privilegium maius*, a suspicious Charles IV had it examined by none other than Petrarch, who declared it a counterfeit. It was Charles, ironically, who provoked this surprising assertion of Habsburg supremacy. As part of regularizing the election procedures for the Empire in his Golden Bull of 1356, Charles had excluded the Habsburgs from the exalted ranks of the prince-electors.

Thanks to such slights, Charles and his son-in-law developed a rather testy relationship, and the emperor brushed off many of Rudolf's pretensions, particularly his use of the iconography of the imperial crown, scepter, and sword. However, he let Rudolf get away with the title "archduke," and henceforth in all of European history it was only the Habsburgs who ever used this title. Though the *Privilegium* was an invention, that did not hinder Rudolf from persisting in its claims, nor undermine its import for the dynasty. One of the more practical provisions of the *Privilegium* was to affirm the unity and indivisibility of the Habsburg patrimony. The *Privilegium* did not promote primogeniture per se (which was not yet a firmly established custom in the German cultural orbit), but it did insist that the oldest brother must have the highest authority, albeit with the other brothers consulting in major decisions. Symbolically, the *Privilegium* expressed the Habsburg sense of a special mission and status. Though they were not entitled to call themselves kings, the Habsburgs claimed a similar level of prestige and authority. Rudolf here formulated an enduring precedent for his family. In terms of regnal power, the *Privilegium* also proclaimed the Austrian ruler's jurisdiction over all courts in his land, and his rights to land usage such as forestry and hunting. In this way it helped strengthen the dynastic state, by enumerating the sovereign's powers, the heritability of the patrimony, and the relationships between the various parts of the patrimony, their ruler, and the emperor. It is thus in Rudolf's reign that the notion of the "House of Austria," encompassing not just the family but all its possessions, began to crystallize.

Rudolf died in Italy in 1364, on his way to Milan for his brother Leopold's marriage to a Visconti heiress that would help establish Habsburg claims to territory in northern Italy. The trail that Rudolf blazed for future Habsburgs makes him the most important member of the family between his grandfather, Albrecht I, and his grandnephew, Friedrich III, nearly a century later. Besides upholding the family's claims to preeminence even while it was shut out of the German kingship, he pointed the way to other, further developments. In 1364 he signed a mutual inheritance treaty with the Luxemburgs and the Angevin dynasty of Hungary which prefigured the Habsburgs' eventual acquisition of the Bohemian and Hungarian crowns in subsequent centuries. Bringing Tyrol into the house, he gave the family an almost uninterrupted string of land from east to west across the Alps, looking both north into Germany and south into Italy. And of course he is one of the key founders of the Habsburg mythology that would be further developed by his successors, including Friedrich III who fully legitimized the *Privilegium maius* after he was crowned emperor in 1452. Rudolf, then, represents a belief in and promise of future Habsburg greatness—even though his own life was too short to complete any of the ventures he had begun. So short, indeed, was his time in charge that he never managed to sire an heir and hence ensure the succession. Rather, once he was gone, the dynasty stagnated.

Division in the dynasty

With a few minor exceptions, the next two generations of Habsburgs hit low water marks in all sorts of ways: their competence, their achievements, their contributions to the dynasty's furtherance. By the first decades of the

1400s, the male members of the family had degenerated into a fractious rabble. Rudolf's younger brothers Albrecht III and Leopold III at least showed some positive attributes, though it is their fault that the patrimony began to split. Albrecht was 15 when Rudolf died, Leopold 14. The former was a reserved, passive character, while the latter went too far in the other direction, being combative, ambitious, and obsessed with chivalric values, to his ultimate doom. In their early years the brothers attempted a kind of corulership, and the family made some important territorial gains. The thriving city of Freiburg im Breisgau came into the house in 1368, and would remain there for centuries. In 1382 Trieste and parts of inner Istria also submitted to the Habsburgs, seeing them as a counterbalance to Venice's expanding power along the Adriatic. By 1379, however, their joint rule was not working out, largely because of Leopold's aggressive ambitions. Contravening Rudolf's explicit instructions in the *Privilegium maius*, the brothers negotiated a division of the family's territories.

The partition treaty signed at Neuburg in Styria in September 1379 resulted in the formation of the separate "Albertine" and "Leopoldine" branches of the family. Albrecht kept Upper and Lower Austria as well as the Salzkammergut, while Leopold got Styria, Carinthia, Carniola, Tyrol, the Vorlande, and the Adriatic areas. The Albertine branch managed to maintain primogeniture such that the domains stayed in the hands of the oldest son, but the Leopoldine branch subsequently split further into Tyrolean and Styrian lines. It would not be until 1496, when only the Leopoldine Styrian line survived, that all the Habsburg domains were reunited under one ruler. In the Neuburg treaty, Albrecht and Leopold tried to maintain the fiction that their now-divided lands all made up parts of one united realm, and that they would all be kept within the Habsburg inheritance. But in practice their politics soon diverged and the branches rarely collaborated over the next century. The Albertine branch tended to be allied with the Luxemburg dynasty, which for several decades held the imperial crown as well as those of Bohemia and Hungary. The Leopoldine branch tended to look west and south, routinely scrapping with the Swiss and the Venetians. The two brothers themselves took opposite positions in the bitter papal schism of 1378, with Albrecht towing the Luxemburg line in favor of Pope Urban VI, and Leopold supporting the Anti-Pope Clement VII. Though such patrimonial divisions were not uncommon among medieval German families, it is unquestionable that in this case it weakened dynastic solidarity and the chances of advancing the whole house's interests.

One of those interests decisively damaged in this time was the family's position in Switzerland. Leopold went to war in 1386 against the Swiss Confederacy, gallantly but fatefully leading his own squad of knights at the battle of Sempach. There he was killed and the Habsburg troops decimated. Trying to undo that loss, Albrecht in 1388 sent some 6,000 men to battle at Näfels in the Glarus Valley, where again they were overcome by farmers wielding axes and spears. These two disastrous defeats nearly completed the process of pushing the Habsburgs out of Switzerland, though it was not until 1415 that the Swiss achieved the symbolic victory of taking Habsburg Castle. With Leopold's death, Albrecht became the warden of Leopold's four sons. These sons, with perhaps too much of their father's bellicosity in them, eventually fell into what amounted to a civil war involving also Albrecht's son Albrecht IV. This period, the first decade of the 1400s, was a terrible time in the Habsburg lands: robber knights marauded because there was no acknowledged judicial authority; famines, epidemics, floods, and an earthquake swept the countryside; and the nobility were able to assert their interests against the disorderly Habsburg rulers.

Though the civil war was inexcusable, the branches' divergent interests are more easily understood. The Albertine line in Upper and Lower Austria fought against the Hussite rebellion that spread in Bohemia and Moravia after 1419 following the execution of the religious reformer Jan Hus at the Council of Konstanz. The Styrian branch of the Leopoldine line had to deal with the rising power of the Ottoman Turks, whose raids up the Balkans were encroaching on central Europe. The Tyrolean line was preoccupied by fighting the last battles with the Swiss. Two of Leopold's sons divided the Leopoldine inheritance: Ernst "the Iron" ruled Styria, Carinthia, and Carniola, and was reasonably competent, while his brother Friedrich IV, in Tyrol, was notoriously inept.

Ernst "the Iron" (1377–1424) elevated the cities of Graz and Wiener Neustadt into the seats of his government, and also built up a state structure that would make Inner Austria one of the most cohesive Habsburg lands until it was dissolved as an entity in 1619. He promoted economic activities such as iron production, asserted the right to levy taxes and to make church appointments, and repeatedly attempted to establish jurisdictional supremacy for himself in a variety of domains. The most vexing problem in this regard was land controlled by the counts of Cilli within Ernst's broader territories. Possibly as part of his campaign to project Habsburg authority over these enclaves of Cilli lordship, Ernst revived use of the lofty title "archduke." Ernst was also the first Habsburg to face the Turks in battle, a calling which would become defining for generations of his successors. His work in strengthening the Inner Austrian domains was essential in that territory's enduring obligation to oversee the war against the Ottomans.

Ernst's younger brother, Friedrich IV (1382–1439), managed to bungle almost everything he touched. Only toward the end of his life did he salvage anything from his reign. Emblematic is his involvement in the Council of Konstanz in 1415. Friedrich decided to stand firmly behind the anti-pope John XXIII, who was one of three popes the council was trying to depose. As a result of his obstructionism, Emperor Sigismund declared Friedrich an outlaw, and all his possessions in Tyrol and the Vorlande forfeit. Friedrich was attacked from all sides, thanks to Sigismund's promise that any conquests made would pass to the victors as fiefs of the Empire. It is at this time that the last Habsburg possessions in the Swiss lands were lost. Scrambling to hold on to anything when even his own subjects in Tyrol had deserted him, Friedrich had to pay his brother Ernst a sizeable sum in 1417 to get Ernst to surrender the authority that the Tyrolean estates had conferred upon him. Friedrich then in 1418 had to pay even more money to clear his name from Sigismund's imperial ban and get back some of the other territory he had given up. During these years on the run (literally and figuratively) Friedrich earned his nickname in Habsburg history as "Freddy with the empty pockets." Once Ernst died in 1424, though, and after his final reconciliation with Sigismund in 1425, Friedrich became the elder of the house and warden of Ernst's two sons. By the time of his own death in 1439, Friedrich had repaired some of the damage he had done to his government, and left his own son Sigismund in a far better place than the bleak years around 1417.

Albrecht V (1397–1439)

As the Leopoldine lines flailed, the Albertine branch remained relatively tranquil. Albrecht V proved an able ruler, achieving a tight alliance with Emperor Sigismund and then regaining the imperial crown for his own family for the first time in more than a century. Albrecht had a sharp mind, particularly in relation to military matters, was enterprising, brave, and doughty. He employed intelligent advisors and led financial and legal reforms in his territories. His smartest diplomatic move was strongly supporting Emperor Sigismund as the latter faced the growing threat of the Hussite rebellion in the 1420s. In gratitude for Albrecht's military support also against the Turks, Sigismund married his daughter to Albrecht in 1422 and named him his heir. When Sigismund died in 1437, then, Albrecht was quickly named the new king of Hungary in January 1438. In March that year he was elected German king as Albrecht II. From 1438 all the way to 1806—with only a brief Wittelsbach interlude 1742–5—every ruler of the Holy Roman Empire was a Habsburg. Interestingly, Albrecht took several weeks to think over whether he wanted the honor, given the very difficult task of trying to rule the Empire. One of the biggest problems was the deficiency of the crown's resources. In the century since the Habsburgs had last occupied the throne, the Luxemburg emperors had continued the practice of alienating imperial property from which the crown could have drawn an income. Other sources of weakness were the lack of an administration that could adequately enforce the king's will, the pressing threats from the Hussites and the Turks, and Albrecht's own position controlling territories that were all peripheral to the main areas of the empire.

Still, he could not resist the offer. He then set about trying to secure the crown of Bohemia, to which he was entitled as Sigismund's heir and thanks to the Habsburg-Luxemburg inheritance treaty Rudolf IV had arranged back in 1364. The Catholic members of the Bohemian estates duly chose Albrecht as their king in the summer of 1438, but the Hussites rejected him. Albrecht defeated his opponents in a battle, but not decisively enough to eliminate the Hussite challenge fully. Since he was foremost a soldier, Albrecht then turned to face the Turks. He led an expedition against them in Hungary, where in 1439 he died as a result of dysentery. He had been a king for only a year and a half, but over the decades of his reign in the Austrian duchies he had registered some respectable achievements. He made progress in repairing the damage done during the days of the intra-family conflicts, restoring order and increasing the authority of his supreme court over the nobles and the clergy. The responsibilities of his government expanded because of his defense needs, and he hired more officials and advisors. The government's budget doubled especially thanks to the wars with the Hussites. Such financial exigencies demanded effective administration, which fortunately Albrecht had. His advisor Berthold von Mangen helped increase government income through taxes on townspeople and Jews, through tolls and even indemnities paid in court cases. Finally, in the long-term dynastic perspective, Albrecht's reign was most important for renewing the Habsburg claim on the imperial crown—and for uniting it with the crowns of Bohemia and Hungary, which would come to pass again only in the following century under Ferdinand I.

Dynastic strategies

In the two centuries from Rudolf I to Albrecht V, the Habsburgs deftly practiced a number of key dynastic strategies, but failed quite spectacularly in others. Representative of this mixed record are the family's efforts at dynastic production and reproduction. Rudolf I's rise to the German kingship brought a corresponding jump in prestige that for a few generations opened up the family's marriage prospects to some of the other leading dynasties of central and western Europe. For example, Rudolf married his children into the royal lines of Bohemia and Hungary, and Albrecht his children into the royal lines of Hungary, France, and Aragon. Once the Habsburgs were shut out of the kingship after 1308, they were then demoted somewhat as marital prospects. Rudolf IV still managed to marry Charles IV's daughter, but it was the astute politicking of Albrecht V's marriage back into the Luxemburg line that enabled the Habsburgs to recapture the imperial crown. Even without that crown, though, they remained one of the leading families in the German lands thanks to the acquisition of Austria in 1278. This was the most notable territorial expansion of this time, followed closely by Tyrol's coming into the house after 1363. Against these successes must be set the gradual loss of the family's position in their original Swiss homeland, which had two long-term effects. On the one hand, the family's solidifying power base in Austria, on the periphery of the Empire, enabled it greater autonomy in imperial politics. On the other, this peripheral location also naturally limited the dynasty's power in the Empire once it regained the crown. The last crucial issue of production and reproduction at this time was the failure to maintain dynastic solidarity and an undivided patrimony. Territorial partition diminished the family's status and resources as a whole, and also spurred the infighting over multiple decades in the fifteenth century.

In the processes of legitimacy and loyalty creation, the dynasty claimed a distinct status even though here, too, it exhibited trends common to the era. Rudolf I's rule proved vital in fashioning many of the foundations for the dynasty's legitimacy. Most lasting of these was Rudolf's reputation for piety, which was cultivated during his life then heavily propagandized later. This reputation grew out of oft-repeated stories such as one in which Rudolf, out riding his horse on a hunt, came across a priest bearing a consecrated Host who needed to cross a river. Rudolf lent his horse to the priest, then forever after refused to mount the steed, since it had ostensibly borne the body of the Lord himself. Another legend configuring a special relationship between God and the Habsburgs holds that when Rudolf was crowned king in the cathedral at Aachen, a cloud appeared in the sky in the form of a cross. Such stories served to reinforce the idea that Rudolf was exercising God's power on earth, that he would rule in accordance with and be legitimized by Christian precepts.

The Habsburgs' claim to the imperial crown which Rudolf I established also became a central plank in their legitimation strategies. That claim had to be legitimized itself, though, to justify the dynasty's worthiness for the imperial title, especially given the allegations that Rudolf was but a "poor count." Hence the family began in these centuries fabulistic genealogical researches to weave an ancestry back through the Carolingian and Merovingian kings, Roman noble families such as the Colonna, and Trojan luminaries. The idea was that as descendants of Charlemagne and Hector, the Habsburgs had a natural claim to primacy. This grew out of the common medieval notion of nobility that an illustrious bloodline legitimized leadership. The *Privilegium maius* was another audacious gambit to assert the Habsburgs' legitimacy. The falsified approbations of Caesar and Nero and the invented title of "archduke" adhered in that document to Austria itself—but Rudolf IV identified himself and his dynasty with the territory and so claimed its special privileges for himself and his family. The bargains with provincial elites were a further way of gaining loyalty and legitimacy. In most of these examples, the dynasty's legitimacy and loyalty depended upon the relationship with the upper echelons of society. There was at this time very little need to justify rule to the masses.

A number of these medieval Habsburgs clearly exemplified typical medieval notions on the role and image of the sovereign. Rudolf I, for instance, unmistakably wielded the ruler's sword: he was the chief of the war band, present on the battlefield with his soldiers in the fight against Otakar. He also wielded coercive justice, restoring peace by rooting out the robber knights left over from the Interregnum. The role as military leader was fundamental to most other Habsburg heads of the family too, from the knightly sallies of the first Friedrich and Leopold on to Albrecht V, who met his end campaigning against the Turks. However, Rudolf's common touch and his easy interactions with all kinds of people evinced a less grandiose image of kingship than his Hohenstaufen predecessors had propagated. Though myth-making plays a role here too, Rudolf as a ruler worked to display the Christian virtue of modesty, at least according to an incident in the conflict with Otakar. In 1276 the Bohemian king was required to swear an oath of loyalty to Rudolf. At this ceremony, Otakar appeared in ostentatious kingly regalia while Rudolf dressed in gray, ordinary apparel. The subtext to this ceremony was that the quarrelsome king had to submit to the authority of the man he had previously slandered as no more than a poor count. Albrecht V also demonstrated a surprisingly clear conception of both his authority and his duties as a ruler. His relatively conscientious government was exemplary for a medieval prince in its objectives of ensuring the peace and fostering the commonweal. He also upheld the prince's duty to protect the Christian faith by leading a war against the "heresy" of the Hussites, and by supporting the church reforms that spread from the Austrian abbey of Melk throughout the southern German lands during this time.

Another trend generally visible in medieval rulership also appears in Austria, namely the gradual move toward territorial lordship. This is the emerging idea that a ruler exerts authority over an increasingly defined geographical space rather than merely over different groups of people who acknowledge him as sovereign. The trend can be seen in the Habsburgs' efforts throughout this period to strengthen the institutions and boundaries of their various Austrian lands, whether the two Austrian duchies, or Styria, Carniola, etc. In this process they were also cementing the notion of the dynasty as specifically "Austrian" rulers. The *Privilegium maius* again played an important role here, and showed Rudolf IV's particular conception of the ruler. With this document, he made a claim for the primacy of princely power, of the prince's majesty and sovereignty over his own lands and subjects, even in relation to the emperor and the pope. The *Privilegium* further defined the special status of Austria, and took a significant step toward associating the dynasty with that territory. The theme of prestige and honor also points to the personal aspects of rulership, which lingered despite the evolution of territoriality. Personal bonds remained central to medieval social systems. One of the essential values undergirding such bonds was honor. The ruler was supposed to treat his vassals and subjects honorably, but also defend the honor of his own line. That preoccupation with honor helps explain Johann Parricida's murder of Albrecht I, since he considered himself slighted by Albrecht's actions. It also motivated Friedrich I's crusade to keep the imperial crown within his house.

The dynasty's institutionalization of its rule during this period led to comparatively strong regnal authority, though government was still quite limited. Besides upholding peace and justice, the ruler was supposed to maintain roads and bridges, levy agreed-upon taxes, administer the realm's finances sensibly, and employ able counselors. Habsburg rulers consistently sought to augment the fiscal resources of their government. This was part of the motivation behind Rudolf I's long campaign to regain lost royal lands in the Empire. Expanding tax authority was another frequent strategy. Rudolf IV for instance introduced new consumption taxes, reduced tax exemptions for the clergy, and asserted his own authority over that of local nobles to collect taxes in cities. Albrecht V's tax reforms raised revenues that helped meet the rapidly expanding costs of his government. Once Tyrol came into the house, regalian rights over its rich mines provided a solid stream of income for the Habsburg line who ruled there.

Despite these improvements, an inherent flaw in much medieval governance was insufficient oversight. As an example, Albrecht V's financial officers typically paid for expenses in advance, and later collected the corresponding taxes. This enabled them to collect more money than they actually paid out. Other ways that dynastic government increased its reach were through the codification of rights and privileges. For instance, Rudolf IV granted privileges to the Tyrolean cities, issued a number of ordinances to encourage rebuilding of structures left neglected because of the Plague's mortality, and loosened restrictions on guilds to free up markets. Rulers such as Rudolf IV also sought to consolidate their regnal power by insisting that their own legal jurisdiction and courts had supreme authority over competing aristocratic or ecclesiastical jurisdictions. The above developments apply primarily to the family's patrimonial lands, since they made little impact on the governance structures of the Empire during this time.

Part of government's increasing penetration into society was an ongoing elaboration of legal practices that delimited in what ways the prince could act and over what territories he had authority. That touchstone of medieval Austrian political development, the *Privilegium maius*, is relevant once more, since it helped define the legal relationships between the regions and their ruler. Thus while the Habsburgs made progress in various aspects of institutionalizing rule, in reality governance was a negotiated coordination among various communities and rights-holders (such as towns, clergy, and nobility) in the areas under Habsburg overlordship. In other words, members of the dynasty could not merely assert their will, and they certainly did not manage to create a single government but rather several; the different Austrian provinces retained distinct identities and institutions. Though certainly the most ambitious Habsburg rulers such

as Rudolf I, Albrecht II, or Rudolf IV chafed at having to share power
with other elites, they also typically respected the need to work with a
consultative body that represented their subjects' interests. Doing so was
a common norm across Europe.

The principal locus of the sovereign's negotiation and coordination with
these other power elites was the estates bodies, the representative groupings
of the various "orders" in society such as the nobility, the clergy, and the
commoners. The estates bodies in the Austrian lands coalesced over the
fourteenth century and became quite forceful in the fifteenth. The largest
landowners (often referred to as the magnates) and the high clergy (abbots,
bishops, but not parish priests) typically carried the most weight, but the
interests in these estates were not monolithic. The petty nobility would
often resent the magnates, and in some estates bodies, such as in Tyrol,
towns were included. The estates in general exercised authority over some
tax levies, and defended landowners' feudal jurisdictional competencies
(over the administration of justice, for example) from the prince's authority.
Habsburg rulers also typically had to acknowledge a role for the nobility in
military matters, some foreign policy issues, and even marital arrangements.
Albrecht I had repeated problems with Austrian nobles because he did not
always respect their rights in these areas. After several uprisings, he won
them over via a combination of suppression and concession, and learned
better to coordinate his rule with them. The high nobles mediated disputes
for Albrecht II's sons and then in the family's fratricidal war in the early
1400s. In the latter case the estates acted as guarantors of treaties the
Habsburgs signed.

Coordination with other interest communities could also provide mutual
benefits. One example is Rudolf IV's negotiations with the Tyrolean cities,
to whom he granted privileges in return for their recognition of him as
ruler. Another is Albrecht V's convoking of the estates, who granted him the
money he needed for his military ventures while also successfully insisting
on oversight powers on his government's finances. Coordination with the
Church likewise proved advantageous if occasionally tense. Rudolf I worked
hard to build a close relationship with the pope, to gain support within the
Empire and for his son Albrecht's succession. This relationship boosted
the Habsburgs' religious credibility, since the Church helped legitimize the
dynasty's rule. Albrecht I's kowtowing to the megalomaniacal Boniface VIII
is further evidence of the utility of papal endorsement to the status-seeking
dynasty's imperial claims. Habsburg pride would never permit a complete
subordination to the papacy, however. Hence it was more typical that the
dynasty insisted on the secular ruler's particular prerogatives vis-à-vis the
Church. Both Ernst and Albrecht V independently promoted ecclesiastical
reforms in their lands. Albrecht V in particular regarded religion as a
matter of state, and his belief that the Church should serve his dynastic
interests marked some of the first steps on the long road toward making a
state church in Austria.

It is only in retrospect from the family's subsequent history that these medieval Habsburgs seem important. Though the achievements of Rudolf I and Rudolf IV, among others, in anchoring the dynasty's rule in Austria are not inconsiderable, they are also not especially remarkable. The dynasty expanded its patrimony, grounded its legitimacy in piety and an imagined ancestry, moved toward territorial lordship, slowly increased its administrative control of its territories, and struck adequate bargains with the other power elites in its dominions. In none of these common practices of dynastic rule did the Habsburgs make extraordinary advances. Similarly, supplying three emperors over this century and a half did elevate the Habsburgs to the upper echelon of German families. But there is nothing in the period that sets them dramatically apart from the other leading families such as the Luxemburgs or the Wittelsbachs. The string of Habsburgs from Rudolf I to Albrecht V in short exemplify most of the typical contemporary trends of dynasties. It was only in the next two generations that the family was to make the leap into a truly higher status. The Habsburgs at this time were but one of several contenders for leadership; they had not yet figured out how to make themselves a necessity in European politics.

CHAPTER TWO

Austria's destiny (1440–1519)

In the autumn of 1473 the city of Trier witnessed an astounding display of princely riches—but it did not come from the Habsburgs. Emperor Friedrich III and his son Maximilian could only look on in envy as Charles the Bold, the Duke of Burgundy, made his entrance into the city accompanied by a retinue of some 13,000 people and, according to some accounts, 400 wagons full of treasures. Clad in raiments woven with gold and jewels, bearing a sword that had the entire Lord's Prayer written on its hilt in diamonds, Charles's exaggerated pomp was calculated to show off the wealth and power of Burgundy.[1] And yet he needed the cash-strapped Habsburg emperor, who could raise Burgundy into a kingdom and perhaps promise Charles the succession to the imperial crown. In return, Friedrich III demanded to marry his only son Maximilian to Charles's daughter Marie, Europe's richest heiress. After extended talks, Friedrich departed suddenly at night with no explanation, leaving Charles to pay the bills. This was typical of Friedrich's tactics: he had a habit of stalling until he was the last man standing. In this case, as in so many others, it worked. In 1477, finally, Charles and Friedrich did sign a marriage treaty by which the Habsburgs gained much of the priceless Burgundian inheritance. Twenty years later, Maximilian arranged another pivotal marriage treaty to give his own son Philippe the conjoined crowns of Castile and Aragon. The Habsburgs had maneuvered themselves into becoming the most important family in Europe.

This eventual outcome is all the more surprising given that Friedrich and Maximilian failed in so many of their other objectives. Friedrich was usually a man to whom things happened rather than who made things happen. Maximilian was nearly the opposite in character, always trying to do too much, hatching grandiose plans that frequently unraveled. They pose one of the most striking father-son contrasts in Habsburg history. Friedrich for much of his long life fiddled while Austria burned around him, and all but ignored his duties in the Empire. Beset on all sides—including by his brother—some of Friedrich's problems were of his own making, but he also had to contend with pugnacious estates bodies and adversaries in Bohemia and Hungary. Maximilian benefited from relative quiet in the Hereditary Lands and so turned his unflagging energy to reform projects in the Empire and military adventures in Italy. His institutional innovations in their Austrian power base helped the family become major players in pan-European politics for the first time. The resultant, sharpening rivalry with France then brought the Habsburgs the vital alliances that were Friedrich's and Maximilian's chief long-run contribution to the dynasty.

Friedrich III (1415–93)

Friedrich was the son of Ernst the Iron of the Styrian line of Habsburgs. His rule has long been criticized for its periodic anarchy, the atrophy of monarchical power in Germany, and drift for most of the Habsburg domains. While some of this is true, Friedrich had an extremely difficult role to fulfill with the limited resources of Styria at his disposal. For all his many disappointments, he also racked up some successes that proved beneficial to the dynasty, particularly reuniting the Austrian territories and bringing the Burgundian inheritance into the house. Friedrich's very long rule as emperor-king can be divided into two broad periods. The first went from his election in 1440 to 1471, during which Friedrich (see Figure 2.1) was tormented by unrest in Austria and intra-family conflicts that led him to neglect events in the Holy Roman Empire. The second phase extended from 1471 to Friedrich's death in 1493. During this time his attention returned to the Empire, where he attempted to restore some central authority, to Burgundy, and to Hungary, whose audacious king managed to conquer Vienna.

Friedrich was a beefy, rather ponderous man with an introverted personality. This meant that he fell conspicuously short of contemporary ideals of the majestic sovereign. He was criticized during his own lifetime as stingy, unforgiving, and oafish. He was given the nickname "Arch-sleepyhead" (*Erzschlafmütze*) for appearing to prefer tending his garden to actually governing. This was never a fair accusation, however. Friedrich was rarely that withdrawn from ruling. Many official documents surviving from his reign testify to his personal involvement with decisions. On the positive side, he was undeniably well educated and highly cultured. He was also patient and stubborn—in fact, tenacity may have been his greatest strength. Friedrich's ruling style has long been viewed through the prism of a phrase that he wrote in his notebook: "Happy is he who forgets what cannot be changed."[2] His fatalistic lack of initiative was informed by the deep-seated conviction that his dynasty had a divine mission that would

FIGURE 2.1 *Friedrich III, nineteenth-century illustration after a portrait attributed to Hans Burgkmair. Image courtesy of the Österreichische Nationalbibliothek.*

guarantee triumph in the end. Friedrich's famous ruling motto conveys this sense of mission: the AEIOU, that Austria was destined to rule the entire world. This belief in ultimate, God-granted victory may have partly been a post-hoc rationalization for his own impotence, of course. But given the upheavals of his century, and the weakness of ruling institutions such as the Empire, by some measures Friedrich's hands-off approach to events he could not control was sensible.

Until the 1470s, Friedrich's rule in the Austrian lands was nothing less than a disaster. These decades were ridden with the chaos of intra-family feuds, traitorous advisors, rebellious mercenaries, utter fecklessness on Friedrich's part, and assertive estates bodies that complicated what little central authority he could claim. The nearly never-ending drama seriously weakened the dynasty's control of its realms, and for significant stretches his actual ruling powers were barely notional. Yet Friedrich was consistently guided by one paramount goal: to reunite all the Austrian territories of the family in his own hands. The fact that by the end of his life this actually came to pass is testament less to Friedrich's skill than to his stubbornness, and to regular invaluable assists from the fortuitous deaths of his opponents. Friedrich became Duke of Inner Austria in 1435, gaining the majority of the Styrian line's lands while his brother Albrecht VI got the leftovers—which proved a source of dispute. For all the responsibilities he was to exercise over his lifespan, Styria as a power base was woefully inadequate, and this helps explain why his leadership was often so feeble.

Early on in his reign it fell to Friedrich, as the oldest male Habsburg, to act as warden for two underage heirs in the dynasty after their fathers died. Both of these occasions resulted in absurd, protracted turmoil. The slightly tidier one involved Friedrich's wardship over his young cousin Sigmund, from the Tyrolean line of the Habsburgs. In 1443, when Sigmund turned 15, the Tyrolean estates demanded that Friedrich end his wardship, but he refused. Friedrich's evident and ignoble strategy was to hold Sigmund as a kind of prisoner until he handed over some of his domains to the Styrian line. This blackmail actually worked. Sigmund gave various properties to Friedrich's land-hungry brother Albrecht, retaining Tyrol and parts of the Vorarlberg for himself. Problems with Sigmund would return to haunt Friedrich in subsequent decades, but at the time this seemed an optimal outcome, since Friedrich got a monetary payment out of Sigmund and also managed to tamp down Albrecht's incessant pressures to carve more for himself out of Friedrich's lands and authority.

This pattern of Friedrich cynically using a young Habsburg heir as a pawn in his own schemes repeated itself with the posthumously born son of Friedrich's uncle, the German king Albrecht V. In this case, though, there were many more, equally cynical and even more avaricious players in the game. When Albrecht died in 1439, his widow Elisabeth chose to make Friedrich the warden over her son, who has become known as Ladislaus Postumus. As heir to the Albertine line of the Habsburgs, as well as to the crowns of Bohemia and Hungary, Ladislaus became a very high-value bargaining chip in the effort to take over that inheritance. This resulted in an (at least) five-way competition over Ladislaus between the boy's mother, Friedrich, and nobles in Austria, Bohemia, and Hungary. Friedrich essentially held the boy captive to rule Upper and Lower Austria in his name. In 1444 the Hungarian estates elected Ladislaus their king, but Friedrich still would not hand him over. Meanwhile, the Bohemian warlord Jiří [George] z Poděbrad demanded to become Ladislaus' governor. In 1452 nobles from the Austrian estates rallied into a league with the support of Bohemian and Hungarian nobles to wrest control of Ladislaus from Friedrich. When Friedrich refused to negotiate with them, they sent an army to attack. Friedrich was besieged in Wiener Neustadt, and seeing himself trapped, he agreed in September 1452 to hand over the boy. Ladislaus was taken to Prague, where he was crowned king.

As contentious as his short life was, Ladislaus' death ignited further feuds. This unfortunate pawn of others' lust for power died in 1457, probably of the plague. Since Ladislaus was the last of the Albertine Habsburg line, the remaining family heads—Friedrich, Albrecht, and their cousin Sigmund— began a lamentable fight over his Austrian inheritance. Sigmund and Albrecht soon reached an agreement whereby the former renounced his claim in return for territorial compensation from Albrecht. Friedrich and Albrecht then made a deal to divide the inheritance between them, but this did not settle the conflict. Moreover, the estates in Upper and Lower Austria refused to acknowledge either of the two brothers as the new ruler. Law and order in the territories evaporated, with no legitimate authority to enforce it. Unemployed soldiers terrorized and plundered the countryside. Albrecht used the chaos to construct an alliance with Austrian nobles and Jiří z Poděbrad (who was now king of Bohemia) to depose Friedrich in 1461. Vienna also rebelled against him, and he was trapped by enemy forces in the Hofburg in 1462. As Friedrich was running out of food, one of his loyalists convinced Poděbrad to switch sides. The Bohemian king sent a force that rescued Friedrich from Albrecht's siege. Friedrich was still faced with having to accede to some of Albrecht's demands—until another seemingly miraculous rescue in the form of Albrecht's sudden death in 1463. Predictably, Sigmund then declared his intention to fight Friedrich for his own share of Albrecht's inheritance. Sigmund was in no position to make that happen, though, since he also had Pope Pius II (who had formerly been his and Friedrich's tutor) threatening war against him for having taken the Bishop of Bressanone prisoner. Hence he was forced to settle with Friedrich in 1464, by which the latter, at long last, assumed sole rule of the formerly Albertine lands of Upper and Lower Austria plus Vienna.

The decades of disorder in Austria lasted a few more years, however, as from 1469 to 1471 Friedrich had to contend with an uprising involving his own traitorous former military captain, Andreas Baumkircher. The grievances of the uprising were the collapse of law and order associated with Friedrich's misrule, but also some things for which he was not strictly responsible, such as harvest failures and epidemics. The whole conflict was encouraged by Mátyás [Matthias] Corvinus, the Hungarian king. By 1471 the quarreling parties had fought themselves to the negotiating table. At that point, with uncharacteristic alacrity, Friedrich ordered Baumkircher taken prisoner, and without even a trial had him beheaded. Though this settled the latest bout of unrest, the years of contested rule and breakdown in central authority had taken a terrible toll on the Austrian lands. One lasting outcome was that in the absence of strong princely rule, the estates' power increased significantly, something with which future generations of Habsburg rulers would have to contend.

Friedrich was elected German king in 1440 and ruled for 53 years—and yet could claim very few achievements for that long tenure. The electors chose him largely because his territories placed him in a strategic position to deal with the growing troubles on the Empire's eastern flank, namely the chaos in Bohemia, the oncoming Turks, and what proved to be a rising power in the Hungarian kingdom. In the middle 1400s the Empire had many widely acknowledged internal problems as well, such as miniscule revenues for central institutions and frequent conflicts among the overlapping competencies of the various governmental powers in Germany, including the crown, the electoral princes, the imperial diet, and cities. Ruling the Empire was not impossible, and Friedrich was never entirely powerless. Distracted by crises in Austria, however, he lacked both the ability and the will to seize the initiative. After a few initial years of engagement, by 1444 he withdrew from German affairs and did not set foot in the Empire for the next 27 years. He did nonetheless journey to Italy in 1452 to become the last Holy Roman Emperor—and the first and only Habsburg—who was crowned as per tradition by the pope in Rome. This gave him added prestige and the right to designate his son as successor. In the years that he neglected imperial affairs, wars routinely broke out involving Brandenburg, the Palatinate, Swabia or among the Italian cities. This chaos, Friedrich's disengagement from it, and his years of ignoring pleas for increased involvement in the Empire motivated an inconsequential effort to depose him in favor of Jiří z Poděbrad.

It was only in June 1471, when the situation in Austria had stabilized, that Friedrich returned to the Empire, calling for an imperial diet meeting in Regensburg. His primary motivation for calling this Reichstag was to raise a military force to deal with the Turks. In 1453, when he had learned that the Ottomans had finally overrun the ancient Christian citadel of Constantinople, Friedrich reportedly broke down weeping—but he could not be motivated to muster an army to respond. By the 1470s, the Turks were encroaching on his own lands. In order to grant money for a military campaign, the diet insisted on several reform projects. Among these was one to reorganize the justice system in the Empire so that the diet would have more influence over the courts and the emperor less. Friedrich strongly resisted this proposal, understandably, since it would have reduced his powers over peace and the administration of the law. The outcome of his renewed engagement with the Empire turned out to be as dissatisfying as his previous forays. He was granted not a major offensive force to counteract the Turks, but only a few thousand men to serve as border defense. Relatively few of them ever materialized. Given the Empire's institutional impasses, Friedrich's decision to keep his distance from its politics and rest on his laurels as emperor was comprehensible if regrettable.

Perhaps Friedrich's single greatest achievement—bringing the Burgundian inheritance into the Habsburg dynasty—demonstrates how his tactics of tenaciously waiting for his enemies to implode proved rewarding. Over the century prior to 1470, the cadet line of the French Valois dynasty had built up a large, very rich, but scattered and loosely connected set of dominions in what is today the Netherlands, Belgium, Luxembourg, and parts of northern France. Taking as their primary title the dukes of Burgundy (which was a duchy subject to the French king), they were also vassals to the Holy Roman Empire by virtue of ruling over the county of Franche-Comté as well as the Low Countries. Since 1467 the ruler had been Charles the Bold, who was determined not only to continue adding territories to his patrimony, but also to settle his ducal inferiority complex by being raised to the title of king. Charles acquired Habsburg lands in 1469 when Sigmund of Tyrol mortgaged territories in Alsace, Sundgau, and Breisgau to him in return for 50,000 gulden. Sigmund, who resembled his equally spendthrift and bumbling father (he of the nickname "with the empty pockets"), needed the money because of his ongoing battles against the Swiss. Charles also began negotiations with Friedrich to have his various acquisitions of imperial fiefs legitimized, and then to gain a royal title. He needed Friedrich for this because the emperor still had some acknowledged authority as the supreme temporal power in Europe. Charles also knew that there was no way his brother-in-law Louis XI, the French king, was ever going to agree to a Burgundian kingdom on France's eastern borders.

Friedrich's abrupt departure from the splashy summit meeting in Trier in 1473 delayed but did not derail his plans to marry Maximilian to Charles's daughter. Sigmund, who wanted back the lands he had mortgaged, formed an alliance with several cities threatened by Charles's expansionist designs and went to battle against him in 1474. Friedrich also summoned the Empire to raise an army after Charles invaded near Cologne in 1475. Friedrich himself, at 63 years old, led his troops. This two-pronged attack regained Sigmund his lost lands, and forced Charles back into negotiations with Friedrich. In 1475 they successfully concluded the marriage agreement. Charles, taking his own "bold" nickname too seriously, then went on the warpath again. He was killed besieging the town of Nancy in January 1477. This set off a mad scramble to claim the immensely valuable inheritance. Louis XI mobilized his troops and intended to marry his own son to Marie, who, however, was actually in love with Maximilian. Maximilian had just turned 18, and Friedrich directed him to rush to Bruges, where his wedding to Marie took place in August 1477. The marriage was the easy part; Maximilian had to spend the next several years on the battlefield and at the negotiating table to secure the inheritance, as will be described below.

Though Friedrich demonstrated that he could not adequately govern his existing territories, that did not stop him attempting to acquire more. After Ladislaus Postumus's death, Friedrich, Albrecht, and Sigmund all mounted preposterous and unsuccessful bids to take the Bohemian crown. Friedrich then made a claim for the Hungarian kingship, and was even elected by a splinter group of nobles. However, the majority of the Hungarian estates supported Mátyás Hunyadi, the son of the former regent. Though only 14 when he came to the throne, Mátyás turned out to be one of the most impressive statesmen of the entire fifteenth century, and he quickly secured his rule. In 1463 he made a deal with Friedrich whereby the Habsburg turned over the Hungarian crown and acknowledged Mátyás as king, but held on to some territory on the Austrian-Hungarian border and also retained succession rights upon Mátyás's death. This was only the opening round of the long duel between these two. In 1482 an armistice with the Turks on his southern flanks freed Mátyás to attack Friedrich with his famous Black Army, perhaps the best fighting force of its day. Mátyás's troops overran parts of Lower Austria, Styria, Carinthia, and Carniola. In 1485 he conquered Vienna, then in 1487 Friedrich's main residence city of Wiener Neustadt, which caused Friedrich to flee to Linz. Mátyás took for himself the title of Archduke of Austria. Friedrich could do nothing militarily to stop this humiliation. He did refuse Mátyás's demands to renounce their 1463 treaty by which the Habsburgs had inheritance rights in the event that Mátyás failed to produce a legitimate heir, which indeed Mátyás was lacking.

Meanwhile, Friedrich took care of his own dynastic succession issues quite neatly. In 1486, after careful politicking, the imperial electors accepted Maximilian as the King of Rome, which was the traditional title for the acknowledged heir to the German crown. For their part, the electors were evidently hoping that Maximilian, who was young and energetic, would more assiduously pursue imperial reforms. For his part, Friedrich was hoping that now the Empire would mobilize troops to help him regain the lands lost to Mátyás. That help never materialized, however. Thus the only thing that Friedrich could do was wait—a strategy that again worked for him. As conveniently predicted by one of Friedrich's astrologers, Mátyás died in 1490. Maximilian then led an army to retake the lost Austrian lands. He hoped to push even farther east to claim the Hungarian crown for himself, but he ran out of money to pay his soldiers. The Hungarian magnates instead chose the reigning Bohemian king as their next sovereign.

Also in these last years, Friedrich had to deal with his wayward cousin Sigmund in Tyrol. Sigmund, now senile and chronically insolvent despite

Tyrol's rich mines, had been selling off his lands to raise funds. The Bavarian Wittelsbachs had been eagerly buying, hoping to make Habsburg possessions in Swabia and the Alps their own. With help from the Swabian cities, Friedrich put together an army to resist the Wittelsbachs and restore order in Tyrol. In 1488 he drove out the corrupt and incompetent advisors who had been running Sigmund's domains. A temporary regency by the Tyolean estates took over governance until 1490, when Maximilian convinced Sigmund to sell him the ruling rights to Tyrol. Once this deal was completed with the approval of the other members of the family in 1492, the entire Habsburg patrimony was reunited after the previous century's fragmentation. This cooperation with Maximilian was smoother than some of their relations in the years before Friedrich died. They both needed each other—Friedrich for help against Mátyás, Maximilian for help in Burgundy—but their interests did not always converge. In the end, perhaps prioritizing the future of the dynasty, Friedrich sometimes forewent his own objectives in order to support Maximilian's.

In the first months of 1493, Friedrich's health worsened rapidly, and a stroke in August finally felled him. He had outlasted nearly all the other men who had crossed him: his brother, Charles the Bold, Jiří z Poděbrad, Mátyás Corvinus, Andreas Baumkircher, and many others. Though he pales as a personality when compared to the likes of Charles or Mátyás, Friedrich's patient, sometimes indolent, always obstinate policies had placed his dynasty on the brink of world power. He played a long game, one with many short-term reversals but a few major, durable victories. Maximilian capitalized on those victories, and his own status as one of the dynasty's most brilliant figures is built on a foundation Friedrich laid.

Maximilian I (1459–1519)

Maximilian has been stylized into the "Last Knight" in Habsburg lore. The idea is that he represents a final flowering of chivalric derring-do in the early bloom of the Renaissance. He did indeed pride himself on his manly skills of swordfighting, horse riding, hunting and jousting, at least until his youthful vigor began ebbing as he neared 40. He also led his troops into battle personally, often taking enormous risks, including once in 1504 when he was pulled off his horse and almost hacked to death by Czech mercenaries until his cavalry rescued him at the last minute. Another aspect of his life that looks more like a medieval king than a Renaissance prince was the itinerant nature of his rule. His was government on the move. Maximilian said of himself, "My true home is in the stirrup."[3] In some years it was uncommon for him to spend more than a single night in one place. But he was also an innovative, forward-looking man deeply intrigued by new ideas. His involvement with humanistic trends in art and philosophy, and his engagement with Renaissance artists put him at the forefront of central European rulers of his day. Even his military thinking was not completely rooted in the past: his use of artillery was advanced for its time. One of his long-term projects was reforming the German *Landsknechte*, the mercenaries, into a more effective fighting force. So, although Maximilian was neither the last knight nor fully the first prince in the early modern sense, the fact that he straddles these two appellations is most truly indicative of his character.

Like his father, he was a big, robust man; he had a ship's prow of a nose, and a jaw with a slight Habsburg jut. With his energy, rashness, and volatility, he did not resemble his father. Throughout their lives, Friedrich and Maximilian often did not see eye to eye. The father considered the son a reckless adventurer and withheld funds from him, hoping that shutting off Maximilian's cash flow would moderate his ambitions. However, his very name, with its whiff of maximalism, points to his boundless ambition. It was an unprecedented moniker for a family previously populated with so many Albrechts, Rudolfs, Friedrichs, and Leopolds. More than any Habsburg before him, Maximilian played on a political field encompassing all of western Europe. His horizons were wide, politically but also intellectually. As might be expected, he was also an unapologetic egotist. In accordance with typical dynastic thinking, his own personal interests were to him inseparable from the interests of the areas he ruled. Machiavelli met Maximilian several times and considered him an excellent ruler with "infinite *virtù*" (in that acme of Machiavellian encomiums) but noted accurately that one of Maximilian's greatest faults was that he could not handle money.[4] His dreams—for reforming the Empire, conquering Italy, capturing the papacy—always outstripped his resources. But few men have so embodied the changeability of their age, or left a stronger mark on their family.

After Maximilian raced to Bruges to marry Charles the Bold's daughter Marie in 1477, he then immediately had to fight off rival claimants to the Burgundian inheritance. He beat back the French armies in 1481 and won a settlement by which he surrendered only Artois and the original duchy of Burgundy to Louis XI. At much the same time as dealing with the French attack, Maximilian also had to respond to revolts that broke out in the Low Countries. The revolts were motivated by protests against the costs of the war with France, but also as an assertion against the new ruler of cities' and estates' privileges, which Charles the Bold had sharply curtailed. Then in 1482 Maximilian sustained a brutal blow politically and personally: his wife Marie died, having given birth to their son Philippe in 1478. Maximilian had married at the age of 18, become a father at 19, and a widower at 23.

The resistance to Maximilian from the Flemish estates grew even stronger. They demanded to take over as wardens of Philippe and ultimately to make him Marie's heir, which Maximilian naturally rejected. He went to war against the estates and defeated them in 1485 to preserve his status as ruler. The increasing taxes he levied, the presence of his foreign troops in the country, and his attempts to reduce the estates' privileges all sparked yet another uprising, in which representatives of the cities of Bruges and Gent took Maximilian prisoner. In 1488 for several weeks he was held hostage in a pharmacy on the main square of Bruges as the leaders of the revolt badgered him for the concessions they wanted. He had to watch as his officials were tortured and even beheaded in protest against his government. Not surprisingly, he feared for his own life. He wrote a desperate letter asking for help from his father, which was smuggled out in a sympathizer's shoe: "I estimate that without money to run my own administration and protect the life of my son, I must surrender him and swallow my anger, for otherwise they will give me poison to eat and kill me. [. . .] This is my last letter, once and for all."[5] While Maximilian was undoubtedly afraid, the rebel leaders generally treated him with respect and even accepted him as the ruler. This letter was partly scare tactics to get help from his father. Friedrich, though pinned down by troubles with Mátyás Corvinus and in Tyrol, did get an army organized to come rescue his son. Finally Maximilian and the rebellious cities of Ypres, Gent, and Bruges made peace, though it was not the end of unrest in the Burgundian lands.

Maximilian's troubles were a harbinger of the Habsburgs' long, turbulent, but sometimes profitable rule over the Low Countries. A fair portion of those lands—principally what is now Belgium and Luxembourg—would remain in the dynasty up until 1797. Besides giving the family territory in some of the richest parts of Europe, it also opened it up to greater influence from the wealth of French and Flemish culture. The dynasty thereby became a conduit for transmitting vital intellectual and artistic trends from its western possessions further east into the Hereditary Lands. Without weakening its anchor in Austria, however, the Burgundian lands did draw the Habsburgs more deeply into the political orbit of France and England than ever before. Indeed, conflicts between France and the Habsburgs would convulse Europe for the next two and a half centuries. In fortunate contrast to the restless Low Countries, and even to Friedrich's time, the Austrian domains under Maximilian were relatively quiescent. With Friedrich's death in 1493, Maximilian became the single ruler of all the Austrian domains, unifying them under one person for the first time since Rudolf IV in the 1360s. He made Tyrol and specifically the city of Innsbruck his base, since Vienna was too far east for easy connections to his interests in the Low Countries and Italy. Tyrol was also the goose that laid the silver egg thanks to its silver (and other) mines, as well as its location on major north-south roads over the Alps. Besides exploiting Tyrolean revenues to fund his political schemes, Maximilian's main concern in Austria was to streamline the territories' governance; he made some lasting changes which are discussed below.

From the time he became King of the Romans in 1486, Maximilian was far more deeply engaged in the affairs of the Holy Roman Empire than his father had been. He said he wanted to be the greatest emperor since

Barbarossa. He was also eyeing the threats from France and the Ottomans and wanted a strong Germany to resist both. Strengthening the Empire meant reforming its institutions. There was a widely acknowledged urgency to improve administration, the justice system, finances for imperial governance and defense. Maximilian tried to harness German national feeling to these ends, declaring for example that "My honor is German honor, and German honor is my honor."[6] What came to frustrate him repeatedly over several decades was that the imperial estates—the nobles, prelates, and cities—had very different notions of what reform should look like. They disagreed with Maximilian's equation of his own person with German interests, as implied in the preceding quote. He wanted more effective central institutions to bolster his own power, to help with his schemes in his patrimonial lands and elsewhere. The solution most princes naturally preferred was that they, and not the king-emperor, should exercise control over strengthened imperial institutions. The negotiations between Maximilian and the estates took place at several assemblies, now formally constituted as Reichstags. The reforms ran into such a complicated constellation of competing interests that many of them were applied only in a piecemeal fashion.

The most important Reichstag meeting was held in the city of Worms in 1495. This diet did inject some new life into the Empire's institutions. A new imperial high court called the *Reichskammergericht* was created, capable of hearing appeals from the many lower princely courts that continued to exist. Unfortunately for Maximilian, the estates sought successfully to limit the crown's power over this court in several ways, including restricting his right to appoint its judges. More positively from Maximilian's point of view, the Worms diet did agree upon a new, regular tax called the "common penny" to raise revenues partly for imperial defense. Resistance to this tax was so widespread that after four years it was not collected again. Demonstrating a schizophrenia as both centralizing German king and territorial prince resistant to that centralization, Maximilian himself balked at introducing this tax in Austria.

At the diet of Augsburg in 1500 there was an attempt to create the *Reichsregiment*, an executive organ for the whole Empire that would have been controlled by the princes and decisively curbed the crown's power. This innovation also never really got off the ground. Another reform advanced in 1500 and 1512 was to establish regional "circles" (*Reichskreise*) for administrative reorganization. What lasted from these two decades of reform initiatives was that while the king-emperor retained a *primus inter pares* position, the Empire now had a consolidating set of common institutions in which he had to share governance with the estates. Maximilian was not satisfied with these outcomes, and he excoriated the German princes (calling them "those German beasts") for foiling his imperial ambitions.[7]

For 20 years beginning in 1495, Maximilian was mired in a series of destructive wars from which he gained very little. Most of these conflicts involved competition with the French Valois kings over influence in Italy.

Maximilian was intent on asserting his rights over the old imperial territories in northern Italy, and thereby shutting the French kings Charles VIII and Louis XII out of the region. One of his gambits was to ally with Ludovico Sforza, the Duke of Milan, and to marry his niece, Bianca Maria Sforza, whose dowry he coveted. There was never love, or even affection, in this marriage. Though Bianca Maria was admittedly a shallow, selfish woman, Maximilian treated her poorly; in his chronic financial straits, he forced her to downsize her household. She had to let go of many servants, several ladies in waiting, as well as two organists and some dwarfs. At one point she had so little money that she was even forced to pawn her underwear to creditors. Maximilian himself fought in a few campaigns in Italy against the French, but was repeatedly humiliated. He could not prevent Ludovico Sforza from being captured by his French opponents in 1500, for example, which gave the Valois control of Milan. The imperial estates refused to send money and troops for these expeditions, and Maximilian almost simultaneously had to fight a new war against the Swiss. He considered these defeats around 1500 the low point of his entire life.

With his characteristic, quixotic vainglory, however, he did not give up his aims. He instead began making shrewder use of diplomacy than arms. He managed to break the alliance between his two main opponents in Italy, France and Venice. Coveting Venetian territory, he helped arrange the League of Cambrai in 1508 that joined him with France, Spain, and the papacy against Venice. The ensuing war was brutally destructive and prolonged because the alliances kept shifting. Eventually even the truce with France broke down, and Maximilian then looked to England to support a joint attack on Paris. Bloodied and exhausted, Maximilian and Louis XII signed a truce in 1514, but this proved only a temporary respite in the Habsburg-Valois wars over Italy. He kept fighting Venice until 1516 when he finally gave up, having amassed crushing debts because he had relied on just the income from his Austrian territories to pay for these wars. Also in the last decade of his life, Maximilian took a step that erased the old king-emperor distinction in the Empire. Because he could never make it to Rome to be crowned by the pope, Maximilian simply declared himself "emperor elect." He even briefly entertained the idea of getting himself elected pope. Maximilian's last big project before he died in 1518 was to ensure that his grandson Charles V would be elected to the German throne. He initiated the campaign of bribing the electors that Charles then completed.

Dynastic strategies

From the dynastic point of view, whatever mistakes they made as rulers were more than recompensed by Friedrich's and Maximilian's remarkable success in securing marital alliances and reuniting the patrimony. Neither man was fortunate in the most basic reproduction of the dynasty: each had only two children who lived to adulthood. Maximilian, as Friedrich's sole heir, had the future of the dynasty on his shoulders. Of Maximilian's two children, Philippe lived just long enough to propagate productively, while Marguerite became a vital ruler and advisor to Maximilian and later her nephew Charles. Where the Burgundian marriage gave the Habsburgs rich if unruly lands at the very heart of western Europe, it was the marriages that Maximilian arranged that catapulted the family into European preeminence. The Burgundian possessions put the Habsburgs into direct conflict with France, and it was a quest to counter French power that joined the houses of Austria and Castile-Aragon.

With Fernando [Ferdinand] of Aragon, Maximilian arranged a double marriage whereby his son Philippe married Fernando's daughter Juana [Joanna], and Maximilian's daughter Marguerite married Fernando's son Juan [John], in 1496. Because Fernando could not produce a male heir, this marital alliance poised the Habsburgs for takeover of the Spanish kingdoms. Once Philippe died in 1506, Maximilian took responsibility for the marriage arrangements for several of Philippe's children. In 1515 he concluded a mutual succession pact with Vladislav II, the king of Bohemia and Hungary. This led to another double arrangement by which he married his granddaughter Maria to Lajos, son of Vladislav, and his grandson Ferdinand to Anna Jagelló, Lajos's sister. Maximilian lived to see his descendants take over Spain, but not Bohemia and Hungary. Many of these people are depicted in Bernhard Strigel's famous portrait of circa 1515, reproduced on this book's cover: Maximilian and his first wife Marie, their son Philippe, their grandchildren Charles and Ferdinand, as well as Lajos Jagelló.

Dynastic solidarity in Friedrich's time hit a nadir, with his brother and cousin both working against him. But thanks to stubborn strategy and also luck (such as Ladislaus Postumus's early death) Friedrich, then Maximilian, managed to gather the various Austrian duchies along with Tyrol back into their hands. They deserve major credit for reassembling the patrimony and for laying the groundwork for binding the Austrian provinces more closely together with some shared institutions. Friedrich and Maximilian's relationship is instructive in another way concerning dynastic solidarity. The two were not particularly close, and yet they worked together quite earnestly. They were motivated by a deep, overarching loyalty to the interests of the dynasty itself. Maximilian and his own son Philippe did not get along well, and when he met his grandson Charles their interaction was cold. In all these cases, the corporate enterprise of the dynasty trumped individual personalities and allayed temporary spats. After settling the intra-family feuds of the fifteenth century, this usually tight dynastic collaboration became a Habsburg hallmark.

Such success as the dynasty had during this period was not solely due to male heads. How a dynasty uses its daughters or younger sons is an important way of judging its rule. In this regard the family's interests were particularly well served by Maximilian's daughter Marguerite. She was instrumental not just as a pawn in marriage—though she was that. At 3 years old she was engaged to the dauphin of France, who later repudiated that arrangement, and Marguerite was married instead to Fernando of Aragon's son Juan. He died six months after their marriage, so then in 1501 she was married again to Philibert II of Savoy, who also did not last long, dying in 1504. Widowed twice by the age of 21, she refused Maximilian's attempt to marry her now to Henry VII of England. Instead Maximilian made her regent of the Netherlands in 1507, where she ruled until 1515, and again from 1519 to 1530. She proved one of the most sagacious and adept rulers the family ever had in the Low Countries. She somehow managed to keep the peace in the restless territory even as wars were being fought around it. She also served as a major patroness of the arts, oversaw the education of several of her brother's children (including Charles V), and provided Maximilian with valuable advice—all on top of sewing linen shirts for him. Esteemed even during her own time for her negotiation skills, she worked to smooth things over between the Habsburgs and France in preparation for an attack on Venice around 1508. She additionally handled treaty talks with Henry VIII over several years, and had her hand in the deal for the Hungarian double marriage. Maximilian called his daughter "the wisest woman in the world."[8]

Friedrich and Maximilian strengthened the dynasty's legitimacy claims both legally and symbolically. As emperor, Friedrich formally recognized the *Privilegium maius* and made it a part of imperial law. Thereby all Rudolf IV's imagined privileges and prerogatives of the dynasty became reality. Making the *Privilegium maius* official meant that the Austrian archdukes now had a more solid legal basis to raise new taxes, tolls and fines, to grant titles of nobility, and to name officers such as judges and notaries. Also, though his manipulation of Ladislaus Postumus was distasteful, it helped maintain the Habsburgs' legal claims to the crowns of Bohemia and Hungary. Friedrich's shoddy rule undermined his legitimacy in both the Empire and Austria (hence the various attempts to depose him), but he seemed to want to compensate for these practical shortcomings with an aggressive insistence on his symbolic legitimacy. Both Friedrich and Maximilian believed very strongly in the divine mission of their family, that it was predestined to rule. That destiny was supposed to legitimize nearly all the family's political projects, no matter how outlandish or temporarily stymied. Friedrich's use of the AEIOU motto also plays a role here. This acronym was taken up into the dynasty's mythology as a bold assertion of Habsburg primacy. It is not clear that the meaning with which it was subsequently freighted was actually in Friedrich's mind as he began using it, since his interest in it may have been more narrowly rooted in his fascination with magic and numerology.

Friedrich's court was meager and did relatively little to represent Habsburg power symbolically. His main architectural legacy was his palace in Wiener Neustadt, featuring the AEIOU motto in its decoration. The one outstanding figure in Friedrich's court was Enea Silvio Piccolomini. Besides serving as a particularly valuable advisor and private secretary to Friedrich, Piccolomini wrote fairly widely, including travel descriptions of the Danubian lands, a didactic work on the proper education of princes, and even some love poetry. He later became Pope Pius II. Piccolomini helped arrange the Concordat of Vienna in 1448, which was important for the Habsburgs' legitimizing relationship with the Church. According to the Concordat's terms, Friedrich gained three new bishoprics in Austria whose nominations he would control, including one for Vienna, which had previously been subject to the bishoprics of Passau or Salzburg. This was a coup not only for Vienna's prestige, but also for Friedrich's authority over the church officials in his lands. The power Friedrich gained to nominate bishops in his territories was a further step in state control over the Church. Moreover, it benefited the Empire, since similar nomination rights were extended to other German princes. The Vienna Concordat in fact served as a basic imperial law guiding relations with the papacy up through 1803.

It was Maximilian, influenced by Italian Renaissance courts, who truly began the glorious Habsburg tradition of artistic patronage. The function of such patronage, for Maximilian and for the dynasty more broadly, was not mere display. Certainly the art itself was supposed to make the ruler look good; effusive symbolism linking him and his family with divinity as well as with virtues such as wisdom, clemency, piety and valor were blatant propaganda. This was not mass propaganda aimed at the general population, however. Few people ever actually saw the art that such rulers commissioned. Rather, patronage was targeted marketing, configuring the dynasty's status to other elites. In addition to the symbolism of its imagery, art propagandized in another way, demonstrating the ruler's wealth and power—but also his cultivation. In Renaissance ideals, the prince was supposed not only to collect and sponsor art, but even to practice it, to develop a taste and facility with painting, music, poetry. Maximilian subscribed to all these ideas, and particularly in his last decade he set about elaborating a cultural legacy that would do him and his family honor. He assembled a circle of regionally important humanists including Johannes Cuspinian, Georg Tannstetter, and Johannes Stabius who authored their own scholarly works and contributed to Maximilian's projects. The artists he patronized included Hans Holbein the Elder and Albrecht Dürer.

Maximilian employed artists such as Dürer and Hans Burgkmair on an elaborate series of publishing projects designed to extol himself and his dynasty. Like his father, Maximilian's liquidity problems meant he built very little. His main architectural legacy was some Renaissance structures in Innsbruck. Instead he consigned his grandiose architecture to paper. Most impressive was an enormous woodcut depicting a triumphal arch: evoking Roman models, the design built in a family tree linking the Habsburgs back to Julius Caesar and Alexander the Great. There was also a project for a triumphal procession, never finished, whose 147 woodcuts assembled a bevy of luminaries from myth and history who (at least on paper) all paid homage to Maximilian. King Arthur was there, also fancifully included in the Habsburg ancestry, as well as kings from far-off Calicut bringing gifts of elephants to propitiate the great Austrian ruler. He commissioned two heavily illustrated, fantastical narratives known as the *Weißkunig* and the *Theuerdank* to tell a fabulist version of his life. These projects show Maximilian engaging in a kind of Renaissance self-fashioning. Though physical structures would have had greater monumental value, that Maximilian published rather than built actually shows his modernity: he harnessed the burgeoning medium of the book to project his power and image.

Friedrich and Maximilian in some ways occupied opposite poles on the spectrum of the ruler's function and image. Friedrich was reactive; Maximilian was hyper-active. Though certainly Friedrich's resources and institutions were wanting, he nonetheless often seemed content with the merely ceremonial aspects of rulership. He was perhaps less interested in actually governing than he was in simply holding the title. His approach even aroused anger during his lifetime. Friedrich's reign came as central regnal power in many European polities was generally expanding and affecting wider populations. A renewed interest in Roman law helped codify the legal powers and obligations of the monarch. There was both resistance to and acceptance of this phenomenon. His many disputes with the Austrian estates came not so much from protests over his rule but over his *mis*rule. With the Ladislaus affair, for example, they believed that their sovereign's actions were harming the genuine interests of the realm. In a similar fashion, the imperial estates lamented Friedrich's neglect because they expected their emperor to *lead*, even despite divergent political interests.

Maximilian's difficulties in the Empire especially came because he tried to do too much. His idol was his father-in-law Charles the Bold, which helps explain both his desire for martial heroics and his attempts to imitate the brilliance of the Burgundian court. He took seriously the emperor's role as the defender of Christendom. His life-long dream to lead a crusade against the Turks was continually undercut by a shortage of funds, but he did mount a rather paltry campaign in 1493. Maximilian, with his ceaseless warring and schemes, may come across as a man of the deed, but he did spend considerable time behind a desk dealing with paperwork. This is another way that he was not just the last knight, leading from horseback in some idealized medieval fashion. His masses of letters—communicating with the papacy, local officials in his realms, or his allies, for instance— point to a more bureaucratic style of kingship. Because of institutional changes in those realms, Maximilian also had more levers of government than any Habsburg before him.

One of Maximilian's long-standing projects was more solidly to institutionalize his rule in his various territories, including the Empire. His goal was to build up the territorial basis of his own authority, but beyond that to strengthen his dynasty's hold and to make government more responsive over the lands it ruled. Though he intended to strengthen central government, his reforms were not part of a meticulous plan. Rather, they were generally temporizing, like much of his rule. Fundamentally, Maximilian hoped to improve his tax base and create a standing army, modeled in part on what Charles the Bold had done in Burgundy. Maximilian was not fully able to unify the government of his lands, typically because of estates' resistance. But he did manage to consolidate key administrative functions for all the Austrian provinces in Innsbruck and Vienna. He created central offices to deal with political, judicial, and financial matters. He tried for a time to establish institutions that would oversee all his realms and serve him, combining his government in the Austrian lands with that in the Empire. The Hofkammer, from 1498, was supposed to handle finances for both the Empire and the Hereditary Lands, though the imperial estates rebuffed Maximilian's plans. He established a court council and chancellery that did coordinate political affairs across his lands, however. The idea to fuse imperial and patrimonial government evinces Maximilian's typical contemporaneous conception that government was inseparable from the ruler. It did not matter that his Hereditary Lands and the Holy Roman Empire were distinct polities in all sorts of ways; they were unified through his person, and should be governed through joint institutions controlled by him. While his control over the coalescing institutions of the Empire was weak, his innovations in Austria provided an enduring, formative basis for the dynasty's government. In the broadest perspective, they were a step in the transformation of states from feudal personal relationships, in which government is carried out by the sovereign's vassals, to a more modern, bureaucratic form in which government is carried out by professionalized officials.

Friedrich did much less to shape governing institutions either in the Empire or the Hereditary Lands. He did not attempt to hinder the budding constitutional processes relevant to the imperial justice system. After 1471, when he became more engaged with German affairs, he did try to steer those processes in a direction favorable to him and his powers. His more consistent administrative ventures involved attempts to improve his finances. Friedrich imposed fees for all kinds of official acts such as granting court decisions, privileges, and fiefs. These fees were widely resented as greedy, but particularly in the Empire Friedrich's tax income was so low that he had to raise revenue somehow. The Empire participated much less in the development of regularized, recurrent taxes that was spreading elsewhere in Europe, including even in the Austrian domains. As an example, the crown's annual revenues in Germany amounted to a paltry 2,000 to 5,000 florins. Even lesser German princes could count on around 30,000 florins a year. Tyrol alone brought in more than 100,000 a year for the Habsburgs in the 1480s, added to another 150,000 or so from the rest of Austria. Kings in places such England, France, Castile earned 300,000 to 900,000.[9] One reason Tyrol was so valuable to the house was that the ruler's regalian rights over the mines supplied a substantial income with no need to get the estates' consent.

The actual income from those mines was still never enough to pay all of Maximilian's expenses. Though his revenues compared favorably with those of the French and Castilian monarchs, he was always short of funds. The mines, therefore, became even more valuable as collateral for loans. Maximilian began the dynasty's long relationship with the Fugger family of bankers, who attached themselves to the Habsburgs like a parasite to a host. Maximilian essentially gave the Fuggers control over Tyrol's copper and silver mines. Of revenues from those mines, 50 percent would go to the Fuggers, 18 percent to Maximilian, and 32 percent to the mining contractor.[10] Deals such as this made the Fuggers immensely wealthy. Another prominent banking family was the Gossembrots, one of whom actually became Maximilian's highest financial official. Interestingly, despite his huge debts, Maximilian played the new game of international finance fairly well, since in contrast to his Habsburg descendants he never once had to declare bankruptcy.

Most of this money went to pay for his hectic foreign policy, in particular for armies. Maximilian was one of the few Habsburgs with real military talent, and he used it to institute the famous corps of infantry troops, the *Landsknechte*, mercenaries who formed the backbone of many German armies in the sixteenth century. Although they were several steps short of constituting a dynast's standing army, the *Landsknechte* were part of the evolution toward the establishment of coercive forces under monarchical control.

The Habsburg domains were not unusual for this era in that their governance was not consolidated and standardized across the different domains. Other dynasties in the fifteenth century such as the Valois, the Luxemburgs, and the Jagiełłos faced similar difficulties trying to rule composite monarchies of loosely connected territories that already had some traditions of governing themselves. In short, at this time there was very little coincidence between the dynasty's interests and the interests of the dynasty's dominions. Those dominions did not identify with the dynasty per se, and the dynasty as yet had not assimilated them into a more cohesive, more tightly bound state with some connective identity rooted in the dynasty. The attempt to coordinate administration with local elites, to negotiate the relationship between the powers of the ruler and the estates, to try (often in vain) to raise money from diverse and disjointed domains for the ostensibly unifying dynastic enterprise—these were the challenges of dynastic sovereigns in this era. What was more distinctive for the Habsburgs, however, were the particularly vigorous estates bodies that Friedrich and Maximilian had to deal with first in Austria, then in the Low Countries.

During the many years of Friedrich's weak government, the estates in most Austrian provinces developed competence and assertiveness in handling their own affairs. They became more organized and started meeting more regularly. They also established bureaucratic offices to oversee aspects of their own administration. When Maximilian inherited, he always recognized that the estates, whether at the imperial level or in the various provinces of his rule, were indispensable partners in governance. In many cases, Maximilian left the estates to govern themselves as long as they provided money when he asked for it. In fact, it has been said that the various Austrian estates deserve a large part of the credit for the consolidation of more centralized rule in the Austrian provinces, but via an accumulation of power in representative bodies, rather than in princely ones. The estates' partnership with the dynasty did not always work smoothly, of course. When they tussled with Friedrich's or Maximilian's government, it was usually because the estates viewed that government as infringing upon their established rights and privileges, or as somehow failing to carry out its basic responsibilities.

Friedrich III's achievements are almost wholly dynastic, since his governmental legacy in both the Empire and the Austrian lands is negligible. He renewed the Habsburgs' claim on the imperial kingship and contributed to its becoming nearly hereditary to his dynasty. He made major strides in reuniting the patrimony and then in extending it through the Burgundian marriage. He kept alive the family's claims to the Bohemian and Hungarian crowns, and resolutely asserted the idea of its special mission and status. Maximilian I had more to show for his reign than did Friedrich, though his reach far exceeded his grasp. Nonetheless, his ambitions were much more expansive than those of any previous Habsburg. He was a contradictory, charismatic personality who did not finish what he began, but still built much of what enabled his dynasty to prosper in coming generations. His marital arrangements were momentous. His cultural legacy was unprecedented within the dynasty. His institutional reforms, fractional as they were, were important to the Empire and fundamental to the Hereditary Lands. He undoubtedly spent too much time pursuing that old knightly mania for battles, and neither in war nor reform did he routinely succeed. Ultimately, despite their unshakeable belief in the Habsburg mission, neither Friedrich nor Maximilian came close to realizing the prophecy of *Austriae est imperare orbi universo*, that it was Austria's destiny to rule the whole world. Together, however, they did lay the groundwork for the dynasty's next generation, for whom that destiny almost seemed possible.

CHAPTER THREE

The greatest generation (1516–64)

Charles V's personal insignia depicted two columns and the motto "Plus oultre," a French version of the Latin phrase meaning "further beyond." The two columns recalled the Pillars of Hercules, and when linked with the motto, Charles's insignia suggested the semblance of this Habsburg emperor with the mythic hero, in daring and geography going far beyond any monarch who had come before him. The symbolism was in many ways accurate. Charles's globe-spanning empire was larger than any preceding European ruler could claim. It required of him burdens that only a Hercules could have supported. It brought the Habsburgs further toward the fanciful Austrian destiny of ruling the world than they might ever have realistically imagined. Every member of this generation was a king or a queen. The heads of the family, Charles and then his brother Ferdinand, were conscientious, impressive rulers over Castile-Aragon, the Holy Roman Empire, Austria, Bohemia, Hungary, and more. Their sisters were Maria, Queen of Hungary and Bohemia, who also served the family as a very capable regent in the Netherlands; Éléonore, Queen of Portugal and later of France; Isabelle, Queen of Denmark, Sweden, and Norway; and Catalina, Queen of Portugal.

This incomparable profusion of eminence demonstrates and also explains the dynasty's exalted position during this period. The Habsburgs attained so many crowns because they were viewed as an answer to many needs. A wealthy ruling family, with lots of foreign allies, was seen as vital for a realm because the family would be better able to defend it from threats, and conduct that defense in part from the family's own resources. This is a major reason why the dynasty came to rule in Bohemia and Hungary. The Habsburgs were also more successful as a "ruling corporation" because they were at this time more cosmopolitan than any of their rival dynasties. Charles, Ferdinand, and their sisters typically grew up in one land but adapted to the cultures of many others, enabling them to serve as sovereigns from Portugal to Poland and Sweden to Sicily. But with the remarkable fortune that gave this generation of the dynasty so wide a territorial reach came innumerable challenges. Charles had to confront conflicts with France, the widening religious schism in Germany, restless estates in a number of his realms, and the Turkish threat in the Mediterranean. Ferdinand dealt with many similar tests, plus a battle for the Hungarian crown and repeated Ottoman onslaughts. The demands, particularly on Charles, proved far beyond what any man could manage in the sixteenth century. By many measures, though, he and his brother represent an unequaled peak in the dynasty's history.

One might envision the man who presided over the largest European empire since Rome as magnetic and domineering, but Charles was not. He was brave in battle, and possessed a deep sense of honor, but he mostly came across as reticent, melancholy, a man of few words. Some people who met him even considered him a little slow. Slow he was not, rather, deliberate. He strove, in his vast responsibilities, to be meticulous and rational. Part of this was the image he wanted to project, of the somber sovereign conscious of his dignity. But the image did, in some ways, accurately reflect the man behind it. The important thing to understand about Charles's character is that he was just not a brilliant personality, not a Napoleon, a Peter the Great, not even a Maximilian I. His life is the story of an unextraordinary man saddled with extraordinary power and responsibility.

Ferdinand was much more sparkling. Though Charles (Figure 3.1) was not unintelligent, Ferdinand (Figure 3.2) was quite sharp. He was also more voluble and approachable. He was described as a small man with lively eyes. He was generally moderate in his ruling style—less imperious than Charles—and, unlike Charles, he was also moderate in his appetites. Where Charles spoke French best, Spanish very well later in his life, and German less fluently, Ferdinand's language ability was often remarked upon for his facility with French, German, Spanish, Italian, and even Hungarian and Czech. The contrast in the brothers' manners was summarized by the Venetian ambassador Mocenigo, who knew them both: "The emperor [Charles] is wise and cautious in his speech, and keeps many things in his breast. The king [Ferdinand] speaks more freely and rarely holds back from saying what is in his heart."[1]

Charles and Ferdinand did not even meet until 1517, and then only briefly, so that over the course of their lives they actually spent very little time together. Once Ferdinand acquired the Bohemian and Hungarian crowns his interests were not always consonant with Charles's. It is remarkable, therefore, how they forged a generally close and cordial working relationship. The key explanation is the dynastic norm of loyalty. Charles was always the elder brother, head of the family, and moreover the emperor. Ferdinand owed him allegiance and obedience. Charles had enough confidence in Ferdinand that he let his younger brother handle the affairs of the Holy Roman Empire while he himself concentrated on other

FIGURE 3.1 *Charles V at Mühlberg, by Titian (1548). In the collection of the Museo del Prado, Madrid. Image courtesy of the Bridgeman Art Library.*

matters. Indeed, in 1524 Charles wrote to Ferdinand that "there is no one in the world I love and trust as much as you."[2] It is true that he did not give Ferdinand much room for maneuver, expecting him more to carry out orders than take the initiative, at least until the later 1540s.

The two did have disagreements, such as over policies toward the Turks and the Protestants, or Charles's attempt to have his own son Felipe [Philip]

FIGURE 3.2 *Ferdinand I, engraving by Hans Sebald Lautensack (1556). Image courtesy of the Österreichische Nationalbibliothek.*

succeed him in the Empire, rather than Ferdinand's son Maximilian. Ferdinand's tactic in these instances was usually not to resist openly, but to stall, to misdirect, to persuade. As a ruler, Charles tended to be obdurate, while Ferdinand was more adaptive. Though certainly this stemmed from their characters, it also stemmed from the nature of their authority. Charles was the emperor, the protector and guardian of Christian Europe, whose massive duties justified ultimate command. Ferdinand was a ruler more neatly through others' grace: he represented Charles in Austria, and had to acknowledge the Bohemian and Hungarian estates for their role in giving him those respective crowns. In many ways Ferdinand, with his more modest, flexible personality, was more successful in meeting his objectives than was Charles.

Charles V (1500–58)

Charles was raised in the Netherlands under the eye of his accomplished aunt Marguerite, Maximilian I's daughter. She and his principal tutor Adrian of Utrecht, who later became Pope Hadrian VI, instilled in him the chivalric values and love of pomp characteristic of the Burgundian ruling style, as well as a conscientious attitude toward governing, a profound piety and sense of duty to the Church. All of these attitudes would stamp his reign. He came to the throne of Spain at age 16. He had never set foot in the country in his life. There was initial resistance among the Spanish nobility to the succession of this "foreigner"—they in fact preferred Ferdinand, who had been raised in Spain. Upon his arrival in Spain in 1517, Charles went to visit his mother Juana, whom he had not seen since he was a small child. On the pretext of her mental problems (she is known to history, with debateable fairness, as "Juana the insane") she was confined to a convent in Tordesillas, which conveniently cut her out of the succession. By May 1518 Charles and his advisors had resolved to eliminate another possible threat to Charles's position as king, and so sent Ferdinand to Germany.

Not long after Charles had taken up the Spanish crowns, Maximilian I died, and Charles was chosen *in absentia* as the new German king in June 1519. His election was blatantly bought. In total, some 835,000 florins were paid, a sum never equaled. More than half of the total came as a loan from the Fuggers. The other two main candidates for the honor, François [Francis] I of France and Henry VIII of England, could not compete monetarily. The fact that the most illustrious kings of Europe sought the imperial crown demonstrates its immense prestige at this time; after Charles, it was never again so prestigious. The symbolic value of the German kingship helps explain why it was so coveted, even though the position's powers were so limited. In fact, as part of the *Wahlkapitulation* (the "electoral capitulation" the imperial princes demanded in return for his election), Charles had to accept a number of restrictions on his power. These included allowing the electoral princes some role in foreign policy, and sharing some of his governing responsibilities with the ill-defined Reichsregiment grouping of princes. Still, only the king-emperor could represent Christendom, and Charles, with his vast dominions stretching from the Atlantic to Austria, and the Low Countries to the Mediterranean, attained a profile nearer to that of Charlemagne than any emperor before or since.

The size of that empire meant that Charles had to divide his time among his realms, as well as rely on viceroys or governors to carry out his will in his absence. For instance, though he ruled Castile-Aragon for nearly 40 years from 1517 to 1556, during that time he spent a total of only 17 years there. This compares to 12 years he spent in the Low Countries and 9 in Germany. His inability to be everywhere at once also forced Charles to become a good delegator. He depended throughout his life on smart, trusted advisors such as his chancellor Mercurino Gattinara or his brother Ferdinand, and able governors like his aunt Marguerite and his sister Maria. It was during the seven-year stretch that he spent in Spain, from 1522 to 1529, that he finally became more Spanish, learning to speak Castilian well and adapting his government to Spanish conditions. Thanks to his efforts in this regard, Charles became more popular in his Spanish kingdoms, and overall under him Iberia enjoyed a time of relative peace and prosperity. Still, Charles and his government always remained cosmopolitan. He always had people from Burgundy, Spain, and Italy in his high court councils.

The predominance of foreigners in Charles's court, and his quick switch in focus to Germany shortly after he arrived in Spain, helped provoke a sudden flare-up of resistance to his rule. This was the revolt of the *comuneros*, which broke out in 1520. It was motivated by politically inept decisions Charles had taken in the years just prior, such as making the young Walloon nephew of his close advisor Chièvres the new archbishop of Toledo, and enfeoffing another noble from Savoy with all of Yucatán and Cuba. Disgruntlement over the way he had sidelined his mother Juana and shipped off Ferdinand also raised tempers in the Cortes (i.e. estates meetings) of Castile and Aragon. A last insensitive action was that Charles summoned the Castilian Cortes to ask for new taxes just before he left the country to be crowned king of Germany.

As soon as he was gone, a number of towns drove out the royal governors and formed their own communal government (hence the name "comuneros"). The revolt was never a very coherent movement. The rebels' demands included that the cities, via the Cortes, should have more authority vis-à-vis the crown, that the king had to stay in Castile but the foreigners in his cabinet had to leave, and that taxes should be reduced. Charles's regent, Adrian of Utrecht, sent out a force to put down the uprising. It nonetheless spread from Castile to neighboring provinces such as Extremadura and Guipúzcoa, and grew more radical, challenging not just royal power but the high nobles as well, threatening social revolution. At that point the high nobles, who had been sitting on the fence, came into the fray against the rebels. Some of the cities that had rebelled, such as Burgos, recoiled from the radical demands and came back into the royal camp. The royalist army then met the rebels' ragtag band of local militias, laborers, and lesser gentry at Villalar in April 1521 and decisively defeated them. The revolt's main leaders were captured and executed.

As all this was going on, there was a simultaneous but not associated revolt in Valencia, known as the revolt of the *germanías*. In that city, nobles fled because of an outbreak of the plague and a rumored Turkish attack. The city guilds then took up arms with the idea of overturning noble dominance in favor of a more republican government. This revolt was suppressed by Charles's viceroy in October 1521. With the defeat of the *comuneros*, the Habsburg succession in Spain was secured and royal power strengthened. Henceforth the cities' influence in government would be reduced, though the Spanish monarchs would continue to have to collaborate to some extent with the nobility and the towns. Also, from this point on, the more isolationist forces in Castile that had resented foreign influence were marginalized; Castile would become ever more drawn into events elsewhere in Europe. By the time he arrived back in Spain in April 1522, Charles presided over a tamed Castile that henceforth became the "treasury and sword" of the Habsburg kings, as a sixteenth-century bishop observed.[3]

In contrast to his initial unfamiliarity with Spain, Charles had grown up in the Netherlands, and knew its culture and circumstances very well. That does not mean, however, that he was able to rule more strongly there than elsewhere. He coveted the territory's enormous wealth to fund his imperial ventures, but not surprisingly the people resisted having to contribute to his constant wars. Charles's very capable regents were his aunt Marguerite from 1517 to 1530, then his sister Maria of Hungary from 1530 to 1555. They had to manage the difficult situation as Charles sought to reorganize the administration of the territory, which comprised a highly decentralized patchwork of governing structures and communities who tenaciously defended their rights and interests. The reorganization did little to strengthen Charles's power. It gave each province its own representative body, which in turn gained increased control over finances. One area where Charles was more assertive was with religious politics. Referring to Protestantism, he said that "What is tolerated in Germany must never be suffered in the Netherlands."[4] Hence he introduced the Inquisition in 1522, ordered that heretical books be burnt, and instituted the death penalty for heresy in 1550. Naturally none of this managed to prevent the gradual penetration of new sects into the area. By the end of Charles's reign, his high taxes, repressive religious policies, and delicate relations with the more assertive provincial bodies all set the stage for the open conflict that would erupt under his son Felipe II.

Whether in Spain, the Low Countries, or Germany, Charles's subjects often resented his multiple commitments to his other realms. There is no question that his empire was too vast to be governed effectively, encompassing too many competing (even contradictory) interests that he as the sovereign somehow had to reconcile. It is also unquestionable that these multiple commitments distracted Charles from being consistently engaged even during crises. The key example is Charles's rule in the Holy Roman Empire, which came at one of the most disruptive times in all of central European history, with the outbreak of the Reformation. Charles believed that it was his duty to protect Christianity, but this does not mean he was fanatically orthodox. He had been raised in the humanistic piety of the Renaissance, influenced (as was Ferdinand) by the ideas of Erasmus. He honestly believed that the Church needed reform.

For a long time, Charles hoped to arrange a peaceful resolution to the religious conflict in Germany. Yet he did come to regard Luther's ideas as heresy, and openly proclaimed that he would feel "shame" if he let them spread throughout Christianity. Indeed, one of the reasons Charles came to oppose the Reformation is because he saw it breaking apart Christian unity. And because religion in the Reformation was inextricably intertwined with politics, Charles also accurately saw that the spread of Lutheranism undermined the unity of the Holy Roman Empire. German princes used Protestant ideas as a pretext to resist the emperor's power. He long hoped that the pope would call a general Church council, to organize the combat against Protestants, but also to address some of the legitimate grievances the Lutherans had raised. The pope consistently refused, however. The unwillingness of the antagonists to compromise—including Charles, who insisted that Luther must simply renounce his teachings—was one of the key reasons that the Reformation not only splintered Christendom but also wrecked Charles's reign as emperor.

Charles met Luther personally at the Reichstag in Worms in April 1521. Luther gave his statement of principles, including the famous "here I stand, and can do no other." Charles heard him out, but then saw no alternative other than to declare him an outlaw. At that point, Luther came under the protection of the Elector of Saxony, and his ideas continued to spread. Luther was not the only issue at this diet, since there were other problems in the Empire during the 1520s. The imperial knights, who were the lower nobility, revolted in 1522–3. In 1524 the Great Peasants' War broke out. Charles was in Spain during both these events, so they were dealt with by the princes; their successful suppression of both uprisings helped bolster the princes' power within the Empire. Charles next engaged German events at the Diet of Augsburg in 1530. By this time the Protestants themselves had begun to split, into factions around Luther and Ulrich Zwingli. Charles's goals at this diet were to raise money for the fight against the Turks and also to try to foster some sort of religious compromise. He failed at both. The Habsburgs' one major success from this diet was that Ferdinand was elected King of the Romans, Charles's successor, in 1531. Throughout the rest of the decade Charles was distracted by his wars with France and the Turks. He pledged not to use force against the Protestants, but the religious conflict continued to escalate in part because of Protestant actions such as seizing Church lands.

In the next decade, after more failed attempts at reconciliation, Charles turned to a military solution. The Diet of Regensburg in 1541 did see some good-faith negotiations from both the Catholic and Protestant sides, but even the agreement reached on certain points was then rejected by both Luther and the pope. Pope Paul finally in 1545 did call a council to meet at Trento, now in Italy but then part of the Empire. The Protestants refused to attend. Extremists increasingly drove politics. Several German princes and cities formed the Schmalkaldic League as a kind of defensive alliance against the Catholics, and also made a pact with Charles's arch-enemy François I. When two more electors converted to Protestantism—the archbishop of Cologne in 1543 followed by the Elector Palatine in 1547—Protestants now had a majority in the imperial electoral college. This was a major threat from the dynastic perspective, since it meant that the electors could well choose a Lutheran as the next emperor, and the Habsburgs would lose the title. Charles now determined to go to war—not, he said, against Lutherans specifically but against the rebels of the Schmalkaldic League. He assembled his own alliance including the slippery Moritz of Saxony, who wanted to replace his cousin as elector of that territory.

At the battle of Mühlberg in April 1547, Charles won what he regarded as the greatest victory of his life. Believing it God-given, he reportedly paraphrased Caesar, proclaiming, "I came, I saw, God conquered."[5] It was after this battle that Titian painted his well-known portrait of Charles on horseback, styling him not just as a Roman emperor but also as the defender of Christianity. This was the high point of Charles's authority in the Empire, but that did not enable him to solve its many problems to his satisfaction. He advanced proposals to strengthen the governmental cohesion of the Empire, but even the Catholic princes resisted this as a power-grab by the emperor. He also encouraged the Reichstag to develop what became known as its "Interim," an agreement by which Catholic principles were reemphasized while conceding to the Lutherans their right to have things like clerical marriage and communion in two kinds. Rather than a basis for reconciliation, the Interim just proved a further step toward separation.

Events over the next several years were a disaster for Charles and ultimately convinced him to abdicate. When Charles publicly aired his desire that the imperial crown should alternate between the Spanish and Austrian branches of the dynasty, princes Protestant and Catholic alike protested at the idea of being ruled by a Spaniard. Under the leadership of Charles's traitorous former ally Moritz of Saxony, several rebellious Protestant princes made an alliance with the new French king, Henri II. In February 1552 Moritz's forces staged a surprise attack on Charles, who was in Innsbruck, and almost captured him. In a humiliating turn of events, the great victor of Mühlberg was forced to flee over the Alps into Carinthia. That same year Henri launched an assault on several cities in Lorraine. Ferdinand now took over the negotiations to achieve a settlement with the Protestant princes and Moritz, while Charles suffered another embarrassing defeat when he tried to retake the city of Metz from the French in early 1553. From this point onward Charles, deeply depressed about the situation in the Empire, let Ferdinand manage events there. It was Ferdinand who negotiated the Peace of Augsburg in 1555. This was a "religious peace" which later became known by the formula *cuius regio eius religio*, meaning that a ruler had the right to decide whether his territory (and hence his subjects) would be Catholic or Lutheran. Charles was disgusted with the outcome of Augsburg and refused to sign the final documents, leaving that to Ferdinand. It amounted not only to a defeat of Charles's desire for unity and harmony in Christendom. Augsburg was also a seminal moment in the ongoing erosion of the imperial office's authority.

Much as the religious splits in the Empire tormented Charles for several decades, so too did the never-ending feuds with the French kings, particularly François I. This conflict became Charles's chief foreign policy preoccupation. The wars were almost always started by François, a proud, duplicitous, unrelenting character who, though usually defeated by Charles, somehow always lived to harass him again another day. François's aggression is at least partially understandable in that France was nearly surrounded by Habsburg territories on its northern, southern, and eastern borders. But the conflict between the Habsburgs and France went back to Maximilian's time, and would persist into the eighteenth century and beyond. Charles and François fought over competing claims to Navarre, Burgundy, and northern Italy, especially Milan. Having already lost the imperial election to Charles in 1519, François seized upon the unrest of the *comuneros* revolt to attack Navarre in 1521, but his forces were successfully repulsed by a Spanish army. Northern Italy then became the scene of the two sovereigns' recurrent wars. As one of the richest, most urbanized parts of Europe at that time, it was a worthy prize. Charles particularly coveted the duchy of Milan because he regarded it as the key strategic link between his lands in southern Italy (which he had from his Spanish inheritance) up through Tyrol, Franche-Comté, and finally to the Low Countries.

In contending for control of northern Italy, Charles had to compete not just with the French but with the papacy as well. François attacked Milan in the autumn of 1524, but then in spring 1525 was resoundingly defeated by Charles's armies at the battle of Pavia where François himself was taken prisoner. François signed the Treaty of Madrid with Charles in 1526 in which he renounced his claims in Italy and Flanders. As soon as he was free, he repudiated the treaty, even though Charles still held his two sons hostage as "guarantees." Meanwhile, Pope Clement VII, afraid of Charles's growing power in Italy, was supporting the French. Charles sent an army to Rome to intimidate the pope, but when its troops did not receive their pay, they mutinied, and sacked the Eternal City in May 1527. The pope had to take refuge in the Castel Sant'Angelo for nine months. Charles apologized, but this event scandalized Europe. The French again invaded Italy in 1527, and once again were beaten in 1529. Another treaty, known as the Peace of Cambrai or "the Ladies' Peace" was now negotiated by Marguerite, Charles's aunt, and Louise of Savoy, François's mother—though of course it did not last. Clement at least reconciled with Charles enough to crown him emperor in Bologna on 24 February 1530. It was Charles's 30th birthday, and the last time a Holy Roman Emperor was crowned by the pope.

François scandalized Christendom for his own part when he began collaborating with the Ottomans against Charles in 1534. He then broke the Peace of Cambrai by attacking northern Italy again in 1536. At this point Charles, anachronistically but admirably, offered to fight François in a duel, "with swords, capes and daggers . . . on land or on sea, in a closed field or in front of our armies, wherever he chooses," as a way "to avoid the deaths of so many people," in Charles's own words.[6] The new pope, Paul III, forbid such a resolution. Exhausted and out of money, both monarchs gave up the fight in 1537 in an agreement arranged by Éléonore, François's wife and Charles's sister. Predictably, François again went on the offensive in 1542 in both the Netherlands and Italy. For this campaign, Charles managed to rally to his side large forces from the Empire, as well as Henry VIII of England, and together they invaded France. François, who clearly never knew when to stop, tried attacking Naples again in 1544 but was forced back. François died in 1547, having caused untold death and suffering with his wars, and leaving the Habsburgs firmly in control of Milan and allied with Florence and Genoa. His son and successor Henri II resumed the conflict in 1552 when he allied with the Protestant princes and attacked Metz, Toul, and Verdun.

As the professed defender of Christendom, Charles also had to take on the external threat of the Ottoman Turks. However, he devoted much less attention to this opponent than to many of his others. He made a few forays against the Turks when circumstances permitted, primarily in the Mediterranean, but apart from in that theater he did not see his realms' interests as seriously threatened by them. He generally left Ferdinand to fend for himself against the sultan's encroachments in central Europe. Turkish naval power increased substantially in the first decades of the 1500s, leading to the capture of the fortress of Rhodes in 1522. The Turks also struck an alliance with pirates along the Barbary Coast of northern Africa, who preyed on shipping in the western Mediterranean and assaulted some Spanish coastal towns. In 1534 Charles signed a peace treaty with François, which freed him to turn to the growing naval threat. The Castilian Cortes voted him extra funds, and he seized some of the wealth coming in from the Americas. Once he made an alliance with Genoa, which put its large navy at his disposal, all the pieces were in place.

Charles determined to attack the pirates' base of Tunis, which became one of the most resounding, if short-lived successes of his reign. With an enormous fleet of nearly 400 ships and some 30,000 men, Charles personally led the assault on Tunis in July 1535. His forces easily won the day, though the pirate leader Barbarossa escaped, retreating to Algiers. The victory at Tunis was immensely satisfying to Charles, and it was eulogized throughout southern Europe. It did very little to sap his enemies' strength, however, and the pirates raided the Spanish and Italian coasts in 1536 and 1537. It was not until October 1541 that Charles was again able to cobble together enough money and allies to mount another large invasion fleet. This time he set off to conquer Algiers despite the late season. In contrast to Tunis, this expedition was a catastrophe: a storm hit the fleet, casting 150 ships ashore, and many men were lost. Charles had to pull out, embarrassed. In subsequent years, the pirate raids continued, and in 1551 they wrested Tripoli from Spanish control. In the end, Charles's engagement with the Turkish threat yielded results no more positive than most of his other endeavors.

One of the most striking things about Charles's reign from the perspective of world history is also one of the things he was least interested in, namely the conquest of America. But the massive gains Spain (Castile, really) made in the Americas took place largely during his time. Firmly established in the Caribbean already by 1508, it was in 1519 that Cortés began his subjugation of the Aztec empire, just a few months before Charles was elected emperor. In 1535, as Charles was capturing Tunis during a lull in his fights with François, Pizarro was conquering the Incan empire. The territorial acquisitions—made in the name of the king of Castile and the Christian religion—were achieved by fewer than 1,000 conquistadors. And though Charles himself had little to do with it, it was also during his reign that the structure for governing this new empire was elaborated. For all the impediments of distance and limitations of technology, that government was impressively efficient and reasonably fair. Impressive, too, is that it accepted Charles's sovereignty, a testament to the strength of the monarchical idea. Both New Spain (i.e. Mexico) and Peru were organized as separate kingdoms ruled by the king of Spain, but governed by his viceroys in conjunction with councils called *audiencias*. The powers of the viceroys and the *audiencias* were designed to check and balance each other, largely so that the viceroy would never become too independent.

One instance where Charles did take a direct interest in the affairs of "the Indies," as they were known, concerned the plight of the native peoples: what rights did they have, and could they be enslaved? Slavery had technically been illegal since the time of Fernando and Isabel, but nonetheless the Indians came to be used as forced labor under the system of encomiendas. In this system, colonists were granted tracts of land as well as dominion over the tract's indigenous inhabitants. To remedy this situation, the "New Laws" of 1542 abolished encomiendas and declared all Indian slaves free. Charles's support for these propositions was not wholly humanitarian, since the Spanish monarchs feared that the encomiendas could become hereditary and give rise to a territorial nobility in the Americas that could then challenge royal power.

Charles also intervened in the famous debate involving Bartolomé de las Casas in 1550. Las Casas argued that Indians were inherently free and deserved the same rights as any citizen of Castile, while his opponent Sepúlveda claimed that they were simply savages and therefore devoid of rights. Charles was inclined to support las Casas' position, and he decreed that until the Indians' legal position was fully resolved, conquests had to stop. Of course, actual enforcement of these laws and values from the distance of Europe was impracticable. Charles's greatest interest in the Americas was in the money it provided for his military campaigns in the areas that truly mattered to him. From the large, growing influx of American silver and gold to Europe, Charles in the 1530s received on average 324,000 ducats a year, which had grown to an average of 871,000 a year by the time he abdicated. The truly massive flows of specie to the Spanish crown would wait until Felipe II's reign.

To his credit, Charles recognized early on that his vast dominions could not be ruled as one unit, nor even by one man. This is one reason why in 1522 he negotiated a treaty with Ferdinand by which the latter would act as Charles's regent in the Austrian Hereditary Lands. Even at the time both brothers foresaw that this was more than merely a temporary arrangement, and indeed it marks the division of the house into Spanish and Austrian branches. Late in his life, more convinced than ever of the impossibility of unified governance for his territories, Charles came to further conclusions with Ferdinand. Charles was particularly concerned to keep the Burgundian lands within the dynasty, and he feared that Ferdinand lacked the resources to do so. Hence he awarded the Low Countries to Felipe, thinking that with Spanish wealth Felipe should surely be able to defend them against all threats. Because it gained not only Burgundy but also the Italian possessions, the Spanish branch became the "senior" of the house, with the richer patrimony. In a particularly controversial idea, Charles wanted Felipe to take over as German king after Ferdinand's death so that not even the imperial crown would belong firmly to the Austrian branch. Their sister Maria had to sort out the argument this caused between the two brothers. Charles finally backed down, realistically seeing that the electors would not support Felipe's candidacy.

These last arrangements were a prelude to Charles's abdication. This was gradual but started in 1555, and is essentially unique in European history, with the only real analogue Diocletian's retirement as Roman emperor in 305 CE. He had already reached the decision to abdicate by 1553. His health was bad, with gout and hemorrhoids, and he led his last battle in 1554 from a litter. He was also dealing with serious bouts of depression, occasionally locking himself in his rooms and refusing visitors. He felt himself a failure, with the Peace of Augsburg the final insult.

In October 1555 Charles gave an emotional speech to the Estates General of the Netherlands in Brussels in which he reflected on his life, and then formally surrendered to Felipe rule over the Low Countries. Charles and his audience were in tears, and the old emperor had to lean on the shoulder of the Dutch nobleman Willem of Orange for support—the same Willem who would later become one of Felipe's bitterest antagonists. In January 1556 he gave up his Spanish possessions, and in September of that year renounced his imperial title. By 1557 he had retired to the monastery of Yuste in Extremadura. Contrary to myth, he did not lead a truly monastic life there, since he had a retinue of 60 people to serve him, and enjoyed luxuries like lobster for dinner. He also continued to follow politics, advising Felipe. He finally went *plus ultra* into death in September 1558. Though he felt he had little to show for his life, in one way he was a great success: he never shirked his titanic responsibilities. His devotion to duty would make him a paragon for future Habsburg rulers confronted with seemingly insurmountable challenges. Indeed, it is as an archetype that Charles made his greatest impact on history. He was the last great western emperor, and a reminder of the time when much of Europe counted a Habsburg as sovereign.

Ferdinand I (1503–64)

Ferdinand's difficulties in assuming rule of the Austrian lands were very similar to those Charles had in Spain. One might think that as a Habsburg, Ferdinand would not have been regarded as a foreigner, as Charles was in Spain. But since Ferdinand had grown up in Spain and arrived with many Netherlanders and Spaniards in his court, he encountered a xenophobic resistance. That was not the only source of opposition. In the years between Maximilian's death in 1519 and Ferdinand's take-over in 1521, the estates had once again asserted their authority in governance. Lower Austria and Vienna were in open revolt by the time Ferdinand arrived in the country. His first task was to suppress the revolt. He brought several nobles and townspeople to trial, and had a number of them executed, including the mayor of Vienna. He then began the process of improving his German, becoming familiar with the local situation, and developing a working relationship with the estates.

Though he was technically Charles's regent in the Hereditary Lands, it was not long before Ferdinand acquired a set of domains uniquely his own. In August 1526 the young king of Bohemia and Hungary, Lajos II, was killed and his army annihilated by the Turks at the battle of Mohács. Now the many years of Habsburg marital alliances and inheritance treaties regarding Bohemia and Hungary finally paid off. Already in October 1526 the Bohemian estates chose Ferdinand as their king; besides the inheritance treaty the Habsburgs had made with Lajos's dynasty, Ferdinand was also the dead king's brother-in-law.

Ferdinand's succession to the Hungarian crown was much more difficult. Late in 1526 the majority of Hungarian nobles actually chose the Hungarian magnate from Transylvania, János Szapolyai, as the new king. Thanks in part to the politicking of his sister Maria, Lajos's widow, a smaller group of nobles elected Ferdinand. It was not just the marital treaties that brought these territories into the house—Ferdinand also had to resort to arms. The dispute with Szapolyai over rule of Hungary lasted many years. Ferdinand defeated him on the battlefield in 1527 and was then actually crowned king, but Szapolyai managed to flee and continue the fight. He gained support from François as well as Sultan Süleyman, essentially making himself a vassal of the latter. By the early 1530s Ferdinand controlled only a relatively small slice of western Hungary and Croatia in addition to Upper Hungary, today's Slovakia. Transylvania was Szapolyai's, and the rest of the former Hungarian kingdom was occupied by the Turks. Through a 1538 treaty Szapolyai granted Ferdinand the inheritance of Transylvania, but after Szapolyai's death in 1540 Ferdinand did not have the resources to try to take it. Szapolyai's son instead became the voivode of Transylvania, with the Turks' assent.

Hungary would remain divided into three until the end of the seventeenth century. But Ferdinand had nonetheless laid the foundations of the Habsburgs' monarchy in the Danubian lands, which would long outlast the family's temporarily more prestigious Spanish claims. The conditions under which Bohemia and Hungary were joined to the Habsburg patrimony—as two separate, independent kingdoms—profoundly shaped the development of the dynastic state. The overriding reason why the Bohemian and Hungarian nobilities chose the Habsburgs was because they hoped that the family would be strong enough to fight off the Turks. Apart from that common interest, though, relatively little connected Bohemia, Austria, and Hungary in the sixteenth century.

The lands of the Bohemian crown were themselves a composite monarchy of several diverse provinces. Bohemia proper and Moravia had a Czech-speaking nobility, a reasonably well-integrated governmental structure, and quite assertive estates. Silesia and Lusatia were more decentralized, mostly controlled by a number of independent German-speaking noble families. As a whole, the complex of Bohemian lands was prosperous, with an economic base of mining and textile manufacturing. Hungary, too, was a composite monarchy, made up of what are today the countries of Hungary, Slovakia, much of Croatia, plus Transylvania (now in Romania). The upper nobility in Hungary—the magnates—were very influential and a major counterweight to royal power. Apart from some mining in Upper Hungary, Hungary's economy was overwhelmingly agrarian, though even that was seriously damaged by the Turkish wars. Transylvania had long enjoyed considerable autonomy from the crown, and it remained particularly feudal, with peasants subject to harsh conditions compared to countries farther west.

In population, Bohemia carried the greatest weight. According to figures from the end of the sixteenth century, it had about 4 million people, compared to 2 million in the Austrian lands, and a little under 2 million in Hungary. A clear-eyed assessment in 1530 would have questioned whether it was even worth taking up the burden of governing this disparate conglomeration. The Bohemian estates remained very jealous of their rights and dubious of this foreigner who wore their crown. Ferdinand made a number of concessions upon taking over, including acceptance of the Hussite church (the movement descended from the fifteenth-century reformer Jan Hus), but he still had to suppress militarily a nobles' rebellion in 1547. Hungary was divided, exhausted by war, but like Bohemia run by a nobility that clung to its considerable autonomy. Ferdinand had to take this patchwork of domains and try to forge it into some kind of workable realm, most immediately so that he could resist the Turkish offensive. That he managed to secure Hungary and Bohemia for his dynasty and mount an adequate defense with limited resources is evidence of his political adroitness.

The formidable fortress of Belgrade had fallen to the Turks in 1521, and then the Hungarian army was defeated in 1526. Vienna and the Austrian lands stood next in line for the Turkish thrust into Europe. Here, too, Ferdinand was operating from a position of serious weakness. His realms' population was less than 7 million, compared to the Turks' nearly 20 million. The sultan could easily muster an army of 60,000 men while it was only under extraordinary circumstances that Ferdinand could raise as many as 20,000. The first half of the 1500s in many ways saw the zenith of Ottoman power. Under perhaps the greatest of all sultans, Süleyman, they were pushing to the west into Europe, to the east against Persia, and into the Mediterranean as well. While conquering the Austrian lands was actually not a major priority to the Turks, Ferdinand legitimately saw them as an enormous threat. In this fight, Ferdinand could count on very little help from Charles. His brother was preoccupied with the fight against France and had little reason to care about Hungary since it did not belong to him. Given that Charles and the Holy Roman Empire provided little money for an offensive, Ferdinand had to raise his own funds. In 1523 he announced a "Turkish tax" that everyone down to 12-year-olds had to pay. An indication of the lack of centralization in his lands was that he had to go the various estates separately to request funds, traveling in turn to the capitals of Innsbruck, Linz, Zagreb, and so on. These efforts still raised too little, and he had to begin borrowing heavily from the Fuggers.

The most dramatic moment in Ferdinand's conflict with the Ottomans came in the autumn of 1529 when they besieged Vienna. Süleyman fell upon the city with more than 100,000 men and 300 pieces of artillery. Before he arrived, Ferdinand had been pleading for aid from Charles and the Empire, but little help came. Vienna had to withstand Süleyman's weeks-long onslaught alone. The city nearly fell, but then as the October rains came, the sultan decided to cut his losses and withdraw. This close call was sufficiently alarming that in 1532, as the Turks were again advancing north, Charles himself led an army of around 100,000 into Austria to do battle. The Ottoman forces were bogged down nearly all of August trying to conquer the little fortress of Kőszeg in western Hungary. They finally gave up in September, pulling out and avoiding a major engagement with Charles's army. Vienna was not directly threatened again until 1683. Nonetheless, in subsequent years Ferdinand tried and failed to retake Buda, in 1541, and lost the Hungarian cities of Pécs and Esztergom to Süleyman in 1543. In 1547 he saw no alternative but to sign a truce with the Turks that required him to pay a humiliating annual tribute of 30,000 florins to the sultan. In the 1550s Ferdinand reasserted his claims on Transylvania and war resumed. Here again the Habsburg cause was helped by the heroic resistance of several Hungarian towns against overwhelming Turkish superiority. In 1552 the town of Eger fended off a siege, with the women and children even helping out from the castle's battlements. In 1556 at the battle of Szigetvár 2,300 Hungarian and Croatian soldiers badly bloodied a Turkish army 100,000 strong.

The wars had predictably terrible consequences for the lands that suffered through them. Central and eastern Hungary, the areas occupied by the Turks, emptied as people of all classes fled or died. The sixteenth century in general is associated with the phenomenon known as "the second serfdom," in which the situation of peasants in eastern central Europe worsened compared both to peasants in western Europe and to their own situation in the previous century. The forced labor requirements (often known by the term *robot*) were ratcheted up, sometimes to more than 50 days a year. Hungarian peasants in many cases lost their own land and became a noble's property. Local nobles' authority increased, with the power to render court decisions on their domains and even to make their own laws. Towns and cities in the region typically declined as well; Vienna, for example, was hurt by losing its markets further east. From being in many ways the heart of central Europe, the Habsburgs' Danubian domains after the Turkish invasion sat on the very edge of Europe, peripheral to much of the commerce and social developments happening further west.

Ferdinand was similar to Charles in that he remained a devout Catholic but also believed some reform of the Church was necessary. Throughout his life he was inspired by Erasmian teachings of tolerance and peace. These teachings informed his politics but also his hopes for a Catholic reform that might heal the rift with the Protestants. Though he is often seen as somewhat more tolerant of Protestantism than Charles, Ferdinand nevertheless used the 1521 Edict of Worms to ban the printing, sale, and possession of Lutheran books and writings in his lands. He even had Lutheran preachers and sympathizers arrested. He clearly did not want Protestant ideas to spread, and he hoped that correcting some abuses of the Church would forestall them. So besides joining Charles in calls for a Church council to respond to some of the Protestants' complaints, Ferdinand implemented reforms to improve the training and performance of the clergy in his lands, accepting for example the idea of priestly marriage. Three times over the course of his reign he also ordered "visitations" that surveyed the state of churches and the clergy, trying to identify problems and deficiencies. He also promoted measures to try to ensure Catholicism's ongoing vitality and sway, for example inviting the Jesuits into his lands.

In attempting to keep his realms Catholic, though, Ferdinand was facing an uphill battle. Lutheranism made strong inroads into Austria, Anabaptism less so. But by the 1550s, of the Austrian lands only Tyrol and Carniola remained majority Catholic. Styria and Upper Austria had become mostly Lutheran and some two-thirds of the population of Vienna was Protestant. Catholicism had all but disappeared in the lands of the Bohemian crown, replaced by Lutheranism and the various sects descended from Hussitism. So Prague was only about 5 percent Catholic at this time, and until Ferdinand appointed a new archbishop for the city in 1561, that post had been vacant since 1471. Elsewhere, Catholics amounted to no more than a third of the population. In the lands of the Hungarian crown, Croatia remained staunchly Catholic but other areas did not. Lutheranism made inroads, but it was really Calvinism that conquered Hungary. Most of the nobility and the clergy became Protestant, and it has been estimated that only 10–15 percent of the total population remained Catholic.[7] This meant that Ferdinand had to be very careful about insisting on his dynasty's Catholicism. Many of the estates organizations throughout his domains were now dominated by Protestants, who went over to the new creed often as a show of resistance to the sovereign's power. Coordinating government with Protestant-dominated estates forced Ferdinand to moderate his own attitudes and policies.

The situation with the Turks and the Protestants also related to Ferdinand's politics within the Empire. Because quite a few princes, including several electors, had adopted Lutheranism, they consistently pressed for concessions before they would grant any revenue to combat the Ottomans. In the 1550s, as Charles gradually gave up on trying to run the Empire, Ferdinand's own authority and independence from his brother's policies increased. That Ferdinand was the primary negotiator on behalf of the emperor for the Peace of Augsburg was a major boost to his prestige. And indeed, Augsburg was an important achievement, even if Charles considered it a defeat and Ferdinand (along with many others) considered it only a temporary solution. Augsburg did guarantee religious peace in Germany for the next several decades. Ferdinand, though, continued to hope that the Protestant-Catholic schism could be healed and unity restored to Christendom. He took over as king following Charles's 1556 abdication, but was not officially crowned until 1558.

His own stint formally occupying the imperial throne was relatively short, lasting only until his death in 1564. The events and achievements of that time were modest. Ferdinand as emperor struck a less martial tone than did Charles. Undoubtedly he had learned from his brother's mistakes, but his own resources were too limited to pursue Charles's constant military engagements, nor was his personality so inclined. Under Ferdinand the position of the emperor lost some of the prominence and centrality it had had under Charles; this was partly due to Ferdinand's self-understanding as a ruler, but also to the debilitating events of Charles's reign. The imperial diet and supreme court continued to bolster their authority vis-à-vis the emperor, though Ferdinand also strengthened his own governing council. His assumption of the crowns of Bohemia and Hungary diverted his attention away from German affairs somewhat. His general objective was to maintain religious peace, but his relationship to the papacy was as frustrating as Charles's. Some Catholic reform proposals he had drafted were rebuffed by the Council of Trent, and he largely gave up on it after 1563. From the dynastic perspective, the imperative was to assure that his son Maximilian would be granted the succession, which transpired in 1562, though not without considerable hand-wringing from all sides over Maximilian's ambiguous religious attitudes (as detailed in Chapter Five).

Dynastic strategies

Ferdinand was more successful than Charles at the most basic element of dynastic reproduction: Charles had only 4 children who survived to adulthood, while Ferdinand had 13. All those offspring proved very useful in diplomatic and other politics. Two of his daughters were married to the same Polish king, and several others went to Italian noble families such as the Medici and the Gonzagas. Ferdinand managed dynastic matters on the whole quite intelligently, to arrange marriages and to ensure family unity on divisive issues like religion. With the perspective of hindsight, it may seem strange that he backslid into the practice responsible for so many troubles in the previous century, namely dividing the inheritance among his sons. The oldest son, Maximilian, got the Bohemian and Hungarian crowns in addition to Lower Austria. Ferdinand the younger received the Vorlande and Tyrol, and Karl Inner Austria. Ferdinand senior included various provisions in his will to try to prevent this divided inheritance from splintering the house. He laid out rules to keep inheritance within the family, and admonished the brothers to work together in the common interests of the dynasty, specifically to help Maximilian against the Turks. Division of inheritance was still not uncommon among German families of this time, and it had an additional appeal to Ferdinand in that it enabled him to spread his debts among the three sons.

Given the enormous additions to Habsburg lands in this generation, it became an absolute imperative to maintain control of that territorial complex in its entirety. The division of the house into Spanish and Austrian branches was one practical response, though it posed particular challenges of assuring dynastic solidarity in the coming generations. Charles's steps to ensure territorial integrity and familial loyalty include giving his son a thorough education in ruling. This conscientious program for Felipe, embodied in Charles's many letters and in the tutors he appointed, was a sterling example of dynastic reproduction. Another wise policy at which the Habsburgs were particularly successful was in using regents who represented the interests of the ruler and the dynasty without aggrandizing their own power. The Habsburgs were somewhat unusual in that they regularly let women act as regents. From 1526 until she died in 1539, Charles's wife Isabel of Portugal was his regent in Spain while he was away. Charles also appointed his aunt Marguerite as regent in the Netherlands, the position she had held under Maximilian. She served Charles equally well. She helped complete the negotiations with the electoral princes to get Charles elected as German king. She was also one of the two women behind the 1529 "Ladies' Peace," one of the periodically broken truces Charles signed with François. Margaret negotiated this peace with her childhood friend and former sister-in-law Louise of Savoy, François's mother.

Marguerite's successor as regent in the Netherlands was Maria of Hungary (Figure 3.3), the sister of Charles and Ferdinand and widow of the Hungarian king Lajos II, to whom she was betrothed when she was just 6 months old. She was as politically astute as Marguerite, as well as being extremely intelligent and cultured; she had an interesting circle of humanists in her court and was admired by Erasmus. Maria however lacked Marguerite's diplomatic finesse, displaying instead a strong authoritarian streak. That may have been necessary in helping her weak, inept husband try to rule fractious Hungary before he died. Maria was then instrumental in getting Ferdinand elected to the Hungarian throne. In 1531 Charles asked her to take over in the Netherlands, and for the next 24 years she doggedly defended his interests there. For instance, she fought with the provincial governors to preserve Charles's right to make appointments to municipalities and bishoprics. She could also resist Charles's plans, however, as when she deliberately dragged her feet on the idea of marrying their sister Christina, the widow of the king of Denmark, to Henry VIII. It has been said that Maria was the one advisor Charles would not argue against.

FIGURE 3.3 *Maria of Hungary, artist unknown. Image courtesy of the Österreichische Nationalbibliothek.*

She is also notable in the dynasty's history in that she was reasonably open to Protestant ideas and had some Protestant preachers in her circle. She remained a committed Catholic, though Ferdinand had his doubts about her. When Charles abdicated, she pleaded with him to let her retire as well. She complained about the particular challenge of being a woman in politics, writing that if ever things go wrong, "It is not difficult to make people believe that the woman who heads the government is to blame for everything, and for this reason she is hated and held in contempt by the people."[8] Maria spent her last years in Spain with her sister Éléonore, François's widow.

The breadth of Charles's territories, his status as a kind of second Charlemagne, and the growing religious splits forced some adaptation in the dynasty's legitimation strategies. Nearly everywhere the inheritance or election that had given him such a vast realm went unchallenged on principle. But while the legitimacy of his rule was not questioned, his rule itself—his actual policies—were almost continually challenged. The problem was the association of Charles with the ideal of the universal monarchy. This ideal had long roots back into medieval times, with contributions from among others Dante and Enea Silvio Piccolomini. It was called "universal" for two reasons. First, it held that the universal monarch should be the supreme political authority, such that even all other kings would be subordinate to him. Second, it implied that the universal monarch's authority necessarily extended over all of Christendom. The simplest formulation was that humankind should be one flock united under one shepherd. Implicit here is an aspiration for harmony among Christians, a new era of peace that would unite them against their enemies, chiefly the Turks. Universal monarchy, with its hint of unitary political power, was seen as threatening by all sorts of other powers (such as François I or even estates bodies) and by religious schismatics.

Charles, however, never aspired to absolute authority over the European continent. He personally subscribed to only portions of the idea of universal monarchy. As an ideology of legitimation, Habsburg universal monarchy was truly propagated by others, most notably Charles's chancellor Mercurino Gattinara in the 1520s. Gattinara made an explicit analogy between Charles and the emperors of Rome, as one ultimate ruler for all of Europe. This aspiration was patently unworkable, as even Gattinara acknowledged. Charles's interests in his different realms were too disparate, his power in each too limited, for him ever to have united them into one cohesive imperial unit. Moreover, he had no wish to unite his own realms, let alone subjugate others. The many wars he fought were consistently defensive, initiated by his opponents. Charles himself also never developed a coherent, unified imperial policy. The affinity of his politics with the ideology of universal monarchy basically rests with the harmony and defense of Christianity, as he himself stated in 1521: "In defense of Christendom I have decided to pledge my kingdoms, dominions and friends, my own body and blood, my soul and my life."[9] Thus though Charles regarded universal monarchy as an impossible dream, this idea was still used both to justify his rule and to oppose it. The idea did not fully disappear from the dynasty even after his death. Its affinity with the imperial ideology—that the Holy Roman Empire and its ruler were the heirs to the ancient Roman Empire—persisted into future generations of Habsburgs. As a polemic, the allegation of a tyrannical universal monarchy was also used against Felipe II.

Whatever his ambivalence about universal monarchy, Charles's court definitely had imperial overtones. Charles helped establish the style of subsequent Habsburg courts, which became famous for their grand, impressive, but also highly ritualized and somber ceremonial that imposed a notable distance between the monarch and his subjects. Though it was long thought that this ceremonial derived from the Burgundian court, in actual fact it was an amalgam of ideas and traditions cobbled together by Maximilian and Charles. It also continued to mutate over the years. Ferdinand first brought the Burgundian style to Vienna in the 1520s, and Charles imposed it on Felipe II in 1548. Because of the Spanish Habsburg court's wealth and prestige, the ostensible Burgundian style became the dominant trend in court etiquette of the day.

Charles's cultural patronage furthered the imperial image. He commissioned martial sculptures by Leone Leoni that made him look like a Caesar, and tapestries to depict his victories at Tunis and Pavia. Charles showed his excellent taste by hiring Titian to do several masterful portraits. Highlights of Ferdinand's court patronage include bringing the painter Arcimboldo to Vienna, and commissioning the Belvedere in Prague. A pavilion designed for his wife Anna, it is one of the greatest exemplars of Italian Renaissance architecture in central Europe. He was in general quite engaged with intellectual currents such as humanism. He boldly but unsuccessfully tried to convince Erasmus to come to the University of Vienna. He did nonetheless attract a number of other humanist scholars. Ferdinand's court was understandably less imperial than Charles's, but not less cosmopolitan. There were always a significant number of Spaniards, though as time went on it also included people from the Austrian lands, the Low Countries, Bohemia, and to a lesser extent, Hungary.

The differing ways that Charles and Ferdinand were depicted artistically point to their mildly divergent conceptions of the function and image of the ruler. The most iconic portrait of Charles is Titian's depiction of the emperor on horseback at the battle of Mühlberg, the regal, victorious, Christian warrior. Influenced by the dying chivalric culture of Burgundy, Charles did still see himself as a warrior king. He led his own armies into battle, and his offer to duel his archrival François I expresses this knightly vision of leadership. Charles's conception of his authority was not unitary, however. He saw himself, in accordance with contemporary understandings, as the sovereign of distinct realms, not of one united realm. He was often the sole link between the different areas and peoples that he ruled. This idea of the dynastic sovereign as a sufficient bond among multiple realms persisted until the very end of the Habsburg dynasty. Though Charles respected his domains' distinct identities, he also regarded them as his personal dynastic possessions. He felt entitled to use their resources for his own goals. This is how funds from the Netherlands could go toward fighting the Turks, when the Dutch people actually had little at stake in that conflict. Charles's diverse subjects certainly recognized that they had few common interests other than a shared sovereign. For this reason the Spanish would resent Charles's dedication to matters in Germany.

In contrast to Charles, artistic depictions of Ferdinand lack the martial and Roman-imperial overtones. Though he also became ruler of a composite monarchy and even emperor, he never had the inflated self-conception nor the propaganda campaign to portray himself as the great, chivalrous warrior king. Another way that Ferdinand's relative modesty and acceptance of ruling norms revealed itself was in his ready acquiescence to Charles's leading role. As the oldest male Charles was considered the "father" of the family, to whom Ferdinand owed obedience.

Where Charles and Ferdinand did coincide was in their ideas of the ruler's role vis-à-vis Christianity. Their engagement with religious issues was informed by the traditional conception of the sovereign as protector of the Church. This conception pertained most strongly to the Holy Roman Emperor, regarded as the highest secular leader of the western Church and obligated to further the Christianization of the world. Charles and Ferdinand fulfilled both roles in relation to the Turks and Islam. But during their lives this traditional conception faced radically altered political and religious circumstances. With the Reformation, Christendom became not one but many, and no one ruler could represent it. This is one reason why the universal, religious pretensions of the emperorship subsided after Charles. And yet Charles until the 1550s clung to this supposed duty to preserve the unity of Christianity. Ferdinand pragmatically adapted: as his lands and subjects became religiously highly pluralistic, he relaxed his belief that he was obligated to protect them from heresy. These rapidly changing ideas on the ruler's role in regard to religion became a shifting ground underneath the dynasty. Subsequent generations of Habsburgs had to reconsider their own attitudes toward God and toward their duties as secular leaders. The transforming religious landscape also impacted the dynasty's legitimation strategies; the Austrian Habsburgs in particular were forced to modify their approach in the next century.

Another area where the dynasty had to adapt during this time was in governing a vastly enlarged set of domains. The distances between Habsburg domains—from the New World to Spain to Austria—and the time needed to traverse those distances, posed a challenge that no modern rulers had ever had to face. It routinely took eight months for a letter to get from Peru to Spain, for example. The challenge was not insuperable, but it helps explain Charles's attitude toward governance. He tried to improve the institutions of the places he ruled, but he never tried to fuse them all into a single administration. Neither Charles nor any other European ruler of his day would have had the idea of creating a unitary state out of such territories. This said, he did oversee the development of some structures that would enable him better to exercise his rule over his expansive lands. His (and Ferdinand's) preferred modus operandi was to expand on existing institutions, tweaking them to serve their own interests more effectively. An example is the council system in the Spanish monarchy, which Charles then brought into the Low Countries as well. Under this system there was a council for each individual land within the monarchy, plus some that dealt with the monarchy as a whole. These councils were generally advisory but could also fulfill administrative functions. An example is the Council of Finance in Spain, which was created to rationalize the financial state of the monarchy, and had powers to manage the credit operations necessary to keep the crown solvent. The councils interfaced with the viceroys or regents that governed the various territories in the king's name when he was absent. In running this system, several key secretaries who were responsible to Charles acted something like modern governmental ministers.

On the whole, this setup provided very thorough governance, in the sense that it attended to most matters that could possibly concern the king and his rule over the territories. It was admittedly very slow, and sometimes featured more discussion than action. It also produced a tremendous amount of paperwork, on a scale never before seen in any European state. Though Charles's court was itinerant, his records became stationary. In 1543 the fortress of Simancas near Valladolid in northwestern Spain was selected to archive governmental paperwork, marking an important moment in the evolution toward the bureaucratic state. Above all the other governance structures Charles did have a rudimentary centralized administration, under the imperial chancellery led by Gattinara and others. But in reality Charles's realms remained a very loose dynastic confederation.

To answer the Herculean task of governing such an empire, Charles built on some solid and some weak foundations. He had an excellent diplomatic corps inherited partly from his grandfather Fernando of Aragon. For his vast defense commitments, Charles had to depend, like monarchs before him, on ad hoc arrangements. He had no standing army, but he could rely on experienced, professional soldiers from the famous Spanish *tercios* as part of military forces. Similarly, when the time came for major naval expeditions such as against Tunis, he had to contract with private ship owners to use their vessels. To pay for all of this, he had a major advantage in the form of a sales tax in Castile, the *alcabala*, which raised a lot of revenue and did not require the Cortes' approval. Income from the Americas was fairly modest in Charles's reign, so he also heavily taxed the Netherlands and his Italian possessions. None of this was enough, so Charles resorted to enormous borrowing, particularly through bonds known as *juros*. By the end of his reign, repayment of these bonds ate up more than 60 percent of the crown's annual revenue in Castile, and he had to pay a similar percent in interest. Charles complained desperately of his financial problems, as did many other rulers at the time and since. But this complaint has to be put in perspective: he lived in incredible luxury for his era, by one count spending some 150,000 maravedíes a day while the average worker in Castile would have earned one maravedí a day.[10]

Ferdinand's governance was likewise a patchwork collection of disparate kingdoms, counties, and archduchies with very limited centralization. These realms' main common interest was the Turkish threat; their diverse other interests, institutions, and social structures inhibited the development of any joint institutions. Nonetheless, the governing arrangements Ferdinand established proved reasonably effective in contemporary comparison. They also set a basic template that lasted for the Habsburgs' Danubian domains until the eighteenth century. He created a privy council to advise on the main issues of his combined realm of Austria, Bohemia, and Hungary. Staffed with trained jurists, it was the only body that had jurisdiction over the entire monarchy, but it lacked executive power to enforce its decisions. Tellingly, there were no Hungarian or Bohemian members of the privy council. Ferdinand also created the Hofkammer (the treasury) to deal with revenues and expenditures, and it too was responsible for Austria, Bohemia, and Hungary together. Another relatively centralized institution was the Hofkriegsrat (founded in 1556) that oversaw all military matters for his realms. This war council took charge of recruitment, arming and provisioning of troops for his realms. It deserves some of the credit for successfully resisting Turkish military power.

The limitations of Ferdinand's government are easily illustrated. The Hofkammer and the Hofkriegsrat actually had to share competencies with similar bodies in Styria, Tyrol, Bohemia, etc. Vienna's position as capital was also hardly dominant. It is only after the immediate danger from the Turks receded in the 1530s that it increasingly became the seat of Ferdinand's government. It still had to share economic and governmental power with other cities such as Linz, Graz, and Innsbruck, however. A good example of how Ferdinand's government remained profoundly patrimonial was that public revenues (such as taxes) were undifferentiated from private revenues (such as income from his own estates or regalian rights). In effect, all monies went into one pot and he spent it as he saw fit. Ferdinand's was also not a fully professionalized bureaucracy in the modern sense. Though it acquired more university-trained jurists and a more formal structure, it was still a set of personal arrangements to serve a sovereign rather than an impersonal state. Moreover, Ferdinand's bureaucratic structures comprised only around 100 people, and the estates and the local nobility still controlled much of the appointments and governing structures at regional and local levels. Hence the penetration of the central bureaucracy was quite limited; nobles' courts still held first judicial jurisdiction in many areas, for example.

The monarch's direct administrative powers were mostly confined to the areas of the mines, customs, and the mint. But there were still some vital changes here: in Ferdinand's reign can be said to begin the formation of an "Austrian aristocracy," a circle of nobles from around the Habsburg lands that became instrumental in serving the monarchy.

Political power in composite monarchies such as Charles's and Ferdinand's has to be understood as having three layers, and it is through these that the monarchy was governed. The top layer was royal power. In general, Charles's authority was more strongly vertical than was Ferdinand's, at least outside the Empire. Nonetheless, even in Castile where royal power was strongest, Charles's central institutions were quite weak. In the middle layer were the organized groups such as estates and cities that had distinct legal rights and typically had to negotiate with the king over the exercise of those rights. In Spain, the regional Cortes and the cities enjoyed significant autonomy from royal power and operated much of the local government. An example of that autonomy is that in Salamanca province, two-thirds of the territory was subject to the judicial and financial authority of the Church or aristocrats. In Aragon and Valencia, the crown had jurisdiction over fewer than half of the towns, the others being free towns or under the jurisdiction of aristocrats. The bottom layer was that of the local nobility, who in both the Iberian and Danubian domains exercised almost unregulated control of their own lands. In Charles's and Ferdinand's time (as well as before and after), the Habsburgs' governance was really a series of contracts between these different layers of power, farming out a great deal of administration to lower levels out of both custom and the inadequacy of central institutions. An example is the *encabezamiento* system of taxation, whereby town councils negotiated with the crown over the taxes they owed, but were then left responsible for collecting those taxes.

Charles and Ferdinand both worked conscientiously with the various estates bodies in their domains, even if they found them aggravating. They tried to limit but not eliminate the estates' influence. In Castile after the *comuneros*' revolt, the estates were fairly docile, and through preferment, nobles were co-opted into the dynasty's rule. Ferdinand's relations with the representative bodies in the Danubian realms were much more complicated. The different parts of his dominions all maintained their own diets, from Tyrol to Carinthia and of course Bohemia and Hungary. The estates retained strong powers over raising revenue, and even the actual collection of that revenue was typically handled by the local nobility. So besides the never easy task of getting the estates to agree to taxes, Ferdinand had to ensure that not only would the taxes be collected, but that his share of the revenues would be sent to him. As further evidence of the limitations of centralized governance in the Danubian domains, Bohemia and Hungary retained separate chancelleries (executive organs) into the 1600s. The estates in these two kingdoms were simply too powerful ever to accede to a more vigorous standardization that might erode their own privileges. The estates in Bohemia were very assertive, sharing power with the king in administration, justice matters, and appointing officials. After the failed Bohemian estates revolt of 1547, Ferdinand did manage to limit some of these powers. But he was more successful in some areas than others. In Silesia, for example, he had to tolerate the continued existence of separate princely courts of justice.

"I had great hopes—only a few have been fulfilled, and only a few remain to me," Charles lamented at his abdication in 1555.[11] Charles's blessing was to be given greater power and possibilities than any European ruler between Charlemagne and Napoleon. His curse was that the demands on and challenges to that power were so great that failure was almost inevitable. He eventually realized this, which is why he abdicated and divided his inheritance into Spanish and Austrian domains. Where he saw his reign as full of failure, however, it is also possible to see this period as one of absurd success for the dynasty. All across Europe, Habsburg heads wore the crown. Castile and Aragon were firmly secured for the family, and therewith the rich overseas possessions. Bohemia and Hungary came into the family's hands. The last pretense to the old ideal of universal monarchy attached itself indelibly to the dynasty. Habsburg armies won major victories against the French and the Turks. Charles and Ferdinand both elaborated reasonably effective governing structures that anchored their power base. Indeed, while so much of the focus in Habsburg history during this time is on Iberia or Germany, in the Austrian Hereditary Lands Ferdinand was furthering probably the most impressive and durable dynastic consolidation from the late Middle Ages into the early modern period. Even though Charles was so disappointed at seeing Christendom splinter, the dynasty's handling of the religious schism cannot be counted as a complete failure. Ferdinand's politicking was instrumental to the Peace of Augsburg, which bought the Empire a measure of religious peace for decades. Still, the Reformation was an earthquake under the Habsburgs' feet, and for the next hundred years the dynasty grappled with its impacts.

CHAPTER FOUR

The European superpower
(1556–1621)

He has been portrayed as a tyrant, a fanatic, a megalomaniacal warmonger plotting the takeover of Europe from the sinister fastness of his monastery-palace El Escorial. This, thanks to the Black Legend, is the popular image of Felipe II, the most misunderstood of all Habsburg rulers. According to this old calumny, Felipe II was merely the most ferocious of the whole degenerate line of Spanish Habsburgs, who ruled over a Spain trapped in obscurantist backwardness, terrifyingly powerful but condemned to a long, agonizing decline. This much is true: Felipe II in particular, and his dynasty in general, lost the media war. The Spanish Habsburgs failed to counter the negative propaganda in their own time, and it has tainted their image ever since. In fact, government in Castile-Aragon was never so authoritarian or absolutist as has been alleged; Felipe II believed in rule by law more than most contemporary sovereigns. And while the religious culture of the monarchy did become more virulently Catholic during his reign, that was in keeping with trends throughout Europe, where religious splits were widening and intolerance intensifying. Similarly, the Spanish Inquisition was never as nefarious nor as ham-fisted as, say, the Monty Python depiction of it. The image of hordes of heretics being burned at the stake is wrong, and torture was not standard practice. Spain was also never so benighted and sealed off as has been assumed. Censorship was not any more widespread there than in other European countries of the day, and the Iberian realms retained deep and long-lasting cultural and economic links to Italy, the Low Countries, and even to France.

Felipe II was thus not a villain, but a tremendously hard-working monarch with tremendously great wealth because of Castile's taxes and the New World's silver. As his resources expanded, so too did his strategic vision. He contended with a rebellion in the Netherlands, opposition and unrest in France, Turkish assaults in the Mediterranean, piratical

depredations in the Atlantic and Caribbean, and a feisty adversary in
Elizabeth I's England. Habsburg Spain was the first truly global power,
and so Felipe had enemies everywhere. He chose to take them all on, to the
lasting detriment of his Spanish subjects and of his reputation. Yet he felt
he had no choice: he was steeped in dynastic thinking that impelled him to
defend his rights as monarch and to protect the Catholic faith. Correcting
the misunderstandings of Felipe II requires a recognition of his motivations,
his many positive accomplishments, but also of his many disasters. His son,
Felipe III, was but a pale shadow of the father, a king as dilettante rather
than ruler.

Felipe II (1527–98)

Felipe was a slight, fair-haired man of below average height. He spoke
quietly, and rarely displayed more emotion than a faint smile. Because of
this intensely reserved outward image, he was something of a mystery to
his contemporaries and to later commentators. But it is a mistake to assume
that the image is the man. Felipe's famously frigid demeanor was the wall
he put up between his inner self and the public figure that, as the king, he
had to be. He did feel intense emotions, perhaps above all in his love for
his family, but also in the strength of his commitment to his faith. He was
not the bloodless, coldly calculating sovereign, but rather strove to project
an image of the king as rational, fair, and diligent. His sense of duty to his
subjects, to his realm, and to his dynasty was immense, even crushing. He
nearly always strove to do what he deemed legally and morally right by the
interests of his state and his house. He venerated his father and felt bound to
continue his policies and match his majesty. But Felipe (Figure 4.1) was not
a battlefield commander. His brand of leadership was from behind the desk,
and from there he worked harder than any other monarch of his day. It is
true that his bureaucratic attention to the minutest details created massive
logjams of paperwork. His indecisiveness, though, would have afflicted any
prudent person faced with such weighty decisions, shifting scenarios, and
scanty information. Felipe's job was to rule the most expansive empire the
world had ever seen, and in many ways he was swallowed by that job.

Charles V gave Felipe quite explicit instructions for how to rule in a
famous letter of 1543. One mark of Felipe's sense of duty to his family is
how deeply these instructions shaped the monarch he became. Charles told
Felipe always to keep God highest in his mind, to listen to his most trusted
advisors, not to show anger, not to offend the Inquisition, not to allow
heretics into his realms, and to dispense justice without corruption. Religion
really did suffuse most aspects of Felipe's decision making. Contrary to
some depictions, this did not make him either a fanatic nor the lap dog of the
pope. Many rulers were swayed by religious thinking in this time, and Felipe

FIGURE 4.1 *Felipe II, by Sofonisba Anguissola (after 1570). In the collection of the Museo del Prado. Image courtesy of the Bridgeman Art Library.*

readily bucked the papacy when he thought it necessary. But he believed that he did have a duty to God to rule justly, and by doing his duty to his God he was also doing his duty to his subjects. Felipe's meticulousness certainly could become counterproductive micro-management. As one example, while he was absorbed in the preparations for the 1588 Armada, he was also corresponding with the pope about how the clergy in Spain dressed.

Felipe's bureaucratic, desk-bound style stemmed partly from his personality, since he was generally uncomfortable dealing with people. He preferred instead to deal with papers and a small circle of people he knew he could trust. That he was quite firmly rooted in Spain (which he never left after the age of 32), with a more stationary capital in Madrid, grew from his style of rule. It also contributed greatly to the Habsburgs becoming more Castilian, which they had not truly been under the cosmopolitan Charles V. This "Castilianization" of Felipe was actually an intentional plan through the first decade or two of his life. Partly to rebut earlier allegations that the dynasty was "too foreign," Felipe stayed in Spain until he was 21 and was always surrounded by Spanish advisors. One outcome of this process was actually that Felipe became "too Castilian," since he spent very little time in his other realms and did not know them well. Related is the fact that he only learned to speak Castilian fluently.

That Felipe was almost constantly engaged in wars major and minor stems not from any Castilian imperialism. In fact, he hardly ever waged a war for conquest, and his policies cannot legitimately be called expansionist. As a Venetian ambassador observed, in words that accurately expressed the king's own thinking, Felipe sought "not to wage war so he can add to his kingdoms, but to wage peace so that he can keep the lands he has."[1] Here again Felipe's actions are attuned to the instructions Charles left him, namely to keep the dynastic territorial complex intact, and not to permit heresy in those lands. These goals led Felipe to define his (and hence his monarchy's) interests in ways that could provoke wars, and which indeed could seem aggressive to his opponents. He fought so often because his interests stretched farther across Europe than any other sovereign's of his time, and like any other sovereign he tried to defend them. But neither Felipe nor Spain itself were particularly militaristic.

Moreover, Felipe's empire was not merely "Spanish." It was actually a collaboration between Castilians, Catalans, Portuguese, Dutch, Italians, Germans, and others. Though Castile was the home turf of his monarchy, and supplied a large portion of revenues and manpower, Castile itself was an insufficient base for all the major actions Felipe undertook beyond Spain's borders. Accordingly, the power of Spain during Felipe's reign, while much greater than that of any other European state in this time, was never as great as hindsight and Felipe's propagandizing opponents made it out to be. Some of those major actions were quite ludicrously audacious given the limitations of Felipe's power—but they nonetheless stand for good or ill as the signs of the much-feared (though never realistic) Habsburg hegemony of Europe. The boldness and size of his projects very closely correspond to the income from American silver. An increase in silver inflows in the middle 1560s gave Felipe the means to respond with a military crackdown in the Netherlands, and then in the 1580s another large silver inflow gave impetus to such projects as the first, famous Armada of 1588, as well as the subsequent, forgotten ones. In addition to these major conflicts, there were also ongoing skirmishes particularly with English, French, or Dutch pirates. Though Felipe's foreign policy seems dominated by disasters, particularly in the Netherlands and with the failed Armada, there were some notable successes too, as with Lepanto and the acquisition of Portugal.

The confrontation between Felipe's monarchy and Muslims—whether the Ottoman Turks or the *morisco* population within Spain—was a frequent point of concern for the first 20 years of his reign. The concern was justified, since the Turks regarded Spain as their chief adversary in Europe, and utilized a variety of means to weaken it. For instance, the problems with the North African pirates that had plagued Charles V continued under Felipe. These pirates, who were allied with the Ottomans, raided Felipe's lands unremittingly, whether in Iberia or Italy. In 1561, for example, they assaulted shipping around Naples, in 1566 off Málaga. They made raids into the interior of Andalusia, too, carrying off thousands of captives. In response to such attacks, Felipe began a long-term plan of building up the Spanish navy. Spanish naval power in the Mediterranean faced a serious test in 1565 when the Turks launched an all-out attack on the Knights of St. John on Malta. The victory of the Christian powers in this battle was a minor miracle. There was also the serious challenge of the Islamic population inside Spain itself. These people were the remnants of the former Moorish kingdoms that had ruled in the peninsula for hundreds of years until 1492. The *moriscos* ostensibly had converted to Christianity, but in very many cases they continued practicing Islam and even speaking Arabic.

Though their existence had been begrudgingly tolerated, with the growth of the Turkish threat in the western Mediterranean the Muslims within Spain came to be seen as a serious security problem. This was not without reason, since some among the *moriscos* did serve as Turkish spies or coordinate raids for the North African pirates. There was even a scheme associated with the attack on Malta to use them as a foothold from which to attack Spain itself. These fears led to a campaign of repression that forbid the use of Arabic, traditional dress, and even customs such as their baths. The *moriscos* rose in revolt from 1568–70 in what is known as the rebellion of the Alpujarras, the latter a name for villages in the mountains of Granada that were an epicenter of the revolt. Some 25,000 of this population had taken to arms by 1569. Suppressing the revolt proved difficult because most of Felipe's armies were active in the Netherlands. Since he did not have a standing army in Spain, he had to resort to conscription in the form of the old feudal levy, which raised only 16,000 troops instead of the 40,000 he had hoped for. Finally he called in his half-brother Don Juan de Austria, who led a systematic, brutal campaign, at one point killing the entire population of the town of Galera, some 2,500 people including women and children. Starting in 1570 more than 100,000 of the surviving *moriscos* began to be resettled elsewhere in Spain, dispersing them away from the areas nearest the coast. The final solution to Spain's *morisco* population came only in 1609, during the reign of Felipe III, when they were actually expelled from Spain.

The Alpujarras revolt also played into the major engagement with the Turks during Felipe's reign, the naval battle of Lepanto. The Turks had taken

Cyprus from Venice in 1570. The Venetians then beseeched Pope Pius V for help, who in turn beseeched Felipe. Felipe had to be convinced, and he was not enthusiastic for a crusade against Islam. But in 1571 the papacy, Venice, and Spain formed the Holy League, which that spring began assembling a huge fleet with the original intention of retaking Cyprus. Don Juan was put in supreme command, in which task he performed admirably despite being only 24 years old. In October 1571, off the Greek coast at Lepanto, the Turkish and Christian fleets met: Don Juan had approximately 207 ships, 70,000 men and superior firepower, while the Turks had around 250 ships and 75,000 men. Miguel de Cervantes fought in this battle, which proved a historic rout: the Turks lost around 150 of their ships and some 30,000 men killed or wounded, compared to the Holy League's loss of 17 ships and some 7,500 men. The great victory set off a wave of jubilation throughout Christendom, and began a myth that Lepanto had conclusively annihilated Turkish sea power. In fact, the Ottomans rebuilt their fleet by the next year, and the Christian powers never managed to retake Cyprus. Nonetheless, by the later 1570s Spain and Turkey basically agreed to disengage. Turkey turned eastward to its fight with Persia. Spain turned west and north to the Atlantic and the Netherlands, and the Mediterranean was no longer a major theater of conflict.

The Spanish Habsburgs' attempts to suppress the revolt in the Netherlands lasted roughly 80 years and bled both men and treasure. It was the graveyard of their reputation and ultimately of their dominance in Europe. The conflict was not constant; there were various respites as both sides licked their wounds, only to return to battle later. Nor was it an unending campaign of repression on the part of Spain. There were periods of moderation as well. But once the rebellion had broken out, a final suppression would have been nearly impossible, since the territory was so far away from Castile and was surrounded by so many potential allies. The causes of that rebellion are multitudinous, but can be boiled down to a few fundamental elements. Unlike Charles V, who had grown up in the Low Countries, Felipe was perceived there as a foreign ruler, too thoroughly Spanish to understand the issues of the territory. His efforts to milk this rich province via taxes to pay for the dynasty's far-flung foreign policy ventures also aroused resentment, as they had even under Charles. But changes in governance under Felipe caused increased friction with the estates and the high nobility. The real power of governance in the Netherlands lay with a few members of the Council of State who were especially trusted by and loyal to Felipe. This exclusivity cut out many other nobles from government, and hence from the political influence they thought they deserved.

Though Felipe's rule was by no means absolutist, like his father Charles, and great-grandfather Maximilian, his general objective was to make government more responsive to his will, which could conflict with the province's established privileges. Resistance to the foreign king and his taxes then combined with religious cleavages to make the rebellion particularly intractable. Lutheranism and Anabaptism had been filtering into the Low Countries for some time, and resentment was growing over the Inquisition's tactics against them. The prospects for rebellion greatly escalated after 1559 as the numbers of militant Calvinists grew and started preaching active resistance to the Catholic king.

In the first years of the 1560s the Dutch nobility were pressuring Felipe both to remove Cardinal Granvelle, who was essentially the prime minister in the territory, and also to moderate the Inquisition. Revolt truly burst out in 1566 when mobs of Calvinists attacked Catholic churches. Felipe was shocked by this action, and so authorized the Duke of Alba to take a military force to the Netherlands to contain the rebels. Alba arrived in the summer of 1567 and set up what he called the "Council of Troubles," but his opponents called it the "Council of Blood." This body convicted approximately 9,000 people of crimes and executed or exiled over 1,000. The symbol of Alba's harshness was that he arrested two prominent nobles whom he not altogether fairly accused of treason, the Counts of Egmont and Hoorn, and had them beheaded on Brussels' Grande Place in 1568. Another noble who became a leader of the revolt, Willem of Orange, fled to escape capture. This severe response met with resistance both inside and outside of Spain. Margherita [Margaret] of Parma, Felipe's half-sister and the regent of the Netherlands, resigned in protest over Alba's harsh tactics. In Spain there was a tussle between two factions: the faction surrounding Alba insisted on a hardline crackdown of the revolt, while the faction surrounding the Prince of Éboli was more moderate, advocating for a negotiated solution. Felipe's own stated justification for the crackdown was simply that it was necessary to suppress a rebellion. His unstated justifications—which however he entrusted to Alba—also included rooting out heresy and centralizing the obstreperous Dutch provinces into a more unified and pacified kingdom.

Felipe downplayed the religious objectives of the crackdown in part for reasons of international politics. He was understandably worried about reaction from France and England to what could be seen as a crusading army in northern Europe. Its presence there did not fail to provoke a response: English and French pirates began harassing Spanish ships, cutting off sea communications between Spain and the Low Countries. Dutch pirates known as the "Sea Beggars" captured the city of Brill in 1572 and declared that Willem of Orange was now their sovereign. Alba's repression failed to subdue the rebellious sectors of the population (by no means the majority), and his attempt to institute a new tax to make the Netherlands pay for its own military subjugation incited further resistance. Felipe recognized that Alba's policies were not working and so took a more moderate course, appointing as governors first Luis de Requesens, and then Don Juan. Just as the conflict was subsiding somewhat, Felipe's 1575 bankruptcy meant he could not pay his troops, and so they rioted. In November 1576 they attacked Antwerp, killing some 8,000 people. This incident has become known as the "Spanish Fury" even though most of the soldiers were either Germans or Walloons. Partly in response to this atrocity, the estates of the 17 Dutch provinces demanded that Felipe withdraw all his troops and accept the religious situation there. Felipe intended to meet these conditions, but neither Don Juan nor the militant Calvinists agreed, so they both kept up their attacks. By the late 1570s the situation was dire for all sides. What had begun as a nobles' movement to assert their rights and privileges had become a widespread rebellion in which the chances for reconciliation had dissipated. At the end of the decade, the rebels openly rejected Felipe's sovereignty and began calling for a new king.

Willem of Orange made a complete break with Felipe in 1580, after Felipe had offered a reward for his assassination. That break took the form of a proclamation in 1581 by the Dutch States General that declared Felipe's sovereignty over the Netherlands ended. This was of course not the end of the conflict, and in the 1580s under the brilliant politician and military leader, Alessandro Farnese (who also happened to be Felipe's nephew), Spain came close to victory over the rebels. Farnese set about creating a split between the nobles in the south of the Low Countries, who were mostly Catholic, and those in the north, mostly Calvinist. In the 1579 Treaty of Arras, Spain agreed not to station troops in the territories that signed the treaty, and even to pay the nobles' previous military expenses. In response, nobles in the northern provinces announced the Union of Utrecht to defend their autonomy and the Protestant faith. Felipe had Willem of Orange assassinated in 1584, and by 1585 Farnese's military campaign had reconquered the cities of Bruges, Gent, Brussels, and Antwerp. One reason for his success, besides his own cunning, was that increased silver revenues boosted Felipe's resources at this time. By the end of this decade Farnese was advocating that Felipe agree to the terms of allowing private Calvinist worship while still remaining sovereign of the north, but Felipe rejected those conditions. He instead ordered Farnese to send his armies into France to aid the Catholic side in France's civil wars in both 1590 and 1592, which diverted the focus from the Netherlands and helped keep the revolt there alive. Farnese himself died in 1592, but he had succeeded in splitting the Low Countries in two, such that Spain still controlled the southern portions. Neither he nor any of his successors were able to recapture the north.

With the benefit of hindsight it is clear that Felipe could never have completely subdued the rebellion by force. He himself probably recognized this at certain times, which is why in 1573 he directed Requesens to take a more moderate line. There are a number of reasons, then, why he persisted, and why defeat became inevitable, even though it did not arrive until 1648. Felipe refused to negotiate because he simply could not stomach the idea of having "heretics" as his subjects. He held stubbornly to the idea of *un rey, una fe, una ley* ("one king, one faith, one law").[2] The religious differences exacerbated the strife, as throughout Europe at this time confessional compromise was extremely difficult to achieve. Additionally, the Netherlands were hazardous terrain for any military, with lakes and marshes that created serious challenges, especially for moving artillery. The distance of all these events from Spain also posed difficulties that were nearly insurmountable for the age; Felipe was always far away from the situation, and yet he was the one who had to make the final decisions. There can be no question that the Dutch revolt seriously undermined Felipe's entire reign and Spanish Habsburg power more generally after he was gone. It brought him into direct conflict with England and provided more flashpoints for conflict with France. It also disrupted Spain's commerce, not just with Europe, but with the Americas as well. Moreover, it was the source of exhausting military expenditures. Felipe's debacle in the Netherlands, motivated largely by what he identified as his dynastic interests, ended up profoundly debilitating the dynasty.

An indisputable success for Felipe was that he achieved the age-old dream of unifying the Iberian peninsula under one ruler. This came about as a result of the death of the Portuguese king Sebastian in 1578, killed leading a reckless crusade in Morocco. He left no heir, and much of the Portuguese nobility was also killed or captured. Felipe then moved methodically to take over Portugal, staking his claim to the succession via his mother, the Portuguese princess Isabel, and his first wife, María of Portugal. His claim was stronger than that of the other main contenders, only one of whom— António, the Prior of Crato, a bastard relation to the Portuguese royal family—put up a real fight for the crown. Most of the Portuguese nobility and merchants favored Felipe, though the towns supported António. In the summer of 1580 Felipe sent Alba into Portugal with an army, and he quickly routed António's paltry force. This was not so much an army of conquest as an army to secure Felipe's legitimate claim. He was then officially chosen by the Portuguese Cortes in 1581 as the new king. It was also not a conquest because Felipe did nothing to subjugate Portugal. In fact, he capitulated in terms of letting the nobility keep all their old privileges. He promised that the Cortes would only meet in Portugal, that laws for Portugal would never be made from outside the country, that all officials handling Portuguese business would be Portuguese, and that the viceroy would likewise either be Portuguese or a member of the royal family. Felipe, in short, did nothing to centralize or integrate Portugal into his other Iberian kingdoms. This was purely a personal, dynastic union.

Portugal was joined to Spain as part of the Habsburgs' empire from 1580 to 1640. The union brought notable benefits, but also some drawbacks. The nobility had quickly gone to Felipe's side because they thought that Spain's military might would be able to protect Portugal's colonial interests and that access to Spanish silver would benefit the Portuguese economy. Spain, too, benefited from access to the large Portuguese fleet, markets in Asia, and lucrative trade in spices. The conjoined monarchy could plausibly claim to dominate the Atlantic, and attained a near monopoly in all American trade. Moreover, the Iberian king was now truly a global monarch, claiming all of the Americas as his territory, as well as patches of Africa, India, and Asia. The Habsburg empire became the first on which the sun never set. On the other hand, with only slightly augmented resources the king now had to defend an even greater expanse of the planet's surface, and his enemies soon began preying on the Portuguese overseas possessions. Dutch and English pirates assaulted Brazil, for example. Felipe himself came to Portugal and remained there from 1580 to 1583, even contemplating for a time making Lisbon his new capital. That reorientation of the monarchy's interests more firmly toward the Atlantic and its overseas empire is one of history's great could-have-beens, but in the end Felipe returned to Castile.

Though pirates and the Armada are some of the most indelible images of Felipe's reign, these were only two elements in a much more complicated relationship with England. From 1554 to 1558 Felipe was in fact King of England by right of his marriage to his cousin Mary Tudor, the English queen. Mary was Catholic, like her mother Catalina [Catherine] of Aragon, Henry VIII's first wife. As queen, Mary launched a campaign of forcible re-Catholicization in England that earned her the nickname "Bloody." Felipe was in England from 1554–5 and then again in 1557, and actually counseled her to take a more restrained course. Felipe's claim to the English royal title died with Mary in 1558, after she failed to produce an heir. Her half-sister Elizabeth I then became queen, and while the idea was floated to marry her to Felipe, neither of the two parties was especially interested. Relations between Felipe and Elizabeth remained on reasonably good terms until the late 1560s when her encouragement of piracy and the Dutch revolt caused an abrupt about-face. John Hawkins and Francis Drake were raiding Spain's settlements in the New World from the late 1560s. Drake captured a major treasure shipment in Panama in 1572 and then attacked the colonies from the Pacific side during his circumnavigation of the globe from 1577 to 1580. Elizabeth's concern in the Netherlands was to see Felipe withdraw his armies there, which were dangerously close to England, and she gave financial support to Willem of Orange.

In the middle years of the 1580s the conflict with England intensified, leading up to the impossibly bold sailing of the Armada. In 1585, retaliating against England's sponsorship of piracy, Felipe seized any English ship in Spanish ports. That same year, Elizabeth sent several thousand men to the Netherlands to secure Dutch ports against Spanish attack, and she authorized Drake to go raiding in the Americas. Spain got involved in a plot to have Mary, Queen of Scots, seize the English crown, but the conspiracy was exposed and she was executed in 1587. By this point Felipe had resolved to go forward with the plan to send an invasion force to England. Its primary purpose was not to conquer England. Rather, the hope was to stop aid for the Dutch rebels, and the pirate assaults on Spanish shipping. The plan envisioned sending a fleet of ships up from Spain to guard another fleet of barges that would take Farnese's army in the Netherlands over to the English shore. The odds on this idea actually working were very long though not nil. A number of fatal miscalculations made the odds even longer. Felipe was the only person who had all the information to coordinate the whole operation—but he was far away from the action. The two commanders, Medina Sidonia for the fleet and Farnese for the army, could never overcome the difficulties in communications between their forces. Farnese was also never able to secure a deep water port for the fleet, which meant it would be forced to anchor where it was vulnerable to attack from English ships. The enormous difficulties were fairly obvious, and caused Medina Sidonia to fall into despair when offered command. It was an offer he could not refuse, though he was convinced before the Armada ever left port that it would fail.

Felipe, too, was aware of the problems, but insisted the plan go forward. His unrealistic belief that God would sort it all out is one of the final reasons why the Armada failed. Nonetheless, it set sail from Lisbon in May 1588 with 130 ships and some 25,000 men. It reached the English Channel in July, but catastrophically allowed the English fleet under Drake and Lord Effingham to escape to windward of the Spanish ships, which afforded them an enormous advantage in the ensuing combat. The fleet made it to its rendezvous point with Farnese in August—but Farnese could not sail the barges with his troops out to meet the fleet because he had no protection from the lurking Dutch ships. Soon the English began sending fire ships into the Armada, and then a great storm came and drove it east and north, away from its target. Medina Sidonia decided that his best course of action was to sail all the way around the British Isles and thence home. It is to his credit that the disaster was not worse. The losses were considerable: the loss of ships and experienced seamen was a major blow to commerce with the Americas, the loss of reputation was a terrible personal blow to Felipe, and the loss in a great endeavor was demoralizing to Spain itself. The Armada's defeat was seen as a turning point after which Habsburg Spain never quite regained its enterprising triumphalism. It was also seen as a victory for Protestants everywhere. A Huguenot commander wrote to Elizabeth's spymaster Francis Walsingham, "In saving yourselves you will save the rest of us."[3] In some ways, though, Spain recovered quite quickly. Felipe assembled a new, smaller armada in 1596, intended to occupy Ireland, and then another large one in 1597, but both were again scattered by storms.

Felipe's last decade is a depressing story of troubles at home, defeats abroad, and his own failing health. In 1591–2 there was an uprising in Aragon mostly among the lesser nobility who feared their privileges were being curtailed. Those privileges were both extensive and extremely feudal: lords had almost complete authority over their vassals, and royal power was weak in the territory. Felipe intended to impose his jurisdiction there to a greater degree, beginning with appointing a non-Aragonese official to be viceroy. Felipe's treacherous former secretary, Antonio Pérez, who because of his scheming had been imprisoned on and off, escaped his jail and fled to Aragon to foment unrest. Felipe sent an army in to capture him and quell any rebellion. Ultimately there was no major fighting, and Pérez was forced to flee to France. In June 1592 Felipe summoned the Aragonese Cortes to resolve the conflict. He ended up conceding to the nobility most of their old privileges, and strengthened the crown's power only modestly, gaining for example the right to appoint the chief judicial official. This was another chance, as with Portugal, where Felipe could have driven a harder bargain and integrated the realm more tightly under his authority. He did not do so because that was not his conception of his monarchy. He continued to view his realms as separate, with their own governmental systems, tied together only through him as king.

In his last years Felipe also had to worry more about France than in the previous three decades. His armies had defeated Henri II at St. Quentin in 1557, leading to the treaty of Cateau-Cambrésis in 1559. One of the outcomes of that treaty was that Felipe married Henri's daughter Élisabeth of Valois. She died after 9 years aged only 23, but Felipe truly loved her, and their daughter, Isabel Clara Eugenia, was very dear to Felipe. Henri's death in 1559 was notoriously gruesome: at a jousting tournament that was part of the marriage celebrations for Felipe and Élisabeth, his opponent's lance pierced Henri through the eye. After that time, France descended into the chaos of its own religious civil wars, and the French kings were mostly concerned with internal matters. Felipe was directly and disastrously pulled into French politics again after Henri III was assassinated in 1589. Henri of Navarre had the best claim to the throne, but he was a Protestant, and Catholics, including Felipe, could not tolerate the idea of a Protestant on the French throne. Felipe's worry was that France would then enter the war in the Netherlands and threaten Spanish interests in northern Italy. So he used Farnese's army to press the claim of Isabel Clara Eugenia. There was little chance of her ever being accepted, however. In 1593 Henri of Navarre converted to Catholicism and was crowned king in 1594. To rally France to his cause, he then declared war on Spain in 1595. Thus Felipe was at war with the English, the Dutch, and the French simultaneously. This vast overextension helped cause Felipe's fourth bankruptcy in 1596.

That bankruptcy did convince Felipe to start reducing Spain's commitments, in part to prepare the ground for his son's succession, since Felipe could feel his own end was nearing. He arranged for Isabel Clara Eugenia to marry Archduke Albrecht of the Austrian branch, and made them co-regents of the Netherlands. This was a way of distancing Spanish authority from the territory, though Albrecht and Isabel did not have ultimate decision-making authority. It proved to be only a temporary solution. In 1596 Felipe also received a humiliating blow when the Earl of Essex captured the port of Cádiz in Andalusia and held it for 17 days—a foreign power managed to take an important Spanish city. Felipe sent the ill-fated armada of 1596 in retaliation. In these last years Felipe was chronically ill with several ailments, including gout and a blood disease. After an attack of gout in 1596 he could not use his right arm, and fell into depression. He made peace with France in 1598. In June that year he knew he was failing and so retired to the Escorial. He was bed-ridden for the last 53 days of his life and died in September 1598. In the context of the dynasty's history, Felipe was in some ways extraordinary, thanks to his longevity and particularly his immense influence. In other ways, though, he was very much like some Habsburgs who came before him (such as his father), and many who came after: he diligently worked to promote his dynasty's interests, but those often proved inimical to his realm's welfare.

Felipe III (1578–1621)

Felipe III came along at a very difficult time for Spain, and he was definitely not up to the task of addressing the monarchy's problems. The epithet of the time was *poco rey para tanto reino* ("little king for a lot of kingdom"). He was not a dolt, but was simply very lazy. He understood politics and the affairs of state, but was just not interested in them. He preferred gambling, bullfights, and especially hunting. Once, in the autumn of 1603, he hunted for 15 straight days, leaving at 4:00 in the morning and not returning until 11:00 at night.[4] Though not a bad man, he should never have been king. Felipe II was all too aware of his son's character. This consummately conscientious monarch lamented not long before he died, "God, who has given me so many kingdoms, has denied me a son capable of ruling them."[5] Though he was not the genetic calamity that were either Felipe's mentally disturbed first son Don Carlos or the last Spanish Habsburg king, Carlos II, Felipe III contributed very little to the dynasty and its realms. His reign can be succinctly summed up as a time of exhaustion, misrule by his favorite minister, and holding actions with regard to Spain's foreign policy interests.

In the 1590s, while Felipe II was still alive, there was a dawning sense that Spain was in crisis. The problems were legion. Grim conditions in the countryside caused many peasants to migrate to the cities. This led to an agricultural dearth such that Spain could no longer feed itself. Food shortages reached near-famine levels in the late 1590s. In 1596 the plague struck, and epidemics afflicted the country periodically over the next several decades. When combined with the final expulsion of the *moriscos*, it is estimated that Castile lost some 600,000 people, or one tenth of its population, during Felipe III's reign. High taxes and rampant inflation also hurt the overall economy. The productive classes were too small to support the large, parasitical nobility. There was a lack of investment in projects such as irrigation and infrastructure. A plan to make the Tajo river navigable so that one could reach the sea from Toledo went nowhere in part because of fatalistic attitudes like those of the theologians who proclaimed that if God had wanted the Tajo to be navigable, he would have made it so. The enormous wealth of American silver was spent mostly on the military and not more productively. And even the value of its colonies was declining for Spain in these years. Their populations also decreased, their demand for goods produced in Spain declined (demand was supplied instead by the English and the Dutch), and silver shipments dwindled. Awareness of these problems did spark reform proposals from people who have become known as the *arbitristas*. Their ideas included rationalizing the tax system in Castile, reducing the size of the court and government expenditure, and repopulating the countryside, but not much came of these proposals.

Felipe III came to the throne at age 20. Several of his father's key advisors were removed from court or demoted, though he retained a few competent and honest counselors to serve him. Unfortunately his main advisor, and the man as much as anyone who can be said to have ruled Spain at this time, was Francisco de Sandoval y Rojas, the Duke of Lerma, a venal, incompetent, detestable human being. He was Felipe's close friend and favorite—and that is the only reason he held his position, since he certainly did not merit it through experience or ability. He was Felipe's *valido*, akin almost to a prime minister, for 20 years to 1618. Lerma was not much more interested than Felipe in actually governing; his primary interest was the exercise of power. He came from a noble family of modest means in Valencia, and was 25 years older than the new king. Felipe II, before he died, had already cautioned his son about Lerma's influence. During his lifetime, too, Lerma was widely reviled by all those outside the immediate circle he corruptly promoted. And those he promoted were often as inept as he was, except at enriching themselves. Lerma's main achievement was to extricate Spain from some of the wars in which it had been embroiled. While this was helpful, he did not use the respite from battle to rebuild and reform the country in any significant way. After 1615 Felipe began to acknowledge the deficiencies in Lerma's rule, and Lerma was ousted three years later, replaced by his own son.

That the later Habsburg kings relied on such powerful *validos* is not surprising. Besides the fact that the dynasty's heads somewhat lost their taste for governing, the monarchy's government had grown too large for one man to oversee. Felipe II had assumed a huge burden of work, but even he depended on capable, often non-noble, university-educated secretaries to help him. Under his successors, the aristocracy reasserted itself both through the office of the *valido* and through the council system. The *valido* controlled access to the king (Lerma even tried to limit the queen's access, since she opposed him). He also controlled the patronage system, managing the client relationships by which government in the early modern state often operated. Where a *valido* such as Lerma neglected day-to-day governance, the councils controlled much of the actual administration of the realm. These were captured by the high nobility, which then ran the state even more openly in their own interests. Lerma never had complete authority over the councils, which could and did take decisions without him. The Castilian Cortes, too, saw their power grow under Felipe III as they were convened more regularly to raise taxes.

Financial problems and an acknowledgment that Spain's military power was being exhausted led to a policy of peace abroad. An armistice was signed with England in 1604. A brief, somewhat successful offensive against the Dutch ended after a drop in American silver revenues and a mutiny by the troops. The state bankruptcy of 1607 also forced a change in policy. The Netherlands' regent Albrecht counseled peace, and arranged a truce in 1609 that was to last 12 years. As part of this truce, Dutch sovereignty was recognized, which in itself was a major blow to Spain's prestige, though it was still not the last act in the conflict. The Dutch continued their depredations on Castile's and Portugal's overseas empires regardless. Also, Henri IV of France was assassinated in 1610, which put that rivalry to rest for a time. In 1612 a double marriage was arranged: Felipe's daughter Ana married the future Louis XIII, and Felipe's son Felipe IV married Élisabeth, Henri IV's daughter. This was a marital treaty that did not result in success for the Habsburgs. Its intertwining with the Bourbon dynasty eventually helped bring about the end of Habsburg rule in Spain.

At home, Lerma decreed the final expulsion of the *moriscos* from Spain in 1609. His motivations were partly to distract from Spain's other troubles, but also to expunge Islam once and for all from Spanish soil. The *moriscos* were still feared as a kind of fifth column for Turkish (or even French) interference, and because they amounted to one-third of Valencia's population and one-fifth of Aragon's, they were viewed as a real threat. In all, some 300,000 people were deported, mostly to North Africa. This expulsion brought bad but not terrible economic effects. While some areas became depopulated and experienced labor shortages, the *moriscos* were too marginal to the Spanish economy for major disruption. Persistent economic problems in Catalonia, however, contributed to a banditry problem there, as royal power was relatively weak on the ground. Castile continued to suffer under taxes that burdened it disproportionately: in 1610 Aragon, Catalonia, and Valencia contributed only 600,000 ducats to the state budget, while Castile contributed 5.1 million. Castile, in effect, massively subsidized the defense of the other realms. Lerma and Felipe did not use the financial crisis to instigate meaningful reforms but took the easy way out and simply debased the currency. Even in peacetime Felipe III continued to spend extravagantly on his court, not separating public revenues from private. On his deathbed in 1621, he proclaimed, "Oh, if God would give me life, how differently I would govern!"[6] He at least recognized his failings, but given that one of those failings was inconstancy, it is not likely that even had he lived longer he would have mended his neglectful ways.

Dynastic strategies

Felipe II's long travails in marriage and producing an heir demonstrate the strength of dynastic norms in guiding his behavior. They also humanize a man whose image is too often distorted. Felipe married four times because his wives and sons kept dying. One of the seminal episodes in the stories of the Black Legend—and indeed a major, terrible moment in Felipe's life—was the drama surrounding his firstborn son, Don Carlos. Carlos was genetically the outcome of a husband and wife (María Manuela of Portugal) who were cousins. From infancy he had physical problems, with an abnormally large head and a frail body. His mental disturbances were widely noted already in his mid-teens, as he gained a reputation for being erratic and cruel. The reality cuts a notable contrast with the character from Schiller's play (and Verdi's opera), who is a dashing crusader for liberty in the Netherlands. Schiller and Verdi were correct insofar as Carlos hated his father, and he did involve himself in the Dutch conflict, possibly even making contact with the rebel leader Egmont. Felipe's response to Carlos's many outrages was fairly lenient, but in 1568 he was finally convinced that he could never let his son become his heir. On the 18th of January that year Felipe had Carlos imprisoned and visited him one last time; his reasonable justification was that Carlos was a danger to the public welfare. In prison, Carlos went through a series of hunger strikes and extreme cures and weakened himself so much that he died in July of 1568. Contrary to legend, there is no reason to believe that Felipe had him killed. Actually, Felipe grieved very deeply—and part of his grief may have been that of the father whose sense of kingly duty impelled him to lock up his son for the good of the realm.

An unyielding dynastic imperative then dictated Felipe's remaining marriages. He sincerely loved his third wife, Élisabeth de Valois, and probably would not have married again after he lost her had he not needed an heir. In 1570 he took his fourth wife, his niece the Archduchess Anna of Austria. She was the daughter of his cousin, Maximilian II, and his sister María. In a classic example of how power buys privilege, the pope granted Felipe the dispensation to allow a marriage between such close relatives. This marriage produced Felipe III, his father's fourth son but the only one who lived to adulthood. Despite such obviously risky outcomes from consanguineous marriages, the Habsburgs persisted in them. Felipe III also married a cousin, for instance. The justifications were primarily twofold. One was that the Habsburgs insisted on marrying into other families that were both Catholic and close in rank to themselves—and there were very few such contenders. Indeed, the dynasty's exalted view of itself meant that to its members, there were in truth *no* other families of equal rank. The second reason was to solidify dynastic solidarity between the two branches of the family. Here the marriages can be counted a success: the extent to which the family maintained, if not a unified front, at least a coordinated one, is remarkable.

Here again dynastic norms were decisive. Habsburg heirs received an education to inculcate a sense of family allegiance. One example is how after Charles V died, Felipe II treated his uncle Ferdinand deferentially. Ferdinand became the acknowledged head of the family, even though the Spanish branch was generally considered the "senior," certainly the richer and more powerful. Ferdinand, inaugurating another Habsburg practice to ensure solidarity, sent his children to the Spanish court for a time, as subsequent Austrian Habsburgs would continue to do. The intra-family marital alliances also worked to coordinate dynastic policy. At Felipe III's court his wife, Margarete of Styria, and his aunt and grandmother in one, Empress María, Maximilian II's widow, both represented the interests of the Austrian branch. María, in particular, worked closely with the Viennese ambassador to Madrid for some 20 years. Though excluded from formal political power, Margarete and María did exert considerable influence. They constituted one of the main forces of resistance to Lerma's iniquity, such that Lerma expressly (and unsuccessfully) tried to forbid Margarete from speaking to Felipe about political matters. She pressed her husband to govern more conscientiously, and the Venetian ambassador described Margarete as "capable of great things."[7]

In another sign of successful dynastic management, the Habsburgs continued to find ways to make even younger or distant members useful to the family. The string of accomplished Habsburg women who acted as regents in the Netherlands continued with Margherita of Parma, an illegitimate daughter of Charles V and therefore Felipe II's half-sister. Felipe II loved and esteemed his daughter Isabel Clara Eugenia: he sought her political advice and even let her help him with his paperwork. He actually had much more confidence in her than he did in Felipe III. Together with her husband and cousin Archduke Albrecht of Austria, she also became an able governor of the Netherlands. Another of Charles's illegitimate children, Don Juan, became the talented military commander at Lepanto and in the Low Countries. Relations between the heads of the two branches did occasionally hit rough patches. Felipe II and Maximilian II definitely did not like each other, and Felipe III started maneuvering to grab the Austrian line's titles as his cousin Rudolf II's reign collapsed.

Catholicism also became a major Habsburg norm to reinforce family solidarity as well as dynastic legitimacy. One reason for the trust and respect between Felipe II and Ferdinand was that they trusted each other's religious stances. Being a Habsburg meant being a strong Catholic. From two potentially divergent branches, this ideology helped coordinate the whole family into what was seen by contemporaries as one symbiotically connected international unit. The dawning of the Counter-Reformation precipitated a change in the Habsburgs' religious legitimation strategies. Prior to Charles V the dynasty had espoused fairly generic ideas about divine right and the prince's duty to protect Christianity. As religious conflict sharpened in Europe, though, Felipe believed it was in the best interests of his subjects that they remain Catholic. He considered it his right to decide on the religion of his realms, but also his duty to protect his subjects from heresy. Like many religious people at all times, Felipe felt that *his* faith was the true one, the only true guarantor of society's moral fundament and cohesion. He watched the French Wars of Religion with alarm, convinced that religious pluralism would lead to disunity and violence in his own realms. In these ideas, Felipe was in the mainstream of his day. What was different about him was that he had the resources plus the will to assert Catholicism's primacy.

His belief in the dynasty's mission to defend Catholicism does not mean that he was a crusader looking to conquer souls or annihilate infidels. Many of the actions that might be seen as religiously motivated—war with the Turks, English, or Dutch—were really driven by security concerns. He did not mount a major assault on England until 1588 despite its ostensibly heretical status, and after Lepanto his combat engagements with the Turks and their allies in North Africa were few. In the Netherlands, countering Protestantism was one consideration. A bigger one was suppressing what he considered an unlawful revolt against his authority and discouraging rebels elsewhere. Religion was *a* motivation but not *the* motivation for Felipe's politics. Like his father, he had numerous and bitter clashes with the papacy. He in fact went to war with Pope Paul IV in the 1550s. For his own reasons, Felipe sought to block papal attempts to excommunicate Elizabeth I of England in 1561 and 1563. That Felipe was not some simple-minded crusader is also shown by the fact that Spain implemented the Council of Trent's decrees quite quickly after 1564. This is evidence for his conviction that some kind of reform was necessary within the Catholic Church. Moreover, he carried out these reforms not in submission to Rome but partly to increase his own power, since he had insisted throughout the Council that the crown control many aspects of Church governance in Spain. In sum, as devoted as he was to the Catholic Church, it never trumped his dynastic considerations, and Felipe never served it blindly. Neither was the victory of the Counter-Reformation one of his overriding political goals.

Felipe's great monastery-palace of El Escorial is often taken as the symbol (rightly and wrongly) for both his court and his religiosity. Felipe made Madrid his capital in 1561, then purposefully placed his palace outside the city as a way of distancing the monarch from the typical political intrigues of the capital. In keeping with the somber style of the monastery-palace and the Burgundian tradition, Felipe's court was solemn, but it was not unrelentingly grave. Thanks to his well-rounded education in history and the arts, his cultural patronage was dazzling. He assembled the Habsburgs' first great collection of art, stocking it with portraits of his family and many religious paintings. Felipe loved Titian's work, met the painter several times, and commissioned paintings from him. The king's sharp eye for quality was also captured by Hieronymus Bosch. El Greco moved to Spain during Felipe's reign, and though the king was not a particular fan of the Greek painter, Greco's painting "The Dream of Felipe II" became one of the most striking political and religious allegories of Felipe's kingship. Research in math and science bloomed in Spain at this time. Charles V and Felipe both employed the renowned Andreas Vesalius as their court physician. El Escorial itself was conceived as a Christian Olympus, a temple to the arts and sciences, embodied above all in its stupendous library. While there were attempts to close off Spain from some potentially heretical external cultural influences, that did not impede the blooming of the illustrious Golden Age of cultural production. Felipe III's reign continued the tremendous vitality in this area, as Cervantes and Lope de Vega reached their peak in literature and Tomás Luis de Victoria in music.

Contrary to the Black Legend's slander, Felipe never simply holed up in El Escorial; he left it often to spend time in Madrid and in his other palaces. Nonetheless, that palace and the Burgundian court style did deeply stamp Felipe's image as a ruler. They made him (and subsequent Spanish kings) remote, exalted figures who were rarely glimpsed by the public. Because Felipe's personality was not that of a charismatic battlefield leader (as even his father had been), his majesty depended in large part on this rarified aura. He was *El Rey Prudente*, the prudent king, untouchable, incorruptible, consummately conscientious—an image maintained despite the many rash gambles he took, including three armadas to invade England. It was true, however, that he spent less time hunting, feasting, dancing, jousting, judging, battling—the iconic displays of kingship—and much more time writing. Felipe II was the king as clerk; he claimed once to have signed 400 different papers in a single day. The minions of his government were secretaries, not the traditional, feudal vassals. He was the master of the first great bureaucracy of any modern monarchy. Though his function as sovereign became more workaday, certainly his rule was still personal. The circles of counselors and bureaucrats of which he was the center served to carry out his will. Felipe alone had ultimate authority and responsibility, which he believed were entrusted to him by God.

The evolution of the monarch into chief bureaucrat was fitful, of course. Felipe III's disengagement from governing meant that he reverted to many of the more traditional roles of the monarch in courtly display. The emergence of the *valido*, however, was part of other changes taking place in the dynastic state. On the traditional side, the *valido* was still justified by ideas of divine right. A Spanish priest tried to legitimize this system by declaring that "God chooses the favorite as he does the king."[8] On the innovatory side, the *valido* was associated with the movement away from personal monarchy and toward the monarch representing the apex of an increasingly impersonal bureaucratic apparatus. It also points to the changing status of the nobility vis-à-vis the monarch, since through high offices such as the *valimiento* the aristocracy was incorporated into state administrative structures more directly than before. This change shows that the nobility was not merely subjugated to or conflicting with the crown, but was often actively cooperative in governance.

That cooperation was essential for this reason: the existence of such an entity as "Spain" was quite weak at this time. The monarchy remained a loose collection of realms sharing the same king. Given the great distances between these territories and the primitive state of communications, it made sense to let them govern themselves to a large extent. The system of regional councils (Castile, Aragon, Italy, etc.) that Felipe II had inherited from his father was the principal central structure of governance. They were typically composed of high nobles from the relevant territory who helped represent the interests of that territory in Felipe's court. A professional cadre of administrative secretaries grew up to liaise between the king and these councils. Because the councils could be riven by factional rivalries among their members, Felipe came to depend on a new circle of experienced advisors, many of whom had backgrounds in the lower nobility. Though key decisions were taken at the top, Felipe otherwise pursued very little centralization. His attempt to constrict some local privileges in the Netherlands helped spark the rebellion there, but elsewhere he negotiated more conciliatorily. His power was never absolute. It usually depended on consultation with other elites. He also professed to respect laws, and royal governance was in fact too weak for him ever to impose his will on his realms unconditionally. Only with the Spanish Church did he have thorough control over such things as ecclesiastical appointments and finances.

Though Felipe II's bureaucracy was the best of its day, it was still woefully inadequate for optimal management of the monarchy's affairs. His financial administration epitomizes the strengths and weaknesses of his institutions. He was able to raise greater revenues than any other contemporary sovereign, yet Felipe himself acknowledged that his finances were handled poorly. Revenues roughly quadrupled over the course of his reign. In addition to the old *alcabala* sales tax, other taxes became a heavy burden in Castile. The Cortes approved some of these, but regressively levied them on the lower classes. The contribution from the colonies amounted to a modest income, some 20 percent of total revenues in 1598, less than what Castile paid in taxes. Military expenditures, however, proved the sinkhole of Felipe's finances. Castile spent less than 2 million ducats on the military in 1566 but about 10 million in 1598. Felipe did increase royal control of the military, taking it away from the high nobility. For example, he made manufacture of gunpowder a royal monopoly. But where every government of the time accrued debt, Felipe's was spectacular for its size. He inherited a debt of 20 million ducats from his father, and left Felipe III a debt of 100 million. By 1598 debt repayment amounted to eight times annual revenues. As guarantees for loans, the government often granted its Italian or German bankers the right to administer tax collection, mines, or other revenue sources. This meant that the state did not control revenues, nor did it construct much of an apparatus to oversee their collection; the apparatus belonged instead to the banks. Despite their flaws, the governance structures elaborated in Felipe II's time remained fundamental to the dynastic state's functioning for the remaining century of Habsburg rule in Spain.

Felipe II was one of the most serious, committed, and simultaneously controversial monarchs in Habsburg history. That he was dedicated to his dynasty and left it an illustrious legacy cannot be questioned. His frustrated attempts to produce an heir, his work to maintain solidarity among the Austrian and Spanish branches, his attachment to Catholicism as a source of legitimacy, and his cultural patronage were all undertaken to serve his family and its posterity as much as to serve himself. His governance also became a model. For all its many problems of inefficiency and financial mismanagement, it was nonetheless superior to most of his contemporaries' and many of his successors'. Likewise, though the Armada, the Dutch revolt and multiple bankruptcies stand out as fiascos, in many other ways Felipe's reign has to be counted as among the most impressive in the dynasty's history. When Portugal was added to his other domains, his monarchy not only loomed over Europe but bestrode the world. Besides the incomparable cultural efflorescence, this was also a time of significant economic vitality in much of Iberia. Seville, for example, was the boomtown of the sixteenth century, growing to possibly 150,000 people in the later 1580s, which made it the third largest city in Europe after Paris and Naples. Certainly by the end of his reign the monarchy's problems were mounting. Without minimizing them, however, an honest evaluation of Felipe II would judge him as about the best that could be expected from sixteenth-century dynastic monarchy. That much worse was possible, even habitual, is shown by Felipe III.

CHAPTER FIVE

Division in faith and family (1564–1619)

Maximilian II insisted, "I am neither a Catholic nor a Protestant—I am a Christian."[1] As a ruler, he hoped to foster in his realms the religious harmony that was in his own mind. Yet bridging the divide between the Christian sects proved impossible, and no politician of this time could have achieved it. In truth, Maximilian's own judicious but ambiguous position provided no real solution. As so often in history, the person who tries to steer a course down the middle is attacked by those at the extremes. Thus he was heavily criticized by both conservative Catholics and the most extreme Lutherans, who were unanimous at least in rejecting compromise. These confessional fissures in the Danubian domains bedeviled Habsburg rule for decades, debilitating the best efforts of even an intelligent, conscientious sovereign such as Maximilian. His sons Rudolf II and Matthias confronted the same splits but then only succeeded in creating new ones. Rudolf is one of the most fascinating yet unstable members of his dynasty, the Habsburg Prospero, neglecting affairs of state in favor of his artistic and occult obsessions. And like Shakespeare's magician in *The Tempest*, Rudolf's titles were usurped by his brother. All three men achieved relatively little in the dynastic perspective, leaving a legacy of festering religious conflicts, empowered provincial estates, costly wars against the Turks, and hapless feuds within the family. Maximilian and Rudolf were interesting as individuals but ineffectual as rulers; Matthias was nothing but a bungler.

Maximilian II (1527–76)

The ambiguity in Maximilian's religious beliefs was evident to and troubling for many members of his family. Ferdinand I, in a codicil to his will of August 1555, felt compelled to admonish his son very explicitly to remain a Catholic. Ferdinand wrote, "I've seen a number of things that make me greatly suspicious that you, Maximilian, would fall from our religion and go over to the new sects. [. . .] God grant that this is not so, and that I have falsely suspected you."[2] He had good reason to worry. In the 1550s Maximilian's actions definitely seemed to indicate Protestant sympathies, or at least an antipathy to the pope's Catholicism. Maximilian argued against the Jesuits, defended a heterodox (though not at that time acknowledged Protestant) preacher in his court, and allowed the Lower Austrian estates to accept communion in both kinds, which was associated with Protestant practice at the time. Ferdinand was so disturbed by what seemed his son's wavering Catholicism that he pressed Maximilian's Spanish wife to intervene and make sure he remained a Catholic. He even threatened to disinherit Maximilian if he left the Church.

Nonetheless, despite his reservations about the Catholic Church, Maximilian never became an avowed Protestant. He did have a special dispensation from the pope to take communion in both kinds. And while he sympathized somewhat closely with the Lutherans, he actually disapproved of some Protestant sects such as the Calvinists and the Bohemian Brethren. He more dutifully towed the Catholic line once he was emperor, but he never gave up criticizing Rome's hostile treatment of Protestantism. His reaction to the St. Bartholomew's Day massacre in France—in which thousands of Huguenots were killed in 1572—expresses one of his fundamental tenets. "The affairs of religion," he said, "cannot be adjudicated and dealt with by the sword."[3]

Maximilian's ambivalent religious stance also complicated relations between the Austrian and Spanish branches of the family. Maximilian was married to his cousin María, Felipe II's sister, in 1548 as part of Charles V's tactic to ensure dynastic solidarity between the two branches. For several years beginning in the late 1540s he acted as regent in Spain, but he never liked it there. He found Spanish Catholicism too dogmatic. He was also angered by Charles's idea to alternate the Holy Roman Empire's crown between the two branches of the family. He schemed quite actively to frustrate Felipe's candidacy for the imperial title. Once Maximilian returned to central Europe in 1551, he started making alliances with Protestant princes, in part to expand his own influence and room to maneuver. He was positioning himself as a defender of German interests, and trying to create a balance of power against the Spanish branch. He also came out in strong support of the Augsburg agreement, which was part of his political and religious strategy to appeal to Protestants without abandoning his family's Catholicism. His antagonism toward Felipe and Spain was sufficiently strong that at one point he floated the ridiculous idea to Ferdinand that the German princes should ally with France against Spain—ridiculous because Ferdinand was very dutiful about maintaining dynastic solidarity. This antagonism was mutual, since Felipe complained about Maximilian's unreliable support of Catholicism. His politicking in Germany ensured that Maximilian did receive the imperial crown in

1564 following Ferdinand's death. Maximilian's attitudes toward Spain mellowed enough in later years that he agreed to his two oldest sons being sent to Felipe's court to be educated.

In some ways, the tensions in Maximilian's own religiosity mirrored the complex confessional situation in his realms. Religious pluralism was a fact of life in the Danubian lands that Maximilian, Rudolf, and Matthias all had to deal with. Apart from Tyrol, Catholic observance was in steep decline everywhere, in cities, towns, and the countryside. In Bohemia and Hungary, too, the numbers of Catholic clergy dwindled, and monasteries emptied. In many places, this left a power vacuum that local nobles filled by taking over church lands. This pluralistic situation set the tone for a generally tolerant society, with significant confessional liberty. Catholicism hung on because the dynasty protected it and none of the Protestant sects was dominant enough to uproot it completely. In Inner Austria particularly, Ferdinand I's son Karl was determined to hold the line for Catholicism, even though the estates in his territories were majority Protestant. It was from Karl's line that the aggressive Counter-Reformation would come in the next century. Despite his compromising inclinations, Maximilian's tolerance had its limits. In 1566 at a Reichstag he tried to have Calvinism banned. His motivation was that this sect was not included in the 1555 Augsburg agreement, and hence seemed a destabilizing force.

Like most contemporary rulers, Maximilian viewed religious pluralism as dangerous, and he dreamed of reuniting the various splinters of Christendom. This aspiration always ran against the hard realities of politics. The estates used his compromising inclinations to their advantage. In return for agreeing to financial outlays, they demanded official acknowledgment of religious freedom. Over several years starting in 1568 Maximilian was forced successively to grant freedom of worship to lords and their subjects in many of his Austrian lands, as well as in Bohemia. He made concessions to Catholics, too, such as promising the archbishop of Olomouc that he could persecute Protestants in Moravia. By the 1570s, Maximilian had begun to see that his hope of compromise between the sects was in vain. Instead of trying to mend the splits, his scaled-back goal became keeping the peace in religiously splintered central Europe.

Given this goal, Maximilian was alarmed by Felipe II's actions in the Netherlands. He was deeply opposed to Felipe's military response to the Dutch revolt. His fears were plausible, namely that the armed response against Dutch Calvinists would stir up anger among Calvinists in Germany. He was also worried that Spanish armies straying into German territory could provoke armed resistance, and that as a result of Spanish military recruiting in Germany, Germans could end up fighting other Germans in the Low Countries. This was an extremely difficult situation for Maximilian. He felt the pressures of his own conscience to maintain family solidarity while, at the same time, he was being pressured by the German princes to counteract Felipe's policies. In the late 1560s he repeatedly pleaded with

Felipe and the Duke of Alba to moderate their response, but Felipe rebuffed him with the disingenuous insistence that religion was not an issue in the Netherlands. Maximilian's own attitude toward the revolt began changing by 1571 because of his concern about the precedent the Dutch were setting by revolting against monarchy. Now Maximilian approved Spanish recruitment in Germany (which had been going on with impunity anyway). But this movement toward Felipe's position frayed his relations with the Protestant German princes. There were accusations that Maximilian had become a partner in Felipe's aggression. Characteristically, Maximilian tried to find a middle way, counseling moderation to Felipe while hosting the rebel leader Egmont's son in Vienna after his father had been executed. Also characteristically, this policy did not work. Protestant princes such as the Elector of the Palatinate bucked the emperor's policy when they started aiding Willem of Orange by 1573.

Maximilian's last years saw him defeated and resigned. He was too intelligent a man not to have recognized his own failure. His attempts at compromise and reconciliation remained unworkable. Too few other leaders, whether religious or secular, were interested in such an approach, and Maximilian became largely irrelevant by 1574. He did manage to get Rudolf elected Roman king in 1575, but by then his own health was clearly failing, which also motivated his withdrawal from governance. He had a list of maladies in the years preceding his death: cardiac seizures, urinary stones, and gout, among others. On his deathbed he refused the Catholic last rites. He died as he lived, thus, unorthodoxly. While Maximilian can be praised for finding his own, unique and genuine way to reconcile Catholicism and Protestantism, his personal beliefs did not provide a feasible political basis for wider reconciliation. His tragedy was to be in between competing sects when everybody else, in his family and his realms, expected him to be on one side or the other.

Rudolf II (1552–1612)

From Maximilian's impossible balancing act between warring sides, in Rudolf II's time the Austrian branch itself broke down into warring sides. Rudolf helped cause these problems, and he was certainly not the man to resolve them. There is no question of his intelligence: it was often remarked upon by contemporaries. Likewise, he was an extremely cultured individual, one of the most curious and broadly educated of anyone in the dynasty. He was also known for being relatively personable but shy, and for having an intense pride in Habsburg superiority. Until about 1600 he also had a fairly strong will and was generally attentive to government. If anything, he may have been *too* involved, since he was not good at heeding counselors' advice. He made some decisions (like renewing the war with the Turks in

1593) that might have been avoided with a better-informed and less willful monarch. After that time, the darker sides of Rudolf's personality came to dominate. Already during the war he displayed signs of what has been suggested as schizophrenia. He began ordering that relatively unimportant military victories be celebrated and glorified out of all proportion. Defeats, even minor ones, caused him to fall into a black depression and shut himself off from court. He became deeply distrustful of almost everyone around him, fearing that he was going to be poisoned or bewitched. He drank too much, contemplated suicide, and gave in to superstition. Though he was never perhaps truly "mad" (as critics then and since have claimed), he was undoubtedly a troubled individual. His psychological disturbances did not make him completely incapable of rule after 1600, but on the rarer occasions when he did intervene, it was too often with catastrophic results.

Rudolf's religious attitudes were not unlike his father's. He was undogmatic, moderate, perhaps more committed to Catholicism than Maximilian, though he too refused the last rites. All his adult life he actively disliked the papacy and the conservative Catholic camp, but neither was he a fan of the fissiparous Protestant sects who all claimed their own political rights. His main practical concern was to avoid religious conflict in his domains. Like Maximilian, he feared how such conflict would undermine order and his own power, and make his realms more vulnerable to Turkish attack. Rudolf's main hope in relation to religious pluralism was to end it via compromise. He dreamed of reuniting the splits and making Christianity whole again. Again like his father, though, he had no real plan for accomplishing this goal, nor was it especially realistic. Perhaps the only place where the different confessions amicably got along was in Rudolf's court, since he had Catholics, Utraquists, Lutherans, and Calvinists in his service. Rudolf (Figure 5.1) was ultimately disengaged from the politics of confessional disputes—which meant that he exerted virtually no control over them and events instead swept past him.

By 1600 confessional conflict was sharpening in both the Empire and the Danubian domains. In Germany, a new generation of princes had come to power, one even less inclined to compromise than their forebears who had reached agreement in Augsburg in 1555. All sides were becoming more combative. One of the main disputes was over Protestant princes' continuing seizures of formerly Catholic lands, including the properties of monasteries and bishoprics. The Elector Palatine, a particularly aggressive Calvinist, was often the leader of obstructionist tactics in the Reichstag, refusing to contribute money for the fight against the Turks. A hardening of differences and grudges led to 9 Protestant princes and 17 imperial cities forming the Evangelical Union in the first decade of the 1600s. In response, 20 princes led by Bavaria created the Catholic League. Rudolf played very little role in any of these events. In Austria, the Counter-Reformation was gaining momentum, though its real successes would not come until later. After 1600 in particular Catholicism became more militant, as a number of

FIGURE 5.1 *Rudolf II, bust by Adriaen de Vries (1607). In the collection of the Weltliche Schatzkammer, Vienna. Image courtesy of the Österreichische Nationalbibliothek.*

commanding personalities took the lead to advance its cause. Nobles and churchmen fought for the return of church lands, refused to acknowledge rights of tolerance for Protestants, and more vigorously persecuted "heretics." New schools were founded, most of the time by the Jesuits. Monasteries were reopened, and other orders such as the Capuchins and the Augustinians also expanded their work. Felipe II encouraged these developments, but the stronger impetus came from Rudolf's brother Ernst and his cousins Karl of Inner Austria and Ferdinand of Tyrol.

The Austrian Habsburgs' ongoing struggle with the Ottomans quieted down for several decades after the first years of Maximilian's reign. Once Süleyman I died in 1566, Turkish expansionist fervor waned in the west, and Maximilian signed the Peace of Adrianople in 1568. It was not until 1593 that border skirmishes again boiled over into full-blown war. It proved a particularly pointless affair, producing no major territorial gains for either side. Rudolf had hoped for a grand crusade that would reaffirm his power in the Empire and his own domains, and tried unsuccessfully to arrange a three-way alliance with Muscovy and Persia for a conjoined attack on the Ottomans. His military commanders won no decisive victories, however, and the war's expenses and disruption seriously undermined Rudolf's regime. It helped spark several peasant uprisings. Rural people had many grievances, including the conscription for the army and new taxes to pay for the war against the Turks, but also the worsening conditions of rural life such as intensified forced labor requirements. In 1595 and 1597 gangs of peasants stormed across the Austrian countryside. Rudolf listened to their grievances to an extent, such as promising to help lessen onerous labor requirements (which were really controlled by local nobles), but he also forcibly suppressed the resistance.

The Turkish war also coincided with a rebellion in Transylvania. The province's ruler, Zsigmond Báthory, sporadically acknowledged Rudolf's sovereignty, and accepted help from a Habsburg army to combat the Ottomans. However, that army was also used to promote Catholicism and persecute the religiously pluralistic Transylvania's other communities including Lutherans and Calvinists. This provoked a revolt led from 1604 to 1606 by István Bocskai, a Hungarian lord who had formerly been allied with the Habsburgs. He made league with the Turks, and part of the Hungarian estates rose up against the Habsburgs. These rebels formed an army partly out of armed peasants known as *hajduks*. A roving force of armed, angry rural people posed the danger of a broader social revolution, and so threatened not just Habsburg authority but much of the landowning elite. A split thus opened up among the Hungarian nobles. Much of the Transylvanian nobility supported an all-out war to seize as much of Habsburg Hungary as possible, to make it an autonomous Turkish protectorate. The nobility further west, even if somewhat disgruntled by Habsburg rule, feared more the prospect of Turkish overlordship. An end to both the Turkish war and the Transylvanian rebellion was negotiated in 1606. Matthias, acting sometimes without Rudolf's approval, agreed that Bocskai would be the prince of Transylvania but would renounce his claim to be king of Hungary. Religious freedom for the nobility and free towns was also guaranteed. The peace of Zsitvatorok ended the futile hostilities with the Turks.

Matthias handled these treaties because of Rudolf's incapacity. As his psychological problems mounted, Rudolf began ignoring events in the

Empire and in his own lands. He neglected papers and refused to see his main advisors, but still nurtured an unrealistically grandiose sense of his own authority. There was in short a leadership vacuum, into which stepped Matthias—though the real political mover was his Svengali, Melchior Khlesl. Khlesl was a power-hungry arriviste who came from a family of Protestant Viennese bakers. Educated by the Jesuits, though, he became an ardent and aggressive Catholic Counter-Reformer. He first wormed his way into Rudolf's circle, rising to become an imperial councilor and bishop of Vienna. But then when he decided that Rudolf's rule was spinning out of control, he switched horses to Rudolf's equally power-hungry, but clueless, younger brother. Matthias had been groomed for a career in the Church, but rejected it and sought to concoct for himself a more prominent role in the family's politics than his age, education, or talent would ever have entitled him to. Matthias's political meddling began in 1577 when without consulting either Rudolf or Felipe II, he accepted a provocative invitation from some Dutch nobles to mediate in the conflict there. This was a major breach of dynastic etiquette, and it enraged Felipe, who considered it a betrayal. Matthias was neither intelligent nor well-connected enough to make any real contribution, and was pushed aside by 1579.

Back in Austria after 1581, he eventually became the focus of the dynasty's attempts to salvage their realms from Rudolf's delinquency. Matthias first explored all sorts of schemes to advance himself such as becoming a bishop or even the king of Poland, but succeeded in nothing. In 1595, after their brother Ernst's death, Rudolf made Matthias his regent in Upper and Lower Austria. It was at this time that Matthias came under the influence of Khlesl, who showed that Matthias was as easily manipulated as he was headstrong. Khlesl helped convince him that since Rudolf had no legitimate heir, Matthias needed to assume authority. In 1606, Matthias, his brother Maximilian, and their cousin Ferdinand of Styria carried out a plan (actually devised by Khlesl) to declare Matthias the head of the family.

Rudolf considered this a treasonous break, and the family split soon escalated to armed conflict. In 1608 Matthias contrived for the Austrian, Hungarian, and Moravian estates to support him against Rudolf, but in return he had to promise them considerable religious liberties. Matthias was actually crowned king of Hungary that year, and Rudolf was forced to cede authority in Austria and Moravia as well. He had nowhere else to turn but to the Bohemian, Lusatian, and Silesian estates for backing, which they bestowed only after he agreed to the Letter of Majesty of 1609. This was a major capitulation by the crown to the estates, allowing thorough religious freedoms including the right for non-Catholics to build churches and schools. In 1610 Rudolf tried to use an army that had been assembled to deal with a succession conflict in Germany to overpower Matthias. These troops entered Bohemia but because Rudolf could not afford to pay them, they began plundering. The successive calamities of Rudolf's leadership finally motivated the Bohemian estates to declare him deposed in 1611. Matthias marched in with his own army and imprisoned Rudolf in Prague's castle; Matthias was then crowned the Bohemian king. Rudolf retained only the imperial title until he died in 1612, after which Matthias was elected to the imperial office. It was a sad end to Rudolf's 36 years as emperor, and a shameful debacle for the dynasty—which would not improve under Matthias.

Matthias (1557–1619)

Matthias and his reign are interesting really only for Habsburg completists; he is more typically, and deservedly, forgotten. The ultimate irony is that once he wore the crown he was just as ineffectual as Rudolf had been. The archbishop of Trier reportedly said after Matthias was elected emperor in 1612, "He'll make no great leaps."[4] Even Khlesl complained about how lethargic and disengaged from ruling Matthias was, and explicitly advised him to pay more attention. But since Matthias was more interested in the trappings of rule than in ruling itself, Khlesl took the reins in his own hands. Khlesl assumed power as the director of the Privy Council, and was even referred to mockingly as the "vice-emperor." Unrest in Transylvania continued, and Matthias had to acknowledge the sovereignty of two indigenous princes, Báthory and then Bethlen. Matthias moved the capital back to Vienna from Prague, and ratcheted up the pressure of the Counter-Reformation. He disallowed the construction of Protestant churches, censored Protestant publications, and forbid Protestants the right of assembly. This in turn sharpened religious conflict in the Empire. The 1613 Reichstag in Regensburg broke down amid escalating religious tensions. Khlesl had begun to seem like a comparative moderate, but under threat of a boycott by the Catholic princes, he failed to engineer a compromise between them and Protestants on several matters. Rival contenders to the inheritance of the duchy of Jülich-Kleves nearly provoked a wider European war in 1614; this was a spark in dry tinder that testified to the volatile situation in central Europe.

Capping Matthias's ineptitude was his inability to produce an heir, again a repeat of Rudolf's problems. This uncertainty led to the predictable jockeying for the Habsburg succession, and the candidates included Friedrich V, the Elector Palatine and a Calvinist, as well as Felipe III of Spain, who claimed a right to succeed because he was the grandson of Maximilian II on his mother's side. The fright of a Protestant or a Spaniard becoming emperor helped rally support behind Matthias's cousin Ferdinand of Styria. Felipe was fobbed off via the treaty of Oñate of 1617, in which he received some territories in Alsace and Italy in return for renouncing his claims. That left the way open for the zealous Catholic Ferdinand. Matthias did not die until 1619, by which time he had already been irrelevant for nearly two years. The events of the Prague defenestration, Khlesl's fall from power and imprisonment, and Ferdinand's takeover led the terrifying descent into what would become the Thirty Years' War. As problematic as Rudolf's reign was, Matthias's heedless greed and boundless folly had accomplished nothing constructive, setting the stage for the conflict that would consume the next generation of Habsburgs.

Dynastic strategies

Maximilian, Rudolf, and Matthias are most important in the dynasty's history for the way they managed family solidarity, and for their court patronage. Solidarity within the Austrian branch was unquestionably complicated by its divided inheritance. Relations between Maximilian and his brothers Ferdinand and Karl were actually quite smooth. As their father Ferdinand I had admonished them, they spoke with one voice on foreign policy matters, though Maximilian led. The division even helped Maximilian in some ways, since his own administrative burden was lessened by the younger Ferdinand and Karl governing their own Austrian domains. There were inevitably some disagreements, since the younger Ferdinand, whose territory was the rich Tyrol, sometimes disputed how much he was supposed to contribute to joint military expenditures. Surprisingly, this Ferdinand removed himself from succession possibilities when he married a commoner. In the next generation, as his brothers and cousin ganged up on Rudolf, family unity obviously broke down in some ways. However, solidarity was actually the underlying motivation for this dynastic squabble. Matthias, his brother Maximilian, and Ferdinand of Styria feared that Rudolf's misrule was damaging the dynasty's patrimony and legitimacy. In deposing Rudolf, these three were thinking in terms of the corporate interest, though Matthias's egotistical ambitions were not inconsequential.

The solidarity with the Spanish branch was also often troubled during this time. Maximilian II's wife María, Felipe II's sister, was essential for keeping the relationship amicable. She consistently acted as a vital intermediary and confidante for both kings, and took an active role in matters of state. She held joint audiences with Maximilian, and ambassadors would often speak to her first to find out how best to approach him. She remained a strong Catholic and was therefore troubled by Maximilian's wavering. Her retinue in Austria was almost entirely Spanish, and though Maximilian knew that they were communicating important information back to Felipe and his court, he had to put up with it. Once Maximilian died, María's sons none too subtly encouraged her to return to Spain to rid themselves of her "meddling" in their politics. In 1581 she returned to Spain and embraced her brother after a separation of 30 years. María's Spanish culture did exert a major influence on several of her sons. For example, Rudolf long favored the Castilian language and Spanish dress. He and his brother Ernst spent their adolescent years in Spain, partly because Felipe was grooming them as potential heirs as he still lacked a surviving son.

Rudolf and Matthias had their own problems with inheritance because neither produced a legitimate son. The machinations surrounding his succession poisoned Rudolf's relations with his family members. The fact that Rudolf never married was entirely due to his psychological afflictions. For some 18 years he was engaged to Felipe's daughter Isabel Clara Eugenia, but he could never bring himself to go through with the marriage. His failure to do so is strange for all sorts of reasons. He was definitely capable of sexual relations, since he had several children by his favorite mistress. He also coveted some Spanish territories like Milan, and even hoped to influence Spanish policies in the Netherlands along a more moderate line. His love-hate relationship with Spanish politics— and his frustration that Felipe was unlikely to give him the things he coveted—are part of the explanation why he never married Isabel. In a bizarre twist, however, when Felipe finally married her to Rudolf's brother Albrecht, Rudolf was enraged. Once they were married and became governors of the Netherlands, Albrecht and Isabel also failed to produce a surviving heir. Thus the Austrian primogeniture line stemming from Ferdinand I went extinct. This helps explain why Ferdinand of Styria inserted himself into the conflict between Rudolf and Matthias: he stood to gain the whole Austrian branch's inheritance, which he did once Matthias died.

The impressive royal courts that Maximilian and especially Rudolf kept partially redeem their political faults. Both men were highly literate and refined. Maximilian's largesse benefited the artist Arcimboldo, whom Ferdinand I had originally brought to Vienna, as well as other painters, musicians, and scholars. Two of the most notable scholars were the early botanist Charles de L'Écluse (known as Clusius) and the physician Johannes Crato, who also served Rudolf. Maximilian's intellectual capacity and curiosity enabled him to participate actively in some of the debates sponsored by the intellectuals in his court. He himself took an interest in botany, importing plants from far-away places, including the potato, which he tried to introduce to his lands. One of his lasting architectural contributions is the Stallburg in Vienna, which now houses the Spanish Riding School.

Rudolf's court was the most multifaceted and eccentrically resplendent of his age. Known popularly above all for its occult trappings, including Rudolf's patronage of the magician John Dee, there was much more to it than alchemy. Rudolf surrounded himself with accomplished scholars of Latin poetry, history, math, astronomy, mineralogy, zoology, botany, and geography, among other subjects. The most famous of the scientists in Rudolf's circle were Tycho Brahe and Johannes Kepler. Many of these people were free thinkers in all kinds of ways. Protestants, Catholics, and ambivalents coexisted in a kind of bookish harmony. Rudolf himself read widely in many subjects, and was especially interested in the natural sciences. His cultural collecting was also diverse and edified. He built up an extraordinary collection of paintings, manuscripts, jewels, clocks, scientific instruments and fantastical things such as the narwhal tooth he believed to have magical powers. Among the most famous works that Rudolf commissioned was Arcimboldo's depiction of the emperor as "Vertumnus," a bizarre portrait in which Rudolf's head is made up of flowers, fruits, and vegetables. He also commissioned a crown that much later became the imperial crown of Austria. Its form is a combination of a traditional royal circlet with a bishop's mitre, symbolizing the Habsburgs' divine right to rule. When he coveted a piece, he made sure he got it. One example is when he decided to add Dürer's *Rosenkranzfest* to his collection: he ordered four bearers to transport the painting all the way from Venice to Prague while holding it upright. Not surprisingly, he spent tremendous sums on these acquisitions, so much that contemporaries complained that if he had invested that money in the army he could have beaten the Turks.

The perception that Rudolf misdirected attention to his cultural activities rather than affairs of state applies also to his interest in the occult. This interest had several motivations. It may have some roots in his peculiar relationship to Catholicism, which much like his father's was somewhat conflicted. It was very likely connected to his withdrawal from reality, or even a quest for an alternate reality hidden behind the visible forms of the world. One of the reasons Rudolf was interested in art was because he believed that the greatest artists possessed some kind of supernatural power. So Rudolf at various times had a number of individuals in his circle who straddled some line between mystic, charlatan, and scholar, such as the Englishmen John Dee and Edward Kelley, and the Italian polymath Giordano Bruno. Prague was the center of all this multifarious cultural activity. Where Ferdinand I and Maximilian II had been somewhat itinerant, Rudolf chose to settle in Prague partly because it was much safer: the Turks were sometimes only 100 miles from Vienna's gates. Also, Rudolf found Vienna's Hofburg too cramped as a palace. He preferred the hilltop grandeur of Prague's Hradčany. Finally, Prague was the main city of his richest domain, Bohemia, and by locating there he could cultivate better relations with the powerful Bohemian nobility. Yet as he was progressively deposed from Austria and Hungary, he became almost a hostage of the Bohemian estates. It was only after Matthias took over that Vienna rose into the Austrian branch's definitive capital.

None of these three rulers left an appreciable legacy in building up the institutional structures of the dynasty's rule in the Danubian domains. Their temperaments, but also political circumstances and a paucity of resources, deterred any significant reforms. Money, whether for military enterprises or even basic governance was, as always, a problem. For example, though Maximilian's average annual income around 1570 was

4.5 million florins, he only had roughly 1 million to spend because of fixed costs such as debt service and the military frontier. He did try to scrape together funds by economizing measures, such as issuing decrees about how many candles his household could use. He also pushed through a reorganization of his exchequer in 1568, but it did not measurably improve his financial situation. Financial irregularities hampered the Austrian Habsburgs' government in another way: when bureaucrats' pay was late or partial, it became harder to employ them, complicating the already daunting challenge of finding enough qualified and capable officials to run the administration. In addition to these problems, Rudolf's governance was often stymied by his personal frailties. His irresoluteness was exacerbated by the admittedly fractious confessional politics. As religion became a flashpoint in the relationship between crown, estates, cities, peasants and pastors, the nobles, in particular, were able to exploit these cleavages to assert their rights vis-à-vis royal power. Because of the struggle between Rudolf and Matthias, the estates definitely gained leverage, to resist the sovereign's will and also to protect worship or feudal jurisdictions. There were also some compromises in favor of the crown. In 1578, for example, the estates of Inner Austria agreed to provide regular financial contributions for the fight against the Turks. In return for granting some basic religious concessions, Archduke Karl essentially removed the estates' bargaining power over financial contributions.

From a Habsburg dynast's point of view, governing the Empire was like governing the Danubian domains, only worse. The imperial princes were even more powerful than the provincial estates, and had more constitutional and physical protections. Given that they were less politically astute, had fewer resources and more confessional conflicts, Maximilian, Rudolf, and Matthias all had a more difficult time in the Empire than did Charles V or Ferdinand I. This is not to say that as emperors they had *no* influence. The emperor always had the suasion of both elected and symbolic legitimacy. More than any other prince in Germany, he had political capital and the stature to build allegiances. But apart from the last resort of military action, he had virtually no means of reliably enforcing his will, at least on the larger princes. Maximilian made one of the few bold initiatives of these years, the failure of which illustrates the dynasty's unreliable influence in Germany. In 1570 at the Speyer Reichstag it was proposed that all military matters of the Empire would fall under the emperor's authority, with the potential even of creating a standing army. The justification of course was to bolster the fight against the Turks, but this proposal was rejected on the predictable grounds that it would weaken the power of the diet. Thus the imperial office at this time remained a central focus of the Habsburgs' interests and prestige, but it afforded them relatively little institutional control in German politics.

Maximilian, Rudolf, and Matthias exemplify the limitations of princely power in the face of religious conflicts and assertive estates bodies. They pose a stark contrast to Felipe II, who though he still governed in collaboration with other societal elites, had struck a more favorable bargain with them, which gave him vastly greater resources with which to achieve his objectives. Maximilian, Rudolf, and Matthias did not lack for that ambition. The first two did uphold the imperial ideal of leading the defense against the Turks, and Maximilian certainly subscribed to the hope of healing Christendom's splits. But the political context of the Danubian domains impeded strong leadership. None of these three gave up on the legitimacy of the Habsburg mission and their exalted function as rulers. Catholicism remained a guiding ideology of the family, even if Maximilian and Rudolf were less committed to it. But given the obvious limits on their authority, they had to seek a kind of symbolic consolation. This was clearly the rationale of much of Rudolf's cultural display; he even commissioned a martial bust of himself by the sculptor Adriaen de Vries that was virtually identical to the great, Caesar-esque bust of Charles V by Leone Leoni. Though not nearly as august or puissant as his grand-uncle (and grandfather!), Rudolf still aspired to be like him. His artistic bequest was Rudolf's greatest legacy for the dynasty. Maximilian cannot be regarded as a complete failure either. He prevented violent religious conflict in his lands, and he also deserves credit for his heartfelt, nondogmatic attempts to navigate the confessional splits. The fratricidal machinations of Rudolf's last years did weaken the bases of the dynasty's authority, however, setting the stage for the calamitous tests of Habsburg power in the ensuing decades.

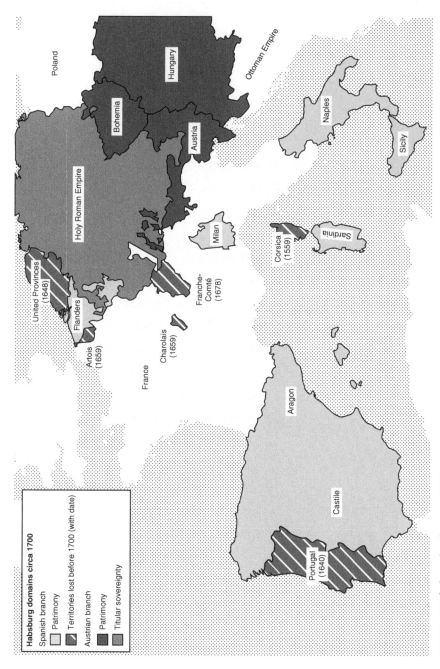

MAP 2. *Habsburg lands circa 1700.*

CHAPTER SIX

Endless war (1619–65)

In Velázquez's *Portrait of Felipe IV* from 1656 we see a man regal, dignified, but beaten. He wears the solemn black usual for the Spanish Habsburg kings. There also is the characteristic Habsburg lip. He gazes, self-possessed, out of the portrait, but it is his drooping eyes that are so striking. They are wells of sadness that bespeak the king's suffering. By the time Velázquez painted this portrait, Felipe [Philip] had lost his beloved first wife and his son, his reformist intentions for his monarchy had collapsed, Portugal and Catalonia had rebelled against him, Castile's wealth and population were exhausted, and he had been defeated in most of his war aims in northern Europe. Despondent, in these years he often turned to a mystic for advice, a nun named Sor María de Ágreda. He once wrote to her, "I don't know whether what is happening to me is real or only a nightmare."[1]

The roughly contemporaneous reigns of Felipe IV in Spain and Ferdinand II and Ferdinand III in Austria were in many ways nightmarish for the dynasty. Almost this entire period was wracked by war. For three decades most of central Europe was a battlefield of the Habsburgs against nearly every major European state. Spain's conflict with the Dutch spilled over into Germany and drew in France. The Austrian branch contended with rebellions in Bohemia and Hungary, and a civil war in the Empire that also provoked an aggressive Swedish invasion. Protestants battled Catholics, entire regions were laid waste, and the Thirty Years' War became history's most destructive conflict until the twentieth century. Felipe's government tried and failed to stanch the brutal drain on its resources, and Habsburg Spain gradually slid from its near-hegemonic position. The Austrian Habsburgs succeeded in eradicating the Bohemian resistance and in propelling the Counter-Reformation in their lands. They had to retreat from many of their advances in the Empire, however. For all that was lost, this period of Habsburg history still left a great cultural legacy and a remarkable record of dynastic solidarity.

Felipe IV (1605–65)

Felipe IV is in some ways the most tragic of all Habsburg rulers. He was intelligent, cultivated, and diligent. He recognized that Spain had been adrift under the negligent rule of his father, and he wanted to correct those deficiencies. But it was his misfortune to rule during a very troubled time— and some of the troubles were of his own making. As his nickname of *El rey planeta* ("the planet king") suggests, Spain's vast empire reached its greatest extent under his reign. Its strategic commitments were likewise vast and simply impossible; there were enemies on all sides. The demands upon his realms and upon him as a monarch proved crippling. This is one reason why Felipe depended upon prominent ministers to do much of the work for him. The most powerful of these ministers was Gaspar de Guzmán, the Count-Duke of Olivares, a canny, controversial politician who is inextricably linked with the first 20 years of Felipe's rule. Though he insightfully identified and energetically attacked many of the issues where Spain most needed reform, Olivares ultimately overreached, and the monarchy almost crumbled. Felipe gave Olivares too long a leash, and was therefore partly responsible for the wreck that resulted from his minister's plan.

Since he succeeded to the throne when he was only 16, the dynasty was fortunate that the new king was astute and took governance seriously. In both these characteristics he was a marked contrast to his father. Though never as deeply engaged with the machinery of government as were Felipe II or Charles V, his rule was nearly as eventful as theirs. It typically receives less attention, though, because it is mostly a litany of defeats, lacking the glories that sporadically brightened his predecessors' reigns. But Felipe IV (Figure 6.1) counts among the most well-rounded of all Habsburg rulers. He deeply loved the arts. He often patronized the theater and even built a few. He liked poetry and favored a few notable poets, including the acid-penned Francisco Quevedo, one of the greatest Spanish satirists, whose relationship with Felipe eventually turned so sour that the king had him imprisoned. And though he spent many hours at bullfights and in the hunt, he did not neglect more cerebral activities. For instance, he dedicated years to his own translation of an Italian historical tome into Spanish. Felipe's taste and cultivation are best seen via his long friendship with Velázquez, many of whose paintings chronicle Felipe's family and court.

Olivares became Felipe's political tutor before Felipe III had died. Olivares came from a prominent noble family that had helped engineer the downfall of Felipe III's venal *valido* Lerma. It is not surprising that a young man like Felipe would be overawed by the acumen of a man like Olivares, who was 34 when Felipe came to power. There is no question that Olivares was a gifted politician, nearly the equal of his great rival Richelieu in France. He was boundlessly ambitious and ruthless, and could be despotic and irascible. But he had vision, an extraordinary sense of how to manipulate

FIGURE 6.1 *Felipe IV, by Diego Velázquez (1656). In the collection of the Museo del Prado. Image courtesy of the Bridgeman Art Library.*

people, and a firm conviction in the greatness of Spain. He worked very hard to realize that vision, which was to rescue Felipe's realms from the humiliation and passivity of the previous reign. Olivares was determined to reestablish Spain's reputation as the leading power of Europe. He did not advocate conquering new domains. Yet his insistence on defending all of Spain's strategic commitments meant that the monarchy had to fight on all fronts, at a time when the economic and social bases of the monarchy's power were already weakening. Nonetheless, Felipe bought into this campaign to restore Habsburg prestige. The partnership between these two men, though it started out as that between mentor and mentee, evolved over the years. Olivares worked to keep Felipe actively engaged in the workings of his government, and it is likely that Felipe's own intelligence and sense of duty ensured that his *valido* was so hard-working. Olivares never truly eclipsed Felipe as the actual ruler, though with historical hindsight it is certain that Felipe delegated too much of his authority to the Count-Duke.

Olivares and Felipe cannot be accused of not thinking big. Their objectives included securing the southern Netherlands, preserving the Castilian/ Portuguese monopoly in the overseas territories, defending Catholicism, and supporting the Austrian Habsburgs. Enormous tasks each in themselves, they also intertwined, which helps explain why Felipe's monarchy was so overburdened. The commitment to the Habsburg alliance was emphasized already in Felipe III's last years, as Spanish money and troops were sent to aid the Austrian cousins in suppressing the Bohemian revolt that was the first stage of the Thirty Years' War. That revolt was viewed by the Spanish Habsburg kings and their advisors as a serious test of the dynasty's power in central Europe, and as an attack on Catholicism. The war with the Dutch resumed in 1621 after 12 years of peace. To Olivares's thinking, the Dutch were the aggressors. Even in the years of peace they had kept up attacks on Spain and Portugal's overseas empires, and had refused to remove their stranglehold on the Spanish Netherlands through the blockade on Antwerp's port. Hence Spain went to war not to reconquer its lost Dutch provinces, but to defend its economic and territorial interests.

When the Habsburgs combined forces, though, it could not help but upset the European balance of power. The Spanish Habsburgs' war against the Dutch, and the Austrian Habsburgs' war in the Empire, dragged in most major powers in Europe. Cardinal Richelieu, leading France, had the old fear of being encircled by Habsburg power, and so began aiding the Dutch and the Habsburgs' other Protestant enemies with funds and diplomacy. In the 1620s Spain and France circled each other warily, avoiding a direct war. England was also hostile because Habsburg power in Germany was seen as a threat to the English kings' possessions there. Initially, Felipe IV's armies won some impressive victories. In 1625 they repelled an English attack on Cádiz and expelled the Dutch from Bahía in Brazil, and Breda in the southern Netherlands. The latter victory occasioned Velázquez's famous painting of the Dutch surrender. There was another series of victories leading up to 1627, closely coordinated with the Austrian branch. Following Spanish naval victories over the Dutch, and land victories by Ferdinand II's general Wallenstein, Habsburg power extended to the Baltic as never before.

By the end of the decade, however, the Spanish monarchy encountered reversals on all fronts. In order to pay for its massive military operations, taxes and borrowing in Spain had skyrocketed. The crown was forced to declare bankruptcy in 1627. Many in Felipe's court, including his greatest general Spinola, commander of the armies in the Low Countries, insisted that now was the time to negotiate for peace. Olivares, however, refused. Then in 1628 the Dutch admiral Piet Heyn captured the entire Spanish silver fleet in Cuba, a terrible blow to the monarchy's already fragile finances. In that year, as well, Olivares committed one of his greatest blunders by diverting troops from the Netherlands for a campaign in northern Italy. After a line of the Gonzaga dukes of Mantua died out, the succession was open to a claimant backed by the French. Olivares was determined to prevent this because he saw it as a dangerous threat to Spain's hold over the duchy of Milan. Spain's action in northern Italy was closely coordinated with Ferdinand II, but it brought them both closer to outright war with France. Moreover, the campaign was an extremely expensive failure, hemorrhaging Spanish resources as the Dutch made new gains in Brazil, and Swedish forces rampaged in Germany. When this Italian conflict was ended by the Treaty of Cherasco of 1631, Olivares had virtually nothing to show for the struggle over the Mantuan succession. Indeed, in later years Felipe IV called this defeat the point "when my monarchy began . . . visibly to decline."[2]

Olivares was not blind to Spain's mounting problems. He launched a number of reforms designed to strengthen Felipe's monarchy. While in many ways smart and well-intentioned, they were also characteristically ambitious and expansive, and so provoked even more trouble for the king and his chief minister. By 1623 Olivares was proclaiming the need to reform the tax system, to end currency devaluations, to streamline the bureaucracy, and to eliminate excessive spending on luxuries. He also called for nothing less than a transformation of Spanish society: he hoped to make the Spanish entrepreneurial merchants more like the Dutch, and simultaneously to reduce the migration to cities that was undermining Spanish agriculture. The success of these reform proposals really depended on events abroad. Not only did Spain need peace to be able to rebuild itself internally, but Olivares needed to curtail the vast sums being spent on the military in order to get the monarchy's financial house in order. Neither came about. As the war progressed and the hoped-for quick victory in Italy was dashed, the most regressive aspects of the tax system were increased, not abolished. Forced to raise ever more revenue, Olivares took steps that were ultimately counterproductive, such as seizing American silver shipments, selling more titles and offices to the nobility, and debasing the coinage.

The signature element of Olivares's reforms was called the Union of Arms, and it was founded on a valuable insight. He wrote that Felipe IV should make himself truly "king of Spain" rather than just "king of Portugal, of Aragon and Valencia, and count of Barcelona," that he should "reduce these realms that make up Spain to the style and laws of Castile."[3] This was not merely an attempt to subjugate all the other realms to Castile, but rather to tie the composite monarchy more tightly together so that the other realms would share the fiscal burden of world power more equitably with Castile. The inequity was serious. In the early part of the seventeenth century, Castile paid some three-quarters of all costs of maintaining the empire, while Portugal paid 10 percent, Naples 5 percent, and Aragon only 1 percent.[4] Olivares's plan was to institute a new property tax across all the realms that would help support a large reserve army. In return for this burden sharing, the people of these other realms would get greater participation in the empire's governance than they currently enjoyed. The plan meant a significant reworking of the monarchy's constitutional relationships. It therefore received a cold response. The realms apart from Castile regarded it as a Trojan horse for complete Castilian domination; the Catalans fought it with special bitterness.

Almost everywhere, in fact, Olivares's reforms sparked resistance, which smoldered into the 1630s. The Portuguese refused to increase financial contributions even to help protect their possessions in Brazil. There were sporadic riots against the idea of union with Castile in various Portuguese towns in 1637, and the Portuguese nobility and merchant classes increasingly began to see the costs outweighing the benefits of belonging to the Spanish monarchy. The Catalans also refused any new subsidies and left Felipe fuming at their intransigence. Rebellion there, too, was brewing. The Union of Arms was not a complete failure, since Naples and the Spanish Netherlands did increase their contributions to the crown. It is perhaps unlikely that the Union would have solved Spain's problems of overstretch, even had the plan been realized as fully as Olivares hoped. It was common in the seventeenth century that provinces would insist upon their contractual relationship to the crown as justification for resistance to growing royal power. The inability to increase the monarchy's cohesion (and hence the effectiveness of the monarch's government) was a major long-term weakness for the dynasty. But Olivares's response to that resistance—intimidation and threats taking precedence over negotiation—provoked serious short-term problems for his own leadership. Besides the growing antagonism in Portugal and Catalonia, his impatient and hectoring nature was making enemies within Felipe's court.

Spain's financial problems motivated truces with England and France in the first years of the 1630s. Nonetheless, Felipe continued to send money and men to help his Austrian cousins in their fight against the Swedes and the German Protestants. In 1634 Felipe's and Ferdinand II's armies won a stunning victory over the Swedes at Nördlingen. This scared Richelieu sufficiently that the years of on-again, off-again French-Spanish clashes now burst into open war in 1635. This was terrible news for both Felipe and Olivares, since it meant a full commitment from their most dangerous enemy; by the late 1630s Spain was fighting a true world war. Spanish and Austrian troops launched an invasion of France in 1637 that failed to make much headway, and though the French won no major victories, a series of lesser defeats took their toll on Spain's power. The Dutch retook Breda in 1637. In 1638 the fortress town of Breisach was lost, which cut the vital "Spanish Road" linking Habsburg possessions from Milan to Brussels. Reinforcements for the war against the Dutch now had to arrive by sea. In 1639 the Dutch beat a Spanish fleet at the Battle of the Downs, and in 1640 repelled a combined Spanish-Portuguese fleet in Brazil. Still, Spain's setbacks have to be set in perspective. It has been estimated that Felipe could put 300,000 men in the field in the 1630s, compared to only 150,000 for France.[5] But because Spanish armies were committed on so many fronts, overwhelming force could not be focused at any one point. Moreover, increasing taxes, more currency devaluation, and declining silver shipments were all sapping Spain's strength at home. Olivares began to seek peace in these years. But in 1640 Felipe and his minister endured two brutal blows to the dynasty's prestige and the monarchy's war effort, the revolts in Catalonia and Portugal.

Catalonia was on the front line of the war with France, yet the province repeatedly balked at contributing money and troops to its own defense. Olivares dispatched an army to fight the French but also force a subsidy from the Catalans. This only exacerbated widespread grievances in Catalonia over such things as Olivares's reform demands and the hardships of the long war. In 1640 peasants rose up and attacked the royal troops, and rebels murdered Felipe's viceroy. They then turned to France for help, and in January 1641 declared Louis XIII the new count of Barcelona. The situation rapidly deteriorated into a civil war as poor people in the countryside and the towns turned on the aristocracy.

Many of the nobles in fact remained loyal to Felipe; without French help there was no realistic possibility that Catalonia would have split from Spain. But the chaos came at a moment when Felipe and Castile were too weak to suppress the rebellion easily. It took more than ten years before the province was pacified. By the 1650s a plague had ravaged the countryside and France, now under Mazarin's leadership, was distracted by its own rebellion with the Fronde. Felipe sent a somewhat weak army that besieged the last rebel holdouts in Barcelona. The city fell in October 1652, and Felipe offered a general pardon as well as promised to respect Catalonia's constitution. Ultimately, the Catalan revolt was not a mass rebellion for separatism. Rather, it was a failed uprising of the disgruntled lower classes, mingled with a conspiracy among a few of the elite, to break away from the Spanish crown. It was, however, a demonstration of the fragility of the ties that bound Spain together as a dynastic state, and of the dynasty's limited ability to strengthen those ties.

The Catalan revolt was actually a lesser disaster than the simultaneous revolt in Portugal, which had deeper roots and much wider support. Portugal was connected to the other Iberian realms only through its monarch, but it depended on their contributions for the defense of its empire. Felipe's sorely pressed monarchy had growing trouble fending off the Dutch predations on Brazil. Olivares also managed to antagonize parts of the Portuguese bureaucracy and the elite throughout the 1630s by appointing Castilians to positions of authority and raising taxes. Olivares was not unaware of this anger, but unwisely tried to redirect it by sending a Portuguese army to Catalonia to help quell the rebellion there. This triggered a coup by

Portuguese nobles in December 1640 in which the Duke of Bragança was named the new Portuguese king. France provided monetary and military support. Felipe's resources were stretched so thin that he could not immediately raise an army to combat this coup. He did try to retake the country in the 1650s and 1660s, however. His armies were defeated by the Portuguese in 1659 at Elvas, and then again in 1663, and finally in 1665 in a battle at Villaviciosa. By now Portugal had allied with England, and Felipe's ministers were convinced that the country had to be let go. The end of the Iberian Union Felipe regarded as one of his worst failures, and kept swearing that he would get Portugal back.

Though the revolts in Catalonia and Portugal were the most consequential of Felipe's reign, there were a series of lesser ones that seemed as if the monarchy might come completely unglued. The Andalusian nobility briefly rose up in 1641, and Naples and Sicily rebelled in 1647. The French tried to encourage Aragon to break off in 1648. There were also smaller revolts throughout the 1630s to the 1650s, as villages, towns, and cities protested worsening socioeconomic conditions, as in Granada in 1648 and Seville in 1652. While these revolts tested the adherence of the various provinces to the Spanish monarchy, they were rarely unified attempts at separatism. In many cases they threatened to slide quickly into the kind of anarchic social revolution that Catalonia's rebellion became. Elites in these provinces, whatever their grievances with the crown might be, still generally saw Habsburg rule as worth upholding. The crown, for its part, promised to respect the provinces' constitutional liberties and refrain from aggressive centralization efforts like those implied by the Union of Arms. Since this arrangement by and large promised to maintain the existing power structure within these provinces, and since there was no realistic alternative for Catalonia, Naples, and the other dominions, membership in the Habsburg dynastic union persisted.

The revolts in Catalonia and Portugal spelled doom for Olivares. Criticism of the count-duke had been mounting for years, from satirists' pens but also from the high nobility. Though Felipe and Olivares had always had periodic disagreements, by the late 1630s their relationship had cooled noticeably. Moreover, the failures of Felipe's government were translating to direct criticisms of himself, as well as privations in his household. He and his family had to sell off jewels, furnishings, and land in a desperate attempt to raise money for their many wars. Felipe finally dismissed his chief minister in 1643, ending their 20-year partnership. Olivares died just two years later, and in his last months he began to go mad. Despite the evident foresight and necessity of his many reform plans, nearly all of them ended in failure. The balance sheet of Olivares's achievements is so consistently negative that he is rarely as esteemed as his contemporary, Richelieu. He was as hard-working as the Frenchman, and less venal, but Olivares's misfortune resulted in Felipe IV's larger misfortune of conscientious governance undone by recurrent disaster.

After he dismissed Olivares, Felipe swore that he would have no other *valido*, but rather manage his affairs himself. He did appoint Olivares's nephew, Luis de Haro, to a position of great influence, and Haro gradually became Felipe's prime minister, but he never fully took over the position Olivares had occupied. It was after 1643, as well, that Felipe increasingly turned to Sor María for advice. He worried that God had begun to punish Spain for deviations from its divine course. He wrote to Sor María in 1645, "All the parts of my Monarchy are in a terrible state, surrounded by wars in every quarter. But I believe that if only I could correct my own behavior, everything will have its own remedy."[6] He was certainly correct that Spain hit a new nadir in the 1640s. Besides the multiple rebellions, there was a major loss to the French at the Battle of Rocroi in 1643. The alliance with the Austrian Habsburgs was also fraying at this time, as the two branches' military objectives diverged. State bankruptcy struck in 1647, then again in 1653. So dire was the financial state of the monarchy that observers reported that on some days the royal household could not even afford bread. Thus Felipe was finally pushed to seek a costly peace. As part of the negotiations at Westphalia, the Spanish Habsburgs made a separate deal from the Austrian branch. The 80-year-long conflict with the Dutch was ended, and Spain officially recognized the independence of the United Provinces. Spain kept the southern Netherlands but gave up other aims such as the opening of the Scheldt River for Antwerp's port.

The treaty with the Dutch did not end the conflict with the French. Felipe hoped to exploit France's own troubles, namely the Fronde revolt, which lasted until 1653. Spanish forces won some notable battles at Barcelona and Dunkirk, but both France and Spain were too weak to deliver a knockout blow, so the war reached an impasse. The tide turned against Spain when England under Oliver Cromwell joined the war on France's side. The English took Jamaica in 1655, then destroyed the Spanish silver fleets in both 1656 and 1657. In 1658 a joint French-English force won the Battle of the Dunes. This led directly to the crucial Peace of the Pyrenees in 1659. Spain was utterly exhausted and the war had to end. Felipe also felt more secure in seeking a treaty because his second wife Mariana had given birth to a son. This was important because per the terms of the treaty, Felipe married his daughter María Teresa to Louis XIV. Without a son, this marriage posed the danger of the Bourbons succeeding to the Spanish throne. Otherwise, the terms were not unfavorable to Spain because France under Cardinal Mazarin's leadership also desperately wanted peace. Territorial losses were not severe. The historic import of the treaty was rather that it sealed the end of Spain as the leading European power. In the remaining four decades of Habsburg rule in Spain, though the monarchy was still sometimes active in broader European affairs, it began to look inward. What it saw was appalling.

Historians have theorized a "General Crisis" of politics, economics, and demographics that afflicted Europe in the seventeenth century. Castile suffered more than most areas. The phenomenon of trying to meet excessive imperial commitments with insufficient fiscal resources, evident already under Felipe II, only worsened. The heavy tax burden increased, much of it borne by the lower classes. Changes in Castile's economic relationship with its overseas colonies also eroded its vigor. After the later 1620s the crown found that it could no longer depend on regular, substantial shipments of American silver; the bullion was sometimes captured by pirates, sometimes fluctuated dramatically in output, and often was quickly reexported elsewhere in Europe to pay other costs. Additionally, the colonies were becoming more self-sufficient economically, and so depended less on Europe for their imported goods. Thus the monarchy benefited less from its colonies even as it had to spend more to defend them against English, Dutch, and French attacks. The colonies' economic maturation accompanied other failures of economic development in the metropole. The American silver was spent less on investments to develop new industries and exports, but instead on consumption and foreign policy ventures.

The silver influx also contributed to inflation and the attendant "price revolution," which was common throughout Europe, but especially deleterious in Castile. Prices there more than quadrupled over the course of a century. These increases impoverished many people in the lower classes, and made Spanish industries uncompetitive. Traditional strengths like shipbuilding and textiles withered. Armaments manufacture declined to such an extent that Spain had to buy many of its military supplies from England and France. Serious maladies in agriculture added to the other problems. A decrease in arable land and outputs meant that many rural people could no longer live from farming, and many people left the countryside. Famines and plague outbreaks repeatedly struck the Iberian peninsula in the first half of the 1600s. Around 1650, bad harvests and disease killed off some 500,000 people, including roughly half of the populations of Barcelona and Seville. This contributed to a terrifying overall decline of the population in many parts of the peninsula. Castile had about 6.7 million people in the 1590s, but only around 5 million in 1665.[7] Relatively little of this decrease came from war deaths.

This dreary picture has given rise to an enduring narrative of decline in Habsburg Spain. Laments of such decline (by Olivares among others) were heard even during Felipe's IV reign and before. And while it is indisputable that Spain by 1659 had fallen from the seemingly hegemonic position of Felipe II's time, an overemphasis on Spanish decline is misguided. First, the most serious of the above problems drained Castile above all, rather than Spain as a whole. Second, Castile at the beginning of its meteoric rise to international prominence—in the opening decades of the 1500s—was a fairly poor country to begin with. It had never been one of Europe's most developed economies. Yet thanks to a strong crown, colonial riches, and high taxes, it managed to support a hyperactive imperial policy for roughly a century. At least as striking as its decline from such a lofty position was

Castile's improbable and vertiginous rise. Third, the focus on decline obscures the many stupendous achievements of Habsburg Spain. That this loose-limbed bundle of realms provided such a solid power base for so many years, despite their limited natural endowments in manpower and wealth, was extraordinary. In fact, the Habsburg kings and their subjects managed to create a reasonably efficient structure for ruling an empire vastly larger than any previous European state. Even in the disastrous last years of Felipe IV's reign, his monarchy was still somehow able to field armies and fleets across much of northern and central Europe, as well as in the Americas. No other king of the time could match it.

Still, even Felipe by the last decade of his life felt that his monarchy was being bled dry by endless war. The goal with which Olivares had begun—restoring Spain's reputation—was palpably lost by these last years. A symbolic moment in that loss was a diplomatic dispute at the London court in 1661. Contrary to a century's practice of giving Spanish diplomats absolute precedence in protocol, on Louis XIV's orders the French diplomatic corps insisted that France receive precedence. The Spanish diplomats protested, and a brawl broke out. Louis then gave Felipe an ultimatum, and since he could not risk a new war, Felipe had to acquiesce. Henceforth the Spanish would be demoted in favor of the French. This deepened the depression Felipe had felt since the mid-1640s, after his wife and son died in short order. By 1665 Felipe was mentally and physically exhausted, much like Castile itself. On his deathbed he expressed the guilt he felt about the crushing toll of taxes and war he had imposed on Castile, but praised what he called "the effort and offering of blood which the Castilians have made and continue to make every day in defense of the Catholic religion."[8] He died just a few weeks after the final, dismaying defeat at Villaviciosa that failed to retake Portugal. In Spanish historiography Felipe IV has sometimes been classed with Felipe III and Carlos II as one of the *Austrias menores*, or minor Spanish Habsburgs. But the pivotal events of his reign, and his attentive approach to kingship and governance, merit a position as one of the most complex of all Habsburg rulers—in part because so many of the decisions he took ultimately hurt his realms and his dynasty.

Ferdinand II (1578–1637)

Ferdinand II was a curious mixture of timidity and intransigence, of personal amiability coupled with near-fanatical intolerance of Protestants. Coming after the conflicted religious attitudes of Maximilian II and Rudolf II, Ferdinand launched the Austrian branch on a new course of aggressive and often single-minded Counter-Reformation. It is with him that the Austrian Habsburgs introduced the especially pompous Catholic piety that so defined the dynasty. He was not an especially astute ruler, but his many political failings were balanced by his decisive victory over the Bohemian rebellion. He came to the throne in August 1619 when he was 41. A small, chubby man, he affected a Spanish-style mustache and goatee. He was a hard worker and well-liked by many people who knew him, but he was no natural politician, owing to his dearth of imagination and excess of stubbornness. An intense, rather suffocating piety was the main element of his personality. He spent several hours a day in masses and prayer. Jesuits made a big impact on his upbringing and education, and continued to be influential in his court. He even said that he wished he had been a Jesuit. He may thus be the most priestly of all Habsburg rulers; despite his two marriages, he generally distanced himself from women and lustful temptations.

His firm moral convictions reflected his strict adherence to Catholic doctrine, which in turn deeply shaped his rule. He was certain that upholding the Catholic Church was his and his dynasty's God-given mission. This literal-minded devotion meant that Ferdinand rarely considered the broader implications of his policies. His inability or refusal to sacrifice dogma to pragmatism often proved counterproductive to his own ends. Apart from matters of religion, he was not particularly strong-willed, and in fact could be pliant and sluggish. His mother basically ruled him until he reached 30, even as he was already archduke of Styria. She pushed him to take a hard-line against Protestants in his lands, something to which he was already disposed after his vigorous Jesuit education at Ingolstadt in Bavaria. So with his mother pulling his strings, he began driving Protestants out of Inner Austria around 1600, trying to bring the province completely back to Catholicism. The Counter-Reformation became the guiding light for nearly all of Ferdinand's politics. While its trends predated him, it was under his rule that more intensive re-Catholicization began.

What he had started in Styria he then pursued aggressively throughout the Danubian domains when, after Matthias's death, he became the head of the Austrian branch of the family. Starting in the 1620s, he burned books, expelled Protestants from his territories, appointed clerics to his ruling circle, and enlisted the Jesuits to convert high nobles in Austria, Bohemia, and Hungary back to Catholicism. The strength of the nobility in Hungary meant that they retained more religious freedom. Nonetheless, wherever he could, Ferdinand ordered churches built to promote cults of Catholic saints and the Virgin Mary. The Church gained a near monopoly on education, to the detriment of freer, nonconformist thinking. Similarly, censorship and a crackdown on book printing began to isolate the Habsburg domains from wider European intellectual trends. Ferdinand's intolerance was not unusual in the context of the seventeenth century, when religious unity was regarded as essential to a well-ordered state. He was just more zealous than most rulers in enforcing religious orthodoxy. Interestingly, Ferdinand was never completely despotic in his Counter-Reformatory ardor, since he allowed some of the Lower Austrian nobility who swore loyalty to him in

1620 to continue to practice Protestantism. He also never hated Protestants personally—he persecuted them because he thought it was his duty.

Ferdinand was elected king of Bohemia in 1617 and king of Hungary in 1618. In both cases, the crown was soon contested, in Bohemia by Friedrich V of the Palatinate, and in Hungary by the Transylvanian prince Gábor Bethlen. But Ferdinand had enough support in the Empire that he was elected there in March 1619 after Matthias died. The decades of weak rule by Rudolf II and Matthias had let more of the emperor's authority drift away, and confessional splits made collaboration with the princes yet more difficult. The confessional splits tended to mirror geopolitical ones, which formed along pro-Habsburg and anti-Habsburg lines. Those in the latter camp feared the concentration of power in the combined Spanish and Austrian branches of the family (since both branches had territory within the Empire), and so sought out the French and later the Swedes as counterweights.

All of these splits played into the disastrous Thirty Years' War, which consumed all of Ferdinand's reign and much of his son's. This conflict began in Habsburg lands and usually centered on the Habsburgs' position in Europe. The dynasty at times collaborated quite closely, but at other times saw its interests diverge. Spain provided consistent subsidies and troops to the Austrian branch, even though Felipe IV was much more pragmatic on the confessional issues than was Ferdinand II. Most of the fighting took place in Germany and Bohemia; Austria and Hungary saw little actual combat, but Austria suffered most from the attendant economic collapse and disease outbreaks. The war can be divided into four broad phases: the initial conflict over Bohemia and the Palatinate to 1625, a less intense period of Danish involvement to 1629, then a hard-fought Swedish invasion to 1635, followed by a direct confrontation between the Habsburgs and France to 1648.

Tensions between Protestants and Catholics in Bohemia had been escalating already in Matthias's last years. Matthias drastically curtailed Protestants' rights to build churches, and their freedom to assemble. Ferdinand, once he became king, had promised to respect the tolerant terms of the Letter of Majesty from Rudolf's time, but began undermining it nonetheless. Protestants' anger at their persecution provoked the famous defenestration of Prague of 23 May 1618. A group of Protestant nobles burst into governmental chambers in Prague Castle and tossed the king's servants, two Catholic nobles—Martinic and Slavata—as well as a secretary, out a window. This was the spark for the Bohemian rebellion and the entire Thirty Years' War. Ferdinand considered from the beginning that the resistance to his authority was not confined to Bohemia, and that other powers were involved, particularly the militant Calvinists of the Palatinate. He commented darkly, "This alarm bell did not ring itself, but was pulled from other places."[9] These forces of resistance combined openly in 1619 when the rebellious Bohemian nobles invalidated their prior election of

Ferdinand and instead chose the Calvinist Friedrich V, the Elector Palatine, as their new king.

Friedrich was the headstrong and politically inept son-in-law of James I of England, on whom he was counting for support in his grab for Bohemia. Some of the Austrian estates also rebelled, supporting Friedrich, as did Gábor Bethlen, who now made a move on Habsburg Hungary. One of the rebel Bohemian nobles raised an army of 20,000 and quickly marched on Vienna, intending to link up with Bethlen's troops. Although he was in dire straits at this point, Ferdinand refused any compromise, insisting that God would protect him. He prostrated himself in front of a crucifix and prayed for hours. His salvation came from more earthly sources, however, namely the alliances he forged with Maximilian of Bavaria, Felipe III of Spain, and the Saxon Elector Johann Georg, who though a Protestant, objected to Friedrich's usurpation of legitimate authority. Where the Spanish Habsburgs provided money and troops, Maximilian really assumed leadership, rallying the Catholic League to defend Ferdinand's power and prerogatives. Ferdinand stayed safely in Vienna while his allies led the war against Friedrich and the Bohemian rebels.

Friedrich in fact did not have much support, since England and France kept their distance so as not to side with a usurper of royal authority. The Evangelical Union of Protestant German princes also resisted taking a side in this fight. Thus when it came to the conclusive clash between Friedrich and Ferdinand, the rebels could mount only a small, amateurish force. The Battle of White Mountain, fought near Prague in November 1620, was momentous only in its consequences; the battle itself lasted barely an hour, after which Friedrich and his routed forces fled. Thus Friedrich became known as the "Winter King," since his reign lasted only one winter. With his convincing victory, Ferdinand set about rooting out all rebellion, which meant hunting down the revolt's leaders, then eliminating the treasonous and heretical strands of Protestantism from Bohemia. The first goal was accomplished quickly: in June 1621, 27 rebel leaders were executed on Prague's Old Town Square, their bodies left to rot on Charles Bridge as a warning.

The fierce, subsequent reintegration of Bohemia took a number of years, but it gave the dynasty greater control over the kingdom than it had ever had before. Protestantism was outlawed; those who would not convert to Catholicism were forced into exile. Bohemia lost some 200,000 of its population over the next few decades partly for this reason. Ferdinand with his own dagger tore up Rudolf's toleration letter. Rebellious nobles' property was confiscated and awarded to other nobles who had been loyal to the crown. The kingdom was given a new constitution in 1627, known as the *Verneuerte Landesordnung*. It made the Habsburgs hereditary rather than elective monarchs, gave the king sole authority over all civil servants in the country, and moved the main governmental office (the Bohemian chancellery) to Vienna. It also significantly weakened the power of the estates as an institution, though they did retain some authority over taxes. German was made equal with Czech as the administrative language. Though Habsburg control over Bohemia still had enough limitations that it was never truly absolutist, the changes after White Mountain were of immense importance. The kingdom was henceforth fused together with the Austrian Hereditary Lands, royal power was expanded, and religious unity restored under Catholicism.

Overconfident from the victory in Bohemia, Ferdinand determined to stamp out resistance in his other domains, including the Empire. For a time, it seemed as if he would become the most powerful emperor in generations. But the gains he made so alarmed the states surrounding the Empire that they intervened. The Swedish invasion in particular tumbled Ferdinand from his peak and brought an even more destructive phase of the war. By 1623, the imperial and Bavarian armies had occupied much of the Palatinate, chasing out Friedrich V, and were assisting Felipe IV against the Dutch. In gratitude for Maximilian of Bavaria's vital aid against the rebels, Ferdinand granted him rule of the Palatinate for his life's duration. This arrogation of imperial and Catholic power antagonized rulers inside and outside Germany. In Germany, Maximilian's takeover of the Palatinate was resented as a violation of the Empire's law. The other princes were particularly alarmed by the precedent of the emperor deposing one prince for another. Encouraged by England and France, King Christian IV of Denmark marched into Lower Saxony and Westphalia in 1625 to defend the Protestant cause. Ferdinand now had to fight in northern and western Germany, and to guard his eastern flank against Bethlen in Hungary. He needed a larger army, and so he turned to Albrecht von Wallenstein, the Bohemian aristocrat who became Ferdinand's gifted but devious warlord.

Wallenstein repeatedly saved Ferdinand's monarchy, yet Ferdinand once dismissed and often distrusted him. Ferdinand, the rather dull, churchly ruler, sometimes actually feared his energetic and audacious general. Wallenstein knew that he was indispensable to Ferdinand and made him pay for that indispensability. A Spanish envoy, describing the relationship between the two men, wrote that "Wallenstein is the sole lord, and leaves the emperor little more than the title."[10] In 1625 Wallenstein raised an army and joined it with that led by the general Tilly, the victor of White Mountain. Together they smashed the Danish king's forces and Wallenstein pushed further into northern Germany. By 1628, thanks to Wallenstein's success, Ferdinand named him "General of the Oceans and the Baltic." Felipe IV and Olivares endorsed a plan to use Ferdinand's now-commanding position in northern Germany to strangle Dutch trade in the Baltic.

In 1629 Ferdinand made a grave mistake that earned him a host of new enemies. Without consulting the imperial diet, the electoral princes, or even some of his close advisors, Ferdinand announced the Edict of Restitution. This edict declared that some 500 abbeys, two archbishoprics, and two bishoprics that had been "secularized" by German princes since 1552 would now suddenly revert to the Catholic Church. Such a reversal threatened the Protestant princes who had seized church land, but also antagonized the Catholic princes because they regarded it as a dangerous overstep for the emperor's authority. The Habsburg presence on the Baltic, coupled with the assault on Protestant princes, induced Gustav Adolf [Gustavus Adolphus] of Sweden to invade Germany in 1630, his army buoyed by huge subsidies from France.

In the early 1630s nearly all the gains Ferdinand had made in Germany were wiped away. Several former allies among the German princes deserted him to make league with the Swedes and the Protestant coalition. At the Battle of Breitenfeld in September 1631 the Catholic forces suffered a significant defeat, with the result that a Saxon army overran Bohemia and Prague, and the Swedes swept into the Rhineland. In 1632 Tilly again lost to the Swedes, and he died in action. Gustav Adolf took Bavaria and came within striking distance of Vienna. Ferdinand had dismissed Wallenstein in 1630 for fear that he was plotting a coup in the Empire, but now desperately needed his leadership and recalled him. The great condottiere quickly reassembled his army, beat back the Saxons, and then did battle with the Swedes at Lützen in November of 1632. Wallenstein was defeated, but Gustav Adolf was killed. The Swedish involvement in Germany nonetheless continued, fueled by ongoing French subsidies. Not long thereafter, Wallenstein began making secret, unauthorized diplomatic contacts with the Protestants and the French. He was seeking perhaps to arrange peace, though rumors swirled that he might even have himself crowned king of Bohemia. He also made his generals swear allegiance to himself, Wallenstein, rather than to Ferdinand. This double-dealing on Wallenstein's part strengthened the case of his many enemies in Ferdinand's court, who now pressed the emperor to remove Wallenstein from the scene. A morally conflicted Ferdinand agreed to Wallenstein's murder, which took place in February of 1634.

Ferdinand now named his son, Ferdinand III, as supreme general, and the heir apparent combined forces with the Cardinal-Infante of Spain, Felipe IV's brother (and Ferdinand III's brother-in-law), in a joint Habsburg attack at the Battle of Nördlingen in September 1634. They won an overwhelming victory, which forced most of the Protestant princes to negotiate for peace, and sharply curtailed Swedish influence. Prodded by Felipe IV, Ferdinand II signed the Peace of Prague in 1635. He proved that he could compromise: he retreated from the Edict of Restitution, and even gave some of his land in Lusatia to Saxony as a price for the armistice. This was a victory for moderates, but it did not end the strife. There was no settlement with Sweden, and the Habsburg victory compelled Richelieu's France to declare war. Ferdinand II did not have long to live by this time. In his last years he experienced major highs and lows, depressed by his many defeats but giddy after the news of Gustav

Adolf's death at Lützen. Before his death in 1637, he used a temporary lull in the conflict in Germany to get his son elected King of the Romans, and thereby secured the Habsburg succession in the Empire. That success alludes to Ferdinand II's importance within the historical context. For all his blunders and provocations, he continued to represent the legitimate authority of the Catholic emperor and the Habsburg dynasty. That the imperial office and the dynasty retained any such authority owed much to Ferdinand's stubborn pugnacity.

Ferdinand III (1608–57)

Ferdinand III was a fairly interesting man, but not an interesting ruler. The mind behind his reign is something of a cipher. The most important ideas and actions came from several of his ministers, particularly the great diplomat Maximilian Trautmansdorff, or Johann Weikhard Auersperg later. Compared with his father, Ferdinand III achieved very little other than a final peace to the Thirty Years' War, which itself should perhaps be enough. In general his politics followed trends laid down during Ferdinand II's reign, including the furtherance of the Counter-Reformation in his own realms, the wearying but close alliance with Felipe IV, and the near-constant threat of Swedish armies. In all these events, Ferdinand III's hand is barely visible. In one recent biography, Ferdinand himself hovers at the edges but is rarely the central player in anything.[11] It is almost as if he were an only intermittently influential spectator at the momentous events that took place while he wore the crown. The picture of Ferdinand's personality is only a little clearer. Here, he was noticeably more intelligent and complex than his father. Though still deeply pious, he was also more pragmatic on religious politics. Ferdinand III's outlook was less clouded by stultifying dogma. He was more curious—he conducted his own chemistry experiments, for example—and well-rounded. Besides being a reasonably competent military commander, he was a gifted composer. Yet despite the major changes that affected the dynasty during his time, he remains among the most indistinct of all modern Habsburgs.

As soon as he came to the throne, Ferdinand III launched efforts to bring the war to a peaceful conclusion. Much as Felipe IV did, though, Ferdinand hoped that his battlefield position would improve just enough that he could sign a more advantageous treaty. This meant that peace kept receding. His armies won some victories over the Swedes in 1636 and 1637, but his opponents then closed ranks. France supplied Sweden with even greater subsidies in return for a promise not to seek a separate peace. By 1639, Ferdinand's prospects were deteriorating nearly as rapidly as those of his brother-in-law in Spain. In that year, the Swedes launched an offensive that took large parts of Bohemia. After 1640, because of Felipe's enormous troubles with Catalonia and Portugal, Spanish subsidies to the Austrian branch dwindled. Over the next few years, the Swedes occupied Silesia and Moravia, again posing a direct threat to Vienna.

Ferdinand was enduring attacks from the east, too, as the Swedes made an alliance with the Transylvanian prince György Rákóczi, who invaded the Habsburgs' Hungarian domains in 1643. Ferdinand appeased him by granting religious freedom in the lands under Rákóczi's rule in 1645, but by then the Austrian war effort, much like the Spanish, was on a catastrophic last slide. In that same year, the combined forces of Ferdinand and his Bavarian ally Maximilian lost an important battle to the Swedes at Jankovice in Bohemia. Maximilian had no choice but to pull out of the war and sign an armistice. In 1648 there was a final humiliation when a Swedish army sacked Prague, plundering much of Rudolf II's great art collection. Spanish setbacks meant that little support could be expected from that quarter, and so Ferdinand took the difficult step of deserting his dynastic ally and making a separate peace.

The negotiations for what became the Peace of Westphalia had proceeded sporadically since 1644 in the two Westphalian cities of Münster and Osnabrück. It was one of the first major international congresses of the modern era, with Spain, France, Sweden, and the Empire the main participants, though the individual German princes were also intimately involved. Ferdinand's main representative at the negotiations was Trautmansdorff, who kept up a copious correspondence with his sovereign about the changing terms of the peace. This correspondence affords one of the clearest signs of Ferdinand as a ruler: he diligently read and analyzed the many missives, displayed a wide-ranging understanding of the politics involved, and in the end did not shy from difficult decisions. The decision to break the alliance with Spain and remain neutral in its war with France was one of the most difficult, and Ferdinand fretted about what it would mean for the dynasty. His hope was to repair the damage done to the dynastic link as quickly as possible. In the treaty, much of Alsace was surrendered to France, which was a blow since it included some of the oldest parts of the dynasty's patrimony. His father's controversial Edict of Restitution was also mostly undone, valid only for properties returned to the Catholic Church by 1624. The powers of the princes within the Empire were increased, and the Calvinist princes were legitimized as they had not previously been. Among other terms of the settlement, Sweden, Bavaria, and Brandenburg all gained territory.

For the Austrian Habsburgs, Westphalia had far-reaching but mixed results. Within the Empire, the dynasty's power was considerably reduced. Ferdinand regarded the treaty as an injury to his personal dignity and to the institutional clout of the emperor. The family did still retain some prerogatives as the de facto hereditary emperors. They could appoint bishops, for instance, and they had significant suasion as the most powerful prince and symbolic head of the Empire. The family's court in Vienna remained the most prestigious in all the German-speaking lands, and so acted as a magnet for many nobles from throughout central Europe. Another sign of the Habsburgs' ongoing weight within Germany was that after 1648 the imperial Reichstag was moved to Regensburg, as close to Vienna as possible without actually being in Austrian lands. On the whole, though, Westphalia furthered a much greater decentralization within the Empire. The cohesion and authority of imperial institutions such as the Reichstag ebbed as the sovereignty of the individual princes was confirmed. The Habsburg dream of restoring Catholicism to its predominance within Germany was also dashed. The dynasty would never be able to rule the Empire with the same kind of power that it enjoyed in its Hereditary Lands. After 1648, therefore, the Austrian Habsburgs focused much more on strengthening their rule in Austria, Bohemia, and to a lesser extent, Hungary. Their ability to do so was partially predicated on Westphalia's terms boosting princes' territorial sovereignty. And though the Habsburg emperors' profile in Germany would periodically rise—as under Leopold I and Franz I—henceforth the dynasty often paid less attention to affairs in the Empire.

The attempts to recover from the upheaval of the Thirty Years' War marked Ferdinand III's last decade in power. The war's destruction was enormous, above all in Bohemia. Hundreds of thousands of people had died, and half of Prague was destroyed. Ferdinand's administration undertook some efforts to rebuild (with measures such as tax exemptions) and to repopulate (with new, firmly Catholic settlers). The characteristic power structure of the dynasty's rule was solidified in these years after Westphalia: the Habsburg monarchs governed in a tight alliance with the Catholic Church and the high aristocracy. Towns and cities throughout much of the Danube lands lost their former vitality as commerce was disrupted by war; when their wealth declined so too did their political clout. In many rural areas conditions for peasants also worsened as their landlords' authority increased. As an illustration, in Bohemia in 1650, 85 powerful noble families controlled 62 percent of all the peasantry.

Ferdinand also had to keep a wary eye on his main enemies, the Swedes. They did not fully withdraw from Habsburg territory until 1650, after Ferdinand paid millions of florins in accordance with the treaty agreement. When Sweden, in alliance with Rákóczi, attacked Poland in 1655, Ferdinand tried to remain neutral, even though some of his advisors urged him to enter the war in contest for the Polish crown. His preoccupations to the north led Ferdinand to resist Felipe IV's urgent requests for help against the French in the later 1650s. In these years the relationship between the Spanish and Austrian branches was at its most strained. There was also a great deal of tension concerning Felipe IV's succession problems. Ferdinand III left the bulk of those problems to his own successor. Weakened by gout and years of military campaigning, he died in April 1657, at 50 years old. He had spent nearly his entire life at war. His main contribution to his dynasty, however, was in finally achieving peace.

Dynastic strategies

These three Habsburgs were intimately, alarmingly connected by marriage and other familial relations. Felipe IV was the son of Margarete of Styria, Ferdinand II's sister. Ferdinand II, for his part, married a Bavarian and an Italian. But then Ferdinand III married María Ana of Spain, Felipe IV's sister. She gave birth to a daughter, Mariana, who later became Felipe IV's second wife. Felipe thus married his niece, before she turned 15 years old. From Felipe's first marriage, to the French princess Élisabeth, came their daughter María Teresa, who went on to marry Louis XIV as part of the Peace of the Pyrenees. María Teresa and Louis were double first-cousins, showing that the Habsburgs were by no means the only practitioners of such consanguineous marriages. From Felipe's second marriage came his daughter Margarita, the charming infanta depicted in Velázquez's *Las Meninas*. She married Ferdinand III's son Leopold I, who was her uncle. These too-close connections were intended to maintain dynastic solidarity between the Austrian and Spanish branches. The balance of power implications in that solidarity were actually one of the causes of the Thirty Years' War. Olivares himself declared, "Not for anything must these two houses let themselves be divided."[12] But the dynasty's cooperation was also often tested by shifting interests in the war. It was with great reluctance that Ferdinand III made a peace separate from Spain in 1648.

Despite (and because of) all the intra-family marriages, Felipe IV was for most of his reign unable to produce a legitimate male heir, which predicament convulsed the dynasty for decades. His son from his first marriage, and his great hope, Baltasar Carlos, died in 1646. This disaster came amidst a string of others, including the rebellions of Portugal and Catalonia. From his two marriages, four sons were born who all died young. Felipe contemplated naming Ferdinand III's son Leopold as his heir around 1656. Ferdinand was resistant to this idea, though, because by that time his own health was failing and his first-born son, Ferdinand IV (whom he had previously tried to marry to Felipe's daughter María Teresa), had died—hence he needed Leopold as his own successor. Finally Mariana produced a son who survived, Carlos II, and he went on to inherit despite his severe mental and physical incapacities.

Ferdinand II's line overcame the succession problems that had plagued Rudolf and Matthias, first of all by dispatching Felipe III's claims to be their legitimate heir. Via the Oñate Treaty of 1617, Ferdinand II granted Felipe III some territory in Alsace and Italy in return for Felipe renouncing his Austrian inheritance rights. Ferdinand also attempted to repair the previous generation's failures in dynastic reproduction by formally declaring the principle of primogeniture in his will of 1621. He realized the necessity of not dividing the family's territories among multiple heirs, and most of his successors upheld this principle.

The threats to the dynasty's legitimacy spurred aggressive but only partial solutions from all three of these monarchs. Those threats came from enemies abroad, such as the Dutch, but also at home, such as Protestants in Austria or Bohemia. The solutions were themselves largely dynastic, in that the Habsburgs remained one of the few binding links among their diverse realms. In Felipe IV's case, his tenacious defense of dynastic prerogatives helps explain why he shackled Castile to decades of devastating wars. Like his grandfather Felipe II, he could not countenance the loss of his dynastic rights to a territory such as the Netherlands. This came also to apply to Portugal. Wedded to the concept of dynastic prerogative in Felipe IV's reign was the idea of *reputación*. The insistence on defending Spain's reputation—on not appearing weak, or susceptible to imperial fragmentation, or enemies' predation—was enunciated most explicitly by Olivares. Of course strategic factors influenced Felipe's foreign policy as well, such as the need to keep open the Spanish Road from Milan to Brussels. It was easier for Felipe to compromise on strategic goals than on dynastic rights, which helps explain the repeated shambolic attempts to retake Portugal.

The divergent legal-institutional arrangements and strategic interests of the Spanish monarchy's realms occluded most formal efforts to integrate those realms. Cultural integration was stronger, however, and contributed to the dynasty's legitimacy and loyalty in a variety of ways. Still strong was the idea of the Spanish monarchy as the standard-bearer and sword arm of Catholic orthodoxy. In this area the Spanish and Austrian branches strongly overlapped. Interestingly, the Austrians were in many ways even more rabid in their insistence on Catholicism, largely because their domains (unlike the Spanish) were so religiously fragmented. Another vital binding agent of legitimacy and loyalty in Spain was the prestige of Castilian culture, which reached its peak under Felipe IV. Felipe in fact regarded it as one of the essential duties of his kingship to sponsor arts and culture. Thanks partly to his support, writers such as Cervantes, Tirso de Molina, and Calderón were widely read throughout Europe. Church figures such as Juan de Palafox, mystics such as Teresa de Jesús, Jesuit philosophers, and the acerbic satires of Quevedo were also part of Castile's ongoing cultural bloom, while the work of Spanish painters attained enormous esteem abroad. Beyond the arts, Iberian civilization under the Habsburgs made notable contributions to fields such as cartography, botany, mining, and metallurgy.

Bound to the cultural patronage were the characteristically impressive royal courts of the Baroque, which also served to enhance legitimacy and loyalty. Here the Spanish court was again influential throughout Europe, and especially to the Austrian Habsburgs. Felipe's court had some 350 principal servants, of whom 47 were designated to wait on the king's table. Adding a few hundred other servants, several dozen clerics, 63 musicians, plus royal officials, the total number of people working in Felipe's household in 1623 was around 1700.[13] This excess was intentional. It was designed to overawe all observers, and particularly to discipline the members of the aristocracy at court. The court functions of magnificent display, showy religiosity, and regimentation of the aristocracy were all explicitly constructed by Olivares. They configured the monarch as the glorious, divinely anointed, untouchable authority over his disparate domains. The palace of Buen Retiro that Felipe constructed was his greatest showplace, decorated by luminaries such as Zurbarán, Rubens, Nicolas Poussin, and the younger Breughel. Nonetheless, the Spanish court was never as extravagant as Louis XIV's in the last decades of the century.

The courts of the Ferdinands were less opulent, but fulfilled many of the same functions. The Viennese court became the irresistible center of gravity for the aristocracy of the Austrian and Bohemian realms, less so for Hungary. Because both Ferdinand II and III had Italian wives, Italian influence swelled in the court and throughout the Austrian lands. This influence was felt strongly in the theater. As one example, the first permanent opera house north of the Alps was constructed in Innsbruck in 1629–30. Ferdinand II never had the kind of funds that Felipe IV lavished on artistic patronage or cultural display, but what money he did have he often spent on music. In 1626 his total tax revenues from Styria and Carinthia were not enough to cover the costs of all his musical performances. Characteristically, Ferdinand II favored music because he believed it aided in the praise of God. Neither of the Ferdinands were great builders, but under Ferdinand II the Capuchin Church in Vienna began to be constructed. It subsequently became the central necropolis for the dynasty's Austrian members. Their two reigns also saw a profusion of pillars erected throughout town squares to depict the Trinity or the Virgin Mary. Veneration of Mary was yoked to legitimacy and loyalty for the dynasty: in the iconography, she was sometimes depicted wearing the same crown(s) worn by the Habsburgs. The Habsburg identification with Catholicism, and religion's role as a force for unity in the otherwise culturally disparate Danubian domains, can also be seen through the many church buildings that were adorned with the family's coat of arms.

Though the Habsburgs prior to Ferdinand II were only averagely pious for European ruling families, with the Counter-Reformation the culture of devotion to the Catholic Church came to define the dynasty and its lands. The dynasty attached itself to central sacraments, such as in the anagram propaganda of "Eucharistia = Hic Austriae," which identified the Eucharist and piety as guiding characteristics of Austria. In reimposing Catholicism throughout its realms, the dynasty promoted a number of saints' cults; though it belongs mostly to the eighteenth century, most notable of the cults was that of Jan Nepomucký, whose Baroque statues are still to be found throughout central Europe. This dramatic religiosity is what gave rise to the image of *pietas austriaca*, the idea that the Habsburgs were more deeply pious (and hence divinely favored) than any other family. Piety was inextricably intertwined with loyalty. To Ferdinand II, being loyal to the king meant being Catholic. Intense Catholicism defined loyalty even within the dynasty, such that piety became an essential socializing aspect for the family's dynastic norms. During this period, the Christian virtues were likewise used to construct the ruler's image in a typically Baroque way. The Habsburgs' incarnation of these virtues justified their power over their subjects. The paramount virtue for the Habsburgs was usually clemency, which as *clementia austriaca* became another foundational part of the dynasty's myth. Though the idea that the Habsburgs were somehow particularly peaceful or forgiving was not new in the seventeenth century, it was now more vigorously promoted. Thus Ferdinand II was portrayed as uniquely clement in that he only had 27 rebels executed in Prague in 1621, rather than pursuing wider, harsher punishments.

As animating a role as *reputación* played in Olivares's foreign policy, it was also important to Felipe's (self-)image as a ruler. He staked a large part of his prestige on military victory, and often yearned for the kind of battlefield heroics of medieval rulers, or even of Ferdinand III. In the later 1620s Felipe wanted to go to Italy or Catalonia to lead armies while Olivares would remain in Madrid handling government. When Olivares rebuffed this plan, Felipe contented himself with staging mock battles at the Buen Retiro palace. He did, however, go to the front in Aragon in 1642 and was there for several years. Though he was obviously influenced by the ideal of the prince as warrior, in reality Felipe spent most of his reign pushing papers. It has been estimated that for much of his reign he worked some 8 hours a day, which in any case better suited his more intellectual character. During much of his adult life he read quite widely, often with the purpose of learning how to be a better monarch. This shows that he staked his reputation also on good governance. With all the troubles that befell his realms, he was consistently plagued by the worry that they came because of his own failings as a man and a king. The evolving nature of royal governance can also be seen through Olivares's function as *valido*. Olivares combined his enormous administrative duties with basic household duties for the king, such as handing Felipe his clothes in the morning. Thus the *valido* was still partly the direct, personal servant of the king, and not a fully professionalized, ministerial bureaucrat in the modern sense.

The institutionalization of the dynasty's rule encountered major setbacks in Spain but made appreciable advances in the Danubian domains. The Union of Arms and many of Olivares's other initiatives were rooted in dynastic agglomerative state building, in that the integration they sought to foster was designed fundamentally to increase the crown's power within the composite Spanish monarchy. But that increase was motivated by dynastic purposes rather than an objective to strengthen the state per se; the intent was to further the Habsburgs' ability to make war and preserve their legitimacy and prestige. The Union of Arms' failure to strengthen the crown can be linked to another problem, namely the nobility's growing control over the central ruling structures. Felipe IV, like his forebears, used the nobility in key service roles to his government. Grandees served as ambassadors and viceroys, they mustered and led ground and naval forces, and they staffed administrative councils. The sheer number of nobles increased—and with them, the governance-delegating networks of client-patronage—because Felipe IV resorted more frequently to selling titles as a way of addressing his monetary shortfalls. In the Danubian domains, Ferdinand II's victory over the estates, and the establishment of Habsburg hereditary monarchy in Bohemia, were a notable boost to royal authority. Because he exiled much of the Protestant Bohemian nobility, and greatly favored the remaining, loyal Catholic nobles, they also became much more firmly integrated into the dynasty's ruling structures than before. Most of the middle and lower tiers of governance remained in their hands, including competencies in tax collection and the administration of justice. So though Ferdinand's power relative to the high nobility did increase, the high nobility's power itself increased relative to those subordinate to them.

Neither of the Ferdinands was a reformer, but they did oversee important developments in the military. The original impetus for these developments was that Ferdinand II had an army wholly inadequate to respond to the challenge of the Bohemian rebellion, forcing him to rely on Wallenstein. The armed force which that warlord provided helped Ferdinand to assert his power in Bohemia and to enforce the *Verneuerte Landesordnung.* In 1635 Ferdinand officially declared that he had exclusive rights over war, trying to sideline the estates, which was an important step on the way to the crown's monopolization of military force. Other subsequent changes under Ferdinand III's reign ensured that colonels would be subordinate to the monarch, which helped create a hierarchical, centralized, and more strictly disciplined professional military. In 1649 Ferdinand III also determined that he would not demobilize nine infantry and ten cavalry regiments, which is usually cited as the nucleus of the Austrian Habsburgs' standing army. Surprisingly, several regiments that first came into existence in the later 1620s lasted until 1918 and the fall of the monarchy. In Felipe IV's monarchy, in contrast, the armed forces became somewhat more privatized than they had recently been, since he had to depend on magnates such as Medina Sidonia to raise an army against the Catalan rebellion. This example points to a larger, contrary trend by which royal power in the Spanish Habsburg state was slowly disintegrating, while in the Austrian Habsburgs' domains it was slowly accumulating.

The ultimate tragedy of Felipe IV's reign is that he exacted such an immense toll on his realms but had very little to show for it. His monarchy was at war for 40 years, the economy was a wreck, the population was depleted and suffering, and Spain lost a lot of the prestige it once had. Felipe must bear much of the responsibility for this bleak situation. Despite the obvious and worsening problems in Castile, the heart of his monarchy, Felipe and his ministers did not meaningfully reduce their imperial objectives until relatively late in the reign. They tried to maintain Spain's enormous commitments even under straitened circumstances, which is the very definition of imperial overstretch. Added to their failure to lessen Spain's military commitments was their failure to reform the governmental and fiscal basis of the monarchy. This latter failure was not for want of trying, of course. What gave Felipe such a woeful countenance in that late portrait by Velázquez is surely the knowledge that he did try to be a good king and yet would be judged a disappointment. He was an intelligent, diligent man who presided over a tremendous cultural bloom, many military victories, and even the expansion of Spain's empire to its greatest territorial extent. But he left his kingdoms in a sorry state, and as his heir, a disabled young boy who would be the dead end of his dynasty.

As the Spanish Habsburgs slouched toward extinction, the Austrian branch survived serious disasters and embarked on solidifying its authority within its own domains. Despite his frequent mistakes and overreaching, Ferdinand II accumulated some important victories. White Mountain helped tighten Habsburg power over Bohemia, and his Counter-Reformation push there and in Austria created a long-lasting confessional and ideological base for the monarchy. The ideal of forcibly restoring religious unity in the Empire under the Catholic Church definitively expired. Though his religious attitudes were not uncommon for his age, Ferdinand II had the mingled fortune and misfortune to be a particularly dogmatic man occupying a political position where less dogma would certainly have led to less conflict. Even so, his faith contributed to the tenacity with which he held to his prerogatives, which ultimately strengthened the dynasty in its patrimonial lands. Ferdinand III regarded Westphalia as a humiliation, but the peace he finally secured was essential for ending the disastrous war and allowing the dynasty to focus on rebuilding those lands. The years 1648 and 1659 may together mark the end of Habsburg hegemony in Europe. Yet to the extent that the Thirty Years' War was a conflict of "everyone against the Habsburgs," it is noteworthy that it took the combined forces of France, the Netherlands, Sweden, and sometimes England to counter the family's power. As Spain was eclipsed, the Austrian Habsburgs now stepped up as the dominant branch of the family. The remainder of the seventeenth century would see them become a great power in their own right.

CHAPTER SEVEN

Rise and fall (1657–1705)

The Siege of Vienna in 1683, with its eleventh-hour victory over the last great Turkish invasion of southeastern Europe, is the most famous moment in Leopold I's reign. But it is not truly the most momentous. That distinction belongs, of all things, to a document. This document begins with a lament about "sixteen years cruel and destructive war," and "how much Blood has been spilt, and how many Provinces have been laid waste." Fortunately, two great men—"the most Serene and most Potent Prince and Lord Leopold" and "the most Serene and most Potent Prince and Lord, Sultan Mustafa Han"—are well aware of "the afflicted condition of their subjects." Moved by compassion, these two illustrious princes are "seriously inclin'd to put an end to such great Calamitys increasing every Day to the Danger of Mankind," and have therefore determined that "solemn Treatys should for this Cause be set on foot, and concluded at Carlowitz in Sirmium, near the confines of both Empires."[1] This document was the Peace of Karlowitz, signed on 26 January 1699 in the town of Sremski Karlovci in what is today Serbia. The treaty not only put an end to the war that began with the Siege of Vienna—it also awarded the Austrian Habsburgs massive territorial gains, and thereby sealed their rise into a major continental power.

This period of the dynasty's history, while usually described as the rise of Austria, is better understood as a shift from being a problem for the European balance of power to being a guarantor for it. While the centuries'-old duty of protecting Europe from the Turks continued, to it was added a new role in countering the aggression of Louis XIV's France. The reigns of Leopold and Louis, cousins and brothers-in-law, are contemporaneous, but the contrasts between the flashy, megalomaniacal French king and the stolid, unadventurous Habsburg could not be more striking. It was nonetheless thanks to his dogged opposition to the French menace that Leopold reversed his family's disfavor in Germany of the previous two generations. Leopold thereby became nearly the last ruler of the Empire to enjoy significant imperial support and dignity. He also succeeded in suppressing two revolts in oft-restless Hungary. Where the Habsburgs still remained a problem was with the Spanish branch's succession, the uncertainty of which seesawed Europe between the threats of Bourbon and Habsburg hegemony. The formerly dominant Spanish branch degenerated at this time into a burned-out shell. Despite Leopold's limitations, he was reasonably competent as a ruler and happily fortuitous in his circumstances and astute underlings. Only the opposite can be said of Carlos II, in whose infirm body the Spanish Habsburgs expired with a whimper.

Leopold I (1640–1705)

Leopold reigned for 47 years, longer than any other Habsburg of the early modern period. The ironic thing about him was that the outsized role he had to play as emperor and monarch—defending Germany from the French, defeating the Turks, grappling for the dynasty's Spanish lands— was too big for the rather unassuming man himself. He managed in most cases to make the best of it, however. He has been described as one of the ugliest members of his line: since both his parents were Habsburgs, Leopold (Figure 7.1) was over-endowed with the family's idiosyncratic physical attributes, namely a dramatically protuberant lip and jaw. He was fairly slight and never physically robust. He had originally been groomed for a Church career, but when his brother Ferdinand IV died, the succession fell to him. He remained a somewhat reluctant statesman, often preferring to spend time with his books and music. Like many of his family members, he was intelligent, diligent, and very pious. He was a talented composer, and perhaps undermined his own conscientious ruling by making sure that his musicians were paid first even when his court was strapped for funds. His almost slavish dedication to multiple masses per day, regular visits to monasteries, and frequent pilgrimages drew criticism even from the papal nuncio, since these devotions diverted so much time from his governing. But this ponderousness was a major facet of his character. He was patient to the point of inaction, a shy, deeply conservative personality who became more passive as he grew older. Never a visionary or inspiring leader, his regime confronted its late, serious trials less with alacrity than with indecision.

Because Ferdinand III had not completed arrangements for Leopold to succeed him in the Empire, in 1658 it fell to the young Leopold and his advisors to negotiate with the electors' difficult conditions. The difficulty arose in part because at this time Felipe IV still had no legitimate son, which meant that Leopold could conceivably inherit the Spanish possessions. That in turn would have posed a major threat to the balance of power, and could have potentially pulled the Empire back into the conflict between Spain and France. Thus Leopold was forced to cancel his marriage plans with

FIGURE 7.1 *Leopold I, artist unknown. Image courtesy of the Österreichische Nationalbibliothek.*

Felipe IV's daughter María Teresa (who eventually married Louis XIV) and agree that he would remain neutral in the Spanish branch's ongoing conflict with France. There had been some serious competition for the imperial title, including the Bavarian elector Ferdinand Maria and the long-shot Louis XIV. Hence at the outset of his reign, the 18-year-old Leopold occupied a feeble position in the Empire. A number of German princes then formed the so-called League of the Rhine with Louis XIV and Karl X of Sweden as a defensive alliance against Leopold, to prevent him from violating the terms of the Peace of Westphalia or the Empire's neutrality. Already in his first two years as emperor Leopold was at war, drawn into a conflict in Poland in which he allied with Denmark and Brandenburg against Sweden. This conflict soon stalemated, however, and was ended by 1660.

The Holy Roman Empire in the years after the Peace of Westphalia was not completely moribund and dysfunctional. The Habsburgs did not give up on the Empire; despite lingering hostility of the princes to the emperor's authority, the latter actually experienced a rebound from its low point in 1648. The emperor still held some judicial and foreign policy competencies, and remained the symbolic figurehead. Even if this meant that in German affairs Leopold was mostly confined to the power of persuasion, he successfully managed to rebuild the dynasty's reputation. He did so through effective alliances with the princes and the administrative Imperial Circles. The Catholic princes moved more securely into the emperor's camp, and Leopold continued to assert his right to appoint loyal bishops in the churches under his authority. The most important factor that revived the dynasty's influence in Germany, though, was the threat from France. Around 1648 many people in western Germany looked to France to help protect against the kind of imperial overreach Ferdinand II had attempted. By the 1660s, though, it had become clear that France was more of a threat than the emperor. Leopold by the 1670s adopted a firm policy against Louis XIV, which brought him much support and even something like patriotism. This led directly to the Empire contributing to the campaigns against the Turks, and to the stronger German solidarity embodied by the League of Augsburg military alliance in the 1680s.

Whereas over the previous 150 years the Habsburgs had been viewed as the paramount threat to Europe's balance of power, in Leopold's time that role was taken over by France under Louis XIV. The Austrian Habsburgs became vital partners for a number of allies to resist French aggression. The French king was the son of a Spanish Habsburg mother, and then he married another Spanish Habsburg. Though Louis and Leopold never met, they detested each other. Leopold remained neutral during France's War of Devolution against Spain from 1667–8. He went so far as to draw up a secret treaty (never signed) with Louis whereby the two would divide the Spanish empire in the event that Carlos II died with no heir. In the 1670s Louis renewed his attacks on the Netherlands, and it became impossible for Leopold to maintain his policy of timid neutrality. After the French invaded

Lorraine, a part of the Empire, Leopold initially could not respond since he was dealing with another rebellion in Hungary. But he then overcame his religious reservations to ally with the Protestant Dutch in support of Spain, and German princes lined up as well to repulse the French attacks. As a result of this war, Spain lost the Franche-Comté and several cities in the Spanish Netherlands, and Leopold temporarily gave up Freiburg in southwestern Germany.

The Habsburgs were at war with France several more times leading up to the major conflict over the Spanish succession in 1700. Louis again invaded the Spanish Netherlands in 1683, but Leopold quickly made peace on his western front because he was dealing with the Turks on the eastern front. The Spanish Habsburgs lost Luxembourg to Louis in this War of the Reunions. Many of the German princes were unhappy with what they saw as Leopold's inadequate defense against the French threat. They nonetheless abjured their earlier alliances with Louis against Leopold to regard the Habsburg emperor instead as the captain of German resistance. Louis fortunately refrained from attacking Germany during the Turkish siege of Vienna, motivated by some sense of Christian solidarity that trumped even his normal, egotistical Realpolitik. Leopold pursued his own Realpolitik, however, by strengthening his alliance with William III of the Netherlands, who after 1688 was also king of England. Their mutual interest in countering France induced William also to support Leopold's claims for the Spanish succession. In 1686 the League of Augsburg was formed. It bound several German princes, the United Provinces of the Netherlands, Spain, Sweden, and Brandenburg against France. Leopold rallied Germany in the resulting war, which lasted until 1697. One of Leopold's string of excellent military commanders, Charles of Lorraine, ably defended Austria's interests even though it was having to fight on two fronts, against the Turks and the French. The Treaty of Ryswick required Louis to surrender some of his earlier conquests, but he held on to Alsace and the Palatinate. This treaty, however, was merely a short respite until the War of the Spanish Succession three years later.

The steady defense in the west at this time is a testament to the consolidation of the Austrian Habsburgs' state. That defense was maintained despite recurring troubles on the eastern frontiers. Hungary and Transylvania were one source of instability. Though by Leopold's time the Counter-Reformation had successfully reimposed Catholicism in the Austrian lands and the Bohemian kingdom, Protestantism remained widespread throughout much of Hungary. The high nobility was mostly Catholic (having never left, or having returned), but much of the middle nobility and the wider population was still Calvinist. There were other pockets of religious heterogeneity in Hungary, too, with many Orthodox Serbs and Uniate Ruthenians. This situation was intolerable to a new generation of high Church officials such as the Archbishop Kollonich. Under his watch there were forced conversions to Catholicism, expulsions of Protestants, and confiscation of their property. Protestant pastors were even sent to the galleys for supposed disloyalty to the crown. From the 1680s onward, as Hungary was reconquered from the Turks, in order to repopulate the territory a lot of land was given to Germans. All these measures not surprisingly provoked resistance at many levels of Hungarian society.

The simmering discontent flared into two notable rebellions during Leopold's reign. The first was sparked by the Treaty of Vasvár which Leopold signed with the Turks in 1664. Many Hungarian nobles regarded this treaty as a disgraceful capitulation to the Ottomans, one that sacrificed Hungarian interests to the Habsburgs' focus on the threat from France. Nobles from several families in both Hungary and Croatia—including the Wesselényis, the Zrinskis, and the Frankapans—in 1670 launched an amateurish revolt that included impractical plans like kidnapping Leopold and offering the Hungarian crown to Louis XIV. Leopold's loyalists easily suppressed the plot and the noble conspirators were executed. Leopold, however, did not follow through on his advisors' encouragement to imitate Ferdinand II after White Mountain and definitively crack down on Hungarian liberties. He was plagued by worry over breaking his coronation oath to respect Hungary's laws. He thus stopped short of making the crown hereditary, but did increase taxes. He also centralized some aspects of the Hungarian administration and ratcheted up Counter-Reformatory activities.

Those impositions only provoked more upset, such that parts of Hungary and Transylvania seethed in revolt throughout the rest of Leopold's reign. These revolts were particularly dangerous because they attracted French and Ottoman meddling, which is also a reason why the Habsburgs were never able to suppress them as conclusively as they did the Bohemian rebellion in 1620. At the end of the 1670s Leopold had to deal with a very serious rebellion led by the Transylvanian magnate Imre Thököly. Known as the revolt of the *kurucok* ("bandits"), Thököly amassed an army of possibly 20,000 troops and marauded all along Leopold's eastern frontiers. By 1680 Thököly was openly inviting Ottoman intervention, and so Leopold's advisers pressed for peace. In 1681 Leopold convoked the full Hungarian diet for the first time in 20 years and made a number of concessions. He restored some governing power to the diet, once again made the Hungarian treasury independent of that in Vienna, and promised respect for Protestants' rights to worship. In return, the diet promised to raise troops against the Turks. Thököly and his hardcore partisans refused to give in, and he later fled to Transylvania. In the 1680s, to keep the magnates on his side, Leopold reaffirmed religious freedom in Hungary and the estates' authority over local government. In return, the diet made monarchical succession hereditary to the Habsburgs' male line.

The other major disturbance to the east was the Turkish war, which in 1663 resumed for the first time since Rudolf II's reign. Throughout the Thirty Years' War, the Ottomans had been focused on Persia, which meant that the Habsburgs had little to fear from Turkish armies during that time. When the Ottomans attacked Transylvania in 1663, however, Habsburg, German, and even French forces mobilized via the League of the Rhine, which led to the battle of St. Gotthard in 1664. Leopold's general Montecuccoli won a great victory over a Turkish force twice the size, but Leopold was still fearful of aggression from France to the west. He therefore quickly signed the capitulatory Treaty of Vasvár in 1664, in which he not only failed to capitalize on the St. Gotthard victory, but actually agreed to pay the sultan an annual tribute of 200,000 florins. This craven submission led directly to the nobles' conspiracy in Hungary of 1670.

St. Gotthard and Vasvár were just preludes to the more significant clashes between the Habsburgs and the Ottomans in subsequent decades. A major new Ottoman offensive into Europe was brewing around 1681 at the behest of the sultan's bellicose vizier Kara Mustafa. The vizier openly sided with Thököly and the *kuruc* rebels against the Habsburgs, thereby violating the terms of Vasvár. It soon became clear that the Turks were assembling for a huge offensive against Austria, and once Louis XIV gave Kara Mustafa his assurance that France would not aid Austria or the Empire if attacked by the Turks, the Ottoman war machine rolled forward. Thanks in part to the pope's mediation, many German princes and the Polish king, Jan Sobieski, pledged to assist Leopold.

The famous siege of Vienna took place in the summer of 1683. The Turks had assembled an army of over 100,000 men (though force estimates for this encounter vary wildly) and began pounding the city in July. Leopold wisely fled to the city of Passau with his court, leaving Vienna's defense in the capable hands of Ernst Starhemberg. Starhemberg managed to hold firm until 4 September, when Ottoman forces penetrated Vienna's outer walls and came close to overrunning the city. In desperation, the Austrian commander fired signal rockets from the tower of Vienna's St. Stephen's cathedral, hoping for the immediate arrival of a relief force. Luckily, that force had been painstakingly assembled by Leopold's general Charles of Lorraine. It included contingents led by the Bavarian Duke Max Emanuel III and the Saxon Elector Johan Georg III. Finally Sobieski with his army of 30,000 Poles arrived in the first week of September, bringing the Christian forces' total to around 75,000. Charles lit bonfires on the hills west of Vienna on 7 September to give Starhemberg and the Viennese hope, and then by 12 September the combined armies under Sobieski's supreme command swept down upon the Turks. Kara Mustafa had stupidly failed to fortify his encampment against the attack he knew was coming, and with a well-timed, last-ditch thrust from Starhemberg's garrison as well, the Turks were routed. Kara Mustafa paid for his poor command with his life, but not at the edge of a Christian's blade: the sultan had him strangled.

Even had the Ottomans taken Vienna, they probably would not have held it for long. Instead, the Habsburgs launched a devastating counterattack that erased almost 200 years of Turkish conquests. The Empire, the papacy, and even Hungary rallied strongly to Leopold, supplying men and money as a kind of crusade fever swept Europe. Leopold tried to secure his western frontiers against Louis XIV's opportunist predations by agreeing to a truce in 1684; in so doing, the Austrian Habsburgs temporarily abandoned their Spanish cousins. Louis did attack along the Rhine in subsequent years, but the German princes together with the Netherlands and England managed to fight back while Leopold's advances in the east continued. By 1685 Charles of Lorraine had pushed the Turks out of present-day Slovakia. In 1686 after a terribly destructive siege the Turks lost Buda, and 1687 saw imperial forces take back Slavonia and Transylvania. Most of Thököly's *kuruc* fighters now swore allegiance to Leopold. The Transylvanian diet also recognized Leopold's sovereignty. In 1688 Max Emanuel of Bavaria led the command that succeeded in conquering Belgrade, and the following year drove further into the Balkans. There was even heady talk that Habsburg forces might press all the way to liberate Constantinople.

From 1688 on Leopold had to wage a two-front war against the French and the Turks. Charles of Lorraine went to the Rhine to fight Louis's armies, but thanks to the Habsburgs' surplus of talented military leaders at this time, Ludwig Wilhelm of Baden took over command in the east. Thököly had assembled a new army and with the sultan's help pushed into Transylvania in 1690. Ludwig Wilhelm moved his army there, defeated Thököly, but left Belgrade too weak to withstand a Turkish counterassault in that same year. Then in 1691 at the savage battle of Slankamen Ludwig Wilhelm annihilated a Turkish army, a defeat from which Turkish military power in the Balkans never recovered. In the next few years most of Leopold's armies were focused on the fight against France, but then in 1697 his new general Eugène of Savoy won another astounding victory at Zenta. The Ottoman vizier and some 30,000 Turkish soldiers were killed, many drowning in the river Tisza as they fled the battlefield. The sultan himself barely managed to escape. Leopold took the opportunity to make peace. The 1699 Treaty of Karlowitz confirmed the Habsburgs' huge gains in Hungary and southeastern Europe and established some borderlines that still exist today.

The major events of Leopold's reign took place abroad; within the Hereditary Lands, this was a time of re-Catholicization and recovery. He dutifully upheld the religious peace in the Empire, but in his own lands, and especially in Silesia, Leopold sent around "Reformation commissions" made up of priests, officials, and soldiers to enforce Catholic practice. Thousands of people and families who would not abjure Protestantism were compelled into exile. The lower classes were the most harshly treated, of course, such as by having their Protestant churches demolished. The nobility had more legal authority to resist this coercion, but the dynasty exerted other means of pressure, such as refusing places at court for Protestant nobles, though there were some exceptions. The Jesuits became the vital executors of the dynasty's Counter-Reformation efforts, and Leopold had a number of important Jesuit advisors in his court. The order took control of most of the educational institutions in the monarchy, teaching not only the high born (such as Leopold himself) and aspirants to the clergy, but even some of the lower classes as well. Protestants were not the only targets of religious homogenization; Leopold also expelled the Jews from Vienna in 1670. Hungary, as always, resisted more successfully. By 1700, there were tiny pockets of Protestants in the Hereditary Lands, but the overwhelming proportion of the population was Catholic, a major turnaround from 100 years earlier.

By 1700 the Danubian domains had mostly recovered from the damage of the Thirty Years' War. Economic growth was stronger in Austria than in either Bohemia, where devastation and depopulation lingered in the decades after Westphalia, or Hungary, which was a battlefield for much of Leopold's rule. Signs of progress were a wool factory in Linz, increased trade down the Danube, and the introduction of new crops such as tobacco and potatoes. It was often the high nobility who most successfully took advantage of new economic opportunities, particularly since the towns took so long to recover their economic life after the decades of conflict. Power and wealth continued to concentrate into the magnates' hands, and landlords' authority over their peasants also tended to increase. Some changes came about thanks to the influence of cameralism, which was akin to French mercantilism in promoting ideas for how state policy could boost economic development. Writers such as Johann Joachim Becher and Philipp Wilhelm von Hörnigk argued for the necessity of improving conditions for the agrarian labor force. Hence Leopold issued a series of regulations to limit peasants' forced labor requirements (to only three days a week) and to allow them to substitute cash payments for labor. The fact that the crown could not always enforce these regulations shows the limits of its power vis-à-vis the high nobility. Despite some improvements, at the end of Leopold's reign the Danubian lands remained fairly backward economically, compared to farther west. Though the Austrian Habsburgs now had one of the largest realms in Europe, its population of 9 million was still well short of France's 20 million, and it depended on strong allies for its final battle with Louis XIV over the Spanish succession.

Carlos II (1661–1700)

Even if Leopold was not the most dynamic monarch, he did at least truly rule, unlike Carlos II. The most remarkable achievement of Carlos's sad life is simply that he lived as long as he did, given his physical infirmities, which in some ways mirrored the weakness of the Spanish monarchy during his time. At various points in his 38 years he had dreadful health ailments, including convulsions, intestinal problems, and edemas on his feet, legs,

abdomen, and face. He did not learn to walk or speak until after he was
4 years old. He did eventually learn to read and write, but his education was
often delayed by illness. He had the blondish hair, long face, and jutting
lip common to many Habsburgs, but his jaw problems meant that his chin
was deformed. He was described as being "so ugly it's scary" by a French
diplomat who knew him.[2] In his last years he acquired the nickname "el
Hechizado" ("the Bewitched") because some Spanish nuns decided that his
many problems including his infertility must have come from an evil spell.
He was even exorcised after his death.

The correct explanation for Carlos's problems was his genetic makeup.
Though he was disabled, he was not completely incapable. His development
was slow but he was not unintelligent. He was in fact self-aware, but with
a weak will and an inability to concentrate. He remained mostly a dynastic
figurehead and a political pawn. Until 1677 government was managed
by his mother and her favorites, later by his half-brother, then by a few
reformist ministers, and after 1691 by his second wife. And just as the
sickly Carlos was the unfortunate opposite of his energetic namesake
Charles V (known as Carlos I in Spain), so too was Spain during much of
his reign an unfortunate contrast with its periods of great energy under
the earlier Habsburg kings. A Venetian ambassador wrote during this
time, "Now there are no ships at sea nor armies on land, the fortresses are
dismantled and defenseless; everything is in danger, nothing is protected.
It's incomprehensible that this monarchy survives."[3] There were signs of
improvement in the later years of Carlos's reign, but on the whole he was
the nadir of the Spanish Habsburgs.

Many of those who ruled in Carlos's name provided unstable or outright
inept government. When Felipe IV died, Carlos was only 4, and his mother
Mariana (Leopold's sister), was 31 but had very little political experience
or skill. Mariana had proven herself to be brittle and stubborn, and Felipe
limited her powers as regent. She was supposed to govern with a council
comprising members of the higher bureaucracy in addition to some church
officials and grandees. She preferred to entrust power to her own favorites,
however, the first of which was the Austrian Jesuit Johann Nidhard (also
spelled i.a. Neidhardt) who became in effect her *valido*. He was widely
hated by the Spanish aristocracy, in part for being a foreigner. He was
finally ousted in 1669. Then another favorite came along after 1673, the
oily Andalusian arriviste Fernando Valenzuela, who inveigled his way into
the queen regent's court not through political talents but through marital
connections. He lasted until 1677, when he was forced out.

The man hovering around the edges of power until 1679 was Carlos's
half-brother Don Juan José, Felipe IV's illegitimate son. He was not
unaccomplished: he had held high positions in Felipe IV's government,
including on the council of state, and he served as the viceroy in Sicily
from 1648 to 1651 after he subdued the revolt there. He also served as
viceroy of Catalonia and the Spanish Netherlands. After Juan José's

failures commanding the armies sent to retake Portugal in 1661 and 1664, Felipe's trust in his bastard son waned and he refused to legitimize him. So Juan José was reasonably talented, quite intelligent, very ambitious, but aggrieved by the taint of his illegitimate origins. It was he who chased Nidhard out of the court in 1669, but he did not have enough support in ruling circles to take over the regency and push through his ideas for reorganizing governance. In 1676, though, he did have sufficient backing from the Castilian aristocracy to muster an army and essentially overthrow Mariana and her venal favorite Valenzuela. Valenzuela was sent to prison in the Philippines for ten years, and Mariana was shipped off to Toledo to limit her influence.

Juan José remains a controversial figure: some see his premature death at 50 as cutting short his significant potential, while others regard him as little more than a brutish caudillo who furthered the aristocracy's dominance over the crown. In the two years that he governed before he died in 1679, he did begin some reforms to address the monarchy's major problems of inflation and trade. The next two prime ministers who ran the government also both achieved some effective reforms. The first, the duke of Medinaceli, was the richest and most powerful noble in Castile. He continued to implement the monetary reorganization that Juan José had started, engineering the painful but necessary devaluation of 1680. He also lowered taxes in Castile, the first time that had happened under the Habsburg kings. After Spain's loss of Luxembourg in 1684 to France, Medinaceli was pushed out by the aristocracy and Carlos's queen in favor of the skilled and astute count of Oropesa. He attempted a number of difficult reforms such as making the tax system more equitable and reducing the bloated church administration. These measures predictably angered the clergy as well as the aristocracy, who arranged for his dismissal in 1691. Carlos's second wife Mariana of Neuburg, the daughter of the Elector Palatine, now exercised royal power, together with a faction of German and Spanish nobles. The improvements that Juan José, Medinaceli, and Oropesa had instituted were piecemeal and halting, but they were part of what helped the monarchy begin to recover from its imperial exhaustion.

At the outset of Carlos's reign, the picture was still quite bleak. The population continued to plummet due to famines, plagues, and migration, in both rural and urban areas. The death toll from these calamities during Carlos's years reached approximately 500,000. As one example, by the 1660s the population of Seville, the largest city on the peninsula, may have fallen by as much as half from its earlier peak. The last lights of the "Golden Age" culture, men such as Calderón and Murillo, flickered out. Intellectual life in Spain stagnated under the over-zealous sway of the Counter-Reformation Church, distrustful of ideas from outside such as the burgeoning revolution in science. Agricultural output also languished, and in much of the countryside landlords' despotic control went unchallenged by the anemic royal power. The weakness of leadership, epitomized by the aristocratic factions at court scheming around the monarchical void, was described by the English ambassador: "This country is in a most miserable condition; no head to govern, and every man in office does what he pleases, without fear of being called to account."[4] By the last decades of the 1600s there were some positive developments, however. The peninsula's peripheral areas revived more strongly than Castile did; shipbuilding and port traffic rebounded in the Basque Country, and trade picked up in Catalonia as well. The population began to grow and agricultural and wool yields improved. The currency devaluations of the 1680s were highly disruptive, but helped reduce inflation in the long run. The modest reforms of Medinaceli and Oropesa were ultimately tender green shoots, unable to produce a major advance in the last years of Habsburg Spain.

Defeats by France were a sign of Spanish weakness. Louis XIV's unceasing attacks took a few cities in the Spanish Netherlands in the 1660s. Having France as a common enemy motivated a remarkably quick warming of Spain's relations with the old nemesis of the Dutch United Provinces. By 1676 the Dutch and the Spanish were fighting on the same side—and losing to the French, as when in that year the French navy defeated a combined Spanish-Dutch fleet. In the subsequent treaty Spain lost yet more slices of territory to France. After French forces invaded Catalonia in 1683 the Spanish had to give up Luxembourg in the peace of 1684. War resumed in 1688 with Spain again allied with the Dutch as well as with Leopold and the League of Augsburg. The French captured Barcelona for a time, but by the conflict's end Louis did not press his gains too forcefully. The Treaty of Ryswick in 1697 gave the French half of the island of Hispaniola, which would later become Haiti. Louis, though, as one of the vultures which had long been circling Carlos's frail body, was preparing for yet another conflict: namely, the struggle over the last male Spanish Habsburg's succession.

The claims to that succession were a tangle of dynastic threads. Though there were negotiated attempts to resolve them, ultimately the incommensurate interests of a number of European powers, including the Habsburg and Bourbon dynasties, led to a worldwide war. Carlos II was the nephew and cousin of Leopold I, which was the basis for Leopold's assertion of the Austrian branch's right to succeed in Spain. Leopold in fact intended the Spanish crown for his second son, Karl [Charles], while his oldest Joseph would reign in central Europe. Louis XIV claimed the succession for his grandson based on the fact that both his own and his son's mothers were Habsburgs. The other major claimant was for a time Joseph Ferdinand of Bavaria, a Wittelsbach who was the son of Leopold's daughter Maria Antonia. This meant that Joseph Ferdinand was also Felipe IV's great-grandson. The Bavarian succession was actually favored by the English and the Dutch (after 1688 both ruled by William III) who, for balance of power reasons, wanted neither the Bourbons nor the Habsburgs to inherit Spain. Negotiations over the succession had begun already in the 1660s. Louis and Leopold never quite reached an agreement whereby the

Bourbons would inherit in return for relinquishing a number of Spanish territories to the Austrian Habsburgs. Leopold's advisors recommended that he settle because there would be no way that he could hold Spain in a war. Louis, likewise, was interested in a peaceful settlement because by the end of the 1690s his finances could ill afford another war. William III tried to make still other arrangements without consulting either of the Habsburg branches.

All of this diplomatic intrigue failed to take account of the dominant interests within Spain, and also failed to prevent hostilities. The paramount concern of the Spanish nobility was that the empire's territories not be divided up. They therefore tended to favor the Bourbon succession based on the belief that the Bourbon candidate, Philippe of Anjou, would be a strong king who could adequately defend the realm. Much of the Spanish nobility—including even Carlos II himself—did not trust that the Austrian Habsburgs would rule in the realm's interests, since they would likely be distracted by their holdings in central and eastern Europe. Carlos turned his back on his family to express support first for the Bavarian and then the Bourbon candidate. What seems like dynastic treason can be explained partly by the machinations of the Castilian nobility at court, including the Cardinal Portocarrero, who had his hands on most levers of power. Additionally, Carlos did have a mind of his own, and he turned against the Habsburgs because he actively disliked his second wife, Maria Anna, Leopold's daughter, who was pushing hard for the Austrian succession. In the year or so before Carlos's long-awaited death, he signed three wills. In one will, he named Joseph Ferdinand of Bavaria his successor. In another, his wife and the Austrian faction at court convinced him to name Archduke Karl, Leopold's son, as successor. The final will named Philippe of Anjou. The latter two wills were signed within days of his death in November 1700. By this point Carlos was probably only dimly aware of how he was being manipulated.

War then engulfed the Habsburgs (spanning the reigns of Leopold, Joseph I, and Karl VI) and all of Europe between 1701 and 1714. It might never have happened had not the Bavarian claimant, the compromise third way out of the Bourbon-Habsburg struggle, died in 1699. Both Leopold and Louis then held tenaciously to their dynastic claims to the Spanish succession, rejecting even their prior attempts to negotiate a settlement. Those competing claims mapped onto great power politics. France and most of Spain fought for the Bourbon succession, while the Netherlands, England, and Austria fought against it, and its attendant threat of conjoining the French and Spanish crowns. Germany split, with Hanover, the Palatinate, and Brandenburg siding with Leopold, while Bavaria sided with France. Catalonia rebelled against the Bourbon claimant and recognized Archduke Karl as its sovereign. The war featured a number of shifting alliances and temporary gains for both sides. In its first phase, while Leopold was still alive, the dynasty managed to hold its position in Italy but suffered setbacks in Germany. Even with support from English and Dutch troops, Habsburg forces were often outnumbered by the French, but the Habsburgs had by far the superior generals fighting for their side, including the great Duke of Marlborough and Prince Eugène of Savoy. At the Battle of Blenheim in August 1704, Marlborough's and Eugène's combined armies won a stunning victory that decimated a French army, forced Bavaria out of the war, and saved Vienna from an impending invasion.

The successes Austrian arms achieved in Leopold's last years came almost despite the old emperor. Around 1700, as he neared 60, Leopold became more conservative than ever, and less actively engaged in running his government. Most of his inner ruling circle were likewise old men who were in their positions more through long service and loyalty than skill. Mismanagement and neglect at the highest levels threatened to sink the Austrian war effort. This was especially dangerous after 1703 since there was a new, large revolt in Hungary led by Ferenc II Rákóczi, a Transylvanian magnate (and godson of the earlier troublemaker Thököly). As Habsburg armies left Hungary to fight the French, Rákóczi happily took 10,000 écus a month from Louis XIV to help finance a rebellion to distract Leopold in the east. This revolt would plague the Habsburgs until 1711. Dissatisfied with his father's handling of Austria's precarious situation, Leopold's oldest son Joseph in 1703 pushed out a number of incompetent officials and took over the government with his "young court," which included Prince Eugène among other reform-minded men. Most urgently this new team addressed the monarchy's looming financial disaster by securing loans from England and the Netherlands. Though the old, conservative faction regained the upper hand in 1704, they had only one more year of influence before Leopold died in 1705 and Joseph became sovereign.

Dynastic strategies

It was not solely because of Carlos that the male line of the Habsburg dynasty was teetering on the edge of extinction. Leopold's uncle, younger brother, and his last two cousins in the Tyrolean branch had all died by 1665. Thus when Felipe IV died that same year, Leopold and Carlos were the only surviving males in the entire dynasty. The boon for Leopold from this wave of deaths was that he gained all the Tyrolean lands, and thereby reunited the Habsburgs' central European patrimony under one line. That was little consolation when he could not produce a surviving son until his third marriage. This son became Joseph I, and the third son from this marriage survived to become Karl VI. Leopold was not short of daughters: he had eleven of them, all but one of whom he named "Maria" in his exaggerated piety. Carlos II proved unsurprisingly incapable of producing heirs with his two unfortunate wives. In this last exponent of the Spanish branch, the dynasty's long (and not unusual, for the time) practice of inbreeding took its final toll. That practice helps explain the sudden scarcity of males in the Habsburg line, as well as the family's extremely high rates of infant mortality. Half of all the Spanish Habsburgs' children died before they reached the age of 10, which was twice the mortality rate for children in Spanish villages. A genetic analysis has found that Carlos was as inbred as would have occurred in an incestuous parent-child or brother-sister pairing.[5] Of all the Spanish Habsburgs, Felipe III and Felipe II's son Don Carlos rank not far behind in their level of inbreeding. The sad, self-inflicted end of the Spanish branch recalls the apt words of the historian Marañón, who wrote that of the five Spanish Habsburg kings, "Charles V inspires enthusiasm, Felipe II respect, Felipe III indifference, Felipe IV sympathy, and Carlos II pity."[6]

The Spanish branch's extinction forced the Austrian branch to look elsewhere for its marriages. The Habsburgs increasingly began to marry other German families. Leopold is an example: his first two wives were Habsburgs, and after they died he had to be persuaded to marry for a third time, to Eleonore of Pfalz-Neuburg, daughter of the Elector Palatine, a Wittelsbach. This marriage did assure the survival of the dynasty, producing both Leopold's sons Joseph I and Karl VI. They both in turn also married German princesses, which helped strengthen dynastic connections within the Empire. Leopold's stronger position in the Empire contributed to the dynasty's reproduction in another way as well. He capitalized on the sense of German solidarity against Louis XIV by having Joseph chosen as his imperial successor in 1690. The relative ease of this election, and the not ungenerous terms of the *Wahlkapitulation*, show how much progress the dynasty had made in shoring up its reputation in the Empire since Leopold's difficult election in 1658.

The dynasty's problems with reproducing itself were for good and ill tied to its legitimacy. The family's inbreeding produced a successor, Carlos II, who because of his inadequacies should never have been king, not least because he himself could not produce a successor. But because of the unavoidable dynastic norm of legitimacy, there was no other Spanish Habsburg who could rightfully take the royal title. In adhering to Carlos as heir, the Habsburgs privileged the ruling legitimacy of the family line at the expense of both adequate governance and the survival of that line. In the Danubian domains, both legitimacy and loyalty were expressed by the assertive, triumphant Baroque culture that matched the newly successful assertiveness of Austria on the international stage. This culture fulfilled a vital integrative role for the monarchy. More powerfully than ever before, provincial elites were integrated into the Baroque court, while the provinces themselves were assimilated into the Baroque culture. A highly visible sign of these processes was the increasing dominance of German language and culture throughout the lands of the monarchy. The elite was most subject to this Germanization: the high aristocracy became more likely to speak German, in part because of the heightened profile of the Vienna court. As Leopold's court grew into the characteristic magnificence of the late seventeenth century, it became a magnet for nobles from all the monarchy's lands. They found that by assimilating at least somewhat to German culture, they could enjoy the pecuniary and preferment benefits of the court. The Bohemian and Moravian nobility in particular gravitated more than ever toward Vienna, where some of them took high state positions.

While Germanization and court preferment helped build allegiance to the monarchy, the success of the Counter-Reformation also continued to bolster loyalty and legitimacy. Leopold furthered the practices of Ferdinand II and III in insisting upon Catholic hegemony as an essential fundament of the dynasty's rule. He did not stint on promoting religious processions and other ostentatious displays in which both the Catholic Church's and his own majesty were conflated. Perhaps the most famous example of both the ostentation and the conflation is the great plague column on the Graben in Vienna, whose archetypically Baroque effusion configures Leopold as humbly praying for, and victoriously receiving, deliverance from an epidemic and the Turks. Trumpeting Catholicism was only one part of Leopold's court, which flourished especially after Vienna's 1683 deliverance. As part of managing administration and integrating the nobility, the court centralized and displayed both the monarch's tangible and symbolic power. Though Louis XIV's contemporaneous court was perhaps more lavish and certainly more frivolous than Leopold's (whose court was often described as religiously somber), the Austrian Habsburgs presided over a comparable cultural flowering. The dynasty of course reigned through many other cultural periods, but the monarchy's territorial expansion and gradual but decisive penetration into society during this era forever left its mark on the Danubian lands.

The Habsburg heritage of art and architecture is unmistakably Baroque-tinted. The greatest early influences on the style of the Leopoldine Baroque came from Italy, and there were many Italian artists and musicians in Leopold's court. These artists contributed to the court's lavish operatic productions, which were used to demonstrate the cultural achievements and glory of Leopold's rule. Apart from the Leopold Wing of the Vienna Hofburg, designed by Italian architects, the monarch himself built relatively little. He preferred to spend his always-short monies on music, theater, festivals, and literature; Leopold's book collecting was prodigious. The Baroque nonetheless gave birth to the first great Austrian architects such as Johann Bernhard Fischer von Erlach and Johann Lukas von Hildebrandt, who both continued to work under Leopold's successors. Fischer von Erlach drew up the first plans for the palace at Schönbrunn, which was originally intended to exceed even Versailles's excess, though for lack of funds the palace did not attain its present look until the time of Maria Theresia.

Ecclesiastical architecture in general helped spread the Baroque throughout the Habsburg lands, and with it the dynasty's message of supremacy. A signal example is with the churches of Prague, nearly all of which were rebuilt in Baroque style as part of the Counter-Reformation. Prague also saw one of the first waves of Baroque palace building, which then spread to Vienna and resulted in such imposing structures as the Lobkowitz and Liechtenstein palaces.

As with overblown displays everywhere, the cultural achievements of the dynasty in this era masked an underlying weakness. The Leopoldine Baroque was miles wide and an inch deep. It was an elite culture, the culture of the monarchy's power bases: the dynasty, the high aristocracy, and the Church. It was not the culture of a thriving bourgeoisie because the cities and towns were still small and subdued. So despite the outward impressiveness of cultural achievements in Leopold's time, broader intellectual life was not particularly vital. The same can be said for Carlos II's court in Spain. There the weak monarch ended the great tradition of the Spanish Habsburg court's artistic patronage, and few great works came out of this period. Though there was some activity in the sciences and medicine, on the whole cultural life reflected the king's own dim light.

The court culture of Baroque display was very well suited to Leopold, the small man inhabiting a very large role. Because his personality was nowhere near the contemporary ideal of "absolutism," the awe of the monarch had to be created through the *image* of the monarch. While this was always the function of royal display, in Leopold's case the disjuncture between the image and the actuality was particularly gaping. Festivals, balls, and theatrical presentations were typical ways of literally staging Leopold's majesty. Genealogies, biographies, and other visual representations similarly affirmed that Leopold was not just one unprepossessing man, but rather the current incarnation of his dynasty's authority and mission. Though Leopold owed almost all his symbolic authoritativeness to that dynastic legitimacy, he was not purely a figurehead ruler, as Carlos II was. Carlos's lineage justified him wearing the crown, but it was the fig leaf for others' exercise of power. His person was difficult to glorify, no matter the amount of display. Leopold on the other hand took a more active role in governance. He regarded himself as his own prime minister, and generally resisted letting any one man in his court accumulate too much power. Hence he would dismiss some of his top ministers after a time, such as Johann Weikhard von Auersperg, in part just to churn the power structure. Leopold, though neither a decisive nor an imposing personality, came to play his role rather well. He left much of the actual running of the monarchy to more energetic underlings. He was never a battlefield leader, preferring to pray for the success of his armies from the relative safety of Vienna, surrounded by the iconography of power.

That those armies were so successful points to the most important institutional development of Leopold's time. By the end of his reign the Austrian military was stronger than it had ever been, able to fight and win on multiple fronts simultaneously. The military grew from the small nucleus of the peacetime standing army created under Ferdinand III to one of the best fighting forces in Europe by 1700, with a core of over 100,000 troops. Leopold's great generals Montecuccoli and Eugène instituted key improvements such as a more professional corps of officers who were more tightly bound to their sovereign than were, for example, Wallenstein's men. They made the military for the first time a truly effective tool of state power. Its centralized nature helped strengthen the links between the different realms into a common cause against a feared enemy. Its success showed that the Habsburgs' Danubian monarchy had evolved into something stronger than the Ottomans' war machine. There remained significant problems in raising money, however. The estates retained some power over raising the financial contribution to the military. They sometimes refused to pay up, though by the end of his reign, Leopold's government had whittled the estates' authority down to bargaining over the amount of the contribution.

The military aside, Leopold made few lasting changes to the structures of dynastic rule. He left inefficient practices and institutions untouched— such as the custom that individual army regiments had to collect their own portion of the contribution—despite the very obvious drawbacks of such practices. He did very little to centralize the separate Austrian governments in Graz and Innsbruck under Vienna's power. He never understood finances, and what funds he did have were often poorly managed. He sometimes appointed unqualified or corrupt men to administer his domains, the most notorious being Count Georg Ludwig Sinzendorff, whom Leopold left in office for 24 years despite widespread suspicions that he was embezzling millions from the treasury. There were always audible voices calling for reform; Austrian cameralists such as Hörnigk wrote of the need for Austria to transform its economic and political structures, with the specific goal of generating more financial resources to support the military. The problem was Leopold's personality: he was too mild and too cautious ever to shake things up in a useful way. A Venetian diplomat commented that because Leopold "was afraid of stumbling, he walked slowly."[7]

The fact that separate provincial diets retained varying degrees of authority throughout Leopold's reign shows that there was no unified "Austrian" polity at this time. It was still very much a composite monarchy, never strictly absolutist because the monarch depended on the various local interests such as the estates, magnates, and the Church in order to rule. The magnates were necessary in all sorts of ways. One was purely financial. Because Leopold was chronically insolvent, he needed loans from the richest nobles, such as the 100,000 florins Ferdinand Schwarzenberg provided during the reconquest of Hungary. Wealthy aristocrats were also necessary to fill many of the high administrative offices in the monarchy, since the crown's financial troubles meant that officers sometimes had to cover their own costs. Even more than elsewhere, the dynasty depended on the local nobility for rule in Hungary. The Viennese government was barely represented in many parts of Hungary; authority belonged to the local lord. The Church was still vital to the dynasty as a political unifier and propagandist, yet state control over churches did increase during Leopold's time. Another instance of the limited centralization was that in Hungary the monarch gained the authority (from the estates) to appoint the high clergy. This served a political function to control the church through the appointment of loyalists, and also to increase the monarch's control of Hungary by appointing non-Hungarians to ecclesiastical as well as secular leadership positions.

Where once the Spanish monarchy had had institutions that could fairly successfully channel the sovereign's will, as under Felipe II, by Carlos II's time the structures of dynastic rule had atrophied. The clearest example is with the Castilian bureaucracy's decline in integrity. What had been relatively efficient under his predecessors fell victim to rampant corruption and the bloat of patronage. Some bureaucratic offices became hereditary, a ludicrous practice which allowed a 9-year-old boy to inherit his father's position on the Council of the Indies in the 1690s. Hence even the highest apparatuses of government such as the councils became inefficient and resistant to reform, since the nobles who monopolized them vigorously defended their narrow prerogatives under the existing system. Just as the quality of the monarch himself plummeted at the end of the Spanish Habsburg dynasty, so too did the quality of the institutions for dynastic rule.

As the Spanish Habsburgs waned, the Austrian Habsburgs waxed. Carlos II is one of the best possible arguments against hereditary monarchy as a form of government. His unfitness for rule furthered the nobility's domination over royal power. It also impeded the kind of leadership that might have more vigorously arrested the years of decline and drift. He achieved nothing positive from a dynastic perspective. If anything, his manipulability and disloyalty to a Habsburg succession actually precipitated the dynasty's ejection from Spain and its great empire. Leopold was also not an incisive politician, nor were the Danubian domains especially well governed in his time. But they were governed just well enough to hold together against French pressure, Ottoman attacks, and Hungarian uprisings. Leopold's reign was important for the growth of trends that were to define the Habsburgs' central European monarchy: Baroque Catholicism; the emergence of a Vienna-centered, German-dominated elite culture; a ruling partnership with the magnates of the various realms; and an ongoing negotiation of the constitutional relationship between the dynasty and its realms. Because he was usually more interested in events on his western frontiers than those in the east, Leopold would never have guessed that his greatest legacy was the reconquest of Hungary. After 1700 the Danubian domains were the Habsburgs' main power base, and the center of gravity shifted eastward within those domains, thanks to that reconquest. While Leopold accomplished little in the way of institutional centralization, the fiscal base and cultural-political cohesion of his monarchy helped make it a potent enough player that, though it could not take up the baton of world empire from the Spanish branch, it became almost to the end of its existence an indispensable great power in European politics.

CHAPTER EIGHT

Opulent stagnation (1705–40)

The contrast between Joseph I and his brother Karl VI was the chasm between what might have been and what actually was. Joseph was the mercurial oldest son of Leopold I, shorter of stature, lively, with flashes of brilliance but also of laxity. He ruled for only six years, but in that time he oversaw the beginnings of reforms that, had they been fully carried out, might well have strengthened the dynastic state as never before in the Danubian domains. Karl was actually Leopold's favorite, and resembled his father in so many ways: he was ponderous and ugly, with a meaty, bovine head and the Habsburg jaw. His overriding preoccupation as ruler was to secure his succession—and even in that, his laborious arrangements were wanting. While they were both alive, there was considerable jealousy between these two, and open squabbling over their rights to rule parts of the Habsburg patrimony such as Naples and Milan. Those squabbles did not derail their joint dynastic pursuit, which was the prosecution of the Spanish succession war. Joseph is by far the more interesting of the two rulers; he had genuine promise, though he is often overlooked because of his short reign. Karl VI, on the other hand, was another of the dynasty's yawning seat warmers.

Joseph I (1678–1711)

Joseph's six years on the throne were characterized by the continuing war with the Bourbons, by the energetic rule of the young sovereign and his excellent team of advisors, by his feelings of German patriotism, and also by his incomplete plans for reforming the monarchy. Joseph was unlike both his father and his brother in his (relative) secularism. Though a devout Catholic, he was not educated by the Jesuits. Some of his tutors were in fact enemies of the Jesuits. He was also notably more tolerant of religious minorities than the several preceding generations of Habsburgs. He for instance appointed a Protestant nobleman among his high servants and allowed Lutheran churches to be built in Silesia. Like his father he was gifted musically both as a performer (he played the flute and violin) and a composer. But Joseph's mind was more probing; he was intrigued by rationalist intellectual trends. His allegiance to things German extended even to his marital politics, since he insisted on marrying a German woman. Joseph's character and leadership were not unimpeachable. Another advantage he had over his father and brother—that he was a fairly handsome man—surely aided in his notorious womanizing, which was criticized during his reign. And though he was enterprising and filled with ideas, he sometimes lacked the follow-through necessary to make real changes. During ministerial meetings he would sit doodling on his notes and then leave to go hunting as soon as he could. Though he was in many ways more modern than either Leopold or Karl, in other ways he remained a vain, profligate aristocrat; as an example, he left his last lover a gift of 500,000 florins.[1]

Joseph saw a need for changing how the monarchy was ruled, and he attacked those challenges with more dispatch than his forebears. Joseph's "young court" of reformers was influential already before 1705 over matters such as financing the war effort. Leopold was often not receptive to these initiatives, and there was quite a bit of wrangling among the father and the sons to get the dynasty's affairs in a logical order before Leopold died. In the end, Leopold and Joseph agreed to renounce their claims to the Spanish throne in favor of Karl, and then all three signed the *Pactum mutuae succesionis* which, among other things, assured Karl's heirs the right to inherit in Austria, Bohemia, and Hungary. After this pact was signed, in September 1703 Karl set off for Spain, and never saw his father and brother again.

Once he came to the throne, Joseph built upon the great successes of Eugène and Marlborough to provide strong leadership for the dynasty's war aims. He helped shore up the monarchy's precarious finances by founding the Vienna City Bank in 1706. After the battle of Blenheim had knocked Bavaria out of the war, Joseph wanted to annex that dukedom to Habsburg lands, but he failed to get the assent of the other German princes. He and Eugène then determined that Italy should be the target of a Habsburg military thrust. Aided by troops from Savoy and a sizeable loan from Queen Anne of England, Eugène won a major victory at Turin, which forced the French to withdraw from northern Italy. Habsburg forces took Naples as well. Joseph then sent Eugène to the Low Countries in 1708, where an allied victory at Oudenaarde enabled the conquest of the Spanish Netherlands. It was not an unbroken string of triumphs for the Habsburgs and their allies. In 1707 a combined English-Dutch-Portuguese army lost in Spain and the French pushed again into southern Germany. There was also the scare of the dynasty being dragged into the simultaneous Great

Northern War, which pitted Sweden against Russia, Saxony, and Denmark. Thanks to able diplomacy, that conflict did not spread to Habsburg lands. Nonetheless, by 1709 France's defeats forced it to the negotiating table.

Joseph also dealt decisively with the revolt in Hungary and Transylvania that had begun under Leopold. In 1707 Ferenc Rákóczi, the revolt's leader, declared the house of Habsburg deposed as rulers of these lands. But already by that point the tide was shifting against him. Rákóczi lacked the support of many nobles for deposing the dynasty and continuing the war. Moreover, a plague ravaged Hungary, and Louis XIV's mounting defeats meant he was unable to provide much support. Also crucial, the successes in northern Italy freed up Joseph's resources to suppress the revolt. The rebels' army, though large—tens of thousands at various points—was made up overwhelmingly of untrained soldiers. Hence it was no match for the force that Joseph sent into Hungary. The rebel army was soundly defeated at Trenčín (now in Slovakia) in 1708, and Rákóczi fled into exile. Joseph had to tread somewhat lightly in mopping up the various pockets of resistance, since his English and Dutch allies objected to any harsh treatment of Hungary's Protestants. The pacification was largely successful, even though the final treaty ending the revolt was not signed until after Joseph had died.

By Joseph's time, the dynasty's position within the Holy Roman Empire was firmer than it had been in a generation. Thanks to the German princes closing ranks in the wars against the Turks and Louis XIV, there was respectable solidarity and support for the emperor. Before he came to the throne, Joseph participated in the campaigns of 1702 and 1704 in Germany, which was an intentional strategy to raise the dynasty's imperial profile. As emperor, Joseph managed to convince the imperial diet to grant 5 million florins to support the war effort. In the long run, this temporarily improved position did not translate into major gains for the dynasty. One reason was that the princes still jealously guarded their sovereign rights. The more important reason was that Joseph himself did not really intend to bolster the Empire, but rather to bolster Austria. The idea was to use imperial resources and prestige almost exclusively for the Habsburgs' benefit. Hence to Joseph's thinking (which others like Eugène and Starhemberg subscribed to), victories such as Blenheim—achieved with a measure of German unity—would serve primarily to help him achieve dynastic aims in defeating the French. Joseph's subordination of the Empire to his dynastic aims was not unusual, since other German princes like the Hohenzollerns and the Wittelsbachs did much the same. His strategy might even have borne fruit, except that after Joseph's death Karl largely dropped it.

Though Joseph started some potentially valuable reforms in the administration of the dynastic state, he deserves credit more for their initiation than their fulfillment. He cut away some of the dead wood in top administrative circles, and enlisted a number of excellent minds among his top advisors. He attained markedly increased financial contributions from the estates for the benefit of the crown's income. He failed, though, to secure the universal excise tax that he hoped would be independent of the estates. His administrative reforms included shifting some of Innsbruck and Graz's competencies to Vienna. Joseph was aware of and sympathetic to certain ideas of the Austrian cameralists. For instance, he agreed with the utility of improving the conditions of the peasants, and so on some of his own estates he reduced the requirements of forced labor. Applying those reforms more widely throughout the monarchy did not get very far, however. The nobility, not surprisingly, offered strong resistance to commutation of the *robot* labor requirements. Of these many good ideas, most remained fragmentary as real policies.

It is important to remember that all of Joseph's six-year reign transpired during wartime. His and his ministers' most immediate goals were always directed toward sustaining the military effort. And in that they were largely successful. By 1710 France was on the defensive, though negotiations kept foundering on Louis's resistance to his opponents' demands. Cracks were starting to show in the opponents' alliance, too, since once the French had been expelled from the Spanish Netherlands the Dutch had met their most pressing war aims. After 1710, Britain's commitment wavered as well, since the Tories now controlled Parliament and moved to take Britain out of the war. Before a resolution could be brought to any of the foreign conflicts or domestic reforms, Joseph contracted smallpox during an epidemic that hit Vienna. He died in April 1711, not yet 33 years old. His time on the throne was so short that it is impossible to predict what he might have achieved had he lived longer. Even in those six years, however, he can take credit for strengthening the dynasty militarily and financially.

Karl VI (1685–1740)

Karl VI's reign was marked indelibly by succession issues. First was his improbable and ultimately impossible quest for the Spanish succession. Then, when that hope was definitively dashed, for most of the rest of his life he was preoccupied with his *own* succession—not because he had no heirs, but because he had only a female heir. As he frittered away his nearly three decades of rule extracting worthless promises from other powers to acknowledge the inheritance of his daughter Maria Theresia, the means of making them respect those promises, namely the remarkable military built up during Leopold's and Joseph's time, declined into decrepitude. During his time the Habsburg monarchy stretched its borders to its greatest-yet territorial extent, and the dynasty's display reached an extravagant, overripe late Baroque. Yet those features are mere camouflage for Karl's inadequacy as a ruler. He was dutiful, well-traveled, persistent to a fault, and not dumb, but he did not have good political judgment. His sense of his own limitations did not lead him to be more pragmatic, but to surround himself with mediocre advisors who also had little political talent. He tended to distrust those who were smarter or more capable than himself. He was another Habsburg monarch, much like his father, whose majesty derived more from the size of his wig and the pomposity of his costume than from his own innate qualities. In fact, even in court audiences he was known to mumble unintelligibly through his teeth like a gawky schoolboy.

His involvement in the Spanish succession war demonstrates a few of his good qualities and many of his bad ones. Though Leopold and Joseph had not regarded gaining all of Spain and its empire as a particularly realistic war aim, that goal was nonetheless dear to Karl's heart. He was present for the early part of the war in the Iberian peninsula, landing in Lisbon in 1704. Then, thanks to English and Dutch naval power, he captured Valencia and Barcelona in 1705. He was with the offensive that took Zaragoza in 1706, but a French-Spanish counteroffensive pushed Karl and his forces back to Barcelona, where he remained holed up most of the time until 1711. In 1708 Louis XIV, looking to end the war, signaled his willingness to renounce the Bourbons' Spanish claims in favor of Karl. The English, Dutch, and Habsburgs insisted on substantial war reparations, and that French forces help drive the Bourbon claimant Philippe of Anjou out of Spain. Louis could not accept these conditions, so the negotiations broke down. Joseph's death in 1710, as English and Dutch commitment was already wavering, did not help Karl's cause. If the Spanish war were successful, he would inherit not only in Spain but also in the German and the Danubian domains. He would thereby follow in the footsteps of his namesake Charles V. The renewed prospect of the old Habsburg aspiration to "universal monarchy" was unappealing to the English and Dutch. Since the most serious threat from France had been repelled by 1711, Karl's allies began seeking a separate peace.

Karl was determined to keep on fighting for the Spanish crown even as the other powers made peace at Utrecht in 1713. Karl sent Eugène on one last campaign that year which achieved nothing. The French forces were exhausted and the Habsburg military was hamstrung by plague outbreaks and the estates' refusal to vote another financial contribution. Pressed by his ministers to give up the farfetched idea of taking on France with no allies, Karl reluctantly agreed to end the war in 1714. He stubbornly refused to recognize the obvious, namely that Philippe was Spain's king, and insisted on retaining that now-chimerical royal title for himself. Other than that, the terms of the treaties of Utrecht and Rastatt were a reasonable compromise all around. The territorial partition was not so very different from the plan William III had proposed at the war's outset. The Habsburgs got the formerly Spanish Netherlands as well as large parts of Italy, including Naples, Milan, and Sardinia. France held on to acquisitions such as Alsace, Strasbourg, and Metz, while Philippe renounced his inheritance rights to the French crown.

By war's end, the Habsburgs were definitively ousted from Iberia but remained the predominant power in Italy. While Milan was quite rich, the dynasty was also saddled with particularly poor parts of the peninsula such as Naples. Moreover, all these Italian lands posed serious problems of defense, since the Habsburgs lacked a realistic sea power. Likewise, gaining what is now Belgium was a poisoned chalice. Karl received that territory as a sort of fallback, since for balance of power reasons it could not be given to France or the Netherlands. Here again was a territory far from the dynasty's real power base in the Danubian lands that it would be hard-pressed to defend. That Karl agreed to such strategically ludicrous acquisitions is evidence of his blinding dynastic pride. In a way more medieval than modern, the Habsburgs embraced the old ideology that they could and should rule anywhere, that their inheritance claims must be upheld whether or not they were practical or militarily feasible. A more realistic thinker would have jettisoned the fantasy of the dynastic claims to Italy and Belgium as a springboard back to Spain (a fantasy Karl for a time maintained), and focused instead on amassing a more contiguous territorial realm. But Karl ignored the difficult defense demands of his acquisitions, wedded instead to dreams of prestige and territorial aggrandizement.

As the Spanish succession war came to an end, so too did the Rákóczi uprising in Hungary and Transylvania. Not long after he ascended to the throne, Karl sealed the victory won during Joseph's time by making peace with most of the Hungarian nobles at Szatmár in 1711. Though the Habsburgs had indisputably managed to defeat the revolt, the peace terms were fairly generous. A deal was struck to satisfy both the Habsburgs and the Hungarian nobles. Hungary proper retained much administrative autonomy, tax immunity for the nobles, and respect for religious privileges. Karl also agreed not to insist on the amnesty he had promised the *kuruc* rebels, since many of the nobles who had remained loyal to the dynasty wanted to hold onto the land they had seized from the rebels. The dynasty did assert its authority by having the Hungarian kingdom's financial and military policy run from Vienna. After 1715 a standing army in Hungary was established, made up mostly of non-Hungarian troops. The Hungarian diet also agreed to a regular annual financial contribution. Karl kept Transylvania as a separate crownland and retained the military frontier areas along the Turkish border, ruling both directly from Vienna. On the whole this was an adequate compromise to extinguish what had been a formidable rebellion. It kept the Hungarian magnates on the dynasty's side while also allowing for some of the kingdom's traditional liberties. Part of Karl's motivation for compromise was that he needed the Hungarian diet to agree to the Pragmatic Sanction.

The Pragmatic Sanction was Karl's overriding obsession and the defining feature of his reign. Promulgated in 1713, this was a document that codified the succession rules for the Habsburg lands and served as an essential legal foundation of the monarchy up to its end in 1918. The inheritance issues explain Karl's obsession: after Joseph's death he was the sole living male Habsburg. Moreover, at the time he first issued the Sanction, Karl had no children. His sons all then died young, which made his oldest daughter Maria Theresia his likely heir. He issued the Sanction to affirm the principle of primogeniture, but to apply it both to female heirs and to his own line. He expressly demoted Joseph's daughters to the second line of inheritance even though they were from the elder line. This was really the last act in the Habsburgs' long-running attempts to ensure the inherited unity of their territories over the older practice of partible inheritance. The Sanction also enshrined the principle that the Habsburgs' realms would henceforth be indivisible. This was an attempt to tie the heterogeneous lands together on the basis of law, rather than purely on dynastic personal union. Though the Pragmatic Sanction has sometimes been understood merely as Karl's attempt to have female succession recognized in the Habsburg lands, that is not strictly correct, since there were no legal impediments to such succession in Austria, Bohemia, and Hungary. Rather, the principal effect of the Sanction was to serve as a (flimsy) paper insistence that the diverse lands of the Habsburg inheritance were in fact one unified realm.

Because the Sanction altered the dynasty's legal relationships with its various realms, and altered Joseph's daughters' (and hence their husbands') succession prospects, Karl felt he needed formal approbation of this act. Thus for almost two decades he lobbied to secure recognition from his realms and the other European powers, and he all but mortgaged his house to get it. The Austrian and Bohemian estates ratified it without much trouble by 1721. The Hungarian diet predictably drove a harder bargain, exacting another promise from Karl that the dynasty would respect all of the Hungarian nobles' privileges. Nonetheless, the Sanction was accepted by Hungary and Transylvania by 1723, and in the Austrian Netherlands and Lombardy by 1725. The much more difficult part of this procedure was securing international recognition. Karl made a deal with his old rival Philippe of Spain whereby, in return for recognition, Karl would marry Maria Theresia to one of Philippe's sons. The prospect of a Habsburg alliance with Bourbon Spain antagonized the English and Dutch, who forced an end to the marital pact. They also demanded for their recognition of the Sanction that Karl would have to close down Austria's nascent overseas trading company, a competitor to British and Dutch interests. By 1732 Karl had secured the German princes' recognition, but this too came at a price. He pledged to support the candidacy of Friedrich August of Saxony to the Polish throne, to marry Maria Theresia to a German prince, and to acknowledge the recent territorial acquisitions of the Prussian king.

In his single-minded pursuit of such weightless promises, Karl overlooked the scheming about the future of his dynasty. Both the Wittelsbachs in Bavaria and the Wettins in Saxony, into whose families Karl had married Joseph's daughters, signed secret treaties with France to support their succession claims to Habsburg dominions after Karl's death. Even the deal to marry Maria Theresia to the imperial prince of Lorraine, Franz Stephan, spurred a plot by France and Spain to seize both Lorraine and the Habsburg possessions in northern Italy. So, although the Pragmatic Sanction marked a legal milestone for the dynasty, it also set up the treacherous scrum for the Habsburg inheritance once Karl died.

Karl's most positive attribute as a ruler was that he encouraged economic development and maritime trade in his monarchy, more than any of the Austrian Habsburgs before him. Not all the enterprises he promoted found success, but to his credit he saw clearly the need for pursuing them. He gave his approval to the foundation of a new trading company in Ostende to break into overseas trade with India and China. Though a worthy idea, the company was soon closed down as part of the deal to win recognition of the Pragmatic Sanction. Karl also named Trieste and Rijeka as free ports to encourage trade. He decreed the building of roads to link Vienna to the Adriatic; one of those roads, the "Carolina" going through Karlovac to Senj in Croatia, even bore his name. He founded a small navy, with two warships entering service in 1726. He lowered tariffs, reduced guilds' monopoly powers, and granted concessions to boost a number of small industries. Factories sprung up for glass, textiles, porcelain, tobacco, and iron, among others. Wool production especially benefited, with output more than doubling in Bohemia and Silesia. Most of these enterprises remained small and not especially lucrative, but they were important as early industries in the Habsburg lands. In his economic ideas Karl, like his brother, was influenced by cameralist thinking, which led him to be more attentive to the condition of the peasantry. He advocated limiting peasants' labor obligations, but he did not push liberalization too firmly. He could not antagonize the landed elite who constituted his social and political base.

Karl's government overall resembled his father's, though perhaps more than Leopold, Karl dragged his feet in making difficult decisions. He also tended to resist the advice of what few competent advisors he had. His most effective minister, Gundaker Starhemberg, was a holdover from Joseph's time. Starhemberg presented proposals for ameliorating the monarchy's weak finances, but Karl negligently adopted only portions of his suggestions. Karl actually refused some ideas for centralizing and ameliorating the monarchy's fiscal situation via measures such as a universal excise tax. That fiscal situation in many ways worsened during Karl's reign. The treasury was sapped by Naples' poverty and the high military costs in Belgium. Even the indisputably brilliant Eugène proved that his brilliance was limited to the battlefield. As the president of Karl's war council and one of the main voices in the monarchy's foreign relations, Eugène turned out to be both very conservative and somewhat lazy. His relationship with Karl was rocky, though both men evinced a preference for playing cards or billiards rather than tackling the thorny problem of reforming the monarchy's dilapidated administrative structures. In relation to the Empire, Karl did not advance any of the gains in prestige and solidarity won under Leopold and Joseph. If anything, the other major dynasties such as the Wittelsbachs, Wettins, and Hohenzollerns became more assertive. Though cautiousness was the usual Habsburg watchword in dealing with their heterogeneous monarchy, Karl's rule veered far into the realm of complacency.

Despite that cautiousness, Karl found himself embroiled in several misguided wars. Philippe of Spain broke the peace achieved at Utrecht and Rastatt by attacking Karl's Italian possessions in 1717. Britain, the Netherlands, and France all came in on Karl's side to stop Spain's aggression. By the peace of 1720 Karl traded Sardinia for Sicily, briefly reestablishing Habsburg control over much of southern Italy; he also finally acknowledged Philippe's right to rule Spain. From 1720 through the remainder of Karl's reign, many of Austria's valuable alliances frayed. Because France after Louis XIV's death was less of a menace, British and Austrian interests coincided less. With cooling relations westward, Karl looked eastward, making an alliance with Russia as part of a deal to get the Pragmatic Sanction recognized. The disastrous War of the Polish Succession from 1733–8 then exposed the weakness of the Habsburgs' geopolitical situation. Karl entered the war to support the claims of Friedrich August of Saxony (who was his nephew by marriage) to the Polish crown, against those of the French-backed claimant. Eugène, his days of glory long past, was now a senile 70-year-old, and could not effectively counter France's invasion of Lorraine nor Spain's attacks on the Italian Habsburg possessions. Karl received little support from Britain or the German princes since he had neglected his ties there. In the end, Friedrich August became king of Poland and Karl's son-in-law, Franz Stephan, booted out of Lorraine, received Tuscany as recompense. Karl, for his part, lost Naples and Sicily to Spain but got Parma instead.

There were also two wars against the Turks. The first resulted in a resounding victory, while the second only added to Karl's list of late military debacles. Karl declared war on the Ottomans after appeals from Venice (which had been under attack from the Ottomans since 1714), but also because of his sense of imperial duty to make war on the Turks. Eugène saw his last, heroic triumphs in the battle of Petrovaradin in 1716, in which he routed a much larger Turkish army, and then in the siege of Belgrade in 1717, in which he built up a Danube fleet that again overcame negative odds to take Belgrade's strategically vital fortress. The result was the Treaty of Passarowitz in 1718, which completed the reconquest of Hungary and added parts of Serbia and Wallachia to the monarchy. From this high point, the tables turned in another fight against the Ottomans at the end of Karl's reign, from 1737–9. Karl entered this war to support Russia, which was a foolish maneuver because it was tangential to Habsburg interests, and the monarchy could scarcely afford it. However, Russia was almost his only ally at the time, and he had promised to support it in return for recognizing the Pragmatic Sanction. Eugène had died in 1736, and the Austrian military effort was sunk by inept generals and diplomats. Though Karl's forces won several battles, they lost the peace, having to give up lands gained in 1718 including Belgrade. The worst disaster of this late Turkish war was that it exposed how the once-vaunted Austrian army had declined, which primed Prussia, among others, for attack in the subsequent War of the Austrian Succession.

Karl died in 1740, shortly after eating a bunch of mushrooms that may have been poisonous. Legalistic to the very end, he insisted that his position as emperor entitled him to four—and not two!—lit candles around his deathbed. He never escaped nostalgia for his lost kingdom, either. According to some accounts his last word was a whispered, "Barcelona."[2] His legalistic fantasies—that he was the rightful successor to the Spanish kingdoms, that a piece of paper such as the Pragmatic Sanction could secure his own succession schemes—defined the man and his reign. Had Karl been sharper he might have seen that a strong financial and military basis would have provided more security for his dynasty than the empty commitments to the Pragmatic Sanction ever could.

Dynastic strategies

The Austrian Habsburgs' failures at dynastic reproduction at this time were only somewhat less egregious than those that had ruined the Spanish Habsburgs in the previous generation. Territorially, the indefensible additions in Belgium and Italy were a problematic success at best. The fact that these lands were awarded to the Austrian Habsburgs is however an indicator of the dynasty's indispensability; no other major house could lay claim to them without upsetting the balance of power. The succession issues placed the family in a still more precarious position. The *Pactum mutuae sucessionis* that Leopold, Joseph, and Karl agreed to in 1703 was necessary to sort out the inheritance issues between the two brothers. It included a provision whereby if one line died out, the other would inherit even if the oldest female were the heir. As it happened, neither Joseph nor Karl had a son who lived. Joseph's one son died, and his wife Amalie Wilhelmine of Hannover also died after Joseph infected her with a sexually transmitted disease. Karl's wife Elisabeth Christine of Braunschweig-Lüneburg became so obese that he hoped she might die so he could marry again and perhaps produce a male heir. Part of Karl's ploy with the Pragmatic Sanction was to alter the earlier *Pactum* so that his own daughter would inherit before Joseph's daughters.

Yet Karl's machinations here were singularly dim-witted, since he married Joseph's daughters to the Crown Princes of Bavaria and Saxony, respectively. Those princes were thereby able to raise claims to the Habsburg succession once Karl died, at the expense of his own daughter. Karl also mismanaged the education aspect of reproducing the dynasty. Even though he acknowledged Maria Theresia as his successor, Karl balked at giving her the kind of education she would need as a ruler. As she matured, he actively excluded her from high council meetings and refused to discuss affairs of state with her. He expressed his attitude when he once said that "a realm cannot be entrusted to a mere woman," since she would need "the firm hand of a king" to guide her.[3] His lack of respect for his daughter's potential is the more surprising since he appointed his sister, Maria Elisabeth, to continue the family's tradition of women regents of the Netherlands. She proved an assured and well-loved ruler, in a way prefiguring Maria Theresia's own reign.

The Pragmatic Sanction, tenuous as it was, nonetheless contributed to legitimacy and loyalty for the dynasty. The Sanction was the first law applied to all the lands of the Habsburg monarchy. It aimed to constitute a more unified state—a *Gesamtstaat*, a fusion of the various parts of the composite monarchy—where one had not previously existed, at least in a formal legal sense. The realm itself, as a nascent *Gesamtstaat*, was given legitimation by Karl's proclamation. It was thus a step beyond Ferdinand II's *Verneuerte Landesordnung* of 1627 which joined the Bohemian kingdom to the Austrian hereditary lands. The Sanction's succession provisions also legitimized Habsburg rule by tying the dynasty to that tentatively coalescing *Gesamtstaat*. That Karl sought and received the various provincial estates' approvals of the Sanction was a gesture of loyalty by the dynasty to the elites in the monarchy, and by the elites to the dynasty. Those elites signed off on language in the Sanction claiming that the Habsburgs' monarchy was "indivisible."

More pervasive and probably effective than a legal document in securing loyalty and legitimacy was the ongoing Baroque cultural fusion of the dynasty, the Danubian domains, and their elites. The Baroque court was still essentially equated with the state. This meant that Karl's servants were in most cases there to serve him personally, even if they held official administrative positions. He counted nearly 2,200 servants in his court.[4] Many of them were not ministers or bureaucrats, since the Habsburg administrative apparatus remained modest at this time. They were instead people holding honorary titles or serving the cultural functions of the court such as artists, musicians, and actors. Except when the royal family was out of Vienna, Karl self-consciously adhered to the austere, black-clad Spanish royal style, which speaks to the lethargic conservatism of his court. He also held to the Austrian Habsburgs' Baroque traditions of overwrought piety. Karl continued the practices of washing paupers' feet on Maundy Thursday, for example. His devoutness he demonstrated by building churches, which in their lavishness stand in dubious contrast to ministering to the poor. The most famous of Karl's constructions is the Karlskirche (actually named after St. Charles Borromeo) in Vienna, built from 1716 to 1737 by the architects Fischer von Erlach father and son. This church features two exterior columns which are topped with the imperial crown and are meant to recall the pillars of Hercules from Charles V's coat of arms. That it was built outside Vienna's city walls testifies to the monarchy's confidence that the Turkish threat had been conclusively beaten.

These were the years when many of the grandest Baroque edifices sprung up throughout the Danubian domains. This was a triumphal, self-congratulatory display of the monarchy's elites. Prince Eugène's Belvedere, designed by the architect Hildebrandt, is the most perfect of all palaces in the Habsburg lands. The abbey of Melk, some 80 kilometers west of Vienna, was the high point of church construction. Boasting a dazzlingly gilded church, it is an overpowering assertion of Austrian Baroque Catholicism. Karl himself added to Vienna's palace complex, including the building of the Spanish Riding School, and the Hofburg's impressive library. But closer to his heart was his project to turn the abbey of Klosterneuburg into his own version of El Escorial, a new monastery-palace for the dynasty to replace the one lost in Castile. Vienna during Karl's reign did see a great growth in art and artisans as all this construction took place. Hundreds of artists, many from Italy, found work there, and contributed to the city's Italian cultural flavor. Karl had several Italian court poets, the most famous of which was Pietro Metastasio. Johann Joseph Fux was Karl's court composer and helped stage the extravagant musical performances Karl enjoyed.

Though Joseph may seem more progressive than Karl, they both exhibited quite traditional conceptions of the ruler. Joseph in particular was preoccupied with an iconography that would depict him as no less glorious than Louis XIV. This motivated his (unrealized) plans to make Schönbrunn outdo Versailles. Despite his very short reign, Joseph also founded Vienna's Kärntnertor theater, established an arts academy, and ordered the construction of a new neighborhood outside the old city walls which continues to bear his name. Karl's preoccupation with long-established, even outmoded images of the ruler can be seen in his imperial allusions to Charles V's monarchy. He was a man who looked resolutely to the past rather than to the future. Divine right, untouchable monarchical gravitas, and tradition were the foundations of his conception of kingship. His belief that the sovereign was responsible for the moral/religious practice of his subjects justified his religious control of them, and the close alliance with the Church. For example, Karl for the first time allowed the Jesuits to enter the Military Frontier along the Turkish border, to try to convert Orthodox believers there to Catholicism. He also gave his approval to closing down various Protestant churches, albeit he did at least allow Protestants to worship privately. Thus Counter-Reformation intolerance persisted as an official ideology in the Habsburg lands long after it had started to moderate further west.

Comparing these two rulers' contributions to the institutionalization of the dynasty's rule reveals an unmistakable picture of improvement under Joseph and decline under Karl. Joseph's reforms, though incomplete, made particularly valuable strides in fiscal matters. Besides bringing the administration of war and finance more under Vienna's central control, he and his advisors helped raise the crown's income from around 9 million florins at the end of Leopold's reign to around 17 million by 1708. That increase came in part from the economic growth during Leopold's years and onward, but also from some rationalization of bureaucratic management under Joseph. The founding of the Vienna City Bank in 1706 aided in providing the monarchy with loans. Expenditures still exceeded revenues, however, creating crippling debt in Karl's years. In 1714 the monarchy's debt was 52.1 million florins, but it increased to 99 million by 1739.[5]

By the end of Karl's reign the monarchy's credit was ruined, with much of its income going immediately to debt service. That Karl did so little to remedy this problem is one of the most glaring indictments of his rule. The financial problems meant that even the military, the best-functioning central institution in the monarchy, was seriously impaired. Fiscal constraints limited the maximum number of troops that could be supported to 110,000 or so, a number well short of what France could field. The other problem with the military was that by his later years Eugène had proved that he was a great battlefield leader, but a poor administrator. He failed to modernize the military in important ways, including in its guns, its supply line planning, its provisioning, and the training of its officers. During the wars with the Turks, the French, and the Spanish, Eugène achieved a great deal with modest resources, but in peacetime he achieved almost nothing at all.

Though it is impossible to know what Joseph might have accomplished had he lived longer, during his short reign he tallied some appreciable successes. His armies kept most of the Danubian domains safe from French aggression, and they efficiently suppressed the Hungarian revolt. They won northern Italy too, securing it from the Bourbons' aspirations into Habsburg hands for another 150 years. He employed perspicacious advisors who began much-needed reforms. He was overall quite astute about furthering his dynastic interests, although he himself sometimes lacked the focus for direct management of politics. He could even compromise when necessary. An example of the latter is his refusal to commit too many resources to Spain, which he knew he could never defend. In all of these things—his intelligent identification of key interests, his effective ministerial team, and his flexibility—he far outshined his brother, who surpassed Joseph only in his longevity.

Karl had the luxury of a period of significant stability, with few major external threats. And yet, owing to his own intellectual limitations and his inflated sense of imperial grandeur, he did not see the need to exploit this relatively stable time to address some of his realm's most obvious weaknesses. This is why his was a time of opulent stagnation. Counter-Reformation Catholicism was boastfully triumphant, but its stultifying suspicions, both of outside intellectual currents, and of the remaining large pockets of Protestants in Silesia and Hungary, fed into a slowly gestating discontent. There was also very little effort to streamline let alone centralize his administration and governing institutions. So the Habsburg domains remained considerably more heterogeneous and less cohesive than other large European polities. Karl also lost the momentum of solidarity within the Empire that had been established during Leopold's time. Military momentum was lost as well. The Habsburg monarchy became militarily strong enough to be a valuable alliance partner in European balance of power politics, but never strong enough to be a threat on its own to the other major powers. In many ways, it was a rare, pivotal position that the dynasty occupied, and together with the great size of its territories, this position girded the Habsburgs' status and prestige for more than a century. It is true that Karl had some redeeming qualities, such as his artistic patronage and his commercial initiatives. But he gave little of lasting value to the dynasty beyond his astounding daughter, Maria Theresia.

CHAPTER NINE

Enlightenment and reform (1740–92)

In September 1741 the Habsburg monarchy found itself in a lethal crisis, attacked all at once by Prussian, Bavarian, and French armies determined to dismember the young sovereign Maria Theresia's inheritance. In that month she met the Hungarian diet at Bratislava. There, dressed in the Hungarian style, her infant son Joseph in her arms, she pleaded with the nobility to support her. She used tears. She appealed to chivalrous protection for a young mother. She reminded the nobles of their previous oaths to the dynasty. And they rose, swearing allegiance anew to their queen, promising to raise a massive army of 100,000 men to defend her with their lives and blood. Maria Theresia was then crowned according to custom: wielding the royal symbols of scepter and sword, she rode a horse up a hill of earth brought from all the counties of Hungary, and atop that hill she pointed the sword in the four cardinal directions, pledging to protect Hungary from all its enemies. In this famous, epic moment, Maria Theresia fought with all the tools in her repertoire. She demonstrated the exceptional political skills that would not only beat back the enemy onslaught, but enable her to refashion and revitalize the bases of Habsburg dynastic rule.

In her four decades on the throne, Maria Theresia was motivated above all by clear-eyed pragmatism and a willingness to compromise tradition for concrete, beneficial political ends. She herself was not truly a person of the Enlightenment, nor was she an intellectual. She was a product of the traditional Baroque world of her father, yet her mind was more forward-looking, and she surrounded herself with relatively enlightened advisors. The way she shaped a new image of the sovereign—as the first female head of her house—also shows how she would readily innovate upon older relationships where necessary. Testimony to her success is that she attained a popular esteem greater than that of any of her predecessors, an esteem that lasts until today. Her son Joseph II, on the other hand, through his willingness to throw tradition out the window, earned more enmity than esteem. He was the incarnation of the enlightened despot, aggressively and self-consciously seeking to institute reason and the primacy of the state as the guiding principles of governance. His reforms were intelligent but lacking in finesse, which explains why he achieved less than his mother. Leopold II found a happy medium between his mother's careful political skills and his brother's overweening autocracy. His time on the throne was so short, though, that it mostly involved cleaning up Joseph's mess.

Maria Theresia, Joseph, and Leopold were by no means revolutionaries. They sought to preserve the old dynastic, aristocratic order, but to make it work better, to make it more modern. Their reforms built upon many existing structures while altering them in hopes of improving their efficiency. Though the reigns of these three monarchs have come to symbolize the Enlightenment in the Danubian domains, in truth Enlightenment ideas did not sink very deeply into what still remained a conservative society. Enlightenment ideas in general only reached a small number of people in the urban areas, or in the uppermost social classes. It was mostly the elite who had access to books and other material from abroad that brought in new thinking. In practice, the Enlightenment in the Habsburg lands was state-centric, and the dynasty selected relevant, "enlightened" principles to strengthen its rule. These were never going to lead to more participatory government, such as a stronger parliamentary system, since that would have been viewed as weakening the state rather than strengthening it. Nonetheless, by the end of this period, the Habsburgs' Danubian monarchy was arguably in a better condition than it had ever been. Its economy was modernizing, and it had greatly improved systems of education and governance. The relationship between the Habsburgs and their peoples also profoundly changed: more than ever before, the welfare of its subjects became the dynasty's justifying ideology.

Maria Theresia (1717–80)

Maria Theresia should not be misunderstood: she was fundamentally a conservative. She clung to many of her family's traditions and did not seek radical change. What made her reign so successful was precisely her ability to bridge the old and the new. Thus she held to those dynastic traditions yet innovated upon them. For example, she did not completely remake the power bases of her rule, continuing to rely on the aristocracy and the Church, but she did modernize them. While still acknowledging the privileges of the provincial estates, she centralized administrative structures. And though she respected Catholicism's dominance in society, intolerance of other faiths relaxed. She held to the established conceptions of the ruler's function, but she also feminized them, and emphasized her duty to foster the public good. She was able to act as a bridge because she was at heart a pragmatist. She had an acute assessment of what had to be done in order to accomplish what she wanted. This meant that despite her traditional upbringing, she was open to new ways of strengthening monarchical sovereignty. She was willing to make targeted, cautious changes, and delegate authority to intelligent advisors more progressive than she was. Even her bloodline shows how Maria Theresia was a hinge between her dynasty's past and its future. She was the last progeny of the unbroken line of male Habsburgs stretching back to the thirteenth century. But she founded a new line, the Habsburg-Lorraine dynasty, which was in every meaningful respect a continuation of ancestral traditions.

Martin von Meytens's portrait of 1759 captures so much of this remarkable woman's character. He painted her numerous times over two decades, and some features are constant. She is consistently depicted with her three crowns—the Austrian, Bohemian, and Hungarian—emphasizing both her majesty and her legitimacy. Another constant is her intelligence: in the 1759 portrait, her lively eyes and cooly appraising expression are unmistakable indicators of the perspicacity and insight with which she managed her government. Maria Theresia was obviously self-possessed, confident, and comfortable in her role as sovereign. Though she is depicted regally, with an elegant, powder-blue gown, a robe of gold and crimson, and diamond jewelry, the whole ensemble is not dramatically overstated. In earlier portraits her clothes are more voluminous, her setting more ostentatious. But this 1759 portrait is a more accurate representation of her nature. Maria Theresia (Figure 9.1) was not particularly preoccupied with her looks, at least compared to other women of her class. Most of the time she dressed quite simply, and after her husband died in 1765 for the rest of her life she wore plain black. The scaled-down magnificence of this portrait reflects Maria Theresia's charm and approachability. She was adept at cultivating loyalty among her advisors and her subjects. She forged personal relationships with some very talented individuals. There are also characteristics that the portrait does not reveal. Maria Theresia was tough and dedicated. She fought for her very survival in 1740. She typically spent more than 7 hours a day dealing with affairs of state. In these matters, she proved far more serious and decisive than her immediate predecessors, particularly her negligent father.

All of these admirable qualities served her well as soon as she ascended the throne at the age of 23. Her father had foolishly trusted the promises of surrounding powers to respect the Pragmatic Sanction and a female's elevation as sovereign. Karl VI had also amassed a huge state debt, had dissolved a number of army regiments, and had peopled his councils with fusty old men. Thus immediately when Maria Theresia came to power, she found herself "without money, without credit, without armies, without experience [. . .] also without any counsel," as she complained.[1] All five things were urgently necessary because of the predatory designs of the surrounding powers. Karl Albrecht, the Duke of Bavaria, claimed that his right to succeed to parts of the Habsburg domains superseded Maria

FIGURE 9.1 *Maria Theresia, by Martin von Meytens (1759). In the collection of the Akademie der Bildenden Künste, Vienna. Image courtesy of the Bridgeman Art Library.*

Theresia's because of his marriage to Joseph I's daughter, and because of an old treaty of dubious validity from Ferdinand I's time. France openly supported his claim. Meanwhile, Friedrich August of Saxony and Poland—husband to Joseph's other daughter—announced his own claims. The scramble by surrounding powers to gobble up bits of the Habsburg patrimony was set off in December 1740 when Friedrich II of Prussia seized Silesia. This launched not only the War of the Austrian Succession, but also Maria Theresia's enduring feud with Friedrich. She actively hated him, calling him a "monster" and an "evil man."[2]

In 1741 Bavaria, with French backing, invaded Bohemia while French and Spanish armies attacked in the Austrian Netherlands and Lombardy respectively. This was Maria Theresia's bleakest hour: the Upper Austrian estates and a portion of the Bohemian nobility deserted her for Karl Albrecht. The German electors, too, abandoned the Habsburgs, electing the Bavarian as emperor in 1742. Karl Albrecht's three-year reign was the only interruption in the Habsburgs' rule of the Empire from 1438 to its dissolution in 1806. At this point even many nobles in the Viennese court thought Maria Theresia's was a lost cause. This is when she made her dramatic appeal to the Hungarian diet. That moment actually involved several months of negotiations, in which she had to promise to respect privileges such as the nobility's exemption from taxation. Hungary as a result maintained its separate institutions and constitution from the rest of the monarchy, such that it would escape many of the reforms that Maria Theresia and Joseph II subsequently introduced. But the kingdom's support came at a crucial time, and in 1742 she managed to fight back more strongly against her many enemies. Her armies retook Prague and she was crowned queen there in May of 1743. In that year, too, the British grew worried enough about French aggrandizement that they began aiding Austria more directly via subsidies and naval assistance. The allies' armies conquered Bavaria and beat back French incursions into Germany. Then in 1745 Karl Albrecht died. His heir, desperate to regain Bavaria from Habsburg troops, promised to renounce his territorial claims and to support the election of Maria Theresia's husband, Franz Stephan, as German emperor.

Though her armies fought an inconclusive campaign in Italy, Maria Theresia's main concern was always Friedrich and Prussia. After signing one truce, Friedrich broke it by taking Bohemia and Prague in 1744. Together with her Saxon allies, Maria Theresia was able to push Friedrich out of those territories in 1745. Despite several brutal battles she still could not dislodge him from Silesia, so she had to seek peace. The terms of the Treaty of Aix-la-Chapelle in 1748 were in one way a triumph for the Habsburg queen: she had survived the crisis at the outset of her reign and fought an enemy onslaught to a standstill. She identified the sharpest minds in her circle and empowered them, but ultimate decisions came from her. She played every card she had, and she played them all very well. It was a remarkable performance for a person only in her 20s. She did cede several territories in northern Italy to Spain, but the only major loss was Silesia, which had been one of the most economically developed parts of the monarchy, contributing some 20 percent of the government's total income. Silesia was not just a loss for the Habsburgs, but a long-term gain for the Hohenzollerns and Prussia. It weakened the Habsburgs' position in Germany, just as it also reduced the number of ethnic Germans within the balance of the monarchy's peoples. The monarchy was also set on a long, rivalrous course with Prussia, which would not be resolved until 1866. Maria Theresia was aware of how precarious her situation was. Thus even during the war she set about rectifying her chief vulnerabilities, namely weak finances, inefficient administration, and erratic military competence.

There were multiple influences on Maria Theresia's reforms, including some admixture of Enlightenment theories with a purely practical search for institutions more responsive both to commands from the top as well as demands from below. The overriding impulse was Maria Theresia's businesslike desire to strengthen her state and thereby her authority. The initial phase of reform was led by Count Friedrich Wilhelm von Haugwitz. The most immediate problems to be solved were military weakness and its underlying financial weakness. To address the former, in 1742 Haugwitz initiated the centralization of foreign policy and then military policy into administrative bodies that would have greater authority and effectiveness. Subsequent reforms continued the trend of centralizing lower bodies' authority upward. At the end of the 1740s his plans became more ambitious. Despite some protests among Maria Theresia's top ministers, Haugwitz pushed through a new funding mechanism by which the Austrian, Bohemian, and Moravian estates would approve taxation once a decade rather than annually. Nobles' previous tax exemption was also ended. These steps had two main effects. They provided more money for the military and also minimized the estates' control over raising revenue. Henceforth the central government had much more power in administering tax collection.

Where the initial reforms targeted the monarchy's immediate survival, subsequent initiatives addressed nearly all aspects of Maria Theresia's rule. In the name of efficiency and rationalization, Haugwitz undertook further centralization of governance via the creation of a new Directory of Administration and Finance and a joint Austrian-Bohemian Chancellery in 1749. Reorganization of the councils and other bureaucratic organs continued under Wenzel Anton Kaunitz, the eccentric yet ingenious minister who dominated the second half of Maria Theresia's reign and served both Joseph II and Leopold II as well. Kaunitz was notorious during his lifetime for his sexual escapades and strange health preoccupations; he continually complained of fevers and headaches, feared cool breezes, and ate an inordinate amount of fruit. But Maria Theresia saw past his odd qualities to recognize his consummate competence, describing him as "honest, without ulterior motive or spirit of favoritism, without ambition or party; he supports the good because he recognizes it as such."[3] Kaunitz continued the judicial reforms that Haugwitz had begun, for example by overseeing the implementation of a new Supreme Court that would reduce the power of nobles' and town courts. Measures were also adopted to improve the quality of judges. A unitary codification of law for the Hereditary Lands (embodied in the *Codex Theresianus*) was completed by 1766, and modernization of the penal code abolished torture in 1776.

Besides the reforms carried out at the upper levels of the government, under Haugwitz and Kaunitz there were many measures to improve the lives of the monarchy's subjects. The initiatives in education, religious affairs, and the economy were never merely altruistic. Rather, they exemplify common eighteenth-century thinking whereby reforms for the mass population not only improved their lot but strengthened the state in the process. Through school ordinances decreeing compulsory primary education in Austria in 1774 and Hungary in 1777, the monarchy instituted a school system that was exemplary for its time. Access to education was massively expanded, and curricula were modernized, with greater emphasis on German (or other vernacular languages), math, and at higher levels, science and engineering. As the state became more responsible for education, the Church's influence markedly decreased, which was part of Kaunitz's project to subject Church institutions to greater state supervision. In this the more traditional Maria Theresia took some convincing, but she did authorize a number of major changes. In 1762, based on Kaunitz's plans, a new government department was created to oversee Church affairs. It intervened in a number of ways: it ensured that state courts would try priests in nonecclesiastical matters, it vetted appointees for high Church offices, and it took control of some Church revenues. Kaunitz also imposed limits on the number of religious holidays and monks in monasteries, and ended the clergy's tax exemption. The goal was to reduce the size of the unproductive religious establishment and make it serve the state more efficiently, for example by using priests as teachers to help train professionals for the monarchy's burgeoning bureaucracy.

The economic reforms followed the general trend of cameralist thinking to promote economic and population growth. New governmental bodies were created to encourage trade; they advanced new tariff schemes, whittled away guild privileges, and encouraged shipping along the monarchy's waterways. Modest attempts to support domestic industries focused on textiles or sugar refining, and on the introduction of new technologies. Very few of these reforms reached Hungary, which, like most of the monarchy's economy, remained overwhelmingly agricultural. Improving agricultural productivity went hand-in-hand with bettering the conditions of the peasantry, and in this area Maria Theresia clearly demonstrated her intertwined concern for her subjects and for her state. She saw a boost in profitability from applying various forward-thinking reforms on her own estates. A series of edicts from the later 1750s onwards protected peasants from excessive *robot* labor requirements and other abuses of landlords. Agrarian reform required Maria Theresia to walk a fine line of asserting the state's intermediary role in the relationship between noble landlord and peasant laborer while not antagonizing the aristocracy, nor upsetting the traditional social hierarchy unduly. Thus she supported peasants' freedom to move, to change occupations, and even to marry without their lord's consent, but she also suppressed several peasant revolts that threatened the established order.

Despite the concerted effort of all these reform initiatives, in many ways they remained limited. One way they were limited was in their application. The Italian and Flemish territories were barely touched by most of them.

Hungary was affected more, but still remained administratively and financially distinct from the rest of the monarchy. When the Hungarian diet refused to countenance administrative competency for Hungary being subsumed into Kaunitz's new united chancellery in 1764, Maria Theresia did not press her case. She respected the promise she had made to preserve Hungarian liberties in 1741, and most of the time left the Hungarian diet to its own devices, only summoning it 3 times in 40 years. The reforms were also limited in their scope. They were never exactly avant-garde. Many of the ideas that she or her ministers implemented were actually several decades old, and most were quite narrowly targeted. Finally, her reforms were limited in their actual success. While certainly many improvements were made, the fundamental goal of strengthening the monarchy's power bases was only partially successful. Though revenues more than doubled over her reign, they were still not enough to cover military ventures such as that of 1778–9.

One thing for which Maria Theresia and her advisors cannot be faulted is the way their single-minded pursuit of key goals led them to reconsider long-standing policies. This applies to the domestic reforms as well as to the new international course impelled by the desire to recover Silesia. This desire led to the so-called diplomatic revolution by which the Habsburgs reconciled (at least temporarily) with their old enemy of France. Friedrich's Prussia had instead become the Habsburgs' chief adversary. As Kaunitz himself said, "Prussia must be overcome, if the House of Austria is to survive."[4] This reversal of alliances meant the dissolution of the strategic partnership with Britain, which the empress did not particularly regret since the British had insisted that she give up on Silesia and surrender Bavaria in the 1740s. Moreover, Britain and Prussia began warming up to each other, with the English king pledging not to support Austria's intent to recover Silesia in return for Prussia's protection of Hanover. Initially France was not attracted to Austria as an ally, but Kaunitz's blandishments, and an impending conflict with Britain, brought the French around. Hence in May 1756 France and Austria made a defensive alliance, and this proved an immediate lead-in to what became the Seven Years' War.

That war was another worldwide conflict involving all the major European powers. Friedrich initiated the hostilities when he invaded Saxony in the summer of 1756, which then brought a combined attack of Austria, Russia, the Empire, France, Poland, and even Sweden against him. Maria Theresia signed a new, tighter alliance with France, receiving large subsidies in return for giving up some land in Flanders and Italy. The Austrian and Prussian armies fought a series of inconclusive battles in which the Austrians failed to strike a knockout blow. At Kunersdorf in 1759 Friedrich was almost killed, but the over-cautious Austrian general Daun did not capitalize. Maria Theresia's support of Daun despite his errors was a grave mistake, and a contrast to her normally incisive identification of talent, as she later acknowledged. Meanwhile, France lost repeatedly to

Britain in North America and India, which meant its subsidies to Austria dried up. Maria Theresia's other most important ally, Russia, also withdrew from the conflict after the Tsarina Elizaveta [Elizabeth] died, replaced by her pro-Prussian son Pyotr [Peter] III. Thus in 1763 Austria made peace with Prussia at Hubertusburg, shortly after France and Britain also ended their conflict. Maria Theresia had attained none of her war aims; indeed, Prussia was only confirmed as a great power. The main concession Friedrich granted was to vote for Joseph II as King of the Romans and hence heir to the imperial crown. Though the permanent loss of Silesia was a bitter pill, it is a testament to Maria Theresia's realism that she knew when it was time to let it go and stop fighting.

In the last 15 years or so of her reign, Maria Theresia was less actively engaged in international matters. She tended to leave foreign policy to Kaunitz and Joseph, who became her co-regent. These two men pushed the major adventures of Maria Theresia's late period, namely the first partition of Poland and the war over the Bavarian succession. As a way to keep Ekaterina [Catherine] the Great of Russia from preying on Habsburg territories, Joseph and Kaunitz agreed with Friedrich of Prussia that all three powers would prey on Poland instead. In 1772, out of this first of three partitions, the Habsburgs got the largest slice, Galicia, including most of southern Poland except for Kraków. They also maneuvered to get the region of Bukovina from the Turks in 1774 to tie Galicia to Transylvania. In reality, this was not much of a gain, since the new lands were very poor, and further complicated the monarchy's ethnic makeup, adding many Poles, Ruthenians, and some 200,000 Jews. Maria Theresia protested that this carving up of the sovereign state of Poland was unjust, and that it cost her ten years of her life. But again, she was too pragmatic not to seize the opportunity.

Maria Theresia was just as skeptical of Joseph and Kaunitz's enthusiasm for trying to acquire Bavaria. The reigning Wittelsbach duke of Bavaria died at the end of 1777 with no son, and the next in line, his cousin the Elector Palatine, did not want to take up the inheritance. He thus offered the Habsburgs a trade: they would get Bavaria in return for giving him the Austrian Netherlands. Joseph and Kaunitz readily agreed. Friedrich was wary of any such Austrian expansion, however, and demanded two modest duchies as his price for allowing the trade to happen. Kaunitz and Joseph rejected his demands, which led to war in 1778. This conflict dragged ineffectually through the winter before Maria Theresia gave up on the desultory fight in 1779. The Wittelsbachs retained Bavaria while the Habsburgs acquired some land in the valley of the river Inn, but they also had to acquiesce to Friedrich's seizure of the two duchies he had coveted.

Maria Theresia was devastated by the death of her husband Franz Stephan in 1765. Several older advisors such as Haugwitz died around the same time. Though in these later years she ruled in conjunction with Joseph and Kaunitz, she retained most of the power. In effect, Joseph was the junior partner in the triumvirate, much to his dissatisfaction. Maria Theresia's relationship with Joseph became strained. He often criticized what he saw as the conservatism and empty formalities of her court, complaining of "gossiping and squabbling between one old woman and another."[5] Joseph was impatient for more rapid change, and supported Kaunitz's ambitious reforms after 1765. Maria Theresia did leave certain areas to Joseph's oversight, such as German affairs (since he became the emperor), military matters (he participated in some campaigns of the Bavarian war), and financial management. She even agreed to some of his proposals such as simplifying the staid Spanish court ritual, and reducing the time and money spent on hunting and gambling at court.

However, on many other matters she rebuffed her son, and out of frustration with Viennese politics he often traveled around the monarchy's lands. This was ultimately to his benefit, since he learned much and ranged far afield, going to France in 1777 and Russia in 1780. He got to know the conditions of the monarchy's subjects up close; according to legend, he even helped peasants plow their fields on occasion. And staying out of Vienna helped reduce the frequent spats with his mother. The relationships in this co-regency were certainly productive in terms of the monarchy's policies, but they were also volatile. Maria Theresia, Joseph, and Kaunitz all were known to use threats of resignation as part of the gamesmanship of their unusual joint rule. Still, the arrangement made sense as Maria Theresia aged and withdrew from the daily management of government. She never fully recovered from a bout with smallpox in 1767. She also complained that her many pregnancies had aged her prematurely, and by her last years her body was fragile. The great lady died in November 1780 at age 63, after catching a cold. The dynasty would never again be led by so astute a politician, able expertly to deploy so many tools to achieve her will, whether cold intelligence or occasional feminine guile. This skillful leadership invigorated the structures of the dynastic monarchy that would serve it until its end.

Joseph II (1741–90)

Where Maria Theresia is the most accomplished of Habsburg monarchs, Joseph II is the most controversial. He was unapologetically an autocrat, but one avowedly dedicated to ruling in the best interests of his subjects. He was enlightened, infused with many modern ideas, but not truly an intellectual; he embraced those ideas for political rather than philosophical ends. Many of his reforms—some lasting, some annulled—were smartly attuned to strengthen the dynasty's government. But Joseph's arrogance and lack of political skills counteracted much of what he wanted to achieve. Since his time historians have alternately praised him for being forward-looking and denounced him for his authoritarianism. There is no question that he tried to do too much; he issued some 6,000 edicts in just under ten years of rule. That number illustrates his ambition for reform, which could often be heedless in its trampling of obstacles such as traditional prerogatives. Joseph's reformist inclinations were formed by his own native intelligence as well as by his education under some moderately enlightened scholars. Unfortunately for him, Joseph's intelligence was not one aware of its own shortcomings. Maria Theresia explicitly criticized his biting wit and sarcasm, saying that they were not befitting a monarch, but Joseph took his lack of diplomacy almost as a badge of honor. There was, though, a softer side to his character. He grieved deeply after the loss of his first wife in 1763 (after only three years of marriage) and his only daughter seven years later. He kept some of his wife's and daughter's clothes as mementoes to console him in his chilly second marriage (Figure 9.2).

Joseph expressed his philosophy of rule quite clearly: he identified himself as the chief servant of the state. Because of his great responsibilities, he insisted that he therefore deserved preponderant authority. Joseph did believe in the equality of all people, regarding nobility as essentially meaningless. The true test of a person's worth was in making himself or herself useful to the state—which in practice meant following Joseph's orders. He was intensely self-righteous, convinced that he had unassailable insights as to what his monarchy needed. He expected everyone from his advisors on down to the lower classes to accept his insights without resistance. His ideal was to be able to issue orders which would then be obediently followed. He was not well-disposed toward the negotiating, compromise nature of actual politics and governance. His orders extended into the realm of micro-management, such as with testy directives forbidding military cadets from masturbating, or about the proper hours for illuminating Vienna's streetlights. While such orders may seem despotically arbitrary, Joseph believed he acted for the common welfare. He did not hesitate to overturn the privileges of the traditional elites such as the landed nobility and the clergy when he thought they stood in the way of the public good. His own, sometimes idiosyncratic definition of the public good is what explains his seemingly contradictory path between liberalism and despotism. Ultimately, though he believed firmly in the public good and working for the benefit of his subjects, Joseph did not trust the public; thus he had to define the good for them. This arrogance toward those he purported to serve explains the nature of Joseph's style of rule, and explains many of the mistakes he made.

Joseph's reforms were motivated more by his vision of rational state efficiency than by Enlightenment notions of liberty and equality. He believed that the greatest good would come from increasing the power of good government, which could then order society in a way conducive not only to the general welfare, but also to the appropriate amount of liberty. Unsatisfied with progress under his mother's reign, once he was sovereign

FIGURE 9.2 *Joseph II and Leopold II, by Pompeo Batoni (1769). In the collection of the Kunsthistorisches Museum. Image courtesy of Bridgeman Art Library.*

Joseph leapt at administrative, economic, and social transformation of the dynastic state. The administrative reforms were designed to create more unitary, professionalized ruling institutions across the monarchy's lands. He decreed that German would be the unified language of administration, partly for the purpose of standardizing bureaucratic governance. The state bureaucracy was essential to Joseph's goal of increasing central control. He therefore promulgated new standards for the expanding bureaucracy and the judiciary, and filled many positions with commoners, in accordance with his belief that birth conferred no automatic distinction. More professional judges and lawyers were also introduced as the judicial system was modernized.

The other administrative reforms had similar objectives, such as his plan to institute a standardized land tax across the monarchy. Joseph particularly resented Hungary's special status and tried to undermine it through the elimination of the old county structure and intervention in the noble landowners' relationships with their peasants. However, that special status also meant that his reforms had less impact in the Hungarian kingdom. In other areas, such as in the Italian and Belgian possessions, political power was centralized upward, reducing the legislative competencies of local estates and municipalities. A new criminal legal code was promulgated in 1787, in which Joseph discarded some of the more archaic things that had survived his mother's reforms, such as capital punishment and prosecution for sorcery. It also explicitly trumpeted the principle that all classes were equal before the law. This code exemplifies Joseph's goals of unifying and rationalizing the instruments of rule, which he hoped would simultaneously help unify his realms. He also decreed some progressive improvements in public health, such as opening the General Hospital in Vienna in 1784, requiring every community to have a state-registered nurse and doctor, and sending surgeons abroad to learn the most modern medical practices.

The economic and social reforms were in many cases inspired by Joseph's familiarity with mercantilist ideas. Measures were enacted to boost manufactures, encourage exports, and protect the development of small industries in his lands. He continued to promote agricultural productivity by further improving conditions in the countryside. In the early 1780s serfdom was legally abolished in most parts of the monarchy. Peasants were freed from their ties to a particular plot of land, from the landlord's authority over their marriages and occupations, and in many cases even from the lord's judicial jurisdiction. The *robot* was not fully eliminated, but peasants' options for commuting labor with cash were expanded. The nobility typically resisted this reduction of their power over the agricultural labor force, with the outcome that peasants in more westward parts of the monarchy enjoyed better conditions than they did in Galicia. Joseph also continued Maria Theresia's reforms by bringing many more rural people into primary education. The expansion of education during Joseph's years is a valuable window on the purpose of his reforms. His vision was that education should instill subjects with useful, practical skills, and the values of loyalty and responsibility. Education at any level was thus supposed to produce people useful to the state. Like his mother, he did not favor higher education for purely intellectual purposes. He discouraged the kind of research or free flow of ideas that might question the bases of the monarchy's authority and stability. Instead, higher education's purpose was to turn out neither scientists nor other kinds of scholars, but functionaries who would serve the state.

One of Joseph's most enlightened reforms, his Edict of Tolerance of 1781, also marked one of his biggest breaks with the policy of his dynasty over the previous several generations. Per this edict, the Protestant and Orthodox sects saw a major expansion of their rights throughout the Habsburg domains. Though some restrictions remained, henceforth it was possible to convert into Protestantism or Orthodoxy and to build new churches and parochial schools. Joseph's religious reforms built upon some trends in Maria Theresia's reign, but went further. For example, in 1782 restrictions on Jews were significantly relaxed, freeing them from restrictions on their dress, enabling them to practice new trades, and to attend university. The goal of these reforms was to reduce the institutional and political control of the Church and make it better serve the state and the populace. Joseph closed down some 700 monasteries—over half of the monarchy's total— out of a desire to rationalize Church institutions and promote productive rather than contemplative occupations. He wanted to modernize the Church's teachings and attitudes as well, instituting a system whereby state officials would supervise priests' sermons. He also brought a number of high Church officials such as bishops into state pay and made them swear obedience to the crown. Joseph remained committed to Catholicism, but in contrast to his predecessors in the seventeenth century (or even his mother), religious uniformity was no longer a precondition for societal stability and state power.

This flood of reforms met with increasing hostility after 1784. In that year a rural revolt broke out in Transylvania. Even the peasants objected to Joseph's changes, though in this case their objection was that the reforms did not go far enough. Protesting high taxes and the price of monetary commutation of labor obligations, they rebelled against their landlords. Though Joseph was sympathetic to some of their claims, and dismayed that his attempts to better rural conditions provoked not so much gratitude as unrest, he had to protect the existing power relationships. He therefore suppressed the revolt, ordering that the ringleaders be killed and quartered, their body parts displayed publicly. Joseph did not slow the pace of his edicts after this incident, but in many ways accelerated them, ignoring warnings about possible resistance. He thereby stirred up the nobility and the bourgeoisie in addition to the peasants. The nobles were predictably incensed by the curtailment of their special legal and economic status. As part of a new land survey that would reorganize taxation, Joseph proposed a sharing of peasants' taxes between the state and the landlord. In practice this would have meant a significant reduction in landlords' incomes. Some of Joseph's top advisors such as Karl von Zinzendorf, the president of his tax regulation commission, warned sternly of potential negative consequences—but Joseph then just removed Zinzendorf from his post.

In addition to these grievances, nobles in Hungary protested Joseph's dismissive treatment of the Hungarian and Croatian diets, and his refusal to have himself crowned in that kingdom. Joseph's application of his reform plans to the Austrian Netherlands kindled intense anger across the classes, including the nobility, clergy, and burghers. The nobility and the burghers protested his administrative reorganization that would restrict their privileges, while the clergy objected to initiatives such as his suppression of monasteries. In 1787 the Estates of Brabant angrily accused Joseph of violating their legal rights, and refused to pay taxes. This resistance across many of the Habsburg realms, though very serious, was almost completely uncoordinated. This shows that despite some integration as a result of the state-building of Joseph and his predecessors, these realms remained loosely connected to each other apart from the commonality of the ruling dynasty.

Joseph was so concerned with reform in the Danubian domains that he consistently neglected the Empire, a trend that had been visible under his mother. The Holy Roman Empire had relatively little meaning for Joseph, since he saw his Danubian territories as his real power base where he could rule more effectively. The German princes were all too aware of Joseph's favoring Austrian over German interests. Schemes such as the acquisition of Bavaria aroused alarm about his intentions, and so the Empire became fertile ground for Friedrich's jockeying influence. Friedrich was able to portray himself as more loyal to common German interests than was Joseph, and so helped form the *Fürstenbund* (a league of princes) in 1785 that expressly excluded Joseph. It was formed in part to thwart Joseph's renewed attempts to trade the Austrian Netherlands for Bavaria. He bungled this plan by reneging on his initial promise to give Luxembourg to the French as payment for their acquiescence to the trade, and so it never came about. Joseph also gained a detrimental reputation as an aggressor after he made war threats—which proved empty—against the Dutch to get them to lift their blockade of commerce on the Scheldt river. His foreign policy disappointments mounted because of the military alliance he signed in 1781 with Ekaterina of Russia as a counterweight to Prussia. This alliance ensnared his monarchy in a pointless war with the Turks in 1788, in which Austria had almost nothing at stake.

In this war, the Austrian military performed well despite a lack of good commanders, testament to the successes of previous decades' reform. Nonetheless, in the very last years of his reign troubles abroad and unrest at home threatened to ruin everything that Joseph had achieved. In 1789 the monarchy entered a crisis perhaps as severe as that of 1740 when Maria

Theresia ascended to the throne. Joseph had to scramble to avert disaster. Belgium exploded in revolt and rebels took Brussels. In 1790 they declared independence. Hungary also rose up, and even Tyrol seethed in annoyance against military conscription. Prussia covertly aided the monarchy's rebels, and gave the impression that it might attack directly after making an alliance with Turkey. Joseph's response to the incipient fragmentation was to roll back many of his reforms. He promised to call the Hungarian diet and be crowned there, and he restored the Croatian diet as well. He enlisted the British to mediate diplomatically with Prussia. Joseph recognized that he had overreached and that his actions had provoked much of the upset. He declared to his brother Leopold, "I no longer dare to have an opinion and put it into effect."[6] In 1788 Joseph had traveled to the Balkans to assume (ineffectual) personal command of the military, but there he fatefully contracted tuberculosis. His body weakened by sickness, he died in February 1790, only 48 years old. He requested as his epitaph, "Here lies a prince whose intentions were pure, but who had the misfortune to see all his plans collapse."[7]

In the end, not all of Joseph's reforms were undone. The tolerance edict, the improvement in peasants' conditions, the advances in public health and general education all remained. The most judicious evaluation of Joseph's reforms has to acknowledge that he achieved much and yet also committed many errors. He furthered the growth of a state that would survive some very serious existential crises in the 128 years remaining to it. His attempt to create a more modern, centralized state was not wrong in principle, but was not carried out in an optimal way. Part of Joseph's problem was that despite his maxim of equality, he still believed in the sovereign power of the dynasty above all. This led him to ignore the fact that power in society did not belong just to the dynasty, but was in fact shared with other institutions such as the nobility. Joseph's neglect of this fact goes back to his distaste for political compromise and his infatuation with the idea of reason. He failed to politick in a way that would build widespread support for the vision of the monarchy he wished to impose. In this regard he was a major contrast to his mother, who worked incrementally to make the improvements she identified as necessary. Joseph's reforms provoked resistance to centralization, and that resistance eventually came to be embodied by nationalist movements. However, it cannot be justifiably alleged that his policies were so Germanizing that they ignited the nationalisms that convulsed the monarchy in the subsequent century. There were many other causes of nationalism's growth. In any case, Joseph was not entirely doctrinaire; he actually approved the use of local languages such as Czech or Hungarian in local administration. Finally, the failures of Joseph's reforms cannot all be laid at his feet alone. Though he always took highest responsibility for his ideas and pushed them the hardest, often they were shared by a small circle of his advisors. Hence the term "Josephinism" for this monarch's ideology of reform belongs not just to one man but to several.

Leopold II (1747–92)

The Josephinist ideology, in its most basic ethos of reform, was shared also by his brother. Leopold became head of the family in 1790 under the worst possible circumstances. Many parts of the monarchy from Belgium to Hungary were aflame with rebellion, yet his main tool of coercion, the Austrian military, was bogged down in the Balkans. His chief ally, France, fell into the initial throes of revolution. That Leopold managed quite artfully to put the pieces back together again was due to his sharp political instincts, which resembled those of his mother rather than his brother, and to his long ruling experience. Over 25 years as the Grand Duke of Tuscany, Leopold amassed a very respectable record of reform—and he achieved it without Joseph's absolutist tendencies. Leopold collaborated closely with other ruling institutions in the duchy, in some areas pursuing a decentralization of power. In 1784, for example, he drew up a constitution that would have created a representative assembly. Joseph forbade this step, however, much to Leopold's anger. Leopold succeeded in introducing other reforms such as a new penal code in 1786 which was the first in Europe to abolish capital punishment. In his economic policies, he was the first ruler in Europe to proclaim free trade in grains. He also undertook measures to relax censorship, improve the peasants' lot, and provide for public health. Leopold was an intelligent, well-educated man who understood the value of compromise. He sincerely disliked Joseph for his domineering attitudes and vetoes of the Tuscan reforms.

Once he took over the throne, Leopold undid some of Joseph's most inflammatory policies, but continued with other reforms. He sought to defuse the anger over new tax regulations by revoking them and letting the estates continue to collect taxes. He ended the military conscription in Tyrol that had antagonized people there. He retreated from the agricultural reforms that had upset landlords, though he preserved most protections for peasants. He set about mollifying the various provincial diets. He promised to respect Hungary's traditional constitution, and wisely had himself crowned king in both Hungary and Bohemia, with the official ceremonies Joseph had always refused. He also reversed Joseph's orders making German the sole administrative language, and he restored a number of monasteries to appease the irate clergy. These strategic retreats were accompanied by several advances, such as doing away with Joseph's restrictions on free speech, releasing political prisoners, and making plans to increase towns' representation in the provincial diets. As a result of all this astute maneuvering, Leopold managed to quell the most dangerous revolts in Belgium and Hungary already in 1790.

In foreign policy, too, Leopold trod carefully, working to extricate the monarchy from the mounting threats against it. One reason why he was able to end the Belgian revolt so swiftly was that negotiations with

Prussia and Turkey freed up his armies. Leopold signed an armistice with the Ottomans, and he agreed to give up the most recent territorial gains. He also agreed to the Convention of Reichenbach with Prussia in 1790 by which Prussia agreed not to aid revolts within his monarchy. While these potential conflicts were thereby pacified, Leopold still had to keep his eye on the growing revolution in France. Since the escalation of events in Paris in July 1789, neither Joseph nor Leopold had particularly feared the revolutionary implications for the rest of Europe. Joseph's troubles cannot be equated with Louis XVI's since the latter's involved a mass uprising of the populace, while most of the resistance to Joseph's policies came from the elite. Moreover, Joseph maintained that he had already implemented many of the reforms now being proposed in France. He declared that the Habsburg monarchy would remain neutral. Leopold even commented favorably on the early days of the revolution, seeing it as a model for cooperation between the sovereign and the populace that would result in a more just, peaceful, and beneficent order for all states that followed France's example.

What complicated Joseph's and Leopold's response to the nascent revolution was the fact that their sister Marie Antoinette was queen of France. Leopold advised that she encourage her husband to accept the new proposed constitution. Louis XVI refused and fled Paris in June 1791. Leopold then began modifying his position out of solidarity with his sister. Together with Prussia's king Friedrich Wilhelm II, he issued the Declaration of Pillnitz in August 1791 which called for Louis to be returned to the throne. This document was motivated by Leopold's cognizance that a France in upheaval would no longer be a strong ally for his monarchy. The declaration did not call for immediate war; it was a defensive alliance, and symbolized Leopold's prudent, cautious policy toward the revolution. Unfortunately, that prudence dissipated quickly once Leopold was gone. He died quite suddenly, of natural causes, in March 1792. His son and successor Franz would decisively halt the monarchy's reformist trajectory of the preceding decades.

Dynastic strategies

Maria Theresia was staggeringly successful at dynastic reproduction: over 19 years she gave birth to 16 children, 10 of whom lived into adulthood. One of the most remarkable things about her as a ruler was that she helped raise all these children yet wisely governed a huge monarchy at the same time. Her splendid marriage helps explain both her fecundity and how she was able to manage motherhood and rulership. Her husband Franz Stephan was from an old but not especially powerful dynasty, which meant that the other German princes were not worried about his house uniting with the Habsburgs. As the price for recognizing Karl VI's Pragmatic Sanction,

France made Franz Stephan give up his family's traditional possession of Lorraine, and instead he got the Grand Duchy of Tuscany. He then became the Holy Roman Emperor after Karl Albrecht of Bavaria died, but in practice it was really Maria Theresia who ruled. Franz Stephan acted instead as the paterfamilias for the couple's ever-increasing brood, and he also successfully managed the family's finances, accumulating a large fortune. As testament of Maria Theresia's and Franz Stephan's genuine affection for one another, they shared a bedroom, which was unusual for royal couples of the day.

Maria Theresia used her profusion of offspring very smartly. To solidify the new alliance with France, she married five of her children to Bourbons, most famously of course Marie Antoinette to Louis XVI. Maria Theresia kept up a regular correspondence with Marie Antoinette so that the latter would work for Habsburg interests within the French court. Several other daughters took on important political roles as well. As but two examples, Maria Carolina as queen of Naples largely ran the government there, and Maria Christina was coruler of the Austrian Netherlands. Her children regarded Maria Theresia as a stern but loving mother. She expected strict obedience (personally administering lashes once to Joseph when he was young), and Joseph's first wife admitted that she was afraid of her mother-in-law. At the same time, however, there was an unmistakable maternal warmth about Maria Theresia that has made her the best-loved of all Habsburg rulers. An example of her personal touch was when she rushed to Vienna's Burgtheater in 1768 to announce (with a grandmother's joy and pride), "der Poldl hat an Buam!"—Viennese dialect for "Leopold has a son!" Leopold was equally prolific (his marriage also produced 16 children), and it was his line that guaranteed the Habsburg continuance, since Joseph had no sons or daughters who survived to adulthood.

One of the profoundest changes that took place in the dynasty's rule during this period was with its claims to legitimacy and loyalty. There was a distinct and very of-its-time evolution away from a religious-based legitimation toward a state-based one. The trends within the dynasty mirrored those in intellectual and cultural life across Europe generally, since during the Enlightenment religion came increasingly to be seen as a personal matter, devotion expressed inwardly rather than in outward, Baroque flamboyance. The influence of Jansenism was important, though never totally dominant. Jansenist ideas were associated with rationalist Cartesian philosophy, inner devotion, and the decline of religious politics. Even from the Church itself grew the idea that reason had to govern religion, and the more superstitious forms of worship diminished. Maria Theresia was the pivot in the dynasty's evolution: though she was raised in the Baroque culture of Karl VI and continued to exemplify aspects of that world, she also exhibited traits more in common with Enlightenment ideas. Her traditional attitudes can be seen in her continuing belief in divine right and in the Catholic character of her monarchy. She was an unrepentant anti-Semite, and still quite vigorously distrusted Protestants, forbidding them from taking degrees at universities. She even rejected a plan for a scientific academy because she feared it might open the door to heresy.

The changes in the dynasty's religious attitudes, however, are more striking than the continuities. Those changes are visible at both symbolic and practical levels. Symbolically, Maria Theresia retreated from the earlier ideology of *clementia*, which she associated with the Baroque tradition of extravagant display. She blamed such traditions for the spendthrift ways and lackadaisical management that had put the monarchy in such a bad financial state under her father. Though Maria Theresia was herself devoted to many of the old rites, she and particularly her successors encouraged the decline of the Marian cult and the excessive religious feast days. An example of the practical changes that Maria Theresia wrought is her curtailing of the dynasty's formerly close identification with the Jesuits. While in the earlier part of her reign her personal confessor was a Jesuit, by the end it was a priest of somewhat Jansenist leanings. She also took away the Jesuits' control of censorship, which the two Ferdinands had given them in the previous century. This action went along with the breaking of the Jesuits' monopoly on education and intellectual life, and led to the greater opening of the Danubian domains to intellectual trends from abroad. Joseph, who was far more concerned than his mother to promote a religious practice based on reason, furthered many of these trends, including expelling the Jesuits completely from Habsburg domains.

As religion declined as an ideological support for the dynasty, notions of the state and particularly of service took its place. Divine right became less of a legitimation, and instead the dynasty believed it was entitled to rule based on its service to its subjects. Again Maria Theresia embodies the transition. She wrote that "an almighty hand singled me out for this position without move or desire of my own," obviously alluding to her authority as God-given. Yet she added that "my duty was not to myself personally but only to the public," and that she hoped to be worthy of her special position not just for her own sake, but for those whom God "has set under me."[8] She here plainly expressed the belief that her success as a ruler should be judged on the basis of how well she worked for the public. Joseph went a step further in this conception of the monarch serving the subjects by insisting that the subjects themselves must serve for the benefit of the whole polity. No longer treating the mass populace as an inert producer of wealth, the state that grew under Maria Theresia and Joseph worked earnestly for the benefit of the population as a whole, as seen in the many agrarian, public health, and education reforms. In return, the rulers expected that the population would be loyal to and work for the state.

It was Joseph who sought to replace the archaic personal monarchy with the impersonal state. He declared in a political memorandum of 1761: "Everything exists for the state; this word contains everything, so all who live in it should come together to promote its interests."[9] In this quotation, the monarch himself has been elided. This suggests how the dynasty in the eighteenth century embarked on a campaign of securing a new loyalty based on an identification of the subjects with the governing structures that served the dynasty and the polity. The attempt to bind the heterogeneous peoples together by transferring their loyalties to the overarching state institutions, with the dynasty at their head, was never fully thought through, and certainly never fully realized. But to some extent, the institutions successfully fulfilled this goal. The bureaucracy and the military did integrate people from across the territories into the service of the state and dynasty. The expansion of primary education was also supposed to inculcate a sense of loyalty among the subjects: it was a very concrete example of the state serving them, and therefore deserving their allegiance. Intellectuals such as Joseph von Sonnenfels, who advised both Maria Theresia and Joseph, argued that the state could indeed generate patriotism, and would thereby create a people. Religion was no longer central to this justification of the dynasty's rule, which was now predicated more on good governance and state service. Admittedly the state during this time was still small, and its integration of its subjects into a new relationship of loyalty and legitimacy with the dynasty was fragmentary. Nonetheless, a major change in thinking had taken place.

One part of the integration process that could create a loyal populace was, in Joseph's vision, an overarching public culture in the German language. German was not adopted specifically to benefit the native German speakers of the monarchy, but rather because it was already the primary language of the dynasty, many of the elite, and of the most educated parts of the monarchy's population. As Joseph himself said, "The German language is the universal language of my empire. Why should I negotiate laws and business with one of my provinces in their own language? I am the ruler of the German Empire and therefore the other states which I possess are provinces which must form one complete state, of which I am the head."[10] This quotation reveals that Joseph's motivation for "Germanization" was not nationalist but rather centralist; it was pragmatic, in his view, to standardize and centralize his rule by promoting the German language. It also reveals the personal and patrimonial residues in Joseph's conception of his monarchy. It was not a unified state, since what bound "the other states which I possess" was himself, the monarch. But it was also evident to him that German culture should become one of these unifiers. Hence Joseph throughout his rule promoted German art, such as the German national theater in Vienna, as part of his desire to inculcate a unified and unifying public culture in German. A famous example is that Mozart's opera *Die Entführung aus dem Serail* was written at Joseph's behest, thereby giving rise to what has been called one of the first German operas.

Vienna and the court still acted as the monarchy's unifying cultural center, but the court's lavishness declined from its Baroque peak. Ostentatious display glorifying the monarch diminished precipitously. Instead, the court was more commonly supposed to demonstrate the ruler's enlightened characteristics, not just through symbolic artistic representations, but through tangible achievements such as reformist policies. There was thus an *image* of Enlightenment that served to configure legitimacy, an image that was very different from the Baroque's over-the-top religiosity. The court became more of a private matter for the family. Maria Theresia downsized court staff and functions as part of her cost-cutting inclinations. In her reign the court was almost bourgeois in some ways, much less pompous than under her father. Joseph then very intentionally further downsized the court as part of his simplification ethos, retaining just 92 people in his household as archduke.

Cultural patronage reflected this scaled-down conception of the court. The musical culture of the court also became more private; for instance, Joseph played three times a week in private concerts with the court composer Salieri and a few other musicians. Another example of how the function of court life changed can be seen through portraiture. By the middle 1700s, the portraits of Habsburg family members are less allegorical or self-important, more likely instead to depict the ruler in private life, surrounded by family members. There are several rather domestic portraits of Franz Stephan, Maria Theresia, and their large brood. The 1769 dual portrait of Joseph and Leopold by Pompeo Batoni is likewise somewhat modest in its style (despite the Roman allusions to Joseph's status as emperor). The two young brothers are depicted not with great majesty, but rather with a restrained, uniformed dignity. There was of course more self-consciously impressive cultural sponsorship. Maria Theresia's rebuilding of Schönbrunn Palace forever associates her with Rococo style. For Leopold's coronation in Prague, Mozart's opera *La clemenza di Tito* was commissioned and performed. The reference to clemency in the opera's title also shows how aspects of the traditional dynastic ideology retained some life. On the whole, Vienna during this time enjoyed its most glittering cultural era yet. It had a population of over 200,000 in 1785, and much of the high nobility continued to build extravagant palaces both inside and outside the city.

The legitimating idea of service also largely redefined the function of the ruler in the era. Just as religion lost much of its earlier utility for the dynasty, so too, in a common contemporary trend, did the monarch become desanctified. The older supernatural conceptions of rulership receded, partially replaced by notions of a contract between ruler and ruled. Where Maria Theresia still relied on some idea of divine right, it was only vestigial to Joseph and Leopold. Characteristically, Joseph sought to rationalize this religious exaltation of the ruler by exalting the state instead. He wrote that "serving God is inseparable from serving the state," conflating divinely given authority with that which comes from being the highest servant of the state.[11] In his formulation, the supremacy of the dynasty was supplanted by the supremacy of the state, but the ruler was still deserving of strict obedience because he (and by extension the dynasty) was responsible for the welfare of all the public. This contractual conception was clearer in

Joseph's rule than in Maria Theresia's: very Hobbesian, it held that the sovereign's power should be absolute, based on his great responsibility of serving his subjects. Joseph's overriding principle of efficiency further justified unitary rule.

There was also a change here in the old idea of the Habsburg mission. Less grounded now in religious duties of ensuring confessional homogeneity and combating Islam, the ruler and his dynasty took on instead another burden, namely sacrificing themselves for the state and for the well-being of their subjects. Maria Theresia alluded to this idea with her motherly lament at having to marry her daughters off for political reasons. So rather than the dynasty incarnating the realm, as in previous centuries, the realm was now conceived as separate, served not just by the dynasty but by the subjects too. Even its members thought of the dynasty as less unique (in comparison to other European ruling families) and less holy (in comparison to centuries past), yet it was still elect because of its work for the public. Like that public, though, the dynasty's members in the eighteenth century understood themselves as having private lives that they sometimes had to subjugate in service.

Maria Theresia was certainly new in the Habsburg imagery of the ruler since she was the first (and only) paramount sovereign in the dynasty who was female. This naturally explains her iconographic presentation as the mother of all her subjects, an idea that she herself adopted. She claimed in her *Political Testament* that "I belong to my peoples," and called herself the "first mother" of her realms. This motherly conception was not purely tender, since it came with the idea that she had the authority to command her peoples for their own good, "raising" them in their best interests, which she identified. As an obvious feminization of the medieval representation of the king as father, Maria Theresia's ruling image still presumed a personal relationship between sovereign and subjects. Joseph, again exemplifying contemporary trends, depersonalized the monarchical image via his emphasis on the ruler as the servant of the state. The family metaphor attenuated, replaced instead by the figure of the rationalist sovereign whose governing ideals were utility and efficiency. The change in the ruler's role was thus the move from parent rearing children under Maria Theresia, to supreme administrator directing dutiful citizens under Joseph.

In many though not all ways, Joseph and Leopold consciously jettisoned the hoary traditions of kingship. Joseph in particular believed that reason led one to reject the older, Baroque ceremonial, which he detested. He therefore did away with many of the pretentious court functions of earlier Habsburgs. This is one reason why he refused to have himself crowned king in Bohemia and Hungary. He not only had a personal distaste for ceremony, but believed that it was inappropriate for the monarch as state servant. After 1787 he in fact forbade people to kneel before him, proclaiming that no man should kneel before another, but only before God. His modest style can be seen in that he chose to live not in one of his palaces, but in a relatively

simple house in Vienna's Augarten park. Leopold likewise believed that
nobility was only a social construct and that all people were truly equal
by birth. He, too, espoused the necessity of a social contract, declaring
that the sovereign must share power with a legislative body, and would
forfeit his position if he broke the contract. Leopold's ideas of humanity
and equality were expressed in his instructions for the education of his own
children, which included the ideas that "princes must above all be convinced
of the equality of people," "that everyone has the same rights," and that
princes must have as "their sole passion [. . .] the humanity, compassion, and
desire to make their people happy."[12] Regardless of Joseph's and Leopold's
insistence on equality, they did not remake the social order by trying to
erase noble status; again, they were reformers, not radicals.

Achieving this ideal of ruling in the best interests of all the subjects
consequently required making the institutions of that rule as effective as
possible. Maria Theresia and Joseph have thus been called by some the
true founders of the Austrian state. The burst of "modernization" in the
middle decades of the eighteenth century gave the Habsburg monarchy
institutions reasonably advanced for their time. Centralization of power
was achieved in large part through the growth of a central bureaucracy, in
the Habsburg lands as elsewhere. One estimate has 6,000 members of the
state bureaucracy in 1740, 10,000 in 1762, and 20,000 in 1782.[13] These
numbers increasingly came from people of non-noble classes, which helped
expand the regime's base of support. Joseph's travels around the monarchy
convinced him that the professionalism of local officials was often low,
which inspired his mission to improve the bureaucracy. Thus training was
improved, pay increased and tied more to merit, and a pension system
introduced. These bureaucrats were not personal servants of the monarch,
as in previous eras, but instead served the state. This idea is unequivocal
in Joseph's so-called Pastoral Letter of 1783 in which he gave instructions
to all state officials. Here again he stressed the idea of service, writing that
"he who does not have love for the fatherland and his fellow citizens, who
does not find himself inspired with a special zeal for preserving the good,"
would not succeed in the bureaucracy.[14]

Additionally, the growth of the bureaucracy formed part of the
movement from indirect rule via other power elites to direct rule by the
central state. For instance, the expanded bureaucracy and judiciary, as
well as the peasant reforms, all went some way to reducing the nobility's
administrative authority even on their own demesnes. Eroded also were the
powers of the estates and the particularistic constitutions of the monarchy's
various realms. The dynasty during this period was gradually moving
away from its older supports, the nobility and the Church, instead relying
increasingly on the bureaucracy and the military. This was a trend with
roots in the previous century, and it would continue into the subsequent
one. Direct rule helped the state extract more resources, as in Maria
Theresia's taxation schemes by which the estates would grant taxes in

ten-year intervals. She also reorganized the middle levels of administration to improve tax collection and reduce the estates' influence over it. Taxes in general increased on all classes including the nobility, clergy, bourgeoisie, and peasantry. The reduction of the nobility's and clergy's special tax privileges is another example of the unification and homogenization of the polity and its institutions. Thanks to such measures, the state's income roughly doubled in the first decade of Maria Theresia's reign.

Higher incomes naturally gave the state more resources for expanding its competencies, a development easily traceable with the military. The monarchy could field around 150,000 men in 1740 and some 300,000 in 1790. Military expenditures at the end of Joseph's reign accounted for 65 percent of the total state budget, though characteristically for Habsburg history there was never enough money to pay for it all.[15] Nonetheless, the reforms undertaken in Maria Theresia's and Joseph's reigns made the Habsburg army the second largest in Europe after Russia's. The increased tax revenues in turn supported massively larger conscription. That conscription itself symbolizes the augmented institutions of the dynasty's rule, since it depended on the bureaucracy to keep track of the population eligible for military service. The army was also one of the most successful engines of centralization. More than ever before, the central state was responsible for recruiting, training, and financing the military, sidelining the estates' former authority in those activities. The military grew to perform the crucial integrative role within the heterogeneous realms that it would fulfill until the monarchy's end. An example is that after the 1740s Hungarian generals started rising through the ranks of the army, and Hungarian soldiers began fighting for the monarchy outside the borders of Hungary. In this way one of the least integrated parts of the monarchy became more tightly bound to the center.

It is important to affirm nonetheless that this centralization was partial, and that it had some negative consequences. Centralization was largely limited to the military and the still modestly sized bureaucracy. It affected Austria and Bohemia much more than it did Hungary. And while the court in Vienna did encourage the growth of an aristocracy that belonged to the *Gesamtstaat*, the nobility's interests could remain local as well, such that an aristocrat in Lombardy would have little affinity for, nor interest in, an aristocrat from Transylvania. Similarly, though an ideology of belonging to the supranational state did germinate during Joseph's reign, his aggressive push for centralization stimulated particularistic and localist resistance. So while Joseph held out a model of what a more unified Habsburg state might look like, he also encountered the beginnings of what resistance to that unified state could look like, namely nationally based movements for autonomy. Regardless, even if the vision of a central state subsuming the different realms into one monarchy remained an aspiration rather than an achievement, Maria Theresia and Joseph established a lasting credo by which the dynasty recognized that it had to protect the welfare and interests of the peasants, in addition to those of the magnates. This was part of the attempt to broaden the social supports for the dynasty's legitimacy.

The most important legacy of this period in the dynasty's history was these improved institutional structures that would preserve its rule into the twentieth century. There was estimable progress in other areas too. The Habsburg realms on the whole enjoyed substantial economic growth during this time. Proto-industries bloomed in Bohemia and Upper Austria, often in textiles. The monarchy admittedly missed out on British- and French-style overseas colonization because of its deficient navy. Nonetheless, Trieste grew as the monarchy's major port, and developed a number of small industries. Transportation networks improved and internal tolls were reduced to promote commerce. Literacy grew, not just in the cities but in the countryside as well. Most advanced were Lombardy and Belgium, urbanized, commercial economies that supplied taxes to far-off Vienna but otherwise remained distant and disconnected. The Danubian domains were mostly rural, with Galicia and Transylvania the most backward. And while the onerous *robot* was reduced and peasants' legal rights protected, in many areas the nobility still had great sway. In parts of Hungary, nearly half the land was controlled by just 28 noble families. While this magnate class was becoming somewhat Germanized, it continued to rule over a dizzyingly pluralistic hodge-podge of ethnicities, languages, and even faiths. That pluralism posed few challenges during Maria Theresia's reign, but already in this time, shoots of more assertive national consciousness were beginning to sprout in some areas such as Bohemia. At Leopold's death, the monarchy's population of 26 million people made it the second largest in Europe. Hungary accounted for nearly half that total, with the Bohemian crownlands and the Austrian territories adding another 20 percent each.

Much of what was positive in these developments can be credited to Maria Theresia's leadership. With her, the Habsburg dynasty reached an unequaled apogee of good monarchical governance. She savvily wielded the power given to her, from rescuing the monarchy at her reign's outset, to selecting excellent advisors to manage the task of remedying the monarchy's problems. It was precisely her gradual, conservative approach that enabled progress in rationalizing administrative structures, strengthening the financial base of her state, and improving the welfare of her subjects. This reformist period, it is true, unleashed forces which the dynasty never mastered. Its compromise path of preserving existing structures while encouraging progressive developments was hazardous, since it antagonized both traditionalists (the most conservative nobles) and liberals (for whom the reforms did not go far enough). Maria Theresia managed this contradiction with greater skill than Joseph did; it was largely because of his impolitic impatience that his reforms engendered so much resistance and had to be rolled back.

Where posterity has judged Maria Theresia so positively, Joseph has to be rescued from the harshest critiques of his reign. Those critiques brand him as a blinkered despot trying to meld an unwieldy patchwork of realms into a modern unitary state, when in fact they were far too diverse ever to be so unified. He has been accused of sowing the ultimate collapse of the supranational monarchy in the twentieth century by sparking the centrifugal forces of nationalism with his Germanization campaign. Even his emphasis on improving agriculture has been alleged to have retarded the monarchy's economic development, consigning it to agrarian backwardness in the industrializing nineteenth century. Those charges are exaggerated, but it is undeniable that Joseph tried to do too much too fast. It is also undeniable that his enlightened convictions about equality and greater liberty sat uneasily against his despotic tendencies. It must nonetheless be recognized that however clumsy Joseph's actual politics may have been, his motivations (as he himself suggested) were often good. He did want to create a state that would rule more effectively in the best interests of his subjects, at least as those in power identified those interests. He cannot fairly be faulted for being an idealist, though he can be criticized for his dogmatism and lack of political finesse. The misfortune for himself and for the future of the dynasty was that he recognized his mistakes too late, since after Leopold's brief rule, the vital reformist impetus was lost for generations.

CHAPTER TEN

Revolution and reaction
(1792–1848)

"There are new ideas around, that I cannot, and never shall, approve of," Franz [Francis] I declared to schoolteachers in 1821. "Stay away from these and keep to what you know." This was not advice but an order. "Who serves me," he said, "must teach what I command. He who cannot do that, or comes along with new ideas, can leave—or I will remove him."[1] This quotation illuminates the deeply conservative core of Franz's character. He was suspicious of new ideas, jealous of his status and authority, and demanded unthinking obedience. This was the man who confronted the immense turmoil of the French Revolution and the Napoleonic Wars, clinging to old notions as tightly as he could, trying to remain impervious to the flood of change. As head of the most august dynasty in Europe, Franz has come to symbolize Habsburg hostility to revolutionary popular sovereignty, and the rejection of his three predecessors' reformist spirit.

He was not always such a reactionary. In his younger years he supported agricultural reform, for example. But the upheaval of the Revolution, and the execution of his aunt and her husband the king, horrified him. While his desire to protect his own domains and his authority was understandable, his biggest mistake came after France was finally defeated. After 1815 together with his chief minister Metternich he tried to rewind history as if the Revolution had never happened. The system Metternich created to restore order in Austria and Europe did preserve Habsburg authority, including for Franz's feeble-minded son and successor Ferdinand I. Yet because Franz was trapped by his intellectual limitations and excessive attachment to tradition, he failed to see that the forces of change the Revolution had unleashed were a genie that could not be put back in the bottle. In their stubborn resistance to "new ideas," Franz and Metternich ossified the dynasty.

Franz I (II) (1768–1835)

Franz has dual Roman numerals because he was the second so-named emperor of the Holy Roman Empire, but the first of Austria. One of the defining characteristics of his reign—as for so many Habsburgs—was tenacity. His first two decades on the throne were consumed by wars against revolutionary and Napoleonic France, wars he usually lost until the final triumph. And though he outlasted Napoleon, in all other regards Franz was too small a man for his position. He was described by an observer at the Congress of Vienna as physically slight, as "broken and old" (this when he was in his later 40s), "with a round back and knees bent inward." This observer, an emissary from the Republic of Geneva, went on to say that Franz seemed very shy and awkward, not particularly intelligent, that, in short, "he resembled more a petty bourgeois from a provincial city than a sovereign."[2] This impression is supported by Friedrich von Amerling's 1832 portrait of Franz, in which he looks like a small-time clerk incongruously swathed in royal robes, staring with a strange mixture of arrogance and suspicion at the viewer. Though he was not dumb, he was definitely narrow-minded. His younger brothers Karl and Johann surpassed him in intellectual ability, for which he always resented them. His uncle Joseph and his father Leopold observed that despite the enlightened education they tried to give him, Franz remained rather lethargic.

His ruling principles, though reactionary, were not despotic. For example, he believed in the rule of law, and sponsored important reforms of the legal code in 1803 and 1811. His convictions always returned to the primacy of royal power, which drove a centralizing attitude in his government, and explain his consistent emphasis on obedience rather than innovation. That he was not without some political shrewdness is shown by the mere fact of his survival—and by his selection of Metternich as his chief minister. And while in so many ways he was inadequate as a ruler, Franz (Figure 10.1) did have his positive qualities. One of the most surprising was how deeply his subjects loved him. Perhaps in accordance with some bourgeois streak in his character, he knew how to relate to common people. In Vienna he held regular open-door sessions where anyone could come and tell him about their problems, and during the city's cholera epidemic in 1831, he went around visiting hospitals rather than fleeing the city. He often spoke in Viennese dialect and had an acerbic sense of humor. He was also known to be generous with those in need while he himself lived a somewhat modest lifestyle, avoiding lavish expenditure at court. He was a fairly hard worker, a serious collector of art and books, and he traveled widely around his dominions. Not only his people but his four wives had great affection for him, which he sincerely reciprocated.

That the progressive development of the monarchy during his predecessors' reigns ended so abruptly in Franz's time can be explained in part by his

FIGURE 10.1 *Franz I, by Friedrich von Amerling (1832). In the collection of the Kunsthistorisches Museum. Image courtesy of the Bridgeman Art Library.*

own political inexperience in responding to the French Revolution. It was only a few weeks after Franz succeeded to the throne in March 1792, when he was 23 years old, that conflict broke out with revolutionary France. The subsequent series of wars involved shifting coalitions of Prussia, Britain, the Netherlands, and Russia against France; Austria was the longest-standing opponent on the continent and fought in all the major conflicts. Though the revolution certainly posed a threat to established monarchical regimes, Franz's characteristically unsubtle response was categorical hostility, exacerbated by the executions of Louis XVI and his aunt Marie Antoinette in 1793. His and his ministers' aims were nothing less than to suppress the revolution and return to the *status quo ante*. Thus Austria became not just a polity in the struggle, but an ideological symbol: it represented the resistance of the old aristocratic order against Jacobinism.

In both the military and ideological campaigns, the Habsburgs were repeatedly thwarted by Austrian armies' battlefield losses. Already at Valmy in September 1792 French forces repelled a poorly commanded Prussian/Austrian force. France took Belgium and parts of the Rhineland in 1794, and Prussia signed a separate peace in 1795. Franz participated in the planning of some of the Austrian assaults, but demonstrated that he was no military man. Archduke Karl, the Habsburgs' best military commander, won some victories against French armies, but could not compete with the rapid rise of Napoleon after 1796. In that year the Corsican genius won impressive victories in Italy, pushing the Austrians out of Lombardy, and later captured the key Austrian fortress of Mantua. This led to the treaty of Campo Formio in 1797, by which Franz had to surrender Belgium and parts of Italy, but gained Venice and its territories in Istria and Dalmatia. Campo Formio was not a decisive setback for the Habsburgs, and Franz just bided his time until the next attack. The opportunity came in 1799 with Napoleon's misadventure in Egypt. The War of the Second Coalition proved no more successful than the previous one for Austria. In 1800 Austrian armies were again defeated by the French at Marengo and Hohenlinden, which led to the treaty of Lunéville, wherein Franz had to acknowledge French gains in Italy and possession of the Rhineland. All during this first decade of war the Habsburg monarchy was in serious financial trouble. It amassed huge debts, and depended on vital subsidies from the British for the war effort.

Just as Franz was committed to combating the revolution abroad, so he and his coterie of conservative ministers were determined to stamp out any stirrings of revolt at home. Their campaign took the form of heavy police surveillance and censorship that clamped down on intellectual and political life in the monarchy. Newspapers and journals were shut down and groups of scholars and intellectuals were broken up. Franz evinced a particular distrust of the masons by closing a number of their lodges. Fearful that the French example might stir up the peasantry to press for a complete abolition of feudal agricultural obligations, Franz ditched even some of his own ideas on reducing the burden of the *robot*. This crackdown was measured and never became outright tyranny. Franz and his advisors did not arbitrarily violate laws in order to root out revolutionary sentiment. There were relatively few political prisoners, punishments such as executions were infrequent, and jail terms were usually not cruel. The reaction might have been harsher but for the fact that there was not widespread revolutionary sentiment in the monarchy's realms. Most nobles understandably opposed the Revolution. Though there was some sympathy for French liberal ideas among the monarchy's educated classes, the execution of the French king and queen appalled many. All in all, the Revolution so overturned the existing social order that even most liberals within the Austrian monarchy viewed it as too extreme. It was thus not too difficult for Franz's regime to suppress ferment among the lower classes, and retain the firm partnership with the nobility both to resist revolution and later to construct the postwar order.

One major casualty of the wars against France was German unity. There was for a time in the years right around 1800 a wave of German patriotism that the Habsburgs tried to attach to Franz. That enthusiasm for German solidarity did not translate into political cooperation among the princes, however; the Empire never managed to cohere in the war against France because of many competing interests. Besides the rivalry between Austria and Prussia, many of the other German states such as Bavaria and Württemberg veered off into France's orbit, seeing Napoleon as their protector against the Habsburgs and Hohenzollerns. Moreover, Austria's repeated losses to the French convinced many German rulers that the Habsburgs could neither lead nor protect them. Franz in any case paid relatively little attention to the Empire. Like his predecessors, he consistently neglected it in favor of his own dynastic interests. Thus after Lunéville Napoleon and his foreign minister Talleyrand were at least as influential in German affairs as were any of the German dynasties.

Several events then provoked the final, flailing expiration of the Holy Roman Empire. In 1804 Napoleon was declared emperor of France, which was a terrible affront to Franz, who could not abide that this Corsican upstart would place himself on a level equal to the prestige of the Habsburgs. Franz was also justifiably worried that Napoleon would either take the German imperial title or dissolve the German empire, which would then leave the Habsburgs actually inferior in rank. Thus in August 1804 Franz proclaimed an Austrian Empire, giving himself an ambitious new title without changing much else about his realms. In fact, in his proclamation, Franz explicitly recognized that he ruled over several states, and promised that he would not change any of their constitutions. The legality of this unilateral proclamation was questionable, but it received solid support from the aristocracy and the rest of his subjects, even in Hungary. Franz's assumption of a new imperial title was a naked play for dynastic honor, to ensure that he would remain an emperor regardless of what Bonaparte called himself.

This new Austrian Empire did not fare well in fresh hostilities against Napoleon, the War of the Third Coalition (which also included Britain and Russia) that started in 1805. After a crushing victory over Austria at Ulm in October 1805, Napoleon advanced on Vienna and occupied it in November. The royal family fled, and Napoleon made his headquarters at Schönbrunn. Archduke Karl brought round an army from Italy, and linked up with Russian troops under Kutuzov. They met Napoleon in battle at Austerlitz in December 1805, which became one of Austria's worst defeats. The terms of the subsequent treaty of Pressburg were onerous: Napoleon's allies Bavaria and Württemberg were raised to the status of kingdoms and received a number of Habsburg possessions such as Tirol and Vorarlberg. Franz also lost Venice and the Adriatic territories he had gained in 1797. Together with the French occupation of Vienna, this was a terrible humiliation. It was compounded in July of 1806 when 16 imperial princes organized into the new Confederation of the Rhine under Napoleon's protection, and Napoleon demanded that the imperial crown be delivered to him. This for Franz was the writing on the wall; rather than let Napoleon seize the German imperial title, Franz decided to end the Empire altogether. Thus on 1 August Franz declared the Holy Roman Empire dead at the age of 1006. This act demonstrated a streak of realism on Franz's part. He knew that he could not fulfill his duties to defend the title nor the Empire from Napoleon. He also desperately needed peace, and felt that he had to focus on the interests of his Hereditary Lands. Though he did relinquish the imperial title held by his family for most of the preceding 400 years, he did not relinquish the symbolism: he moved all the old imperial relics and regalia to Vienna, to the seat of the new dynastic empire.

In the years after Austerlitz, there was a halting move toward reforms in the Austrian regime. Much of the impetus came from Franz's brothers Karl, who instituted some military improvements, and Johann, who created nationally based militias within the army as part of a broader effort to foment an Austro-German patriotism in support of the monarchy. There was also a campaign by the foreign minister Stadion to relax censorship and liberalize slightly as part of rallying popular support. There were other pressing problems, such as the monarchy's disastrous financial state, but these reforms remained incomplete because Franz himself never strongly backed them. He was actively suspicious of his brothers' efforts. As Napoleon's war in the Iberian Peninsula heated up in 1808, it became clear to Franz and his brothers that another fight between Austria and France was coming. Prussia and Russia would not join, so Austria ended up fighting alone, albeit with British financial assistance. The conflict proved short and disheartening. Though Karl did inflict a rare battlefield defeat on Napoleon at Aspern in May 1809, his cautious tactics failed to capitalize, and Napoleon then won a hard-fought victory at Wagram six weeks later. Franz personally watched this battle from the sidelines, and left the world a reminder of his sodden phlegmatism when, as Austria's defeat became clear, he supposedly remarked, "Now we can just go home."[3]

Karl then made a truce without Franz's approval—and Franz blamed the disastrous war on his brothers and Stadion, who were all dismissed. Vienna was again occupied by French troops, and the Habsburgs were forced into another humiliating peace. They surrendered parts of Upper Austria and Salzburg to Bavaria, and parts of Galicia to the Grand Duchy of Warsaw. Parts of Carinthia, Carniola, and all of Dalmatia went to Napoleon's newly created Adriatic puppet state known as the Illyrian Provinces. Austria was thereby dismembered, losing its access to the sea. There was even talk of Napoleon's compelling Franz to abdicate, though such did not come to pass. Austria was reduced to a French satellite, its army forcibly limited to 150,000. Worst of all for Franz, he had to marry his daughter Marie-Louise to Napoleon to seal the armistice.

In the government shakeup resultant to this treaty, Franz recalled his ambassador in Paris to become his new foreign minister. This was Klemens von Metternich, the man who would become synonymous with the next 40 years of Habsburg history. Praised and reviled since his own time, Metternich was an unashamed reactionary, a skilled diplomat, an unrepentant philanderer, and a haughty political puppetmaster. As a young man he had been imbued with Enlightenment ideas, but came to privilege reason primarily as it would serve the state and the nobility. He therefore rejected the ideas of revolution and equality because they would undermine the existing social order and the monarchy's exercise of power. He was no crude despot, since he believed a monarch should uphold laws, nor did he ever supplant Franz as the actual ruler of the Habsburg monarchy. He was also not quite as sharp as he considered himself, and as the years went on he betrayed an inability to reexamine his positions in the light of changing circumstances. His immediate goals in 1809 were to win the monarchy a period of peace during which it could rebuild, and then resume the battle against the French menace. His strategy was not to mobilize popular energy—as the Revolution had done, and even as Archduke Johann had suggested—but to rely on slippery statecraft and the rock-solid support of the aristocracy.

Franz was persuaded by Metternich's approach, and the two formed a remarkable working relationship. That relationship was not free from disagreements, and Metternich never had uncontested control in either foreign or, much less, in domestic policy. But Franz's trust of his most famous minister was rooted in their deep, shared conservatism. Metternich expressed his vision in this summary he wrote for Franz: "Your Majesty is the central point, the only true, surviving representative of an old order of things built upon an eternal, unchangeable law. In this irreplaceable role, all eyes are directed at your highest Majesty."[4] To preserve this central role for the dynasty and Austria, Metternich cannily pulled many strings at home and abroad. Domestically, he limited free speech rights, kept personal

control of the secret police, and created a number of central governing
ministries that would tie the various realms, including Hungary, closer to
Vienna. Internationally, he stitched a web of diplomacy that made Austria,
weak as it was after its string of defeats and financial crises, pivotal in the
final alliance against Napoleon. After 1809 Franz wanted to stay out of
war. When in Metternich's view the time came for Austria once again to
prepare for combat, he had to bring Franz around. His means for doing so
included turning Franz against his own empress, who was strongly opposed
to renewed war. Metternich's surprisingly successful strategy ensured that
in accomplishing Napoleon's defeat, and then in engineering the whole
postwar order, the Habsburgs became the crux of the European balance
of power.

As Austria nursed its wounds after Wagram, Metternich arranged for a
rather loose alliance with France. This meant that some 30,000 Austrian
soldiers took part in Napoleon's disastrous campaign in Russia in 1812,
although the Austrians rarely engaged the Russians. In 1813 the Sixth
Coalition formed, bringing together Russia, Prussia, Sweden, Britain,
Spain, and Portugal—Austria was absent until Metternich decided that the
time was right to cut the French alliance and turn on Napoleon. When
Austria reentered the war against France in August 1813, it was suddenly
the leader of the whole coalition, with Prince Karl Schwarzenberg the
senior commander of the armies and Metternich heading the diplomatic
efforts. Franz joined his counterparts Tsar Aleksandr I of Russia and King
Friedrich Wilhelm III of Prussia in the camp outside Leipzig to watch the
so-called Battle of Nations in October 1813, in which Napoleon was soundly
defeated. The allied forces then marched on Paris, taking it in March 1814.
Napoleon abdicated in April. Austria's rather improbable leadership in the
whole effort was confirmed by Vienna becoming the site of the famous
congress to rearrange Europe's chess pieces after the war.

In the 1814–15 Congress of Vienna, amidst all the balls, intrigues and
assorted frivolity, Metternich managed to get most of what he wanted.
The question is whether what he wanted was really the best thing for the
monarchy in the long term. The goal that he and Franz agreed upon was
as far as possible to restore the European order as it had been before the
Revolution. This meant that prerevolutionary leaders had to be put back
in possession of their former principalities, which in turn would mostly
keep to their earlier borders. The whole project was designed to maintain
a finely calibrated balance of power. Thus France was not too harshly
punished. Prussia was rewarded with a chunk of Saxon territory—but
an independent Saxony remained. The problem of Prussian ambitions in
Germany was also dealt with by creating the new German Confederation,
in which Austria would retain nominal leadership while Prussia's influence
nonetheless grew. A new Polish state was constituted, though it became a
Russian satellite. The Habsburgs themselves had to give up their old lands
in Belgium, but instead gained most of Venice's former territory in the

Adriatic as well as other parts of Italy. Those changes made the monarchy at last territorially contiguous, though only marginally more defensible. Metternich did not unduly press for Austrian territorial gains because one of his principles was that Austria should be seen as neither too powerful, nor as too weak.

In hindsight, Metternich's achievements seem much less impressive. The monarchy's new position as the dominant Italian power weakened its weight in Germany and set the stage for repeated problems responding to growing national feelings in Italy. Further, Metternich's and Franz's idea of turning back the clock was only a partial solution. On the one hand, it was reasonable that the pre-1790 European order would be reassembled, since it was neither possible nor in accordance with dynastic rulers' interests to engineer a new sociopolitical system on the basis of the French Revolution's transformations. However, where Franz and Metternich failed was that they preferred to ignore the ripple effects of those transformations, including liberalism and nationalism. The mistake the Habsburg dynasty made was to try to suppress rather than harness the century's political, social, and cultural changes.

The governance system credited to Metternich, which applied both internationally and domestically in the decades after 1815, gradually broke down as the years went by. Internationally, his vision was for Austria to work in concert with the other great powers to combat revolution, nationalism, and liberal stirrings more generally. This was the motivation behind the Karlsbad Decrees of 1819, which clamped down on universities and ratcheted up censorship in German-speaking Europe in an attempt to neutralize patriotic feelings. Metternich and Franz feared nationalism because of its inherent claims for popular sovereignty, which posed a threat not just to monarchy, but especially to supranational dynasties such as the Habsburgs. The Holy Alliance of Austria, Prussia, and Russia was supposed to keep up the fight against revolution, hence military action to suppress revolts in Naples and Piedmont in the early 1820s. After 1825 in particular, Austria formed a closer relationship with Russia because Franz and Nikolai [Nicholas] I shared an abhorrence of popular revolt. Contrary to the view of Metternich as a simple reactionary, he actually advocated reforms in places like Naples so that they would have a professional bureaucracy and a more efficient, equitable legal system, as Austrian dependencies like Lombardy had. Thus though Austrian rule in Italy was unquestionably repressive, its territories were the best governed in the whole peninsula.

Domestically, the last 20 years of Franz's rule were peaceful, a period known as the complacent Austrian Biedermeier. Indeed it was too complacent: while theses of political rights and more participatory government percolated among the growing middle class in much of western Europe, Franz and Metternich remained immobile, and in many ways the monarchy's ruling system stagnated. Franz insisted that his was a government of laws that applied just as well to him as to everyone else, regardless of social class.

Nonetheless, the system that evolved incarnated the conservative ideal. It was a highly paternalistic governing arrangement in which a monarch with greater centralized power relied on a loyal and efficient bureaucracy to rule over a grateful and quiescent populace. This was a time of pervasive though not especially invasive police surveillance. Censorship constrained the University of Vienna, which was not as intellectually vital as universities elsewhere in German-speaking Europe. The minister of police, Sedlnitzky, targeted any documents or even artworks that put too much emphasis on words such as "constitution" or "freedom."

Some reforms were introduced, such as the establishment of the Austrian National Bank in 1816, which helped stabilize finances, and the continued expansion of education, including compulsory free primary schooling for girls. The provincial diets' powers were preserved but only in a limited fashion; they could raise taxes but not veto Franz's demands for funds, and so their sovereign ignored them as best he could. Franz's government was often rather listless and inefficient. He would commission reports but put off reading them, so decisions were postponed and ministerial competencies confused. Little was done to improve the organization of the military, which remained chronically under-funded. This meant that Austria routinely had shortages of soldiers and could not keep up its defense commitments, which undermined its status as a great power. Though Habsburg government resisted adaption to changing circumstances, it cannot be criticized for being unpopular, since most of Franz's subjects respected his regime and revered him personally.

While Franz and Metternich in many ways wanted to return the monarchy to 1790, after 1815 economic change far outpaced the political. The years up to 1848 saw much wider industrialization in the monarchy, above all in Austria and Bohemia, since Hungary remained overwhelmingly agricultural. The Habsburgs' realm as a whole lagged somewhat behind lands further west, but individual territories developed quite vibrantly, particularly Lombardy and Bohemia. Steam engines came into wider use around 1820, and the flourishing textile industry in Bohemia was fully mechanized by about 1840. Mining was important in Bohemia, Moravia, Styria, and Upper Austria; Bohemia alone accounted for 50 percent of the monarchy's coal. Iron production also grew in many of these same areas. The first railway on Habsburg territory was opened between Linz and České Budějovice in 1832, and one between Vienna and Olomouc in 1836. The railways and canals—such as that linking the Danube to the Vltava to the Elbe—gave Bohemian and Moravian industries greater access to distant markets. Steam navigation came to the Danube in 1831. Transportation improvements also helped Hungarian agricultural exports, which expanded rapidly. Sugar refining grew in Hungary and elsewhere. The banking sector also expanded, led by the Rothschilds and a few other houses. Franz took an active interest in many of these economic developments, and sought to encourage more growth as with road and rail expansion.

This robust economic growth was unavoidably attended by important social changes. The population increased significantly, with the monarchy reaching a total of nearly 34 million inhabitants by 1848. Vienna had some 360,000 people in that decade, Prague 115,000. The Habsburg realms remained a dizzyingly complex patchwork of peoples and near-feudal conditions in some rural areas. A traveler to Vienna in the early 1800s was amazed by the diversity of peoples he saw there—Hungarians, Poles, Serbs, Croats, Wallachians, Moldavians, Greeks, and Turks—unlike any city further west.[5] There was nonetheless the slow but steady growth of a bourgeoisie, which often had German as their main language. Some of them were wealthy capitalists, some were middle-class functionaries. While most bourgeois remained loyal to the regime, many could not help but notice how the dynastic monarchy restricted their growing economic clout from translating to political influence. There was also a small but growing working class. Working conditions in the fledgling industries were predictably harsh, with 14-hour days not uncommon until 1839—though in that year children's labor was officially limited to 12 hours a day. Worker unrest grew from isolated miners' protests around 1810 to larger demonstrations, including attacks on machines, in Prague in the 1840s. In the Hereditary Lands, the condition of the peasantry had markedly improved under the reigns of Franz's predecessors. Reforms in Hungary in the 1830s reduced feudal burdens on peasants, such as by giving them greater security of land title, but in Galicia landlords' powers over rural people were still formidable.

In addition to the tectonic societal shifts, developments outside the monarchy also undermined Metternich's system. There were further congresses in Aachen in 1818, Troppau in 1819, Ljubljana in 1820, and Verona in 1822, yet the ability of such meetings of European powers to impose a political vision rapidly diminished. At the Ljubljana congress it was decided that Austria would intervene to suppress the popular revolt in Naples, which earned Franz and Metternich resentment from liberals throughout Europe. The Verona congress determined that France would take the lead in suppressing the revolt in Spain. Britain thereafter withdrew from the Congress System, and Russia's growing weight and assertiveness meant that the system's ability to preserve the balance of power was vitiated. The revolutions in Paris and Belgium, and the uprising in Poland, all in 1830, also posed problems for Metternich. He feared the precedent of another Bourbon deposed in France, and the secession of Belgium from the Netherlands, but he could not risk a war over it. He tried to seal off the Polish parts of the Habsburg monarchy so that they could not aid the Polish rebels. To Metternich's mind that rebellion was a shocking challenge to the tsar's legitimate sovereignty, as well as an alarming pretext for further Russian military gains.

The remainder of Franz's reign also saw a fairly steady decline of Habsburg influence in Germany. Though his constitutional power had vanished when the Holy Roman Empire expired, Franz nonetheless enjoyed a swell of popularity in the years before 1820. For his visit to Aachen for the 1818 congress, he was met with jubilation in the streets. It was almost as if he were still the emperor, and Austria for a time remained the predominant German state. Franz himself remained generally uninterested in German affairs, however, and Metternich's main concern was to make sure that Prussia would not come to dominate Germany. The German Confederation proved a weak association, with an inadequate base of solidarity to combat external threats. Austria could not hold its own, since when in 1830 there was rumor of war with France, Prussia mustered far more troops for Germany's defense than could Austria. By the later 1820s it had become clear that Metternich and Austria had relatively little to offer either the smaller German princes or the segment of the population craving increased German unity. Metternich made sure that the liberal nationalists he despised were closely monitored by the police. Austria was also gradually excluded from the increased economic integration of the various German states. Nascent customs unions among those states began in 1819; by 1830 this Zollverein included a number of the larger German polities and was dominated by Prussia. Though the German Confederation did succeed in preventing any revolutions, and kept Austria influential especially in southern Germany, Metternich himself realized that his German policy was failing in the other goal of averting Prussian preponderance.

Metternich's system was more successful at maintaining Austrian influence in Italy, where there was no other large competing state. Franz also took a greater interest in the Italian situation: he had been born in Tuscany, and he visited Milan and Venice numerous times as emperor. Here, too, the goal was to suppress revolution and bind smaller states in an alliance under Austrian sway. The Habsburg possessions were themselves ruled from Vienna with a strong hand. Vienna sent troops into Italy five times between 1820 and 1848 to suppress uprisings. Sources of resentment among the local population were that relatively few of the bureaucrats and officials were locals, and also that taxes were too high. Thus even though Habsburg rule brought some progress such as improved educational systems and various social services, it was an autocratic government that did not ingratiate itself with either the aristocracy or the middle class.

Just as in Italy, in Hungary stirrings of nationalism and liberalism foreshadowed the explosion of 1848. There was a gradually increasing politicization of the Hungarian population, though the leaders pushing for greater national autonomy were predictably the elites. The Hungarian nobility vociferously protested the introduction of a paper currency in 1811, which was part of remedying the monarchy's anemic financial state. Franz and Metternich forced the scheme through, and after that Franz did not call the Hungarian diet again until 1825. Metternich of course opposed Hungarian autonomist sentiment, fearing its vaguely democratic character and that it might lead to a more vigorous push for Hungary's independence from the monarchy. His response was to assert central control over the Hungarian county governments, increase censorship, and use the secret police to jail activists. Even as Hungarian nationalism was sprouting, so too was that of other peoples within Hungary, most notably the Croats, who objected strongly to the deterioration of Croatia's constitutional status within the Hungarian kingdom and the relegation of the Croatian language to secondary status in favor of Hungarian. Tensions were thus building up not only in Hungary's relationship with the dynasty, but also in the relationships of the various peoples of Hungary.

In the last decade of his rule, Franz became ever more rigid and paranoid. He essentially pretended that the social forces contributing to the revolutions of 1830 did not exist. There was however one major change he had to prepare for, namely his succession. He knew that his disabled oldest son Ferdinand was not capable of rule, but characteristically both he and Metternich opted for the principle of legitimate primogeniture, that the rightful line of succession had to be honored regardless. Thus in the late 1820s, when he was about 36 years old, Ferdinand began to be invited to key council meetings. In 1830 he was crowned king of Hungary to succeed Franz. In 1835, as Franz was on his deathbed, he composed a set of instructions for Ferdinand. They read like a note a parent leaves a teenager before going away for the weekend—yet Ferdinand was nearly 42. Franz wrote, "Rearrange nothing of the state edifice; rule and do not change; hold firm and steadfast to the principles by constant adherence to which I not only led the monarchy through the storms of hard times, but also assured the lofty position that it occupies in the world."[6]

Metternich gave his input to these instructions, and in the note Franz also advised Ferdinand to trust Metternich, "my truest servant and friend," implicitly. Franz's worldview is crystallized in these words. Change nothing; hold rigidly to one's principles; resist all contrary forces. Though he was not always so intransigent, the lesson he learned from the trials he endured was not to adapt but to remain immobile. That obduracy helped him outlast Bonaparte, and his and Metternich's leadership deserves much credit for leading the charge against revolutionary and Napoleonic France. That leadership also brought a good deal of stability to his lands after 1815. Though Franz cannot truly take credit for this, it is even a testament to the relatively mild repression that there was such a cultural efflorescence during his reign, seeing the late apogee of Haydn's, the sum total of Beethoven's and Schubert's careers, and the literary creativity of Franz Grillparzer, Nikolaus Lenau, and others. But Franz ultimately kept looking backward, to an impossible vision of monarchical authority before the age of revolution. That reactionary illusion was perhaps to be expected of the man who was the last Holy Roman Emperor, but it was not a recipe for adaptive leadership.

Ferdinand I (1793–1875)

Ferdinand was purely a figurehead to preserve the appearance of monarchical rule. The true rulers in his reign were his uncle Archduke Ludwig, Metternich, and in domestic matters Count Franz Anton von Kolowrat. This regency triumvirate disliked each other, and largely held the monarchy in stasis until the 1848 upheaval. To his credit, Ferdinand, who is often portrayed as an empty vessel, in that year did recognize that it was time for the old system, and Metternich himself, to go. Thus though Ferdinand was unquestionably unfit, he was not an idiot. In his younger years he suffered from periodic epilepsy, and his normal development was delayed; he learned to walk and talk quite late. His infirmities retarded his progress at school, but he eventually learned five languages, played the piano well, and developed an interest in botany. Nonetheless, the family kept him out of public view for many years. When he did have to appear, such as at his coronations in Prague in 1836 and Milan in 1838, the affair was carefully stage-managed to protect the authoritative image of the king. That image was unprotected within more intimate circles, however. The tsarina of Russia met Ferdinand in Teplice and penned this portrait of him: "Good Lord, I had heard a lot about him, of his little, ugly, feeble form and his big head with no expression other than stupidity, but the reality surpasses all description."[7] Even within his own family Ferdinand received the unkind nickname of "Nandl der Trottel" (roughly, "Ferdy the fool").

Although the sovereign was incapable of rule, the dynasty asserted itself by dictating the composition of the State Conference that actually governed. This body thwarted Metternich's hopes for unfettered power by giving Count Kolowrat significant control over purse strings, and allowing influence from Archduke Ludwig along with Ferdinand's rather dim brother Franz Karl. This was all a recipe for lackluster rule. Kolowrat was somewhat more liberal than Metternich, and their many disputes included his protests about the latter's intransigent attitude toward government reforms. Metternich complained that Kolowrat was so financially stingy that the military was starved. The basic system of government centering on the police, the bureaucracy, and the Church remained intact. Economic advance continued; signs of progress were further railway building, stricter child labor laws in 1842, the foundation of the Austrian Academy of Sciences in 1847, and the first telegraph connection between Vienna, Prague, and Brno in the same year. However, some initiatives that even Metternich and others of the regency supported were stymied by interests elsewhere in the monarchy, such as the plan to join the Zollverein or introduce a customs union between Austria and Hungary. Metternich's abiding attitudes dictated the monarchy's foreign policy: hostility to liberal and nationalist ferment, the defense of monarchical legitimacy, and the preservation of the balance of power.

By the 1840s, however, the Habsburg regime was losing authority at home and abroad. A number of vulnerabilities together explain the outbreak of revolution in 1848. Internationally, Metternich's system was behind the times; Britain under Lord Palmerston called for all European states to adopt constitutional regimes, and even Prussia adopted more liberal reforms. That Austria's pivotal position in European politics had deteriorated was shown by it being mostly ignored in British and Russian machinations over Turkey in 1839–40. Domestically, though there was by no means a deep, coordinated popular anger at the monarchy, there were widespread grievances. Economic conditions slumped in the years before 1848. Harvest failures started in 1845, which caused sharply rising food prices and widespread hunger. Decades of rapid population growth led to a shortage of jobs. Complaints about high taxes were heard across the class spectrum.

The monarchy's finances were precarious, with nearly 30 percent of its budget swallowed by debt service in 1847. This helped precipitate a run on banks because of fears of a state bankruptcy. The estates in Bohemia, Moravia, and Lower Austria had for a number of years been calling for increased power over government budgets, the end of censorship, and the establishment of a more equitable income tax. Conservative nobles not surprisingly objected to pressures from the diets and the Vienna government for further land reform, while liberal nobles were pushing for a more constitutional regime. Elements of the bourgeoisie also wanted to see an end to the more intrusive and autocratic aspects of Metternich's police state. Conspicuously absent in this percolating discontent were calls for overthrow of the regime—most people remained loyal to the dynasty, even if desires for political change were building.

The other factor unsettling the monarchy's politics was the growth of nationalism. In the decades before 1848 groups of elites became increasingly enthused by ideas of national self-assertion. The Hungarians had the most forceful and broadest-based movement. It was still mostly a preserve of the nobility, and even within that class there were conflicts over what the proper attitude should be toward Vienna, and toward Hungary's own national minorities. The moderates included men such as István Széchenyi, a patriotic noble who promoted economic and intellectual reform, a parliamentary government along English lines, and the cultural development of the Hungarian language. Lajos Kossuth was the most prominent member of the radical wing, which insisted on a much looser connection to Austria and possibly even outright independence. The radicals were also typically more vocal in asserting the primacy of the Hungarian language in administration and education, an end to the feudal aristocratic regime, and Hungarians' right to rule over all the minority peoples within the Hungarian kingdom.

Slovaks and particularly Croats objected to the latter claim especially; the modest numbers of Croat noble and bourgeois nationalists insisted that Croatia was a historic state with its own right to rule itself, equal to

Hungary. Among the monarchy's Slavs, the Czechs had the most robust nationalist movement, led by principled intellectuals such as František Palacký. Czech nationalism had progressed from its earliest, cultural phases at the turn of the century into a burgeoning political movement appealing to the members of the educated, Czech-speaking middle classes. Though it contained a strong anti-German sentiment, there were few voices repudiating Habsburg rule. Among the smaller peoples of the monarchy, such as the Slovaks, Slovenes, or Romanians, nationalist sentiment remained restricted to tiny coteries of educated people including priests. Separatism was somewhat stronger in the Italian areas, where radical secret societies were active, and grievances about Vienna's high taxes and autocratic rule were more widespread.

In the years before 1848, these movements were still emergent—but their basic assumptions about the nation as the legitimate basis of political community would come to inform the revolutions in that year. A common denominator was the identification of liberalism with nationalism. These ideas fused claims for equal political rights for all classes, and the possibility of cooperation among those peoples with Vienna, as long as Vienna respected their rights. Nationalism at this time was not inherently antithetical to dynastic monarchy. The problem for the Habsburgs was that since their scattered, multi-ethnic dominions were only weakly connected culturally and institutionally, the dynasty itself formed the main connection. There was only a flimsy sense of unity between Hungarians and Italians or Germans and Poles, beyond sharing the same sovereign. As nationalist movements over the course of subsequent decades came to insist on rights of self-determination, that conflicted with the dynasty's insistence on its historical right to rule.

This confluence of liberalism, nationalism, and material grievances burst into the 1848 revolutions. In some ways, it is incorrect to call them "revolutions," since apart from Hungary and Italy the revolts did not attempt to depose the dynasty. Though demands for change were extensive, they were often also contradictory, as one national group's claims could be incompatible with what another national group demanded. The revolutionary movements were on the whole an amorphous, shifting coalition of interests among the moderate liberals (often doctors, lawyers, teachers, and other professionals), more conservative liberals (who might come from the nobility or the clergy), and radicals (who were mostly students and sometimes workers).

The revolution in Paris in February 1848 was the original spark for similar uprisings across Europe. After some protests in early March, the earthquake struck Vienna on 13 March when large parts of the city rose up and marched on the Chancellery. Soldiers fired on the crowd, and to appease the mob and forestall a further escalation, the Habsburg inner circle decided that Metternich had to go; he fled that same day. The escalation continued regardless: a number of citizens' committees organized themselves to exercise authority in areas such as justice, and to press for a constitution. Kolowrat, still running the dynasty's government, found himself forced to share power with these committees. On 15 March some 20,000 people marched on Buda's castle, symbol of the Habsburg regime. In Prague there were demands for a separate ministry for Bohemia, just as Hungary had. The monarchy's Polish domains saw riots among liberal intellectuals in Kraków and Lviv.

In most of these revolts the demands were similar: trial by jury, freedom for political prisoners, freedom of speech and the end of censorship, abolition of serfdom and tax exemptions for the nobility, plus the creation of legislative assemblies that would represent national groups' interests. Over the next month the royal government developed a constitution for the Hereditary Lands to try to answer some of these demands, but because it did not include wide suffrage and a unicameral house it was rejected. This led to fiercer riots in Vienna in mid-May, and the royal family fled to Innsbruck. In halting response to popular pressure, the dynasty advanced a second proposal for a parliament, for which elections were held in June in the Hereditary Lands. This assembly eventually sat in the town of Kroměříž in Moravia, and is known as the Kremsier Parliament after the town's German name. This was a multinational, cross-class body, but it was never particularly effectual. The court by this point was ensconced in the nearby city of Olomouc. Archduke Johann was now officially the regent, but the various members of the dynasty including the Archduchess Sophie closely coordinated on rule.

The dynasty agreed to a separate government for Hungary in April. According to the so-called April Laws, Hungary was to be governed as a constitutional monarchy in which the monarch's power would be strictly limited. The dynasty soon paid the price for this concession, though, when calls for a similar arrangement for Bohemia raised the possibility of the entire monarchy breaking up. Kossuth was leading the new Hungarian parliament toward creation of a separate budget and currency. Meanwhile, the various non-Magyar peoples objected to the Hungarian radicals' calls for independence from the monarchy, and so started threatening independence from Hungary. The Croats led the charge, naming the general Jelačić their leader. Demands for autonomy from the Slovaks, Serbs, and Romanians followed in May. Kossuth used these events as a pretext for a mass mobilization to defend the integrity of the Hungarian state. By summer's end, radicals in Vienna and Hungary were each other's only remaining allies. The Czechs were not supporting the Hungarian revolutionaries because of the latter's treatment of Hungary's minority populations.

In Bohemia, the revolution split along multiple cleavages. Besides the schism between Czechs and Germans, among the Czechs there was also a split between the pan-Slavists and the radicals. The most influential were moderates such as Palacký, who wanted to preserve the Habsburg monarchy as an association of equal peoples. Indeed, it was he who famously commented that if Austria did not exist, it would have to be invented. In June, Palacký convened in Prague an international Pan-Slav Congress that called for a federal structure in the monarchy, respecting the rights of the historic kingdoms. In this proposed arrangement, Bohemia would have its own parliament on an equal status as Austria or Hungary. Though the Czechs' assertion of their rights was more measured than that of the Hungarian radicals, even the call for a federalization of the monarchy was more than the dynasty was willing to stomach. This congress, and the Prague uprising, was crushed in June by an army led by General Windischgrätz.

Events in Germany ran headlong into the problems of the monarchy's multinational nature. Austro-German liberals looked to the Frankfurt Assembly in their hopes for a more unified Germany. That assembly had as its goals the creation of a federal, constitutional system, with strict observance of the rule of law and individual rights, under a hereditary emperor. For a time the hope was for a stronger confederation that would include certainly Austria and possibly Bohemia. Archduke Johann was chosen as the regent of this embryonic German state in June 1848. The problem with the entire project, from the Habsburgs' point of view, was that if the monarchy's Germans were in any way affiliated with it, then how would the rest of the monarchy's peoples (and institutions) relate to each other if the Austro-German areas belonged to a federated German polity? Though there was a residual identification of the Habsburg monarchy with the old German empire that had expired in 1806, the uprisings of the Czechs, Hungarians, Italians, and Croats all made obvious that the Habsburg monarchy was by no means mostly a German state. The nationally minded political weight of the non-German parts of the monarchy now complicated more than ever before the Habsburgs' pretensions to leadership in Germany.

Secessionist pressures immediately came to the surface in Italy, driven largely by the aristocracy. Elsewhere in the monarchy nobles for the most part supported the monarchy. In the Italian lands, however, they wanted to overthrow it, typically because they felt that the Habsburg state had excluded them from power. Austrian troops were forced to withdraw as Milan and Venice rose in revolt. Then in late March, Carlo Alberto, the king of Piedmont-Sardinia, launched an attack to drive Austria's forces out of the peninsula. His stated goal was to unify northern Italy under his constitutional rule. The Italian uprising and war were short-lived, as Field Marshal Radetzky restored Habsburg control by defeating the Piedmontese army at Custozza in July, and then again at Novara in March 1849. By the end of September 1848 the dynasty was also moving toward war against the Hungarian revolutionaries to stop their moves for independence. The Hungarian rebel army had several indecisive skirmishes with royal forces, but the final battles would not take place until new leadership was directing the dynasty's affairs.

Ferdinand's role in these revolutionary events was mostly that of a spectator. He did not like Metternich and was not sorry to see him go.

Ferdinand was also predisposed to greater concessions in the revolution's early days, to which the other members of his family would not agree. Hence he was taken out of Vienna to Innsbruck, to be further away from where decisions were being made. He later returned to the capital, but then his war minister Latour was murdered on 6 October by a mob. That mob stormed the arsenal, taking weapons and pledging to aid the Hungarian revolutionaries. Ferdinand was angry and disappointed that his subjects had committed this murder, and soon left again for Olomouc. Vienna fell fully into the radicals' control, though not for long. General Windischgrätz arrived with his army, and with the assistance from Jelačić's force of peasant soldiers, Habsburg forces recaptured the city by the end of October.

In November the family decided on a new cabinet that took power in Vienna. Led by the conservative aristocrat Felix Schwarzenberg, the decision was soon made that the reestablishment of the dynasty's control required a change of sovereign. In December Ferdinand had to be convinced to abdicate; he resisted because he thought abdication was inimical to his divine ruling status. But in the end he agreed to step down in favor of his nephew, Franz Joseph. Ferdinand was 55 years old when he abdicated, and lived for another 20 years. His entire reign had been a kind of shadow play staged by Metternich and the dynasty to uphold their legitimist, obsolescent fantasy of absolute monarchy. His abdication did not defuse the uprisings, which challenged the ongoing absolutist fantasy of Franz Joseph's first years.

Dynastic strategies

The dynasty's record of production and reproduction in this time must be seen in the same spirit as Franz's whole reign: its outward adequacy masked real insufficiencies. On the territorial front, the indefensible holdings in Belgium were lost. The compensating stretches of territory gained in the 1795 third Polish partition, and then the old Venetian lands along the Adriatic firmly acquired after 1814, were at least contiguous with the rest of the monarchy, but they added little in terms of wealth or productivity. In his marital and fatherly roles Franz was prolific, siring 13 children with 4 wives. None of these children, however, proved particularly scintillating. Ferdinand came from the second marriage, which was to Franz's cousin Maria Teresa. This close connection helps explain Ferdinand's disabilities, and also why Franz Karl, Franz's second son and a possible alternate candidate for the succession, was dull and not much of an improvement over Ferdinand. Franz, tenacious to primogeniture in his own line and jealous of his smarter brothers Karl and Johann, refused to consider them for the succession. Because Ferdinand remained childless, it was Franz Karl who continued the line; his son Franz Joseph was the dynasty's penultimate

ruler. Of Franz's other children, his daughter Leopoldine notably went on
to become the Empress of Brazil.

There were other tricky succession issues because of Franz's daughter
Marie-Louise, Empress of the French thanks to her marriage to Napoleon.
Marie-Louise's son from that marriage, Napoleon II, was named successor
by his father, which the victorious allies did not allow after 1814. The young
son was then taken in by his Habsburg family, and died at Schönbrunn
in 1832 at age 21. An important moment in ensuring dynastic solidarity
came in Ferdinand's reign with the family statute of 1839, which regulated
succession issues. It also specified rules for territorial inheritance among
the various Habsburg progeny, their rights and duties in relation to the
dynasty, and how the family's head could use its joint funds. The statute
was nothing less than a codification of the expectations for how each
family member would contribute to the dynastic project, specifying a legal
framework for maintaining its corporate interests. The statute governed
such matters for the Habsburgs up to their fall from power in 1918.

The French Revolution and the turmoil in its wake mounted an enormous
challenge to the Habsburgs' legitimizing traditions. Though the dynasty's
response to that challenge for a time offered the possibility of loyalty on
a new basis, ultimately thanks to Franz's and Metternich's conservatism
there was a retreat to earlier traditions, no matter how antiquated. The
experiments around the turn of the century were mostly the product of
thinking by people like Stadion, Archduke Johann, and the Tyrolean
intellectual Joseph von Hormayr. The guiding idea was to create a source
of loyalty to the dynasty that would mobilize the populace and substitute
for French patriotism. Because these men recognized that a French-style
patriotism, based on some core of linguistic and cultural affinity, could
never work in the heterogeneous Habsburg lands, they instead launched a
project to create a loyalty based on what those lands did have in common,
which was the dynasty itself. Johann said that he wanted to make "the
business of the state the business of the nation." He went to Tyrol and
Styria to organize militias for the fight against the French, arguing that
"the nation, the mass, must fight, all for one and one for all," and that
thereby the "Austrian nation" would be "invincible."[8]

The hope was to promote local pride and culture that would raise
troops and motivate resistance, but also build national feeling in support
of Habsburg rule. The government funded various publications, provincial
and national museums, and other cultural activities aiming to create
community solidarity. Johann himself sponsored patriotic art, for example
commissioning the painter Karl Ruß to produce a cycle of paintings
depicting the historical achievements of the dynasty. While Johann's
activities focused on the Austrian lands, Stadion encouraged people in
Bohemia and elsewhere to undertake many of the same activities, so there
were publications in Czech, Polish, and other languages. These projects lost
steam after a few years. Franz was suspicious of their utility and of what

forces they might be awakening that could challenge his rule. Moreover, his jealousy of his smarter brother always inclined him to look askance at Johann's activities.

Franz and his advisors rejected the French Revolution's assertion of popular and national sovereignty, which they understandably saw as contrary to dynastic rule. Their vision of legitimacy was that the dynasty had to be in charge because it had always been in charge. Admittedly, the regime made some claims to justify its rule through its insistence that it protected the public welfare by combating the disastrous chaos and iconoclasm of revolutionary ideas. There was also some recourse to claims of efficiency of rule, that Habsburg administrative sovereignty was justified because it provided good government. Where Maria Theresia, Joseph II, and Leopold II had advanced a particular but explicit notion of a social contract, however, Franz and Metternich downplayed such ideas. Maria Theresia and her sons espoused a vision of the dynasty and its state relatively in tune with its times, whereby legitimacy came from serving the people by fashioning a modern institutional apparatus. For Franz and Metternich, the state would still serve the people—that legacy of the Josephine era persisted—but the paternalistic, autocratic steering of the state was inimical to modern political ideas of liberalism and nationalism, even if it did embrace to a certain extent contemporary economic developments.

The intransigence bordering on fossilization of the dynasty's legitimizing strategies can also be seen in its use of religion. The state by this time had so thoroughly consumed the institutional Church that the latter could hardly be counted as an independent support of the monarchy. The Church did have a significant role in supervising secondary education, but in that sphere, too, it was closely supervised. Promoting Catholic morality and routine observance was still part of the dynasty's ruling ideology, especially as a defense against French revolutionary godlessness. But as Franz's and then Ferdinand's reigns went on, the dynasty's religious attitudes fell more out of step with those of the general population. As religion became more of an inward matter, insisting on conformity—as the regime did, with required church attendance and communion for secondary students— offered another example of an archaic, overly paternalistic attitude toward its subjects. Thus even as the Church and religion became less vital to the cultural, social, and intellectual life of the populace, the dynasty stuck to old habits, including a deep suspicion of Protestant influences.

It is debatable whether Franz truly understood what postrevolutionary patriotism meant. An anecdote attributed to Franz has him asking, when told that a particular man was a patriot, "But is he a patriot for me?" Franz seemed to assume that patriotism could be tied to an individual dynast rather than to a national polity. He maintained an unsurprisingly conservative ideal for his function as a ruler: he rejected the notion of constitutional monarchy. He denied that any other part of society could make rules that would bind the sovereign. His *image* as a ruler was actually less hide-bound.

He affected to remain aloof from the turmoil of his reign, to stand as a stern, but benevolent father over his subjects, who were much like children in that they did not know what was good for themselves. Though his royal function necessitated some distance from his subjects, Franz was in many ways personally more accessible than previous Habsburg rulers had been. He gave audiences several times a week at which he would wear an unostentatious officer's uniform, speak in Viennese dialect (or Hungarian, Czech, or Italian), and genuinely listen to his supplicants' concerns. He did not like formal protocol in general, enjoying more the chance to escape the court and interact with ordinary people. Most of all he preferred to spend time with his family. He was in short an approachable monarch, one who seemed more like a run-of-the-mill bureaucrat, but who earned sympathy for surviving Napoleon's assaults and the deaths of three of his wives. As much as he revered his authority and assiduously defended his traditional prerogatives, Franz was not enamored with glorifying his own person, nor with the symbolic trappings of his authority. This may be one reason why he looks so grumpy in the portrait by Friedrich von Amerling.

Some institutional structures were strengthened during the reigns of Franz and Ferdinand, but very few meaningful reforms were carried out, despite frequent calls for them. The problems of the administration were widely recognized. Archduke Karl in particular proposed various reforms, but was repeatedly rebuffed. He for a time had an ally in Johann Ludwig von Cobenzl, who headed the foreign ministry. But while there were still such reformist minds in government, the monarchy was embroiled in wars that redirected attention to only the most pressing needs. After 1815, reformers were suppressed under Metternich's government. Metternich himself was not inherently hostile to reforms, and indeed long looked to remedy the military's problems. Franz, too, was not categorically opposed to reform, but his governing style was often procrastinating. His overriding approach was to uphold the status quo, which contributed to the political stasis at the monarchy's heart.

Even if the regime was hostile to changes it saw as undermining its authority, it nonetheless provided its subjects expanded services through the burgeoning welfare state in the Hereditary Lands. It offered pension systems, hospitals, charity care for those who could not afford it, and tuition support for needy university students, among other things. The monumental codification of civil law in 1812 was based on the principles of equality of all before the law. A demonstration that the impersonal state would serve its citizens equally was its legal assistance for lower-class people in civil suits. Strict supervision of how noble landlords treated their peasants was also instituted, as were not inconsiderable taxes on the nobility. The dynasty served in new ways, expanding its charitable giving often for programs to help the disadvantaged. Perhaps less benevolently, the police apparatus grew significantly from the kernel Joseph II had established; it was tasked with providing Franz and Metternich a fresh report every morning with their breakfast. The state's scope and penetration further enlarged to promote economic and infrastructural development via railroads, navigation, and postal service.

Such expansion of state activities was generally characteristic of European polities after the French Revolution. One aspect was a gradual move to direct rule, in which specialized bureaucrats implemented the center's decisions in local areas. This was a major change for the Habsburg realms because it attenuated the dynasty's old reliance on indirect rule through the aristocracy. Though the aristocracy overall remained firmly in the dynasty's camp in these years, the relationship altered fundamentally because the dynasty did not need nobles as it had a century previously. They retained some role in administration—particularly high nobles in the most important posts—but increasingly the bureaucracy was staffed by members of the middle class. Bourgeois functionaries thereby grew into an essential support of the regime. They served in the bureaucracy, but they also benefited from the stability of the social order that had allowed them to attain their positions.

This class's growth enabled the ongoing professionalization of the bureaucracy, which in turn promoted the expansion of the state. As schools turned out more educated people, there were qualified candidates for posts, who increased not only the state's penetration into society but the effectiveness of its services. As long as the dynasty provided stability, opportunity for economic gain, and was not overly heavy-handed with the secret police, the middle class was solidly behind the regime. Economic troubles in the later 1840s and a sense that the monarchy had become inexcusably reprobate in its guaranteeing of political rights helped motivate the individuals in the middle class who revolted in 1848. It must be said that all of these administrative structures were still limited, often by the monarchy's financial troubles. Such institutional weaknesses help account for the monarchy's shaky response to the revolutions.

Though with historical hindsight Habsburg history from 1792 to 1848 must be judged unfavorably, fairness requires acknowledgment of some worthy, if transitory, achievements. Despite the many failings of the Habsburgs' state, it managed to mount a nearly continuous resistance against a much larger French polity enflamed with revolutionary fervor, and could then claim victory in 1815. Franz and others read this victory as an affirmation of the eternal resiliency and legitimacy of the dynasty. In some ways, the decade or so after 1815 was also an improbable triumph for the dynasty, since its hodgepodge realm acted for a time as the linchpin of politics on the continent, thanks above all to Metternich's leadership. The later years of Franz's rule, and then the placeholder reign of Ferdinand, were not wholly a time of decline. There were positive developments in the monarchy, such as economic growth, the expansion of a generally loyal middle class, and domestic and international peace.

The problem is that these were years of political stagnation. The Metternich system was both a tactical and an ideological response to the decades of upheaval. Tactically, it sought to restore the *status quo ante* in order to bring peace and stability. Ideologically, the *status quo ante* of dynastic monarchy was conceived as inherently more legitimate than any of the revolutionary or Napoleonic political models. This system did bring some peace and stability, and an adherence to the traditional, supranational bases of rule was in some ways a sensible recourse given the challenges the Habsburgs faced at home and abroad. But in the end, because they were so distrustful of changes whether abrupt (such as the original revolution in France) or percolating (such as the growth of liberalism, or nationalist tensions in Italy, the Czech lands, and Hungary), Franz and Metternich failed to capitalize on the years of stability to adapt in any consequential way, even to accept the modest proposals made by Archdukes Johann and Karl. Franz held to an intransigently antiquated vision of dynastic rule that maintained a reactionary social order for an artificially long time. It was because it resisted adaptation that the monarchy found itself in confrontation in 1848. Not only was there a failure to quell the revolutions in Ferdinand's time, the confrontations between the dynastic monarchy and changing sociopolitical circumstances led to shocks repeatedly throughout the rest of the century.

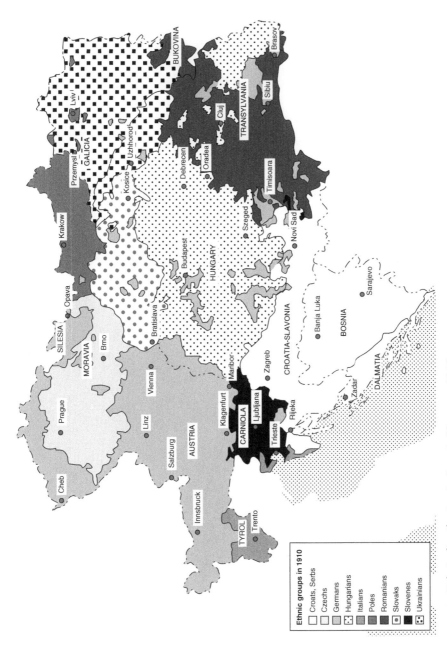

MAP 3. *Ethnic distribution in Austria-Hungary, 1910.*

Ethnic groups in 1910

- Croats, Serbs
- Czechs
- Germans
- Hungarians
- Italians
- Poles
- Romanians
- Slovaks
- Slovenes
- Ukrainians

CHAPTER ELEVEN

To succumb with honor
(1848–1918)

In 1874, greeted by festive fireworks and a representation of the Bohemian crown in flowers, Franz Joseph visited Prague. It was the twenty-sixth year of his rule. For the emperor's arrival, a triumphal arch was erected at Prague's main railway station. It was emblazoned with the slogan, "God bring him luck."[1] As it turned out, that wish was in vain. Throughout his 68 years on the throne, Franz Joseph needed a great deal of luck—but he had relatively little, much of it bad. This was a man who incarnated conservative, dynastic rule, and who endured setback after setback in maintaining the prerogatives of his dynasty. And while bad luck may have played some part in those setbacks, his own poor decisions were even more important. When he came to the throne he hoped to rule with an iron hand, to assert the central authority of the monarchy as never before. This dream also was in vain, and over several decades Franz Joseph saw that traditional authority whittled away by losing territory to Italy, international clout to Prussia/Germany, and governing power to new political parties within his own state. To his credit, Franz Joseph did adapt. He relinquished some—though not all—illusions about what a monarch could be in the late nineteenth century. He never ceded all power, and never became a mere figurehead. He was a multivalent symbol: a symbol of one of the few unifying features of his heterogeneous realms, a symbol of monarchical authority pared down by modern parliamentary politics, a symbol of dynasty as dinosaur in a world so greatly changed from the conditions that had privileged dynasties in the first place.

The Habsburgs' last seven decades of rule were a time of modernization and resistance to modernization. Rapid changes in the economy and society stood at odds with the halting changes in the regime. Where the dynasty dragged its feet in responding to the consequences of the growing political assertiveness of the middle and lower classes, and looked stonily down upon the growing fragmentation of nationalist movements, these two developments precipitated pressures that ultimately the sovereigns and their ministers could not rebuff. Where these decades amounted domestically to a conflictual lurch toward constitutional government, internationally the monarchy's prestige was often in free fall. At times it seemed almost incapable of defending itself, until the final fateful gambit, when the dynasty's attempt to assert its evaporating great power status led to the catastrophic world war that ended the monarchy altogether.

Franz Joseph I (1830–1916)

Franz Joseph (Figure 11.1) was a dull personality, but because of his difficult position athwart epochal change, he is a fascinating figure. His defining characteristics were his sense of duty, propriety, and the legitimacy of his house. He slept on an old iron bed in the Hofburg and never installed a modern bathroom. He rose early every morning and dealt with some 4,000 papers a year. He was no intellectual, but he was not unintelligent. His education was supervised by his mother Archduchess Sophie, and by Metternich. Thus he was inculcated with a deep sense of tradition, of reverence for the established truths of the dynasty and its rule. In contrast to so many of his ancestors, he never learned to love art and music, preferring instead the pleasures of military regimentation and simple domesticity. A bureaucrat's reverence for routine and order guided him. As monarch, he maintained a very formal, reserved demeanor, a kind of rigid professionalism, beyond which very few intimates ever penetrated. He endured a series of personal tragedies, including the final cataclysm that engulfed his subjects and his realm in war, yet rarely betrayed any public emotion. This is what makes him interesting: he was brought up in, and always lived in, an archaic world, one that (as he himself acknowledged late in life) was out of step with his own times. How he negotiated those tensions over his long rule—the longest of any Habsburg sovereign—is a study in an ancient dynasty's confrontation with its own obsolescence.

His uncle Ferdinand's abdication in December 1848, and Franz Joseph's accession to the throne, were arranged by an inner circle of the dynasty that included Archduchess Sophie and the new chief minister Felix Schwarzenberg. Franz Joseph was only 18 at the time of his elevation, a fresh face chosen to mark a change but not a break in the context of revolutionary upheaval. Schwarzenberg and Sophie in the early years of the reign exercised significant influence over the young monarch. His immediate task was to complete the suppression of the rebellions and then institute a vigorous, sometimes brutal restoration of what he intended to be his absolute authority. The revolts in Vienna and Prague had been crushed with relative ease by October 1848, and Radetzky's army in Italy had restored Habsburg power there by March 1849. The bigger problem was

FIGURE 11.1 *Franz Joseph I, photographer unknown (1914). Image courtesy of the Library of Congress.*

the situation in Hungary. The Hungarian revolutionaries led by Kossuth refused to recognize Franz Joseph's authority because he was not crowned king of Hungary. In December 1848 the Austrian general Windischgrätz launched an invasion of Hungary that took Buda in January 1849. Kossuth and his army were forced to flee to the eastern city of Debrecen.

In March a new unitary constitution was announced that would apply to the entire monarchy, including Hungary. Known as the *oktroyierte Märzverfassung* (or "imposed March constitution"), it invalidated the earlier Kremsier Constitution, but actually incorporated some of its features such as the abolition of serfdom. This new constitution was mostly authored by his minister Stadion, yet Franz Joseph never fully implemented it. He did not object to its centralizing aspects, for instance that he would be crowned only once, as emperor of Austria (rather than separately in his various realms), and would have a veto over all legislation. However, as emperor he would have to work with a parliament to whom his ministers were responsible. His objection was that ministers should only be responsible to the emperor and not to the people. Schwarzenberg also recalled the Austrian delegation from the Frankfurt Assembly, and that act, together with Friedrich Wilhelm of Prussia's refusal of the German crown offered him, ended the revolutionary events in Germany. In April Kossuth proclaimed Hungary a republic, formally deposing the Habsburgs. This was too provocative a move, since the major European powers would not support a royal family being forced out in this way. Russia, under the very conservative Tsar Nikolai I, was already making rumblings of intervention.

That intervention became necessary later in the spring as the Austrian forces, ineptly commanded, lost ground to the Hungarian army. Franz Joseph had been pressed by Windischgrätz and Schwarzenberg to accept Nikolai's offer of military assistance, but when he finally did so, he felt it a humiliation that he required outside help to regain control of one of his own realms. In June Russian troops invaded Hungary, but the Hungarians generally avoided pitched battles with the tsar's forces. What truly led to the revolt's defeat was that Hungary was simply weaker than Austria. It lacked international allies and an industrial base with which to support its army. When the Hungarian general Görgey finally surrendered in August, Kossuth fled with loyalists to Turkey and thence to England. The dynasty's retribution for the Hungarian rebellion was swift and terrible: under Austrian military rule, the Hungarian generals were executed, numerous other army officers imprisoned, political leaders who had fled were condemned to death and hanged in absentia, and even moderate leaders were shot.

The dynasty defeated the rebellions of 1848–9, but that did not mean that all the revolutionary goals were defeated. Certainly the visions of the Hungarian or Italian radicals for separation from the monarchy, or even of the Czech moderates for a more federated structure, did not come to fruition. Though at times the dynasty was in serious trouble from the multiple uprisings, the rebels in the various provinces never managed to coordinate with each other. Their respective national goals were often discordant, and even the more widely shared objectives of liberalism were fragmented by class and other divisions. Some of those objectives were achieved, however. Serfdom was definitively abolished. Peasants, students, and workers were politicized as they never had been before. The Kremsier Constitution established a precedent for sharing the monarch's power with an elected, representative assembly. In so many ways, the revolutions' defeat evolved into a long-term victory. Where the dynasty thought it had won in 1849, political forces of constitutionalism and national mobilization could be only temporarily subdued.

Franz Joseph, backed by a few key ministers, now embarked upon a mission to strengthen the dynasty's rule, relying on the bureaucracy and the army. This absolutist reaction lasted for roughly a decade, to October 1860. It aimed to overcome the old faults that had perennially plagued the Habsburg system: a weak monarchical state in which decentralized governance was defended by assertive regional interests such as the nobility. The initial architect of the reassertion of Habsburg authority was Felix Schwarzenberg, a clever, right-wing sybarite who strengthened Franz Joseph's inclination for autocratic centralism. The neo-absolutist regime was inaugurated on 31 December 1851 when a royal patent was issued (known as the "Silvester Patent" after the German term for New Year's Eve) that replaced the imposed constitution of 1849. Authority was now at least theoretically centralized in Franz Joseph's hands. This patent restricted jury trials and joined the judicial to the administrative system for better central control. Ministers were directed strictly by the emperor, and most officials throughout the monarchy were now appointed by him rather than by regional authorities. German became the dominant language of administration and to a certain extent in schools, even in Hungary where it dislodged Magyar. Other laws in 1852 and 1853 were part of the crackdown, such as limiting press freedom and instituting a court system with secret trials. As Franz Joseph gleefully commented in a letter to his mother in 1851, "We have thrown all that constitutional stuff overboard, and now Austria has only one master."[2]

Schwarzenberg died suddenly in 1852; Franz Joseph was always to consider him his greatest minister. The decade of neo-absolutist reaction thus came to be identified with Franz Joseph's interior minister, Alexander Bach, who oversaw the system of police surveillance, bureaucratic centralization, and a resurgence of Catholic domination. The Bach system was no mere throwback to archaic monarchical authority; this was a "modernizing dictatorship."[3] His repressive measures were designed to restore order, rationalize governing structures, and thereby set the stage for further reforms that would strengthen the state domestically and internationally. In many ways, the ideals Bach embodied, and the policies Franz Joseph let him undertake, were inspired by Joseph II's incomplete project. This was to build a centralized state that removed power from local sources to focus it on an efficient bureaucracy and powerful army, which together would ensure not only the dynasty's authority but also the well-being of its subjects. This goal came closer to realization in the 1850s than it would either before or after. And although there were some unquestionably authoritarian aspects to this system, it presided over an economic upswing even while civil rights were curtailed.

Liberals grumbled, but much of the bourgeoisie settled into a familiar pattern for the Habsburg monarchy: meager participation in politics, but acceptance of adequate, paternalistic governance. The Hungarians complained most loudly about their lost freedoms—one tried to assassinate Franz Joseph in 1853, crying "Long live Kossuth!" as he did so—but were kept tightly suppressed. The paternalism was particularly evident in the state's new coziness with the Catholic Church as a strongly traditional ideological ally. After Schwarzenberg died, Vienna's Archbishop Rauscher became a very close confidant of Franz Joseph. The emperor signed a concordat with the Church in 1855 that gave the latter expanded censorship powers, oversight of educational curricula to assure accordance with dogma, and precedence over civil law in areas such as marriage.

This short-lived neo-absolutist period should not be seen as a mere restoration of the *status quo ante* 1848. The old feudal regime was definitively broken, and the landed aristocracy was largely supplanted by the middle class as the dynasty's main support. This was a more modern autocracy, based on an increasingly urban and industrialized society. It was a more centralized autocracy than ever before, but it did carry over from the past the Josephine traditions of rule for the people but not by the people. It may thus seem more backward-looking than the constitutional regimes growing in many western European states. But in fact the years into the 1860s were an essential step toward the modernization of the Habsburg state. Franz Joseph did not long manage to remain the "one master" of Austria, however. His inexperience led to several mistakes that undermined his temporarily consolidated authority.

The first blunder came with the Crimean crisis in 1853. As part of geopolitical jockeying around the declining Ottoman Empire, Russia occupied Turkish dependencies along the Danube. This alarmed Franz Joseph and his foreign minister Count Buol, who themselves were angling for Turkish land in the Balkans. Franz Joseph was also worried about having the huge Russian Empire come right up to his doorstep, since the Slavs in his own lands could start looking to Russia for leadership. Austria arranged a secret deal with Prussia to fight Russia if necessary, and made diplomatic approaches to Britain and France, who after 1854 were at war to stop Russia's preying on Turkey. The blunder came in trying to carve out a middle position for Austria in this conflict. Britain and especially France were never going to adopt Austria as a durable ally, since it was viewed as too repressive an autocracy. France in particular was looking to weaken Austria's hold in Italy. But when in May 1854 Franz Joseph issued an ultimatum to Nikolai to evacuate Moldavia and Wallachia, he thereby alienated his old ally who had sent troops to prop him up in 1849. Nikolai was so angry at what he saw as this betrayal that he turned a portrait of Franz Joseph to the wall.[4] The result was that Austria did end up in the middle, but with no major allies on either side. The amateurish two-timing toward Russia, Britain, and France exposed that Austria was no longer so essential to the European balance of power, and it is from this miscalculation over the Crimean War that the monarchy's steep loss of international prestige can be charted.

The other blunder cost the Habsburgs their three centuries' old possession of Lombardy. Austrian control of northern Italy was deeply unpopular with the people there, made only more so because of Habsburg victories over the Italian revolutionaries in 1849. When Franz Joseph made a state visit to Venice in 1856 he was received coldly, with three-quarters of the Venetian nobility declining an invitation to a court reception. In 1857 he appointed his brother Maximilian as governor-general. Maximilian, as so often in Habsburg history, was more able than his older brother, and also more liberal. He recommended that Franz Joseph grant the people in Lombardy and Venetia concessions in response to their complaints of high taxes and minimal involvement in their own government. Franz Joseph was still intent on pursuing a hard-line, and so missed the opportunity to assuage the building resistance to Habsburg rule. In this volatile situation, Cavour, the prime minister of Piedmont-Sardinia and architect of Italian unification, made a deal with Napoleon III of France for support in a war against Austria. Franz Joseph refused to negotiate, even when offered support from Britain and Prussia, believing that to back down in Italy would compromise his dynasty's honor. When war broke out in 1859, Austria came to rue that it had no allies it could count on.

For all Franz Joseph's idealization of the military, it turned out he could not even count on his own army. His forces struck quickly at Piedmont-Sardinia, hoping to knock it out of the war before France could mobilize. But Franz Joseph's general, Gyulai, was so incompetent that despite major numerical superiority he could not defeat the Piedmontese at the battle of Magenta. A series of command failures torpedoed the dynasty's chances in Italy, until the final one, when an exasperated Franz Joseph came to the front to lead his armies himself. He proved no better a battlefield general than Gyulai. At the battle of Solferino in June 1859, he faced Napoleon III in personal command as his opponent, marking the last time in European history when armies on both sides were commanded by their monarchs. Austria was defeated, and afterwards, Franz Joseph met Napoleon III alone to make many of the arrangements that became the Treaty of Zürich. By this treaty the Habsburgs lost Lombardy, Modena, and Tuscany, and Franz Joseph personally lost much of his credibility as a leader. His initial response, dismissing Bach and shuffling his ministers, was minimal. But the clamor for change could not be silenced; despite his furious resistance, even his bankers were insisting Franz Joseph end the neo-absolutist experiment and introduce constitutional rule.

The steps that the regime took first in October 1860 and then February 1861 did not grant a constitution, but they did move in that direction. The "October Diploma" was an initial step toward reducing some of the monarch's powers. The Diploma appeased the provincial aristocracies, particularly in Hungary, by restoring their traditional rights such as diets. It also created an empire-wide assembly, the Reichsrat, which would have powers in taxation and other economic matters such as customs and currency. This bid for conservative federalization satisfied almost no one, however. For the Hungarians, it did not go far enough toward granting their autonomy. For the Czechs and the Croats, it was incomplete since it did not grant them roughly equal status with the Hungarians. The liberal bourgeoisie was dissatisfied because the Reichsrat would still be too weak, while other elements among the bourgeoisie, mainly the conservatives, objected to the retreat from centralism in favor of federalization.

To this half-measure, Franz Joseph then added the February Patent in 1861, which backtracked on some of October's federal commitments. The Reichsrat gained increased powers above the regional diets, for example. While that adjustment angered the Hungarians and Czechs who wanted increased autonomy, it satisfied the more conservative members of the Austro-German bourgeoisie, who in any case were among Franz Joseph's strongest backers. To benefit them, the February Patent also expanded representation of the urban middle and upper classes. Franz Joseph reluctantly viewed these steps as necessary to shore up support for his regime. But while he admitted that he was introducing some constitutionalism, he also intended to hold tenaciously to his powers, above all over the military and foreign affairs. The next several years were a tentative time, as the monarch felt his way toward constitutional rule, and the aristocracies, bourgeoisies, and national groups within the monarchy similarly explored how the new arrangements would work. Though these October and February decrees did not firmly implant constitutional rule, they established a precedent for the end of absolutism that Franz Joseph was never able to reverse.

As the defeats in the war for Italian unification forced changes on Franz Joseph in 1860, so too did the unification campaign in Germany later that decade. Since 1850 the Habsburgs' authority within Germany continued to deteriorate. Though there were a variety of visions for governance of Germany, they boiled down essentially to two. One was the *kleindeutsch* ("small German") solution in which Austria would be excluded from Germany, and Prussia would be the dominant power. The other was the opposite, the *großdeutsch* ("big German") solution that included Austria; it was supported by a number of other German states such as Bavaria, Württemberg, and Saxony, who feared Prussian domination. In a number of instances, including its failure to enter the Zollverein, Austria botched strategies to strengthen its case for the *großdeutsch* option. One important reason why the Habsburgs' initiatives in Germany were unsuccessful was because of domestic politics: the Austro-Germans were unable to dictate policy in Vienna, and Franz Joseph's attempt at centralism was discredited by 1859. Hence any concerted effort to emphasize Austria's connections to Germany was crippled by the assertiveness of the Hungarians and the growing impact of the Czechs, Croats, and other groups.

The Habsburgs' slow loss of weight in Germany was matched by Prussia's striking rise. Once Otto von Bismarck was named Prussian minister president in 1862, he consistently and decisively out-maneuvered Franz Joseph and his advisors. In 1864, when Austria joined Prussia in an attack on Denmark over its majority-German duchies of Schleswig-Holstein, most of the gains from that war went to Prussia. Prussia at this time also had the sympathies of German patriots more than Austria ever could, since the Habsburgs' state was multinational and viewed as more politically reactionary and economically backward. Some of Franz Joseph's advisors had for several years been advocating an attack on Prussia sooner rather than later to assert Austrian supremacy. That the emperor became convinced of this plan was due not just to Bismarck's skillful stratagems, but also to Franz Joseph's own domestic problems. By the mid-1860s his regime was being challenged on a number of fronts. The Hungarians had been balking at cooperation in myriad ways, including in paying taxes. There was an uprising in Galicia in 1863 and unrest continued to simmer there. The monarchy was also experiencing bad harvests and serious financial problems, for example with mounting state debt. Franz Joseph unwisely decided that war would be the best way of winning back control of events. The idea was that his peoples would rally around him because of the conflict, and that defeating Prussia and Italy would bring large indemnity payments to stave off an Austrian state bankruptcy.

To prepare for war against Prussia, Franz Joseph knew that he had to shore up his western and southern flanks, since he could not risk France or the young kingdom of Italy attacking at the same time. Here again he was out-maneuvered by Bismarck. Prussia signed a commercial treaty with Napoleon III that bought French neutrality in any Prussian-Austrian war, and then signed another treaty with Vittorio Emanuele, the king of Italy, since the latter wanted Venetia from the Habsburgs. Franz Joseph, meanwhile, had to buy French neutrality for himself but at a very steep price, namely agreeing to hand over Venetia even if Austria defeated Prussia. So he guaranteed beforehand an Austrian defeat in Italy, and yet he still sent troops to fight and die on that front. Finally, since Franz Joseph had alienated Russia in the Crimean War, he could count on no support from that quarter.

When war came in June 1866, then, Austria was fighting on two fronts at once, which it could not afford to do. In the Veneto its troops defeated an Italian army, and in the Adriatic the Austrian navy easily bested the Italian.

In Germany, Austria had the support of Hanover, Hesse, and Bavaria, but the Prussians overpowered their small combined army. The crucial encounter was between the main Austrian and Prussian forces in Bohemia, near the town of Sadová. Known as the Battle of Königgrätz, the victory that Prussia won was not overwhelming, but it amounted to a crushing defeat for Austria nonetheless. Though the two armies were comparable in size, the Prussians had better command, troops, and technology. They decimated the Austrian ranks with the needle gun while the Austrians were relying on antiquated rifles and bayonet charges. The multiethnic nature of the monarchy proved debilitating here, too: its military was less well-trained, hamstrung by the many languages of its recruits. Significant numbers of Czech and Hungarian soldiers deserted.

Franz Joseph's chief commander Benedek predicted what would happen in a pitched battle between Prussian and Austrian forces, and warned Franz Joseph in a telegram several days before Königgrätz, but the emperor, motivated by concerns of honor and prestige, insisted that he would not make peace before a battle had taken place. In the end, Napoleon III mediated, and Bismarck did not seek the maximum penalty against Austria. He wanted a quick war that forced Austria out of Germany but would not unduly weaken a future potential ally. This loss to Prussia was the result of long-running trends and the precipitant of others in the monarchy's remaining decades. It signaled the Habsburgs' final expulsion as arbiters of German affairs, bringing to an end roughly four centuries as the first family of Germany. It was a major blow to the dynasty's prestige—though it was Franz Joseph's clinging to such prestige that impelled him to seek the disastrous fight in the first place. Internationally, Austria for a time drew closer to France, since both regarded Prussia as their chief enemy. But after the French republic was declared in 1870, it was unlikely that Franz Joseph could seal a firm alliance with a state antithetical to the principle of dynastic monarchy. He could never get revenge on Prussia either, though he initially wanted it, since the monarchy's financial situation was so precarious.

In 1866 France, Britain, and Russia all abandoned Austria to its fate in a way that would have been unthinkable in the previous two centuries. The decline in the Habsburgs' geopolitical standing continued such that by 1900 the monarchy was clearly no longer in the first rank of powers. The expulsion from Germany also altered the fundamentals of the monarchy domestically. It could no longer pretend to be a German power, and instead had to admit to its hybrid, heterogeneous makeup as never before. Ejected from Italy, shut out of Germany, Franz Joseph turned eastward, looking to the Balkans as the area where Austria could still throw its weight around. That course would draw the monarchy into the final cataclysm in 1914. More immediately, Franz Joseph was forced to acknowledge the limits of his power, and indeed the weakness of his position even at home. Liberals now had greater leverage to demand stricter constitutional government, and the Hungarians had greater leverage to demand more autonomy in that government.

The *Ausgleich* ("compromise") reached with Hungary in 1867 was a major concession for Franz Joseph, and it created the so-called dualist Austria-Hungary that existed until 1918. It was not purely a product of the emperor's defeat at Königgrätz. In fact there had been ongoing negotiations with two key moderate Hungarian leaders, Andrássy and Deák, since 1865. In that year Franz Joseph had suspended the February Patent because it was proving unworkable as a basis of government. The Reichsrat, for instance, was usually blocked by the resistance of one national group or another. In 1867 his chancellor Beust reached an agreement with Andrássy and Deák on granting Hungary nearly all the powers of a separate kingdom, united with the Austrian "half" of the monarchy mainly through the person of the monarch. Franz Joseph went along with this because after the defeat to Prussia he felt he had to secure the Hungarians' loyalty. For their part, Andrássy and Deák did not want to break up the monarchy, seeing union with Austria as Hungary's best protection against Russia. But they did ruthlessly exploit their upper hand, so that Franz Joseph agreed to terms that increased the constitutional constraints on him.

The arrangement was dualist because it was not federalist. Rather than parceling out the monarchy into a structure in which the Austro-German lands, the Czech lands, Galicia, and Hungary-Croatia would all have roughly equal weight, it was divided simply into two, the Hungarian half and the Austrian half. This latter was not really called "Austria" but rather "Cisleithania," meaning "beyond the Leitha River," which was the border between Austria and Hungary. The formal name of the Cisleithanian half was "the countries and realms represented in the Reichsrat," which gives some indication of the insubstantial basis for common identity of those territories. The governmental link between these two halves was also minimal. Foreign and military policy belonged almost exclusively to Franz Joseph. He retained the power to appoint and dismiss ministers, who thus had only a partial responsibility to parliament, and he could reject laws passed by the Reichsrat. There was a joint financial ministry and tariff regime. But details such as Hungary's share of the budget could be renegotiated every decade, which led to repeated political conflicts in the years ahead, so dualism's division of powers was by no means entirely clear.

Nearly everything else was separate. There were distinct parliaments for the Cisleithanian and Hungarian halves, and each half had its own administrative, legal, and school systems. The realm was designated as *kaiserlich* ("imperial") for the Austrian Empire of Cisleithania and *königlich* ("royal") for the Kingdom of Hungary. In practice, dualism meant that the Austro-Germans dominated the other peoples in their half, and the Hungarians the other peoples in theirs. In many ways, Hungary's weight within the Dual Monarchy only grew after 1867, thanks to economic advances that in turn fed into greater assertiveness on the part of the

Magyar elite. That elite asserted itself quite successfully not only against Vienna but also against the national minorities within Hungary. This was not an arrangement that could ever satisfy the Czechs in the Cisleithanian half nor the Croats in the Hungarian half. Franz Joseph was aware of this problem, but chose to ignore it. He said, "I do not conceal from myself that the Slav peoples of the monarchy may look on the new policies with distrust, but the government will never be able to satisfy every national group. That is why we must rely on those which are the strongest . . . that is, the Germans and the Hungarians."[5]

Ultimately, even the Austro-Germans and the Hungarians disliked dualism. The former resented Hungarians' disproportionate weight in the monarchy, while the latter constantly pushed for more autonomy and resisted any changes that would reduce their weight. And virtually all the other national groups detested the arrangement because it unfairly excluded them. Franz Joseph initially made his acceptance of the Ausgleich contingent on the Hungarians coming to an agreement with the Croats and passing a nationalities law. So in 1868 the *Nagodba* ("Agreement") was signed with Croat leaders. It guaranteed some autonomy within the Hungarian kingdom, but its provisions were gradually whittled away by centralizing Hungarian governments over subsequent decades. There was also an attempt at an agreement between Vienna and Prague in 1871, but it never came to fruition. The Austro-Germans were averse to sharing power in Cisleithania with the Czechs, and the Hungarians (led by Andrássy, who at this point was the foreign minister for the Dual Monarchy) opposed it because any moves toward federalism in Cisleithania would likely encourage similar pressures in Hungary, which would undermine Magyar domination of the other nationalities.

The dualist system in sum was both a success and a failure. The failure is easy to pinpoint. After 1867 the two halves of the monarchy became less cohesive with each other, above all politically but also culturally to some extent. The dynasty itself provided the tenuous link. Dualism created as many problems as it solved, since it excluded so many other national groups from its ruling structure. This structure experienced continual tensions and occasional breakdowns. That it could be called a success at all may seem surprising, given the opposition it aroused at the time and the criticism it has received ever since. But the Ausgleich amounted to a constitutional formalization of Hungary's special position in the Habsburg monarchy, a special position dating back to 1527. In that sense the Ausgleich was not new, but rather a codification of prior arrangements. Moreover, it sealed an end to the misguided experiment in neo-absolutism. The resultant Dual Monarchy would, for almost five more decades, provide a partially modernized legal and governmental structure for the political, economic, social, and cultural development of the various peoples bound under Franz Joseph's sovereignty. These decades were a time of by no means constant progress. Still, the monarchy for the most part enjoyed peace abroad, and provided security for a number of smaller peoples who otherwise would have been vulnerable to predations from larger states. At home, while it did lag western Europe, Austria-Hungary was demonstrably more liberal and developed than states to its east or south. For all the political problems dualism engendered, then, the remaining decades of the Habsburg monarchy saw considerable advances as well.

One of those advances was in the economy, which expanded solidly over the course of Franz Joseph's reign. The 1850s saw fairly modest growth but some major projects such as building roads and railways; the Semmeringbahn, completed in 1854, was the world's first mountain railway. Railways spread rapidly over the succeeding decades. It was in the years after the Ausgleich that parts of the monarchy really developed into modern economies. This is the period known as the *Gründerjahre*, or "founding years." Most of the economic development of this time was concentrated in Bohemia and Moravia, Silesia, around Vienna, and in the Hungarian plain. Bohemia and Moravia were the most industrialized parts of the monarchy, accounting for nearly three-fifths of its industry, with Lower Austria coming second. The monarchy's single largest industrial concern was the Škoda factories in Plzeň, which among other things produced most of the military's armaments. Hungary in general grew faster than did Austria. One reason why it did so was the tariff regime making agricultural imports into the monarchy more expensive, which helped Hungary become the monarchy's breadbasket. Overall agriculture formed the largest sector of the monarchy's economy, but farming productivity did increase, especially in Hungary. Land ownership was also still quite concentrated, again especially in Hungary. Areas such as Slovakia, Galicia, Transylvania, and Bukovina remained backward. Many poor peasants from these lands sought to improve their lot by migrating to the monarchy's cities, or to the Americas.

There were also a number of detriments that retarded economic development in the monarchy. It was mostly landlocked, with its main port of Trieste located far from its main economic centers. Its peripheral areas such as Galicia and Dalmatia were poorly connected to the rest of the monarchy because of both a lack of rivers, and mountainous terrain difficult for overland transportation. A relative dearth of mineral resources, political elites entrenched in traditional economic and social structures, and nationalist jealousies that led to unstable politics were also all factors. Moreover, a serious stock market crash hit in 1873, leading to a depression that lasted until 1879, though in the 1880s growth accelerated. By 1914 the monarchy was not economically as large nor as modern as Britain, Germany, or France, but it was still the fourth largest economic power on the continent, significantly more industrialized than Russia. It was the third largest producer of coal, and the fifth largest of iron and textiles in Europe.[6] It had grown soundly for decades, and become more economically integrated despite its political tensions.

Perhaps more impressive than even the economic strides during Franz Joseph's reign was the tremendous cultural bloom. As with the economic modernization that nonetheless left some regions distinctly backward, the cultural bloom, for all its richness and innovation, coexisted with nationalist tensions, political repression, and anti-Semitism. Some commentators have theorized that the monarchy's troubled politics actually encouraged the feverish fecundity of its artistic production.[7] Nationalism, for instance, certainly catalyzed art in a variety of media, as peoples throughout the monarchy strove to create a unique cultural expression for their community. Above the nationally inspired art, though, soared an aspirationally cosmopolitan artistic culture, typically based in German trends and precedents. Space prohibits any more than a woefully inadequate list of great names from this period. The monarchy's eminent writers in German would include Arthur Schnitzler, Hugo von Hofmannsthal, Georg Trakl, Franz Werfel, Franz Kafka, and Marie von Ebner-Eschenbach. Talented visual artists such as Hans Makart and Tina Blau stand not far behind the heavyweights of Gustav Klimt, Egon Schiele, and Oskar Kokoschka. Vienna continued to be a magnet for musical genius, with Johannes Brahms making the city his home from 1869 to 1897. Other Austrians such as Gustav Mahler, Hugo Wolf, Anton Bruckner, Anton Schönberg, Alban Berg, and of course the Strauss family of waltz fame helped define musical culture. Austro-German intellectual life was particularly fecund, with such innovators as Ernst Mach, Gregor Mendel, and Sigmund Freud.

The other nationalities also produced an astonishing array of talent, albeit usually less well-known in the English-speaking world. Hungarian writers such as Géza Gárdonyi, Endre Ady, Mihály Babits, and Dezső Kosztolányi elevated Magyar literature to new heights. A number of Hungarian painters made a mark, such as Mihály Munkácsy, Pál Szinyei Merse, and Jozsef Rippl-Ronai. Several excellent Hungarian architects, including Miklós Ybl, Imre Steindl, and Ödön Lechner created an impressive and influential built legacy. Among the era's notable Hungarian composers were Imré Kálmán and Franz Lehár, plus the early careers of Béla Bartók, Ernő Dohnányi, and Zoltán Kodály. Czech literary output was also splendid, notably the contributions of Jan Neruda, Svatopluk Čech, Božena Němcová, and Jaroslav Hašek, among other writers. The Czechs as always punched above their weight in music, thanks to Bedřich Smetana, Antonín Dvořák, and the beginnings of Leoš Janáček's fame. The less numerous nationalities of the monarchy each had their own artistic scene as well. Kraków, for example, was the Polish cultural capital, and it was crowned by the brilliant, multi-talented writer, painter, and designer Stanisław Wyspiański.

The crucible of the monarchy's fertile cultural stew was Vienna itself. It was transformed during Franz Joseph's reign, from a modestly sized city on the eastern fringes of western culture, to a great, thriving metropolis and harbinger of modernity. Symbol of that transformation was Franz Joseph's decision in 1857 to tear down the colossal fortifications—evidence of the city's former position near the perilous frontier of the Ottoman Empire—and build the roughly circular boulevard known as the Ringstraße. Over the next several decades a series of imposing structures were erected along this street, in historicist styles that referenced the dynasty's geographic reach and centuries'-old authority. The Votive Church was erected in gothic style as a thanksgiving for Franz Joseph surviving the 1853 assassination attempt. A permanent parliament was constructed to look like a Greek temple. The city hall echoed in an elephantine fashion Brussels' medieval city hall. The neo-Renaissance opera house, opened in 1869, was one of the most controversial buildings of the Ring; negative public reception drove one of its architects to suicide.

While these historicist buildings reflected the dynasty's own values, there was more daring architectural work by Otto Wagner, Joseph Olbrich, and Adolf Loos. Franz Joseph hated the latter's building on the Michaelerplatz, across from the Hofburg, for its modern touches such as the lack of window ornamentation, whose lack led the Viennese to dub the building "the house without eyebrows." All this construction was made possible in part by the growth of banks that provided capital to the monarchy's growing economy; they often built their headquarters along the Ring. Noble families also built palaces along the Ring, such as the Colloredos and the Kinskys, but Vienna was growing out of its old character as primarily a seat for the Habsburg court. It was a magnet for people of lower social classes from all across the Habsburg realms. For Jews from the poorest lands such as Galicia, Vienna could provide a very climbable ladder: hence so many of the city's lawyers, doctors, journalists, and intellectuals were Jewish. Many of these same trends applied on a smaller scale to Budapest as well, unified as a single city in 1873. Around 1914, after decades of rapid growth, the twin capitals Vienna and Budapest had populations of 2 million and not quite 1 million respectively.

After 1867 Franz Joseph had to modify his dynastic vocation dramatically to accommodate parliamentary politics. The Reichsrat gained the power to introduce legislation, and its lower house as well as various municipal councils were elected. Suffrage expanded gradually, and with it, mass party politics. In Cisleithania, the Liberals dominated until the 1880s, when more sectors of society began to organize for elections, including the working class and peasant/rural interests. The Hungarian liberals remained predominant past 1900, thanks in part to a suffrage slanted in favor of the upper and middle classes and large landowners. National parties also coalesced in both halves of the monarchy. In Hungary, most parties were explicitly nationalist in that they represented the claims of Hungarian (or Croatian) autonomy. In both Hungary and Cisleithania, social democratic parties campaigning for workers' rights grew stronger as the suffrage was widened. The 1890s in Cisleithania additionally saw the rise of the Christian Socials, a motley collection of peasants, clergymen, and the lower middle classes with a strong current of anti-Semitism. Their leader Karl Lueger was elected mayor in Vienna of 1895, but Franz Joseph, using his constitutional prerogatives, initially refused to appoint him. He was appalled by Lueger's anti-Semitism and populism.

The evolution toward a more democratic state and society was fitful. The monarch, the bureaucracy, and the military remained the key central institutions. Freedom of association, assembly, religion, and the press were guaranteed by law after 1867 but limited in practice. Libel and sedition laws restricted press freedom, and groups that the government considered subversive—which could be anything from nationalists to anarchists—could be broken up and their members jailed. Article 14 in the constitution allowed for emergency powers for the executive, which enabled Franz Joseph to impose his will when necessary. In general, governments in Cisleithania were more liberal than those in Hungary, and the latter was also more strongly centralized. As nationalists, the middle classes, workers, and peasants became more politically assertive in the two decades prior to 1900, each produced their own fracturing tensions on the monarchy's governments. There were a number of long-serving prime ministers in Cisleithania, including Adolf Auersperg from 1871 to 1879 and Eduard Taaffe from 1879 to 1893. In years thereafter, though, prime ministers' tenures were much shorter, typically undone by disputes in the centrifugal politics of nationalism. The principal mode of governing the monarchy became "muddling through" (*fortwursteln*), as Taaffe said.

Franz Joseph grudgingly acceded to these developments. To the end of his days, he disliked the idea of being a constitutional monarch, but he did rule according to the law, helping inculcate a strong legal culture in his monarchy. He adapted to the rising tide of liberalism by emphasizing his position as sovereign above all classes, ruling in the interests of equal application of the laws and an efficient bureaucratic administration that would serve all his subject-citizens. He retained a firm hand over the military and foreign policy, and he could hire and fire ministers at will. However, by the 1880s, as he had already been on the throne for nearly 40 years, he became less directly involved in politics. He tended to let his ministers take the initiative while he still stood at the top of the entire state, for better and for worse. Final decision power rested with him, but as he himself acknowledged when he met Teddy Roosevelt in 1910, he was stuck in his ways and something of an anachronism. Some of his ministers complained that Franz Joseph was too resistant to change, unreceptive to the most audacious ideas for solving the monarchy's structural problems, such as through an increasing federalization. By 1900 the dynasty's primacy in most spheres of politics had receded because of rapid changes in economic modernization, the growth of mass politics, and increasingly assertive nationalist movements. Other elements of long Habsburg practice also faded, such as the privileged place for the Catholic Church, regional elites, and provincial diets.

The emperor's ultimate response to transformations in society and his own political role was simply to soldier on. He was defined by his sense of duty to fulfill the role of monarch and incarnate the supranational politics his monarchy aspired to. He hoped that economic advances, increased public services, and expanded suffrage might weaken the most intransigent nationalist groups. He resisted not only such intransigence but also those voices in the ruling circle who urged him to crack down more strongly on the Hungarians. For example, around 1905 he rejected plans supported by his appointed successor Franz Ferdinand for a military coup against Hungary. His nearly unbreakable routine—reading governmental reports by 5:00 a.m., taking meetings with various officials for several hours after 8:00 a.m., several times a week giving audiences in the afternoon and performing ceremonial functions—left him with an austere life. His son Rudolf wrote of his father in 1881, "He stands lonely on his peak; he talks to those who serve him of their duties, but he carefully avoids any real conversation. Accordingly he knows little of what people think and feel, their views and opinions. Only those people now in power have access to him . . ."[8] Still, the old, bewhiskered emperor symbolized authority, legitimacy, and links among the peoples of eastern central Europe in a way that the vast majority of his subjects respected, despite whatever grievances they may have had about the regime.

As turbulent as were the changes in society, Franz Joseph's domestic life was no more serene. A series of tragedies took their toll on him, until the very last one, Franz Ferdinand's assassination. An underlying misfortune to his whole family life was his unfulfilling marriage to Elisabeth, known as Sisi, a Wittelsbach who became his bride when she was 16 years old. Sisi has been romanticized into a treacly caricature. In actual fact she was an intelligent, self-absorbed, unstable woman who never reciprocated the deep love Franz Joseph offered her. His outwardly stolid demeanor broke completely in his letters to Sisi, addressing her as "my dear, only angel," "my dear, heavenly Sisi," and signing himself, "your little man" and "your poor little one."[9] Sisi, however, deeply resented life at court, especially the early years of their marriage when Franz Joseph's mother Sophie exercised a domineering control. Thus Sisi came to spend much of her time traveling, whiling away her days in Madeira and Corfu. Even then she was not happy, and probably became anorexic.

She did occasionally play an important role in politics, most remarkably when she actively pushed Franz Joseph to conclude the Ausgleich in 1867. She had conceived a love of the Hungarians, advocated for their interests at court, and was rewarded with their love in return, such as at the festive ceremony that same year when she and Franz Joseph were crowned king and queen in Hungary. Because she knew she could not satisfy Franz Joseph's emotional needs, she arranged for him to develop a relationship with a Viennese actress, Katharina Schratt. This became a platonic but very intimate liaison, with Franz Joseph writing to her frequently and confessionally, sharing his heart's concerns, and even matters of state. It was nonetheless a terrible blow for the emperor when Sisi was stabbed to death by an Italian anarchist on the shores of Lake Geneva in 1898. He commented bitterly, "I am spared nothing in this world."[10] Katharina Schratt broke off her own holiday to come console him.

Sisi's violent death was the third such in Franz Joseph's family circle. In 1867 his brother Maximilian, who had become Emperor of Mexico, was executed by a firing squad. Maximilian had a difficult relationship with his older brother. After serving as governor in Lombardy, Maximilian bought into a French plan to create a Catholic monarchy in Mexico, though Franz Joseph did not approve. He lasted only three years on the throne. Once Napoleon III pulled his troops out, support for the Mexican monarchy collapsed. Maximilian was shot and his widow, the Belgian princess Charlotte, reportedly went insane. Franz Joseph learned of his brother's death just a few days after his and Sisi's coronation in Hungary.

A still crueler blow came 22 years later. The marriage with Sisi had produced one son, the crown prince Rudolf, who inherited much of his mother's character. He was highly intelligent but emotionally troubled, moreso as the years went on. Though Franz Joseph had first tried to educate Rudolf as a conservative military man, that was clearly at odds with the boy's character, and Sisi intervened to further Rudolf's education in a more progressive mode. Rudolf came to sympathize with liberal ideas, even to an extent with the aspirations of the monarchy's non-German nationalities. He chafed against his father's stern traditionalism. Franz Joseph excluded him from most leadership roles, so Rudolf dabbled in journalism—writing some articles critical of the monarchy's governance—but also devoted his energies to debauchery. He seems to have contracted gonorrhea, and evidently convinced that he would never amount to anything, in 1889 at the family estate of Mayerling he shot 17-year-old Mary Vetsera (one of his various mistresses) and then himself. The royal family tried to cover up this scandalous murder-suicide, and Franz Joseph tried to remain stoic at the shocking loss of his only son and successor. But this succession of tragedies is one reason why Franz Joseph took on the aura of such an impassive drone, working hard on behalf of the monarchy while retreating into an unfeeling aloofness.

Perhaps in keeping with the dark cloud of such tragedies, Austria-Hungary's last decades are often seen as a textbook case of a state crippled by nationalist dissension. Certainly the growing assertion of nationalist politics, and the mobilization of masses for those politics, posed problems. Yet these developments were neither definitive nor irremediably destructive. Though only about a quarter of the population was Germans, they made up 75 percent of the bureaucracy, and they paid some 65 percent of the direct taxes in Cisleithania, demonstrating their relative preponderance within the Habsburg state.[11] The Polish elite worked to ensure its control over the Ruthenian minority in Galicia, which control the Ruthenians understandably resented. Czechs consistently argued for a restructuring of the political system that would allow them an autonomy comparable to the Hungarians'. There were also often tensions within Bohemia between Germans and Czechs; Germans tended to regard the Czechs as uncultured upstarts. Hungarian leaders pursued a policy of Magyarization to centralize control of the state and restrict the rights of the Romanian, Slovak, and South Slav minorities. Those South Slavic groups of Serbs, Croats, and Slovenes occasionally squabbled and occasionally collaborated. Irredentism among the Italian and Romanian groups was also a concern.

This increasing division of the society along national lines resulted in a complicated, sometimes dysfunctional politics in the Reichsrat. In particularly contentious periods, it could seem as if nationalism was sabotaging the whole monarchy. One example is with the language ordinances proposed by the prime minister Badeni in 1897. These would have required all government officials in Bohemia to learn Czech, which caused a huge uproar among Germans. There were riots in Vienna, Graz, Prague, and other parts of Bohemia, and violence in the Reichsrat itself, which was subsequently closed down for a period. In response, Franz Joseph appointed bureaucrats rather than parliamentarians to run the government, and used Article 14, the emergency clause of the constitution, to pass decrees. After the political firestorm, the language ordinances were revoked in 1899, but then the Czechs began obstructing parliament. For much of the remainder of the reign, the Reichsrat was controlled by bureaucrats rather than elected representatives, undermining the entire parliamentary system and leading to frequent brinkmanship among the national groups. In 1906 there was a parliamentary crisis in Hungary as well, as Magyar politicians advanced revisions to the Ausgleich that Franz Joseph could not accept. The military occupied the parliament in that year and formally dissolved it. There were continuing disputes in the next several years over such matters as Hungary's quota of annual army recruits, which further stressed the monarchy's basic governing institutions. In 1908 the Bohemian diet was dissolved because of obstructionism again over Czech/German language rights there.

But these tensions have to be set in context alongside instances of cooperation, overarching unity, and other societal developments. For example, in Bohemia there were practices such as the *Kindertausch* whereby a Czech family would send its children to live with a German family, and vice versa, so that they could grow up learning each other's languages.[12] An elite, German-centric culture also served as a source of unity. The army, as well, fairly successfully fused the diverse peoples into a functioning body. Rarely were nationalists, no matter how extreme, disloyal to Franz Joseph. Very few voices were calling for the breakup of the monarchy. In many places, too, rural people remained relatively unmoved by nationalist agitation. This was at first a phenomenon of a usually small number of political entrepreneurs, even if its appeal grew by 1900 to embrace mass political parties. The increasing nationalist mass mobilization toward the end of Franz Joseph's reign was by no means unique to Austria-Hungary. It mirrors similar developments in other European societies, including the incorporation of other previously excluded groups into politics such as peasants and industrial workers.

The positive aspects of nationalism should also not be forgotten. For much of this period, nationalism was closely linked to liberalism, and so emphasized ideas such as legal equality and the rule of law, the expansion of education, and social progress more generally. In short, though the politics of the monarchy's national groups grew increasingly contentious, this was still a fairly free society. Parliamentary politics were reasonably democratic (albeit on a restricted franchise), the bureaucracy was for the most part efficient, the press mostly free and the judiciary independent. The Habsburg monarchy was a passably prosperous, modern, functioning constitutional regime with very little likelihood of splintering. According to the 1910 census, which included Bosnia-Herzegovina, the monarchy had a population of 51,390,000, greater than that of France. Of that total, 28,572,000 lived in Cisleithania, 20,886,000 in Hungary, and 1,932,000 in Bosnia-Herzegovina. Some 45 percent of the monarchy's total population were Slavs (see Table 11.1).

Table 11.1 Ethnic groups in Austria-Hungary

Ethnic group by language	Percentage of monarchy's total population
Germans	23.36
Hungarians	19.57
Czechs	12.54
Poles	9.68
Serbs and Croats	8.52
Ruthenes	7.78
Romanians	6.27
Slovaks	3.83
Slovenes	2.44
Italians	1.5
Others	4.51

Source: 1910 Austro-Hungarian census, published in *Geographischer Atlas zur Vaterlandskunde an der österreichischen Mittelschulen* (Vienna: K. u. k. Hof-Kartographische Anstalt G. Freytag & Berndt, 1911).

The monarchy's foreign policy was almost as fraught as its domestic politics, and the two often intertwined. Thanks to skillful leadership by two foreign ministers, Friedrich Ferdinand von Beust and Gyula Andrássy, Austria-Hungary remained neutral in Prussia's war with France in 1870, and then achieved a rapprochement with both Germany and Russia. Their objective was to restore the monarchy to its great power status by improving relations with France, cultivating influence in southern Germany, and acquiring territory in the Balkans. In general terms, the Austro-Germans looked toward the German Empire and wanted a strong alliance with it. The Hungarians were more worried about Russia, but saw a German alliance as an important security guarantee. The Czechs and the other Slavs tended to be much more sympathetic to Russia, in its ostensible role as protector of Slavs, and opposed to Germany. The Poles, however, were caught between their eternal rock and hard place, and so were wary of both Russia and Germany.

While Franz Joseph jealously guarded his foreign policy prerogatives, those did not go unchallenged. As in much of the Dual Monarchy's politics, Hungary often had a disproportionate influence here, in part thanks to the astute diplomacy of Andrássy between 1871–9. But the German liberals also tried to assert parliamentary control over foreign policy after the 1878 Berlin Conference, which Franz Joseph strongly rejected. Both Andrássy and the German liberals got what they wanted in 1879 in the form of the firm alliance Austria-Hungary signed with Bismarck's Germany. This alliance bound the Habsburgs' state to the rising Germany, which brought with it growing conflicts with most of the other European powers. For example, France and Russia allied in 1894, and then Britain compacted with France in 1904 and Russia in 1907. All of these moves were motivated by worries about German ascendancy. Thus the web of alliances was woven that constricted Austria-Hungary into its alliance with Germany, and which would contribute to the outbreak of war in 1914.

The monarchy's moves in the Balkans amounted to its wished-for colonial enterprise. They represented compensation for territorial losses in Italy and elsewhere, and a faltering attempt to imitate the imperialist expansion practiced by the larger European powers. Austria-Hungary faced friction in the region with Russia, which regarded the Balkans as within its sphere of interest especially because of the many Orthodox Slavs there. At the Berlin Conference, it was agreed that Austria-Hungary would occupy the formerly Turkish possession of Bosnia-Herzegovina. This was in part a gambit by Germany, Britain, and France to frustrate Tsar Aleksandr II's desire for domination of the Balkans. Bosnia-Herzegovina was so poor that occupying it brought few tangible benefits to the monarchy. Instead, it heightened tensions with Russia and eventually Serbia. The fact that Franz Joseph made this flawed calculation about the value of this addition to the monarchy suggests that his imperialistic ambitions clouded his judgment.

Domestically, German liberals as well as the Hungarian elites were wary of the venture because it added more Slavs to the population. The Hungarians, moreover, did not want the new territory to fall under the jurisdiction of Cisleithania, since that would have reduced Hungary's overall leverage in the dualist structure. Neither did the politicians in the Austrian half want Bosnia-Herzegovina to go to Hungary. The compromise was to administer it under the Joint Finance Ministry, so that it became an anomalous third part within the Dual Monarchy. For a time, Austria-Hungary worked with Russia to try to define spheres of influence in the Balkans to avoid conflicts. This was reasonably successful until 1908. Serbia at first settled into a somewhat acquiescent role as a satellite of Austria-Hungary. After 1903, however, under its new Karađorđević dynasty, Serbia began pursuing a more strongly nationalistic and Russophile course. There was a trade war between Austria-Hungary and Serbia already in 1906. It originated in a dispute over a customs union between Bulgaria and Serbia, which Franz Joseph's foreign policy advisors regarded as threatening moves toward a potential unified South Slav state. In 1908 Austria-Hungary annexed Bosnia-Herzegovina outright, but without sufficient diplomatic preparation to smooth acceptance by the other powers. Franz Ferdinand and the foreign minister Lexa von Aehrenthal were intent on pursuing a more assertive foreign policy to demonstrate independence from Germany, and affirm the monarchy's vitality as a great power. They also had the idea of creating a South Slav union within the monarchy that would counter the Magyars' prevalence in the dualist structure.

The annexation immediately antagonized the Serbs, who feared that Austria-Hungary was trying to dominate the South Slav region and exclude Serbia. Russia then objected to what it saw as an aggressive act toward Serbia. Turkey and Britain objected as well, since the unilateral annexation violated the terms of the 1878 Berlin Congress. In the spring of 1909, the monarchy responded to the uproar not with conciliation but with an ultimatum to Serbia to back down. Germany added its muscle, issuing another ultimatum to Russia that it would have to abandon its support of Serbia or risk war. Then in 1912–13 Austria-Hungary worked against Serbian interests in the First and Second Balkan Wars, for example by thwarting Serbia's aims of winning access to the Adriatic. This geopolitical contest wove into the problems with the South Slav populations inside the monarchy. There were sizeable numbers of Croats and Serbs in Bosnia-Herzegovina, but also of Serbs in areas that Croats considered part of Croatia. While few Croats wanted to break up the monarchy, many Serb radicals did want out, and they looked to Serbia as their protector. Croat and Serb politicians sometimes collaborated against Vienna, but also sometimes tussled over competing visions for a South Slav state. This contributed to increasing rancor and extremism in the South Slav areas, evinced by several assassination attempts on the monarchy's officials.

By 1914, therefore, the Habsburg monarchy was facing problems on many fronts. Internationally, its relations with Russia were tense, and it could count only Germany as a strong ally. It had irredentist threats from

Italy, Romania, and most dangerously Serbia. Its domestic politics were also troubled. The diets of Istria, Croatia, and Bohemia were all closed down in the years just prior to 1914, and in that year the Reichsrat was also dissolved by the prime minister Stürgkh. It might seem that Austria-Hungary by this point was in a state of terminal decline and dysfunction. There were numerous voices among intellectuals in the Danubian domains claiming that politics were fundamentally broken, and that the monarchy was a relic, especially when compared to the dynamic-seeming behemoth of Germany. Even Wilhelm II, before he took the German throne, opined to Crown Prince Rudolf that the Habsburg monarchy was "rotten" and "near to dissolution."[13] There were undeniable problems, with parliamentary politics in particular obstructed by competing nationalisms. The regime was most retrograde in Hungary, where in 1913 the government of István Tisza interfered with a number of civil rights including those of the press, assembly, and jury trials.

But a more judicious view would recognize that, although the politics were dysfunctional, the state and society were not in death throes. Public goods such as roads, railways, canals, and schools continued to be provided. The bureaucracy continued to function reasonably well to administer government. The state's fiscal basis was admittedly fragile, and the economy was not Europe's most robust, but it still brought great strides in material prosperity to many. Culturally, too, the major cities were incredibly vibrant. Many Austro-German, Czech, Magyar, and other politicians were not certain that the competing national groups could compromise to reform the monarchy's structure—but at the same time, very few of those politicians actively advocated the monarchy's end. Even the difficult relationship with Hungary was amenable to negotiation, as demonstrated by a new agreement in 1907 to increase Hungary's contribution to the general treasury. The greatest failure, and the one that led directly to World War One, was with the monarchy's leadership. The dynasty made decisions that led to its own downfall.

The monarchy's provocative politics in the South Slav lands provided the backdrop to the war, though the immediate spark was of course the assassination of Archduke Franz Ferdinand, whom Franz Joseph had chosen as successor after Rudolf's death. Franz Ferdinand proved a particularly problematic addition to the dynasty's leadership. He was intelligent, but reactionary and authoritarian by nature. He derided the non-German peoples for causing the monarchy's problems, and expressed a quite inclusive set of prejudices against Hungarians, Czechs, Italians, and Jews. He rarely got along with the old emperor, operating a shadow cabinet out of his residence at the Belvedere Palace. Franz Ferdinand had his own plans for reform of the monarchy, and resented Franz Joseph's sclerotic resistance to those plans. After Franz Ferdinand and his wife Sophie were killed by a Bosnian Serb extremist in Sarajevo on 28 June 1914, a number of key leaders were determined to crush Serbia once and for all—even though the

Serbian government was not responsible for the murder. Franz Joseph was not in Vienna as this crisis came to a head, instead summering at his Alpine getaway in Bad Ischl. Though he had for decades generally counseled peace as key to the monarchy's preservation, he had also allowed his ministers to pursue policies in the Balkans for more than a decade that were bellicose, especially toward Serbia. The monarchy's leadership repeatedly spurned compromise, and did so now.

Franz Joseph and Austria-Hungary bear a large share of the responsibility for the disaster of World War One. The emperor was the one who gave the final, fatalistic assent to war. The Habsburgs were admittedly caught in a difficult position. If Austria-Hungary did not respond aggressively, it would effectively surrender its status as a great power. It was well known that war with Serbia probably meant war with Russia, but Wilhelm II assured Franz Joseph of Germany's backing. The emperor therefore determined that the dynasty's honor required military action. There were further motivations as well, including some hope that victory might tame the monarchy's other problems. The regime's leadership drew up an ultimatum deliberately designed so that Serbia could never accept it. When Serbia did reject it, Austria-Hungary declared war on 28 July. The leadership was counting on a short conflict, since the monarchy's finances could not sustain a long one. Franz Joseph might not have been so optimistic, however; the later Empress Zita reported that he told her already at the beginning of the war that he foresaw it ending in defeat and revolution.

The monarchy encountered some very serious problems in the early phases of the war. The military was exposed as well-trained but under-funded. Even Italy spent more on defense than did Austria-Hungary. Hence Franz Joseph's army lacked adequate materiel and weapons. The emperor himself opposed some innovations such as armored cars because they scared horses. The overall strategy was for Austria-Hungary to defeat Serbia quickly and then hold off Russia while Germany delivered a swift death blow to France. This became impossible once the western front stalemated after the Marne, and Austro-Hungarian forces failed to beat Serbia and to repel the Russians in Poland. Because of poor command and a faulty mobilization (itself a result of inadequate investment in locomotives), more than half of the Habsburg army had been killed by the end of 1914. Henceforth many of its troops were hastily trained recruits who could never fully replace the experienced men lost in the initial bloodbath. Then Italy entered the war against Austria-Hungary in 1915, after making extortionate demands for territorial compensation as the price for neutrality. The monarchy found itself fighting a three-front war, in the Balkans, against Russia, and against Italy. It was also clear that it was fighting for its very survival: defeat would assuredly mean dismemberment of large chunks of territory.

In 1915, with German help, Serbia was overrun, and Galicia was won back from Russia. Once Romania entered the war against the Central Powers in August 1916 it was defeated by autumn, with the help of allies

Turkey and Bulgaria. After its early difficulties, Austria-Hungary's military functioned reasonably well, even though its chief general, Franz Conrad von Hötzendorf, committed a number of critical mistakes. Its heavy troop losses made the monarchy ever more dependent on German military assistance, and Germany did not hesitate to exploit that relationship. Germany provided weapons, troops, financial subsidies, and even food aid. It charged high prices for the fuel it supplied, and consistently subordinated Austria-Hungary to German military and policy interests. The longer the war dragged on, too, the more precarious the situation for the Central Powers, since they were particularly vulnerable to the economic blockades mounted by Britain and France. Public opinion in the first war years was generally supportive. The fraternal feuding that had convulsed politics over the previous two decades subsided. But all was not peaceful on the home front; there was still squabbling between Czechs and Germans over the administration in Bohemia, and Hungarians maneuvered to integrate Bosnia-Herzegovina and Dalmatia into Hungary. In October 1916 a socialist agitator assassinated the prime minister Stürgkh. By that time, there was growing dissatisfaction over food shortages and censorship.

When Franz Joseph died on 30 November 1916, the outcome of the war was not yet certain, but it was undeniable by that point that his peoples and his prestige had suffered terribly. He was not blind to this: in the months prior to his death he argued that the monarchy needed peace. The course of events was long past his control, however. Franz Joseph was probably resigned to that fact. A line he wrote to his mother after the defeat at Königgrätz in 1866 gives an important indication to his character. He said, "When the whole world is against you and you have no friends, there is little chance of success, but you have to keep fighting as long as you can to do your duty, and finally to succumb with honor."[14] The old emperor, tradition-bound as he was, set such a high store on the honor of his dynasty that he entered a war whose consequences he himself dreaded. Though Franz Joseph was obsolete in so many ways by the time he died, his loss was still terrible for the monarchy. Once he was gone, so too was much of the long experience, residual authority, and age-old legitimacy of the dynasty. His successor, though much younger and more modern, was not able truly to step into Franz Joseph's boots, nor wear his crown.

Karl I (1887–1922)

After the deaths of Rudolf and Franz Ferdinand, the succession fell to Karl, the son of Otto Franz, one of Franz Joseph's nephews. He was 29 when he came to the throne, and had never been educated to become a ruler. He participated in offensives in Italy and Galicia during the war, so he had seen the frontlines, which assuredly helped motivate his objective of securing peace. Karl's aims were indeed laudable. He hoped to reform the monarchy, to rebalance its structure to answer some of the concerns of the Czechs, the Slovaks, and the various South Slavs. He was also appropriately more up-to-date than Franz Joseph, for instance introducing telephones into Schönbrunn. He and his family lived fairly modestly since many of his subjects were suffering deprivations. However, Karl was regarded even by his underlings as weak and indecisive, and his lack of experience in the monarchy's politics proved damaging. One example was that he agreed to be crowned king of Hungary as soon as possible. In so doing, he had to swear to respect the provisions of the Ausgleich, which effectively countered his own plans for reform, and antagonized many of the monarchy's Germans and Slavs. He also recalled the Reichsrat in May of 1917 to show his support for constitutional government, but it rapidly fell into bitter feuding among national groups.

Even a very skilled politician would have had difficulty rectifying the monarchy's mounting problems in the last two years of the war. Domestic unrest was growing stronger by 1916, motivated by ever-deepening privation. Shortages of many kinds wracked the economy, including of cotton, wool, iron, coal, and troops. These hurt not just the military effort but the general population. The lack of coal meant that people did not have fuel even for heat. Inflation rose rapidly, driven by scarcity and by the government's printing currency to cover its huge debts. People's purchasing power plummeted in the face of a precipitous rise in the cost of living, which by 1918 had increased more than ten-fold over 1914. The food shortages were particularly serious. In part because of manpower shortages, harvests shrunk and production of cereals and grains plunged. Strict bread rations were imposed for soldiers and civilians alike, and people's consumption of meat fell to less than half of prewar levels. Wide segments of the populace were understandably holding the regime responsible for these terrible conditions. Hunger became one of the primary motivators of the growing unrest. Major strikes hit Austria in May 1917, and flared up throughout the monarchy in the months to November 1918. In June 1918, workers at the state railway factory in Budapest rioted until they were fired upon by the military. The next day 500,000 workers around Hungary joined in protests that lasted nine days before they were suppressed.

There was some good news on the battlefield in Karl's first year on the throne. A Russian offensive in the summer of 1917 was repulsed, and then after the October Bolshevik Revolution, Russia left the war with the peace of Brest-Litovsk in December. The Central Powers routed Italian armies at the battle of Caporetto in October. However, Germany's declaration of unrestricted submarine warfare in February 1917—which Karl had opposed—helped bring the United States into the war in April. Another example of Karl's well-meaning but bungled initiatives was the disastrous diplomacy of the Sixtus affair, which broke in April 1918. Karl was sincere about seeking peace, and was irritated by German rejection of negotiations; he complained in particular that Kaiser Wilhelm would not listen to reason in his pursuit of "total victory." Karl therefore reached out to Britain and France via his brother-in-law, Prince Sixtus of Bourbon-Parma. He signaled that he would support a peace in which Germany would give Alsace-Lorraine to France and in compensation Austria-Hungary would give Galicia to Germany. This was a pointless offer, though, since hard-liners in Germany would never surrender Alsace-Lorraine, and anyway it was not Karl's to promise.

The proposal initially went nowhere, until Karl's maladroit chancellor Černin in April 1918 suggested that France had actually offered to reach a separate peace and give up its claims on Alsace-Lorraine. This was a lie and besmirched French honor. It led the French prime minister Clemenceau to publish a letter of Karl's from a year earlier. In the letter, Karl voiced support for France's claims for Alsace-Lorraine, and intimated his receptivity to a separate peace for Austria-Hungary. The publication of this letter was a ghastly humiliation for Karl and briefly roiled the alliance with Germany. He had a heart attack, and Černin threatened suicide. The outcome was even worse for the future of the dynasty and Austria-Hungary as a state. In a shame-faced reaffirmation to Germany of his alliance commitments, Karl surrendered nearly all foreign policy and economic independence, tying the fate of his dynasty to the success of the German war effort. Moreover, his obvious double-dealing caused him to lose all credibility with the Allies, who henceforth saw Austria-Hungary as essentially an appendage of Germany and began to support proposals for the breakup of the monarchy.

By the summer of 1918 the Habsburg dynasty's death knell was ringing. Though Romania and Russia had left the war, in the west Germany was retreating as more American troops and supplies poured in. In the east, an allied army forced Bulgaria out of the war in September, Romania rejoined hostilities on the allies' side, and Turkey signed an armistice. Allied forces were marching through the Balkans toward Hungary. Also in September, Italian and British troops broke through on the Italian front. Non-German troops in the monarchy's armies began deserting in growing numbers. Deprivation and riots on the home front erased whatever legitimacy the regime had left. After Woodrow Wilson promulgated his Fourteen Points in January 1918, they became the basis for the national groups' calls for self-determination. The reopening of the Reichsrat proved not a safety valve for discontent but rather a megaphone for it, and over the summer Slavic politicians' former calls for autonomy became instead demands for independence. The monarchy's top leadership, including Cisleithanian and Hungarian prime ministers, had been insisting that increased autonomy was a nonstarter—but this was a senseless position that only reinforced the propagandistic image of the Habsburg monarchy as a "prison of peoples." It helped the national minorities align their struggle with claims of democracy and liberty. Wilson, who had originally envisioned federalization of the monarchy, in October was convinced by Clemenceau and Lloyd George instead to support independent Czechoslovak and South Slav states.

Karl presided impotently over the progressive hollowing out of the whole monarchical state until there was almost nothing left that he actually governed. At the end of October the nearly 400-year-old monarchy dissolved in a matter of weeks. Karl issued a proposal for federalization on 16 October, but he and his idea were already irrelevant by that point. Gyula Andrássy, the last foreign minister of Austria-Hungary, said that the implicit logic behind the final, futile moves taken by the leadership was that "so that no one can kill us, we'll commit suicide."[15] The initiative was instead firmly in the hands of the various national groups. On 18 October Romanians in Hungary called for union with the Kingdom of Romania. On the 21st the Germans of the monarchy declared their right to self-determination. On the 28th the Czech National Council declared independence, and on the 30th the new Czechoslovakia was officially formed. On the 29th the Croatian parliament formally dissolved its connections to Austria and Hungary and pledged to join the new Yugoslav kingdom. On the 31st the Ruthenians in Galicia announced their secession. On 1 November the Hungarians proclaimed their ties to the monarchy ended, followed ten days later by Galicia joining the new Polish republic. As all this was happening, Karl was still working at his desk in Schönbrunn, but the palace was mostly empty. Only a few loyal servants remained, since even his bodyguards had left. Finally on 11 November Karl signed papers that he was "temporarily" giving up his powers. He never formally abdicated but went into exile, first in Switzerland. Karl twice tried to retake the throne in Hungary in 1921, but after these unsuccessful attempts he was removed by the British to Madeira, where he died in 1922.

Dynastic strategies

In its last decades of rule, the dynasty experienced multiple failures of reproduction in the form of succession crises. Ferdinand never produced a legitimate heir, so Franz Joseph's accession had to be arranged since he was the emperor's oldest nephew. Franz Joseph then had his own reproduction problems, given that his marriage to Sisi produced only one son, which led to succession problems after Rudolf's suicide. Casting about to find a suitable heir led to the choice of Franz Ferdinand, whose assassination obviously resulted in another succession failure. When the mantle finally settled on Karl's shoulders, the dynasty ended up with a monarch who was unprepared to rule, and who moreover was saddled with nearly impossible conditions in which to rule. Beyond the succession issues, there was a different kind of reproduction problem that afflicted the dynasty in these years. This was the reproduction of a ruling style and ideology, of maintaining the Habsburgs' ancient (and archaic) vocation of rule and conviction that they were chosen to do so. Adam Wandruszka suggests that several of the family members' morganatic marriages (including Franz Ferdinand's and Archduke Johann Salvator's) as well as Rudolf's suicide can be read as the Habsburgs shying away from the duties and traditions of the dynastic calling.[16] Johann Salvator renounced his title and his heritage in 1889, jettisoning the Habsburg name to call himself instead Johann Orth. Franz Joseph's determinedly pedestrian inner life, as well as his obvious longing for simple domesticity as in his relationship with Katharina Schratt, also suggest that his dutiful demeanor as majesty was a role he played with no great relish. Against these problems must also be mentioned the deep ranks of the family, most of whom did embrace the privileges of nobility. There were five main branches of the family by the late 1800s, all of whom stemmed from Leopold II. There was the ruling line, a Tuscan line, and a Hungarian line, to name but three; several such branches persist today.

At the outset of Franz Joseph's rule, the dynasty went through many familiar motions of legitimation and loyalty strategies. There was an initial flourishing of courtly life, after the Biedermeier boredom of Franz I and the fallowness of Ferdinand, while Franz Joseph was still young and confident in his eager absolutism. One notable celebration from the middle of the reign was that for Franz Joseph's and Sisi's 25th wedding anniversary in 1879; it can be read as an attempt to configure dynastic legitimacy through longevity. The commemoration included a lavish pageant that paraded through Vienna representing great moments of Habsburg history. Individual family members dressed up as great Habsburgs from the past, so Rudolf donned costumes as Rudolf I and Charles V, for example. Rudolf was also entrusted with an interesting project to help construct a cohesive cultural whole out of the monarchy's multi-national patchwork. This was the *Kronprinzenwerk* (properly titled *The Austro-Hungarian Monarchy in Word and Image*), a 24-volume encyclopedia recounting the historical, cultural, geographical, and natural attributes of the various lands and peoples of the monarchy.

The claims to legitimacy and loyalty were impacted by many of the same changes that buffeted Franz Joseph as man and monarch. By the end of his reign the proud courtly style was almost entirely gone. The aged emperor, sorrowed by his numerous family tragedies, did not go in for spectacle, and so the commemoration in 1908 of 60 years on the throne was more somber. In any case, ostentatious royal celebration as a reminder of an older sociopolitical order was inherently anachronistic by this time. The decline of monarchical display is linked to the broader decline of the aristocratic society, which by the latter decades of the reign was no longer culturally nor politically dominant, even if many nobles retained significant economic clout. The nobility lost control of the regional diets as their personal preserve of political power, and the petty nobility saw the richer members of the bourgeoisie snapping up their old estates. Similarly, while Catholicism remained a basic ideological plank of the regime, and much of the population remained devoutly Catholic, the political relevance of the Church declined.

The monarchy's liberals in particular were solidly anticlerical, and worked to whittle away the Church's influence in education and other fields. By 1900, legitimacy and loyalty could no longer be predicated on the small aristocratic slice of the population, nor on the supposedly divine and glorious origins of the ruling house. Franz Joseph correctly saw that his constituency was no longer the older Habsburg pillars of the aristocracy and the Church. He understood that he was responsible to, had to represent and ensure that the government represented, the interests of a much wider segment of the population.

The movements for German and Italian unification naturally served as competitors to the legitimacy of the Habsburg state and the loyalty of its subjects. After the loss at Königgrätz, the Habsburgs could not look to one of their traditional sources of legitimacy, predominance in Germany. Instead, the dynasty had to recalibrate to a new basis of legitimation. This became a more explicitly supranational one, to protect and serve the smaller peoples of eastern central Europe. The equitable treatment of the various peoples was one of the dynasty's duties—although some (the Germans and the Hungarians) were clearly more equal than others. Likewise, creating a well-functioning state that served its peoples and abided by the laws was another lasting source of legitimacy. Franz Joseph himself came to believe that this was the dynasty's divine mission. Whatever outdated notions he carried in his head, Franz Joseph did recognize two developments that forced him to alter not only his dynasty's legitimacy and loyalty claims, but also his own image and function. First, as the state became impartial and impersonal, it presided over a legally undifferentiated population that in theory enjoyed the same rights. Peasants, workers, shopkeepers, civil servants, industrialists, aristocrats—he had to represent them all. Second, as nationalist politics mobilized ever larger numbers, he had to stand above those divisions too. He learned to symbolize and serve all his subject-citizens. Until the war years these goals were often successful, and Franz Joseph was widely respected as a kind of benevolent (grand)father above the many social and political divisions.

Still, those widening cleavages of class and nation necessarily complicated loyalty to the dynasty. Such cleavages were only exacerbated by the rise of mass politics. Old theses of dynastic sovereignty fell gracelessly on the ears of socialists or proletarian activists. Moreover, the justification for the Habsburg multi-national state was problematic to the Germans, Italians, Romanians, and eventually Serbs who could look outside its borders at consolidating national states in Germany, Italy, and so on. Hungarians' insistence on national autonomy had of course long bedeviled the dynasty. For Czechs, Slovaks, Slovenes, and others, the problem became how the Habsburg state thwarted their aspirations to increased self-governance. The dynasty's attempts to overcome these growing cleavages were only ever partial. The belated ideology of constitutionalism and supranational citizenship, of loyalty to the "imperial" Cisleithania and "royal" Hungary, was represented by the slogan *Viribus unitis*, "With united forces," which was Franz Joseph's personal motto. Not surprisingly, this idea of supranational patriotism for the imperial and royal Austria-Hungary found it hard to compete with Czechs' or Italians' patriotism for a sovereign Czech or Italian state.

The emperor knew that his envisioned mission made the dynasty and its state anomalous in the contemporary context of large European nation-states. But his acknowledgment to Teddy Roosevelt that he was a throwback displayed admirable self-awareness. He did embody many monarchical traditions archaic in the context of the twentieth century. But he never became obsolete, since over the course of his reign he adapted. One aspect of traditional monarchy that he retained was his insistence that the government truly served him and not the state. This attitude is clearest in his treatment of his ministers as personally responsible to him, and not to parliament (or thereby to "the people"). Likewise, Franz Joseph insisted that *he* was ultimately responsible for policies, not his ministers. He could be ruthless in dismissing ministers for whom he no longer had any use. One example was his finance minister Beck, who became tainted by an embezzlement scandal. Franz Joseph summarily sacked him, after which Beck cut his own throat. Franz Joseph's paramount political authority, accountable in the last instance to no one but God, can also be seen through the constitutional clause reserving emergency powers to the monarch. However, when he used the emergency clause, in his mind it was to reboot the political system after narrow, self-serving party interests crashed it. This "reboot" would then restore the system's adequate functioning in the broader interests of all. One of his most old-fashioned characteristics was his preference for a chivalrous culture of the officer corps, who almost like modern knights were bound by loyalty to their emperor-king. Franz Joseph regarded the army as identical with the monarchy, and represented this connection visually by nearly always appearing in uniform when he was in public. Though many state institutions had become impersonal, almost separate from the dynasty, the military had not.

Franz Joseph was not completely traditional in that he participated far less in the Habsburgs' old practices of cultural sponsorship. As a sober, unimaginative military man, he was not especially passionate about art, and the great cultural flowering of his reign came about with relatively little involvement from the dynasty. Another untraditional aspect is that he learned to operate in the constitutional system, and did so fairly effectively given that it was so foreign to his political ideals as a younger man. He even came to support the idea of universal suffrage. His motivations were a comprehensible mixture of benevolence—since he felt that universal suffrage would help incorporate the masses into the state—and calculation, as with his hope that universal suffrage might undermine some of the nationalists' strength. The transition to a constitutional monarchy meant that Franz Joseph exercised power in the first instance because of his function in the governance system, and less because of his traditional dynastic right.

That function was fundamentally to be the neutral, impartial overseer of the government's operation. As such, the monarch's powers became more tightly, legally circumscribed, apart from in military and foreign policy matters. It is true that by its nature, the monarchical system presumed Franz Joseph entitled to his function based on dynastic right. And thanks to those dynastic claims the monarchy still rested on an undemocratic basis, since the Habsburgs were obviously not chosen by a mass plebiscite.

That undemocratic basis the dynasty finessed by holding to the Josephinist inheritance. Franz Joseph believed that his authority was justified by ruling for the benefit of his subjects, that he owed them a prosperous, orderly society, and that they in return owed him obedience. Even more than in the eighteenth century, though the monarch was still conceived as the top of the hierarchy, he was supposed to rule not in the interests of his family or his class but in the interests of all his subjects. As constitutional monarch, Franz Joseph performed his symbolic functions well. His scrupulous observance of protocol, of respect for his duties and those of his underlings, for the legal structure of those relationships, shows how he learned to unite the function with the image of the constitutional monarch. Though his own personal inclinations were often simple and frugal, he knew how to play the role of emperor-king, and so earned the admiration of virtually all his peoples. As the Hungarian Admiral Miklós Horthy remarked, "I never knew another monarch who was the personification of majesty in the way that he was."[17]

By 1900, the Habsburg state had come to serve its subject-citizens perhaps better than it served the dynasty. Though the bureaucracy could be slow, it was generally efficient, impartial, and honest. It compared favorably with the bureaucratic machinery of regimes further west, and was far superior to those further south and east. The state's public benefits were notable, including housing, workers' protection, industrial mediation, and social insurance. The civil service was a common means of incorporating educated people almost regardless of nationality into the state. It was thus one of the more effective centralizing organs of the entire monarchy. By employing not just Germans but members of most national groups, it was at least somewhat representative of the monarchy's cultural and linguistic diversity. And while the bureaucratic structure inevitably broke down under the pressures of the world war, in many regards it actually survived the collapse of the dynasty, forming the backbone of the administrations of the successor states. In this sense the Habsburg bureaucracy has to be seen as one of the dynasty's most enduring achievements. Nonetheless, in the end this respectable provision of public services could not overcome the dynasty's broader problems of legitimacy and loyalty.

Where Habsburg administration proved most rickety and inefficient, to the dynasty's ultimate detriment, was with the state's continuing inability to raise sufficient tax revenues to support its defense needs.

The monarchy in these last decades—as often throughout the previous centuries—could not generate the resources to field an army that could adequately protect its vulnerable geographic position. In Franz Joseph's time the culprit for this deficiency was not only the fragmenting force of regional and national privileges that underlie the monarchy, but also the Reichsrat's cutting the military budget. Hence the military remained technologically backward as well as tactically outmoded in key conflicts. In 1849, with difficulty, it restored the dynastic order, and it could be used against any internal group that would threaten that order. But it proved inadequate in 1859 and 1866. It did manage to fight right up to the end of October 1918 as the rest of the state structure was crumbling. So even if the Habsburg military won very few major battles in World War One without German help, at the same time it was never decisively defeated, and it remained intact until the very end. More importantly, perhaps, the military acted as the most integrative agent of the monarchy's patchwork of peoples. It was overwhelmingly Germanic in character: German was the language of command, and some 80 percent of the officers were Germans in 1906.[18] Yet there were highly ranked Hungarian, Czech, Polish, and South Slav commanders too. Whatever its battlefield achievements, through its highly centralized, cross-class, multinational integration, the military was a vision of what the rest of the monarchy never became.

Franz Joseph's reign, and the stub of Karl's, confronted the Habsburg dynasty with more momentous and comprehensive changes than ever in its previous history. The dynasty's response to these challenges presents a mixed record. The failures are all too obvious. Habsburg monarchs still depended on old ideas of legitimacy that were deeply anachronistic for societies in processes of economic modernization, democratization, and nationalization. The governing structures the dynasty put in place never adequately accommodated these processes. Even though parliamentarism was well-developed—more so in Cisleithania than in Hungary—it was compromised by the defining political arrangement of dualism. The 1867 "compromise" with Hungary was a short-term calculation by Franz Joseph that brought enormous longer-term difficulties, above all in that it simply could not adapt to give national groups besides the Germans and the Hungarians a proportionate voice in governance. The dynasty could not reconcile its traditional, firmly held insistence on paramount power with a fully federal polity. The dynasty also never managed to create an alternative structure to personal union for its diverse territories. Those territories, and their many splintered, nationally coalescing communities therefore lacked both sufficient connection to each other, and a sufficient reason to preserve dynastic rule after enduring the disasters of World War One, a war that was itself triggered in part by dynastic rule. The decision to go to war was a result of the lack of separation between *raison de dynastie* and *raison d'état*. The Habsburgs' own reputation required vengeance for Franz Ferdinand's assassination, even if that was not necessarily in the best interests of the polity and peoples they ruled. Franz Joseph gambled in 1914—as he had several times earlier in his reign, surprisingly for his conservative character—and as so often before, his luck was lousy.

On the other hand, the Hohenzollerns and the Romanovs also failed the tests of societal change and world war. Many other European dynasties, including such old Habsburg rivals as the Wittelsbachs in Bavaria and the Bourbons in France, were no longer in power by the time 1919 came either. In that sense Habsburg failure is not unique. Additionally, during Franz Joseph's time there were any number of positive developments in his monarchy. Besides the adaptation to constitutional and parliamentary politics, social progress was impressive. Economic growth, education, hospitals, running water, sanitation, railways, the public sphere, artistic culture, women's rights, and the middle class all made great strides. There were even some integrative forces within culture and politics. Besides the army and the bureaucracy, there was the prestige of German artistic and scientific culture, relatively free movement across borders that brought people from the far corners of the monarchy to Vienna and Budapest, and a reasonably unified economic space stretching from the Adriatic to the Carpathian Mountains. Franz Joseph himself cannot take credit for all these improvements. But his dynasty's rule—as backward-looking, resistant to change, and complacent as it was—nonetheless provided the stable social and political environment that made those developments possible. Habsburg rule came to an end in 1918 not because of the impossibility of adapting to the future, but because the war concentrated a disastrous storm of factors that simply ran out the dynasty's clock.

Conclusion

The Habsburg monarchy did not have to die. It also could not have continued to live as it had been. Though it was not a failed state in 1914, doomed at the outset of the war, it did have grave problems. The responsibility for many of those problems falls to the dynasty itself, and so it must be judged that the dynasty played a major (though not the exclusive) part in the monarchy's final dissolution. There were serious mistakes in leadership, from Franz Joseph and Karl on down, through the generals and prime ministers. Franz Joseph's decision to go to war partly to preserve dynastic honor was, given the political circumstances in 1914, miscalculated in the extreme. Karl's attempts to secure peace, while wise in theory, were clumsy in practice. The generals were too often wedded to outdated strategies and tactics, the prime ministers to policies that unjustifiably excluded certain groups and parties from adequate influence. The mistakes were thus both structural and individual: the flaws in the dynastic polity itself shaped the decisions its leaders made.

Those flaws were intrinsic to the very nature of a dynastic monarchy. The dynasty did too little to adapt to changing conditions of legitimacy and loyalty by the beginning of the twentieth century. Franz Joseph in particular was too steeped in the conservatism and traditions of his house to change in his basic conception of personal rule. His and his ministers' leadership remained ultimately unaccountable to the public. As parliamentary politics malfunctioned in the last decades, the monarchy's ruling circle responded by governing through administrative fiat, and those in charge of the government were always finally responsible to the emperor. Deep in Franz Joseph's conception, the state still belonged to the dynasty, not to the people, his to govern as he saw fit. But by 1918, people wanted their own states, theirs to govern according to the principles of democratic self-determination.

Though "what if" scenarios are too often idle speculation, it is certainly reasonable to conjecture that had a reformist leader come to power before

1914, the monarchy might have survived the war's cataclysm. This is why the monarchy was not a failed state already at that date. For all the obvious tensions in Cisleithanian and Hungarian politics, governance was never so defective that the national groups really wanted the dissolution of the monarchy. Those tensions were often caused by nationalist or other groups working not against the dynasty, but against each other. The center was not the enemy; rather the other political factions were. The monarchy actually provided a reasonably open structure for political competition, though less so in Hungary. When that competition brought parliamentary politics to a halt, administration and governance did not fall apart. Thanks to the efficient bureaucracy and the (admittedly imposed) caretaker cabinets, government business went on almost as usual. This is what a journalist of the time meant when he described the usage of the article 14 emergency clause as a "round-trip ticket for the constitution," since emergency decrees were always conceived as stopgap measures to ensure the basic functioning of the political system.[1]

Moreover, the problems of national conflict were not always intractable, since compromise solutions were worked out in Bukovina in 1910, Galicia and Bohemia in 1914. Compromise was harder to come by in Hungary, and it is not completely fair to draw long-term conclusions about the monarchy's cohesion just from those late-date agreements between Czechs and Germans. But the point remains that the monarchy's politics were never so "broken" as to be unfixable. It was not until the very last years of the war that nationalist political leaders began advocating for the monarchy's end. In 1918, certainly, their actions played a role in its fall. Even then, the death of the Habsburg state should not be misunderstood. It was not just the nationalisms of the nondominant groups that undermined the monarchy. The nationalisms of the ruling Germans and Hungarians (and to a lesser extent the Poles in Galicia) frustrated the other groups' desires for equitable political arrangements.

The end of the Habsburg monarchy did bring its peoples self-determination, but it also brought a host of other problems. The states that replaced it had many difficulties with their own national minorities: Germans and Hungarians in Czechoslovakia, Hungarians in Romania, Italians in the Kingdom of Serbs, Croats and Slovenes. With the exception of Czechoslovakia, none of the replacement states proved especially stable, all of them succumbing to authoritarian governments before World War Two. Thus many of the monarchy's weaknesses persisted into its successor polities. This fact demonstrates the misguided insistence on the part of Britain, France, and the United States that the monarchy had to be dissolved. The image of the Habsburg state as deeply reactionary and authoritarian—as an illegitimate regime opposed to liberal democracy—was simply wrong, though that perception drove the final decision to destroy it. Further, the Habsburg monarchy's disappearance left an enormous power vacuum, with obviously disastrous consequences for much of the twentieth century. The Habsburg state was an answer to a European problem that even in the twenty-first century has not disappeared: how to maintain peace and stability among the ethnic patchwork of peoples in the eastern and southeastern reaches of the continent.

It has therefore become a scholarly commonplace to assert that the Habsburgs were "a European necessity."[2] It is said that as no family before or since, the Habsburgs became the pivot of the balance of power, counteracting Ottoman Turkey, France, and even Russia; moreover, that they provided reasonably effective governance, and eventually cultural and economic conduits of modernization, for much of eastern central Europe. This assertion is not wrong. But it is important to recognize that the Habsburgs *made themselves* into a European necessity. Through the astute, occasionally ruthless and occasionally lackadaisical exploitation of key strategies of dynastic rule, this family assembled a huge patrimony and reigned for more than half a millennium, a more impressive achievement than any other European royal house can claim. Even if the Habsburgs reached their zenith in the hundred years after 1500, and their success in those years limited some of their options later, there is no question that their manipulation of dynastic strategies could serve as a textbook for dynasts past, present, and future.

The Habsburgs were extraordinarily, improbably successful with production and reproduction of the dynasty, especially up to 1527. Though partible inheritance occasionally fragmented the patrimony, in the end it was always reunited. Marital alliances and sometimes war consistently added more territories. The bonanza of Castile-Aragon and Bohemia-Hungary, all in one generation, remains unprecedented in European history. The Habsburgs managed to bring those realms into the house because they had cannily positioned themselves as a family powerful enough to protect the realms from their enemies. Thereafter, the Habsburgs were usually seen as *too* powerful, and so the great age of territorial expansion through marriage faded. Another reason why it faded was because the Habsburgs' own marital strategies changed. The Reformation limited the Habsburgs' choices, since it reduced the pool of marriageable Catholic families. The pool also decreased because the Habsburgs began considering their status too exalted for almost all other families, even the Catholic ones. This led to the ultimately iniquitous intermarriage between the Spanish and Austrian branches.

That intermarriage helps account for one of the major failures of Habsburg reproduction: not just the extinguishment of Carlos II, but the overall debasement of the family's gene pool. With Maximilian I and his daughter Margarete; Charles V, Ferdinand I and their sister Maria; and then Felipe II, the family for a time had an admirable surplus of talent and ability. They lost it as Habsburgs began marrying Habsburgs. It would not really return until Maria Theresia and her sons, with an infusion of new blood, though already with Franz I's marriages it was lost again. Of course there were other reasons for this diminution of Habsburg *astuzia*. One of them, oddly, was a further element of the dynasty's success at reproduction, namely with inculcating its norms into succeeding generations. With only a few exceptions such as Rudolf II and Matthias's generation, to a remarkable degree the Habsburgs managed to ensure loyalty and solidarity within the family. The downside to the strength of Habsburg norms was that their emphasis on tradition, conservatism, and intense piety meant that few Habsburgs were raised to be bold thinkers or innovators.

Though the Habsburgs are often viewed as not that fortuitous in war, it was occasionally a quite efficacious tool for the family. The most prominent such instances came in 1278, when Austria was brought into the house, and after 1683 as the Ottomans were pushed out of Hungary. The flip side of the family's extraordinary accumulation of territories was the cultural, institutional, and even geographical distance between many of those territories. This not only hindered defense of the realms (as evinced most starkly by the Spanish Habsburgs' Europe-wide and global military commitments) but also the development of the Habsburg monarchical state.

The Habsburgs' prodigious territorial acquisition also limited the techniques they could employ to secure legitimacy and loyalty. In this area the Habsburgs were no more than moderately successful, and by the nineteenth century they had been surpassed by other ruling houses. From the Middle Ages into the early modern period, the family relied on fairly standard practices of dynastic legitimacy, based on claims of divine right, piety, and bloodlines. The Habsburgs did perhaps place more of an emphasis on the idea of their destiny to rule than did other dynasties. All of these were adequate to secure legitimacy and loyalty from the small segments of the population that mattered, particularly the local aristocracies. That these practices in some sense sufficed is seen by the acceptance of Habsburg rule in lands as distant as Portugal and Hungary: in all these places the Habsburgs were acknowledged as the legitimate sovereigns. This was the legitimation of the personal right to rule. The Reformation then impacted the Habsburgs' dynastic strategies, and again not for the best. As society secularized little by little, and after 1648 moved away from religious justifications for rule, the Habsburgs doubled down on Catholicism. Men such as Ferdinands II and III and Leopold I became even more myopically devout, as rulers elsewhere in Europe frequently became more worldly. From medieval personal legitimation, the Habsburgs held on to confessional legitimation longer than most sovereigns. After 1648 they only partially transitioned to territorial legitimation, and never to national legitimation.

The service ethos of Maria Theresia and Joseph II provided the most effective legitimation strategy until the monarchy's end. It was partially territorial, in that it promised good governance to all people who lived in the lands of Habsburg dominion. But of course there was no natural connection between those lands, beyond the person of the sovereign. For all the services the Habsburg state provided, the failures in World War One destroyed such instrumental legitimation strategies. Besides humiliating battle defeats, the breakdown in the most basic functions of food distribution showed that the regime could no longer meet its end of the social contract to serve its people. Once that was gone, the Habsburgs had only the most vestigial legitimacy to fall back on. Because of the diversity of their realms, they could never adopt nationalism as a legitimation strategy.

The impossibility of embracing nationalism should not be seen simplistically as a failure by the Habsburgs. In fact they never *wanted* to pursue national legitimation. Apart from piecemeal efforts by Joseph II, and then Archdukes Karl and Johann in the early 1800s to highlight the Habsburgs' German identity, the dynasty always held itself above national divisions. However archaic, the dynasty's supranational self-conception was fundamental, and fervently believed. That supranational ethos conflicted with one of the fundamental claims of nationalism, that people must be loyal to the cultural collective (usually ethno-linguistic) with which they identify. The older idea that they owed loyalty to some royal who ruled over them because of personal, bloodline-based legitimacy evaporated in the era of mass politics. There was no automatic presumption that the dynastic ruler's interests were identical with (or at least subsumed) those of his increasingly politicized, nationally diversified subjects. The dynasty's position as unelected rulers over large populations was grounded only on consensual acts distant in history, and so that position, and those acts, were unsurprisingly contested in an era of burgeoning democratic politics.

The Habsburgs' supranational profession was also long essential to their function and image as rulers. While the insistence on the imperial German title did divert their attention from institution building in their patrimonial lands, overall the Habsburgs effectively fulfilled their ruling role. Few of them attained military greatness in accordance with long-enduring medieval conceptions of leadership, but individual Habsburgs exemplarily satisfied other expectations. Rudolf I very respectably met his age's demands for a German king. Maximilian I embodied the many-sided Renaissance prince, Charles V was the last great Western emperor despite his reign's tremendous difficulties, and Felipe II personified conscientious, bureaucratic kingship. Leopold I was just competent enough to inhabit the role of Baroque absolutism, Maria Theresia struck the perfect balance between tradition and innovation and became the most accomplished ruler the dynasty ever had, and Joseph II, for all his failures, epitomized enlightened despotism. Even Franz Joseph's grappling with the kind of sovereign he wanted to be versus the kind of sovereign his subjects would let him be showed an admirable accommodation to constitutional monarchy. The Habsburg dynasty, in short, instinctively and adroitly adapted to changing standards of kingship. They made mistakes, of course. The aggressive devotion to the defense of Catholicism led several generations of Habsburgs to engage in all kinds of violence. But the dynasty's consistent sponsorship of cultural production cannot be reproached. Several of its monarchs, including Rudolf II and Felipe IV, stand among the greatest artistic patrons in European history.

It is customary, and somewhat reasonable, to claim that of all these dynastic strategies, the Habsburgs' greatest failure was in building the institutions that would strengthen their rule. And the disappointments here are easy to enumerate. Though the dynasty did establish the Holy Roman Empire as a hereditary monarchy, they had little success in bolstering its central institutions. The Danubian domains themselves had very weak central institutions until the later eighteenth century. From then until the monarchy's collapse, though the state grew significantly, it was never particularly unified nor efficient at extracting the resources necessary for the Habsburgs' military needs. It was always a multiply composite monarchy. Finally, it can be alleged justifiably that the Habsburgs fell in the end because their state was inextricably identified with the dynasty, unlike in most other monarchies by the nineteenth century. The state was created by the dynasty—in that the Habsburgs were not unusual. But their problem was that the state was so tied to them that it had little justification for existence apart from them. Of course that did not mean that their state was ever completely illegitimate. State institutions long provided numerous benefits such as public goods and military security to the peoples of eastern central Europe. By October 1918, however, the ideology of national sovereignty overwhelmed any justification for the Habsburgs' multinational, dynastically entwined state.

The condemnatory verdict on Habsburg institutions should not ignore either the dynasty's successes or its extenuating circumstances, however. There were in fact some striking achievements of Habsburg state-building. For one, constructing "Austria" out of a collection of lands not necessarily destined to be together—Vorarlberg in the west, Tirol and the Salzburger Land in the middle, Styria and Carinthia in the south, and the Austrian duchies in the east—was very impressive, so much so that the modern country of Austria rests comfortably in the Habsburgs' footprint. Additionally, there were a number of Habsburg institutions that were definitely effective in carrying out their sovereigns' will. The Spanish Habsburgs created not only the best bureaucracy in Europe of its time, but also the world's first global bureaucracy to manage their empire. The Cisleithanian bureaucracy of the nineteenth century, if not as innovative, was acceptably competent. For a century, the Spanish Habsburgs had Europe's best military, and then under Eugène of Savoy in particular the Austrian Habsburgs' armies were the equal of any on the continent. And even if the Habsburgs kept losing to Napoleon, they also kept fighting. Despite the military's deficiencies, it always managed to rebound for another battle. Much the same can be said about the performance of Austria-Hungary's armies in World War One.

The extenuating circumstances that force a reconsideration of Habsburg institutional failure are the dynasty's own attitudes toward state-building.

Quite simply, at least until Joseph II Habsburg sovereigns never sought to create a centralized state. They always conceived of themselves as the rulers of multiple realms who had to respect those realms' unique privileges and institutions. The Habsburgs knew they ruled composite monarchies, and did not seriously entertain the idea of trying to forge them into a unitary monarchy. Even if they had tried, it might have been impossible; again, the dynasty's success in amassing heterogeneous territories worked against institutional homogenization. Nonetheless, there were certain opportunities—such as Felipe II's takeover of Portugal, or the suppression of one of the various Hungarian revolts—which Habsburg sovereigns could have seized to pursue centralization to a greater degree. Indeed, there are repeated examples, from Maximilian I onward, of rationalizing and consolidating institutions. But the Habsburgs, for better and worse, rarely chose to push that project very far.

It is all too easy to survey the dynasty with historical hindsight and point out its mistakes. But harping on about missed opportunities, or obsessing over a decline and fall, are not so pertinent in trying to understand how the dynasty actually *conceived of* the above strategies. The truth is that few if any Habsburgs ever really questioned the existing system of their rule. That system had made them who they were, had put them on top, so to speak, and so there was rarely a compelling reason to overhaul it. Moreover, from an ideological standpoint, it would be odd (to say the least) for "winners" like the Habsburgs to consider radically changing things. Their formation—the ideology of dynasty—was legitimized by what had been, by tradition. They were conservatives in the purest sense. The point of the dynasty was to conserve the patrimony and prestige. So while individual rulers such as Maria Theresia and her sons could make significant changes, the thinking behind those changes was not change for change's sake, but rather to tweak just enough to keep the system that put them in power working as well as it could. From the perspective of one of the richest, most powerful, most illustrious families on the planet, if things were not broken (and they were not likely to seem broken to those who were doing very, very well), then why try to "fix" them?

The fact that its traditional ideology and strategies have an almost undying validity for the dynasty can even be seen in the Habsburgs post-1918. Zita, Karl's wife and the last Habsburg empress, never formally renounced her crowns. She was only allowed to reenter Austria in 1982, but was given an elaborate funeral in Vienna in 1989. Her son, Otto von Habsburg, was the rightful heir to the throne, had there been any throne to sit upon. After 1930 he took over as the official head of the house. Further evidence of how, for dynasties, tradition justifies itself, Otto did not renounce his succession claims in Austria until 1961, and he continued to act as the sovereign of the Austrian branch of the Order of the Golden Fleece. Through much of his career, he worked for pan-European causes, supporting European unification and serving for 20 years as an MP in the European Parliament.

He died in 2011 at the age of 98. At his Vienna funeral, the *Kaiserhymne*, the old imperial anthem, was played before his body was laid to rest with his forebears in the Capuchin crypt. Otto's son Karl, a businessman, politician, and former television quiz show host, became the next head of the family and continued to support pan-European and human rights causes.

As the activities of the last several Habsburg heads have shown, the family's supranational vocation has persisted. Indeed, the Habsburgs and their monarchy have often been cited as a model for the project of European unification. That comparison requires some caution. As the Habsburgs themselves found, it may be difficult for people to feel allegiance to an overarching, seemingly shallow identity when it is so much easier to console oneself with narrower national particularity. Some writers claim that cosmopolitanism such as the Habsburgs represented can never generate true loyalty.[3] When we interrogate it more deeply, though, the Habsburg example reminds us that national allegiance was for centuries not an impediment to such a supranational state; it is only in the last 200 years that it has become so. It is therefore wrong to presume that this relatively young phenomenon of nationalism is eternal. The Habsburgs' employment of the old strategies of dynastic aggrandizement may have few lessons to offer most people in the twenty-first century. But their aspiration to a multinational political order, transcending the small minds and restrictive confines of nationalism, is not only still relevant—it is worthwhile.

NOTES

Introduction

1 Wolfgang Reinhard, "Introduction," in Reinhard, ed. *Power Elites and State Building* (Oxford: Clarendon Press, 1996), 6.

2 See Wolfgang Weber, "Dynastiesicherung und Staatsbildung: Die Entfaltung des frühmodernen Fürstenstaats," in Weber, ed. *Der Fürst: Ideen und Wirklichkeiten in der europäischen Geschichte* (Cologne: Böhlau, 1998). Also Hermann Weber, "Die Bedeutung der Dynastien für die europäische Geschichte der Frühen Neuzeit," in *Zeitschrift für bayerische Landesgeschichte* vol. 44, no. 1 (1981), 5–32.

3 I will note that this is by no means a comprehensive list of "the work of dynasties." In particular, I devote little attention to another common strategy, the symbolic representation of the dynasty through art, and cover only superficially the ruling family's relationships with other power elites in the aristocracy and the Church.

4 See Günther Kronenbitter, "Haus ohne Macht? Erzherzog Franz Ferdinand und die Krise der Habsburgermonarchie" in Weber, ed. (1998).

5 See Paula Sutter Fichtner, "Dynastic Marriage in Sixteenth-Century Habsburg Diplomacy and Statecraft: An Interdisciplinary Approach," *The American Historical Review* vol. 81, no. 2 (April 1976), 243–65.

6 See Tanner (1993).

7 See i. a. Vocelka and Heller (1997) and David Armitage, ed. *Theories of Empire, 1450–1800* (Aldershot: Ashgate, 1998).

8 See Rodney Bruce Hall, *National Collective Identity: Social Constructs and International Systems* (New York: Columbia University Press, 1999).

9 Yves-Marie Bercé, ed. *Les monarchies* (Paris: Presses Universitaires de France, 1997) is a useful overview.

10 Wolfgang Reinhard, *Geschichte der Staatsgewalt: eine vergleichende Verfassungsgeschichte Europas von den Anfängen bis zur Gegenwart* (Munich: C.H. Beck, 1999).

11 See Charles Tilly, *Coercion, Capital, and European States 990–1992* (Oxford: Blackwell Publishers, 1992).

12 Weber (1998).

13 Hillay Zmora, *Monarchy, Aristocracy, and the State in Europe, 1300–1800* (London: Routledge, 2001), 30.

14 J. H. Elliott, "A Europe of Composite Monarchies," *Past & Present*, no. 137 (1992), 48–71.

15 Taylor (1948), 10.

16 I will admit to a few additional fudges. Popes and artists, for example, have retained their familiar, Anglicized names.

1. From not so humble beginnings (c. 1000–1439)

1 Herm (1992), p. 33.

2 Günther Hödl, *Habsburg und Österreich 1273–1493: Gestalten und Gestalt des österreichischen Spätmittelalters* (Wien: Böhlau, 1988), 14.

2. Austria's destiny (1440–1519)

1 Dorothy Gies McGuigan, *Familie Habsburg 1273–1918: Glanz und Elend eines Herrscherhauses* (Berlin: Ullstein, 1966), 27.

2 Hödl (1988), 209.

3 Gerhard Benecke, *Maximilian I: An Analytical Biography* (London: Routledge & Kegan Paul, 1982), 13.

4 Ibid., 252.

5 Ibid., 34.

6 Bérenger (1990), 141.

7 Manfred Hollegger, *Maximilian I: Herrscher und Mensch einer Zeitenwende* (Stuttgart: Kohlhammer, 2005), 264.

8 Hermann Wiesflecker, *Maximilian I. Die Fundamente des habsburgischen Weltreiches* (Wien: Verlag für Geschichte und Politik, 1991), 152. See also Sharon L. Jansen, *The Monstrous Regiment of Women: Female Rulers in Early Modern Europe* (New York: Palgrave Macmillan, 2002).

9 Eberhard Isenmann, "The Holy Roman Empire in the Middle Ages," in Bonney, ed. (1999), 261.

10 Bérenger (1990), 139.

3. The greatest generation (1516–64)

1 Alfred Kohler, *Ferdinand I. 1503–1564: Fürst, König und Kaiser* (Munich: C.H. Beck, 2003), 92.

2 Ibid., 103.

3 Lynch (1981)(a), 43.

4 Kamen (2005)(b), 76.

5   Martin van Gelderen, "Wie die Universalmonarchie der Volkssouveränität weichen mußte," in Jussen, ed. (2005), 300.

6   Kamen (2005)(b), 72.

7   Bérenger (1990), 204.

8   Jansen (2002), 102.

9   Lynch (1981)(a), 68.

10 Vocelka and Heller (1997), 67.

11 Cited based on the original text, at http://text.habsburger.net/module/karl-v.-und-der-traum-von-der-universalmonarchie, accessed August 2012.

4. The European superpower (1556–1621)

1   Kamen (2005)(a), 29.

2   José Luis Beltrán, "Un imperio sin emperador," in García Cárcel, ed. (2003), 204.

3   Elliott (1970), 289.

4   Bennassar (2001), 22.

5   Lynch (1981)(b), 14.

6   Manuel Peña, "Felipe III: La búsqueda de la paz y el 'remedio general,'" in García Cárcel, ed. (2003), 294.

7   Magdalena S. Sánchez, "Melancholy and Female Illness: Habsburg Women and Politics at the Court of Philip III," *Journal of Women's History*, vol. 8, no. 2 (1996), 89.

8   Lynch (1981)(b), 16.

5. Division in faith and family (1564–1619)

1   Bérenger (1990), 249.

2   Kohler (2003), 301.

3   Paula Sutter Fichtner, *Emperor Maximilian II* (New Haven: Yale University Press, 2001), 185.

4   Cited after Friedrich von Hurter, *Geschichte Kaiser Ferdinands II und seiner Eltern*, vol. 6 (Schaffhausen: Hurtersche Buchhandlung, 1853), 529.

6. Endless war (1619–65)

1   R. A. Stradling, *Philip IV and the Government of Spain 1621–1665* (Cambridge: Cambridge University Press, 1988), 242.

2   Ibid., 269.

3 Cited after the text of Olivares's "Gran memorial" of 1624, accessed October 2012 at www.guillermoperezsarrion.es/files/2011/07/1624OlivaresGran Memorial.pdf.

4 Kamen (2005)(b), 236.

5 Manuel Peña, "Felipe IV: España entre la realidad y la apariencia," in García Cárcel, ed. (2003), 328.

6 Stradling (1988), 270.

7 Lynch (1981)(b), 127.

8 Stradling (1988), 190.

9 Dieter Albrecht, "Ferdinand II," in Schindling and Ziegler, eds (1990), 130.

10 Johann Franzl, *Ferdinand II. Kaiser im Zwiespalt der Zeit* (Graz: Verlag Styria, 1989), 227.

11 See Lothar Höbelt, *Ferdinand III. Friedenskaiser wider Willen* (Graz: Ares Verlag, 2008).

12 Elliott (1989), 123.

13 Ibid., 145.

7. Rise and fall (1657–1705)

1 Cited after the original text at //www.archive.org/stream/ generalcollectio00lond#page/290/mode/2up, accessed August 2012.

2 Bennassar (2001), 201.

3 Ibid., 200.

4 Lynch (1981)(b), 280.

5 Gonzalo Alvarez, Francisco C. Ceballos, and Celsa Quinteiro, "The Role of Inbreeding in the Extinction of a European Royal Dynasty," *PLoS ONE,* vol. 4, no. 4 (2009), accessed at: es5174.doc10.1371/journal.pone.0005174, February 2011.

6 Gregorio Marañón, *El conde-duque de Olivares* (Madrid: Espasa-Calpe, 1952), 230.

7 Charles W. Ingrao, *In Quest and Crisis: Emperor Joseph I and the Habsburg Monarchy* (West Lafayette: Purdue University Press, 1979), 8.

8. Opulent stagnation (1705–40)

1 Ingrao (1979), 124.

2 Ingrao (1994), 149.

3 Charles Ingrao and Andrew Thomas, "Piety and Patronage: The Empresses-Consort of the High Baroque," *German History,* vol. 20, no. 1 (2002), 38.

4 Vocelka and Heller (1997), 256.

5 Bérenger (1990), 447.

9. Enlightenment and reform (1740–92)

1 Maria Theresia, *Politisches Testament* (1749–50), http://germanhistorydocs.ghi-dc.
   org/pdf/deu/3_AustrianHabsburgEmpire_Doc.1_German.pdf, accessed August 2012.

2 Wandruszka (1964), 143.

3 Jean-Paul Bled, *Marie-Thérèse d'Autriche* (Paris: Fayard, 2001), 137.

4 Ibid., 191.

5 Derek Beales, *Joseph II. Volume 1: In the Shadow of Maria Theresa
   1741–1780* (Cambridge: Cambridge University Press, 1987), 154.

6 Ibid., *Enlightenment and Reform in Eighteenth-Century Europe* (London: I.B.
   Tauris, 2005), 262.

7 Beller (2006), 103.

8 Maria Theresia, *Politisches Testament*.

9 T. C. W. Blanning, *Joseph II* (London: Longman, 1994), 56.

10 Elizabeth Manning, "The Politics of Culture: Joseph II's German Opera,"
    History Today (January 1993), 16.

11 Hans Kluetung, "Der aufgeklärte Fürst," in Weber, ed. (1988), 158.

12 Weissensteiner (2003), 13.

13 Ingrao (1994), 175.

14 Joseph II, "Errinerung an seine Staatsbeamten" ("Hirtenbrief") (1783), www.
    jku.at/kanonistik/content/e95782/e95785/e95786/e95794/e104403/e104407/
    e98359/ErinnerunganseineStaatsbeamten.pdf, accessed August 2012.

15 Bérenger (1990), 530.

10. Revolution and reaction (1792–1848)

1 Beller (2006), 116.

2 Weissensteiner (2003), 49.

3 Walter Ziegler, "Franz I. von Österreich," in Schindling and Ziegler, eds (1990), 313.

4 Ibid., 316.

5 See Blanning (1994), 12.

6 Gerd Holler, *Gerechtigkeit für Ferdinand. Österreichs gütiger Kaiser* (Vienna:
   Amalthea, 1986), 158.

7 Weissensteiner (2003), 78.

8 Ernst Bruckmüller, *Nation Österreich: Kulturelles Bewußtsein und
   gesellschaftlich-politische Prozesse* (Vienna: Böhlau, 1996), 228.

11. To succumb with honor (1848–1918)

1 See Otto Urban, "Navštěvy Františka Josefa 1. v Praze," in Marta Ottlová and Milan Pospíšil, eds. *Umění a civilizace jako divadlo světa* (Prague: Ústav pro hudební vědu, 1993); and Hugh LeCaine Agnew, "The Flyspecks on Palivec's Portrait," in Laurence Cole and Daniel Unowsky, eds. *The Limits of Loyalty: Imperial Symbolism, Popular Allegiances and State Patriotism in the Late Habsburg Monarchy* (New York: Berghahn Books, 2007); and finally Alan Palmer, *Twilight of the Habsburgs: The Life and Times of Emperor Francis Joseph* (New York: Grove Press, 1994), 193.

2 *Briefe Kaiser Franz Josephs I. an seine Mutter*, Franz Schnürer, ed. (Munich: Verlag Joseph Kösel und Friedrich Pustet, 1930), 166.

3 The term comes from Lothar Höbelt, *Franz Joseph I. Der Kaiser und sein Reich. Eine politische Geschichte* (Vienna: Böhlau, 2009).

4 Palmer (1994), 83.

5 Jean-Paul Bled, *Franz Joseph* (Oxford: Blackwell, 1992), 152.

6 Bérenger (1990), 670.

7 The classic English-language work is Carl Schorske, *Fin-de-siècle Vienna* (New York: Random House, 1979).

8 Palmer (1994), 224.

9 Herm (1992), 287.

10 Ibid., 294.

11 Bérenger (1990), 673.

12 See Pieter M. Judson, *Guardians of the Nation: Activists on the Language Frontiers of Imperial Austria* (Cambridge: Harvard University Press, 2006).

13 Sked (2001), 234.

14 *Briefe Kaiser Franz Josephs I. an seine Mutter* (1930), 358.

15 Weissensteiner (2003), 172.

16 Wandruszka (1964), 177.

17 Bled (1992), 211.

18 Bérenger (1990), 601.

12. Conclusion

1 Gary B. Cohen, "Nationalist Politics and the Dynamics of State and Civil Society in the Habsburg Monarchy, 1867–1914," *Central European History*, vol. 40, no. 2 (2007), 270.

2 The term is originally Josef Redlich's, in his *Das österreichische Staats- und Reichsproblem* (Leipzig: Der Neue Geist Verlag, 1920), vii.

3 See, for example, various essays in Martha Nussbaum and Joshua Cohen, eds. *For Love of Country?* (Boston: Beacon Press, 2002).

SELECT BIBLIOGRAPHY

The scholarly literature on the Habsburgs is vast. Because of space limitations, this is *not* an exhaustive bibliography of all sources consulted in the research for this book. Instead I have listed major, mostly recent sources, and noted selected works relevant for specific chapters.

General

Beller, Steven. (2006). *A Concise History of Austria*. Cambridge: Cambridge University Press.

Bennassar, Bartolomé. (2001). *La España de los Austrias (1516–1700)*. Barcelona: Crítica.

—. (2006). *La monarquía española de los Austrias: conceptos, poderes y expresiones sociales*. Salamanca: Ediciones Universidad de Salamanca.

Bennassar, Bartolomé and Bernard Vincent. (2001). *Le temps de l'Espagne: XVIe—XVIIe siècles*. Paris: Hachette.

Bennassar, Bartolomé, Christian Hermann, et. al. (2001). *Le premier âge de l'État en Espagne (1450–1700)*. Paris: CNRS éditions.

Bérenger, Jean. (1990). *Histoire de l'empire des Habsbourg 1273–1918*. Paris: Fayard.

Brauneder, Wilhelm and Lothar Höbelt. (1996). *Sacrum Imperium: Das Reich und Österreich, 996–1806*. Vienna: Amalthea.

Cartledge, Bryan. (2012). *The Will to Survive: A History of Hungary*. New York: Columbia University Press.

Coreth, Anna. (2004). *Pietas Austriaca*. West Lafayette: Purdue University Press.

Čornejová, Ivana, Jiří Rak, and Vít Vlnas. (1995). *Ve stínu tvých křídel . . . Habsburkové v českých dějinách*. Prague: Grafoprint-Neubert.

Duindam, Jeroen. (2003). *Vienna and Versailles: The Courts of Europe's Dynastic Rivals*. Cambridge: Cambridge University Press.

Elliott, J. H. (1970). *Imperial Spain 1469–1716*. London: Penguin Books.

—. (1989). *Spain and its World 1500–1700*. New Haven: Yale University Press.

Erbe, Michael. (2000). *Die Habsburger 1493–1918: Eine Dynastie im Reich und in Europa*. Stuttgart: Kohlhammer.

Evans, R. J. W. (1979). *The Making of the Habsburg Monarchy 1550–1700*. Oxford: Clarendon Press.

—. (2006). *Austria, Hungary, and the Habsburgs: Essays on Central Europe, c.1683–1867*. Oxford: Oxford University Press.

Fichtner, Paula Sutter. (2003). *The Habsburg Monarchy, 1490–1848: Attributes of Empire*. Houndmills, Basingstoke, Hampshire: Palgrave Macmillan.

—. (2008). *Terror and Toleration: The Habsburg Empire Confronts Islam, 1526–1850*. London: Reaktion Books.

García Cárcel, Ricardo, ed. (2003). *Historia de España Siglos XVI y XVII: La España de los Austrias*. Madrid: Cátedra.

Gonda, Imre and Emil Niederhauser. (1978). *A Habsburgok: egy európai jelenség*. Budapest: Gondolat.

Good, David F. (1984). *The Economic Rise of the Habsburg Monarchy 1750–1914*. Berkeley: University of California Press.

Herm, Gerhard. (1992). *Aufstieg, Glanz und Niedergang des Hauses Habsburg*. Düsseldorf: ECON Verlag.

Hochedlinger, Michael. (2003). *Austria's Wars of Emergence: War, State, and Society in the Habsburg Monarchy, 1683–1797*. Harlow: Longman.

Huss, Frank. (2008). *Der Wiener Kaiserhof: eine Kulturgeschichte von Leopold I. bis Leopold II*. Gernsbach: Katz.

Ingrao, Charles W. (1994). *The Habsburg Monarchy 1618–1815*. Cambridge: Cambridge University Press.

—, ed. (1994). *State and Society in Early Modern Austria*. West Lafayette: Purdue University Press.

Kamen, Henry. (2003). *Empire: How Spain Became a World Power 1492–1763*. New York: HarperCollins.

—. (2005)(a). *Golden Age Spain*. New York: Palgrave Macmillan.

—. (2005)(b). *Spain, 1469–1714: A Society of Conflict*. London: Pearson Longman.

Kann, Robert A. (1974). *A History of the Habsburg Empire 1526–1918*. Berkeley: University of California Press.

Komlos, John. (1989). *Nutrition and Economic Development in the Eighteenth-Century Habsburg Monarchy*. Princeton: Princeton University Press.

Königsberger, Helmut Georg. (1971). *The Habsburgs and Europe 1516–1660*. Ithaca: Cornell University Press.

Lockyer, Roger. (1993) *Habsburg and Bourbon Europe 1470–1720*. Harlow: Longman.

Lynch, John. (1981)(a). *Spain under the Habsburgs. Volume I: Empire and Absolutism 1516–1598*. Oxford: Blackwell.

—. (1981)(b). *Spain under the Habsburgs. Volume II: Spain and America 1598–1700*. Oxford: Blackwell.

—. (1992)(a). *Spain 1516–1598: From Nation State to World Empire*. London: Blackwell.

—. (1992)(b). *The Hispanic World in Crisis and Change, 1598–1700*. London: Blackwell.

Macartney, C. A. (1968). *The Habsburg Empire 1790–1918*. London: Weidenfeld and Nicolson.

Okey, Robin. (2001). *The Habsburg Monarchy: From Enlightenment to Eclipse*. New York: St. Martin's Press.

Pérez-Bustamante, Rogelio. (2000). *El gobierno del imperio español: los Austrias (1517–1700)*. Madrid: Comunidad de Madrid, Consejería de Educación.

Press, Volker. (1986). "The Habsburg Court as Center of the Imperial Government," *The Journal of Modern History*, vol. 58, Supplement: Politics and Society in the Holy Roman Empire, 1500–1806, pp. S23–S45.

Ribot, Luis. (2006). *El arte de gobernar: estudios sobre la España de los Austrias*. Madrid: Alianza Editorial.

Schindling, Anton and Walter Ziegler, eds (1990). *Die Kaiser der Neuzeit 1519–1918*. Munich: C.H. Beck.

Spielman, John. (1993). *The City and the Crown: Vienna and the Imperial Court, 1600–1740*. West Lafayette: Purdue University Press.

Tanner, Marie. (1993). *The Last Descendant of Aeneas: The Hapsburgs and the Mythic Image of the Emperor*. New Haven: Yale University Press.

Tapié, Victor-L. (1969). *Monarchie et peuples du Danube*. Paris: Fayard.

Taylor, A. J. P. (1948). *The Habsburg Monarchy 1809–1918*. London: H. Hamilton.

Vocelka, Karl. (2001). *Österreichische Geschichte 1699–1815: Glanz und Untergang der höfischen Welt*. Vienna: Ueberreuther.

— and Lynne Heller. (1997). *Die Lebenswelt der Habsburger: Kultur- und Mentalitätsgeschichte einer Familie*. Graz: Styria Verlag.

Wandruszka, Adam. (1964). *The House of Habsburg: Six Hundred Years of a European Dynasty*. Garden City: Doubleday.

Weissensteiner, Friedrich. (1995). *Große Herrscher des Hauses Habsburg: 700 Jahre europäische Geschichte*. Munich: Piper.

—. (2003). *Die österreichischen Kaiser*. Vienna: Ueberreuter.

Wheatcroft, Andrew. (1995). *The Habsburgs: Embodying Empire*. London: Viking.

Introduction

There is an enormous literature on both kingship and state-building; on dynasties per se it is smaller. The following is a partial listing.

Asch, Ronald and Adolf Birke, eds (1991). *Princes, Patronage, and the Nobility: The Court at the Beginning of the Modern Age*. New York: Oxford University Press.

Blickle, Peter, ed. (1997). *Resistance, Representation, and Community*. Oxford: Clarendon Press.

Bonney, Richard. (1991). *The European Dynastic States 1494–1660*. Oxford: Oxford University Press.

—, ed. (1999). *The Rise of the Fiscal State in Europe, c.1200–1815*. Oxford: Oxford University Press.

Burns, J. H. (1992). *Lordship, Kingship, and Empire 1400–1525*. Oxford: Clarendon Press.

Dewald, Jonathan. (1996). *The European Nobility 1400–1800*. New York: Cambridge University Press.

Duggan, Anne, ed. (1993). *Kings and Kingship in Medieval Europe*. London: King's College London Centre for Late Antique and Medieval Studies.

Henshall, Nicholas. (2010). *The Zenith of European Monarchy and its Elites: The Politics of Culture 1650–1750*. New York: Palgrave Macmillan.

Jussen, Bernhard, ed. (2005). *Die Macht des Königs: Herrschaft in Europa vom Frühmittelalter bis in die Neuzeit*. Munich: C.H. Beck.

Nexon, Daniel H. (2009). *The Struggle for Power in Early Modern Europe: Religious Conflict, Dynastic Empires, and International Change*. Princeton: Princeton University Press.

Monod, Paul Kléber. (1999). *The Power of Kings: Monarchy and Religion in Europe 1589–1715*. New Haven: Yale University Press.

Schneider, Reinhard, ed. (1987). *Das spätmittelalterliche Königtum im europäischen Vergleich*. Sigmaringen: J. Thorbecke.

Shennan, J. H. (1974). *The Origins of the Modern European State, 1450–1725*. London: Hutchinson.

Skinner, Quentin and Bo Stråth, eds (2003). *States and Citizens: History, Theory, Prospects*. Cambridge: Cambridge University Press.

Spruyt, Hendrik. (1994). *The Sovereign State and its Competitors: An Analysis of Systems Change*. Princeton: Princeton University Press.

Tilly, Charles, ed. (1975). *The Formation of National States in Western Europe*. Princeton: Princeton University Press.

Tilly, Charles and W. P. Blockmans, eds (1994). *Cities and the Rise of States in Europe*. Boulder: Westview Press.

Watts, John. (2009). *The Making of Polities: Europe, 1300–1500*. Cambridge: Cambridge University Press.

Chapter 1: From not so humble beginnings

Additional sources

Baum, Wilhelm. (1996). *Rudolf IV. der Stifter. Seine Welt und seine Zeit*. Graz: Styria Verlag.

Brunner, Otto. (1992). *Land and Lordship: Structures of Governance in Medieval Austria*. Philadelphia: University of Pennsylvania Press.

Debris, Cyrille. (2005). *"Tu, felix Austria, nube": la dynastie de Habsbourg et sa politique matrimonial à la fin du Moyen Âge*. Turnhout: Brepols.

Krieger, Karl-Friedrich. (1994). *Die Habsburger im Mittelalter*. Stuttgart: Kohlhammer Verlag.

—. (2003). *Rudolf von Habsburg*. Darmstadt: Wissenschaftliche Buchgesellschaft.

Lhotsky, Alphons. (1967). *Geschichte Österreichs seit der Mitte des 13. Jahrhunderts*. Vienna: Böhlau.

Ritscher, Alfred. (1992). *Literatur und Politik im Umkreis der ersten Habsburger*. Frankfurt: Peter Lang.

Schneidmüller, Bernd and Stefan Weinfurter, eds (2003). *Die deutschen Herrscher des Mittelalters*. Munich: C.H. Beck.

Chapter 2: Austria's destiny

Heinig, Paul-Joachim, ed. (1993). *Kaiser Friedrich III. in seiner Zeit*. Köln: Böhlau Verlag.

—. (1997). *Kaiser Friedrich III.: Hof, Regierung und Politik*. Cologne: Böhlau.

Rill, Bernd. (1987). *Friedrich III. Habsburgs europäischer Durchbruch*. Graz: Verlag Styria.

Silver, Larry. (2008). *Marketing Maximilian: The Visual Ideology of a Holy Roman Emperor*. Princeton: Princeton University Press.

Chapter 3: The greatest generation

Blockmans, Wim. (2002). *Emperor Charles V 1500–1558*. London: Arnold Publishers.

Doyle, Daniel R. (2000). "The Sinews of Habsburg Governance in the Sixteenth Century: Mary of Hungary and Political Patronage," *The Sixteenth Century Journal*, vol. 31, no. 2, pp. 349–60.

Fernández Álvarez, Manuel. (1999). *La España del Emperador Carlos V*. Madrid: Espasa Calpe.

Fichtner, Paula Sutter. (1982). *Ferdinand I of Austria: The Politics of Dynasticism in the Age of Reformation*. Boulder: East European Monographs.

Kohler, Alfred. (2001). *Karl V. 1500–1558. Eine Biographie*. Munich: C. H. Beck.

Maltby, William. (2002). *The Reign of Charles V*. New York: Palgrave.

Rosenthal, Earl. (1971). "Plus Ultra, Non plus Ultra, and the Columnar Device of Emperor Charles V," *Journal of the Warburg and Courtauld Institutes*, vol. 34, pp. 204–28.

Soly, Hugo, et. al. (1999). *Charles V, 1500–1558, and His Time*. Antwerp: Mercatorfonds.

Chapter 4: The European superpower

Allen, Paul C. (2000). *Philip III and the Pax Hispanica: The Failure of Grand Strategy*. New Haven: Yale University Press.

Fernández Álvarez, Manuel and Luis Fernández y Fernández de Retana. (2002). *La España de Felipe II*. Madrid: Espasa Calpe.

Kamen, Henry. (1999). *Philip II of Spain*. New Haven: Yale University Press.

Parker, Geoffrey. (1998). *The Grand Strategy of Philip II*. New Haven: Yale University Press.

Pérez Bustamante, Ciriaco. (1979). *La España de Felipe III*. Madrid: Espasa Calpe.

Rodríguez-Salgado, M. J. (1988). *The Changing Face of Empire: Charles V, Philip II, and Habsburg Authority, 1551–1559*. Cambridge: Cambridge University Press.

Williams, Patrick. (2001). *Philip II*. New York: Palgrave Macmillan.

Woodward, Geoffrey. (1992). *Philip II*. London: Longman.

Chapter 5: Division in faith and family

Edelmayer, Friedrich and Alfred Kohler, eds (1992). *Kaiser Maximilian II. Kultur und Politik im 16. Jahrhundert*. Munich: Oldenbourg.

Evans, R. J. W. (1973). *Rudolf II and His World*. Oxford: Clarendon Press.

Janáček, Josef. (1987). *Rudolf II. a jeho doba*. Prague: Svoboda.

Rill, Bernd. (1999). *Kaiser Matthias. Bruderzwist und Glaubenskampf*. Graz: Styria Verlag.

Vocelka, Karl. (1985). *Rudolf II. und seine Zeit*. Vienna: Böhlau.

Chapter 6: Endless war

Alcalá-Zamora, José and Queipo de Llano, eds (2005). *Felipe IV: El hombre y el reinado*. Madrid: Villaverde Ediciones.

Elliott, J. H. (1984). *Richelieu and Olivares*. Cambridge: Cambridge University Press.

— (1986). *The Count-Duke of Olivares: The Statesman in an Age of Decline*. New Haven: Yale University Press.

Hengerer, Mark. (2008). *Kaiser Ferdinand III. Vom Krieg zum Frieden*. Vienna: Böhlau.

Mears, John A. (1988). "The Thirty Years' War, the 'General Crisis,' and the Origins of a Standing Professional Army in the Habsburg Monarchy," *Central European History*, vol. 21, pp. 122–41.

Tomás y Valiente, Francisco. (1982). *La España de Felipe IV: el gobierno de la monarquía, la crisis de 1640 y el fracaso de la hegemonía europea*. Madrid: Espasa Calpe.

Wilson, Peter H. (2009). *The Thirty Years War: Europe's Tragedy*. Cambridge: Harvard University Press.

Chapter 7: Rise and fall

Kamen, Henry. (1980). *Spain in the Later Seventeenth Century, 1665–1700*. London: Longman.

Mikulec, Jiří. (1997). *Leopold I. Život a vláda barokního Habsburka*. Praha: Paseka.

Redlich, Otto. (1961). *Weltmacht des Barock. Österreich in der Zeit Kaiser Leopolds I*. Vienna: Rohrer.

Ribot, Luis, ed. (2009). *Carlos II: el rey y su entorno cortesano*. Madrid: Centro de Estudios Europa Hispánica.

Schumann, Jutta. (2003). *Die andere Sonne. Kaiserbild und Medienstrategien im Zeitalter Leopolds I*. Berlin: Colloquia Augustana, 17.

Spielman, John P. (1977). *Leopold I of Austria*. New Brunswick: Rutgers University Press.

Chapter 8: Opulent stagnation

Kampmann, Christoph, et. al. (2008). *Bourbon, Habsburg, Oranien: konkurrierende Modelle im dynastischen Europa um 1700*. Cologne: Böhlau.

Redlich, Otto. (1962). *Das Werden einer Großmacht. Österreich von 1700 bis 1740*. Vienna: Rohrer.

Rill, Bernd. (1992). *Karl VI. Habsburg als barocke Großmacht*. Graz: Verlag Styria.

Chapter 9: Enlightenment and reform

Beales, Derek. (2009). *Joseph II. Volume 2: Against the World 1780–1790*. Cambridge: Cambridge University Press.

Browning, Reed. (1995). *The War of the Austrian Succession*. New York: St. Martin's Press.

Capra, Carlo. (2005). "Habsburg Italy in the Age of Reform," *Journal of Modern Italian Studies*, vol. 10(2), pp. 218–33.

Crankshaw, Edward. (1969). *Maria Theresa*. New York: Viking.

Dickson, P. G. M. (1987). *Finance and Government under Maria Theresa 1740–1780*. New York: Oxford University Press.

Koschatzky, Walter. (1979). *Maria Theresia und ihre Zeit*. Salzburg: Residenz Verlag.

Kowalská, Ewa. (2002). "Aspects of Rationality in the Relationship of State and Church: The Case of the Habsburg Monarchy in the Eighteenth Century," *Dialogue and Universalism*, no. 8–10/2002, pp. 41–9.

Szabo, Franz A. (1994). *Kaunitz and Enlightened Absolutism 1753–1780*. Cambridge: Cambridge University Press.

Wandruszka, Adam. (1963–5). *Leopold II*. Vienna: Verlag Herold.

Wangermann, Ernst. (1973). *The Austrian Achievement 1700–1800*. New York: Harcourt Brace Jovanovich.

Yonan, Michael. (2011). *Empress Maria Theresa and the Politics of Habsburg Imperial Art*. University Park: Pennsylvania State University Press.

Chapter 10: Revolution and reaction

Bridge, F. R. (1990). *The Habsburg Monarchy among the Great Powers 1815–1918*. New York: Berg.

Drimmel, Heinrich. (1981). *Franz von Österreich: Ein Wiener übersteht Napoleon*. Vienna: Amalthea.

—. (1982). *Franz von Österreich: Kaiser der Biedermaier*. Vienna: Amalthea.

Roider, Karl A. (1987). *Baron Thugut and Austria's Response to the French Revolution*. Princeton: Princeton University Press.

Rothenberg, Gunther Erich. (1982). *Napoleon's Great Adversary: The Archduke Charles and the Austrian Army, 1792–1814*. New York: Sarpedon.

Siemann, Wolfram. (2010). *Metternich. Staatsmann zwischen Restauration und Moderne*. Munich: C.H. Beck.

Sked, Alan. (2001). *The Decline and Fall of the Habsburg Empire 1815–1918*. London: Longman.

—. (2008). *Metternich and Austria: An Evaluation*. New York: Palgrave Macmillan.

Tritsch, Walter. (1952). *Metternich und sein Monarch*. Darmstadt: Holle Verlag.

Chapter 11: To succumb with honor

Bridge, F. R. (1972). *From Sadowa to Sarajevo*. London: Routledge & Kegan Paul.

Cassels, Lavender. (1973). *Clash of Generations: A Habsburg Family Drama in the Nineteenth Century*. London: J. Murray.

Fejtő, Ferenc. (1997). *Rekviem egy hajdanvolt birodalomért: Ausztria-Magyarország szétrombolása*. Budapest: Atlantisz.

Gamerl, Benno. (2009). "Subjects, Citizens, and Others: The Handling of Ethnic Differences in the British and the Habsburg Empires (Late Nineteenth and Early Twentieth Century)," *European Review of History*, vol. 16, no. 4, pp. 523–49.

Gerő, András, ed. (2009). *The Austro-Hungarian Monarchy Revisited*. Boulder: Social Science Monographs.

von Hirschhausen, Ulrike. (2009). "From Imperial Inclusion to National Exclusion: Citizenship in the Habsburg Monarchy and in Austria 1867–1923," *European Review of History*, vol. 16, no. 4, pp. 551–73.

Komlos, John, ed. (1983). *Economic Development in the Habsburg Monarchy in the Nineteenth Century*. Boulder: East European Monographs.

—, ed. (1990). *Economic Development in the Habsburg Monarchy and in the Successor States*. Boulder: East European Monographs.

Lackey, Scott W. (1995). *The Rebirth of the Habsburg Army: Friedrich Beck and the Rise of the General Staff*. Westport: Greenwood.

Rauchensteiner, Manfried. (1993). *Der Tod des Doppeladlers: Österreich-Ungarn und der Erste Weltkrieg*. Graz: Styria Verlag.

Rothenberg, Gunther Erich. (1976). *The Army of Francis Joseph*. West Lafayette: Purdue University Press.

Wandruszka, Adam and Peter Urbanitsch, eds (1973–). *Die Habsburgermonarchie, 1848–1918*. Volumes 1–9. Vienna: Österreichische Akademie der Wissenschaften.

Wawro, Geoffrey. (1995). "The Habsburg *Flucht nach vorne* in 1866: Domestic Political Origins of the Austro-Prussian War," *The International History Review*, vol. 17, no. 2, pp. 221–48.

Winkelhofer, Martina. (2008). *"Viribus unitis": Der Kaiser und sein Hof. Ein neues Franz Joseph Bild*. Vienna: Amalthea.

INDEX

Lightning Source UK Ltd.
Milton Keynes UK
UKOW06f0952260816

281553UK00006B/96/P